Teaching
INDIVIDUAL
and
TEAM SPORTS

SECOND EDITION

Teaching
INDIVIDUAL
and
TEAM SPORTS

R. T. DEWITT

KEN DUGAN
David Lipscomb College

PRENTICE-HALL, INC., Englewood Cliffs, New Jersey

© 1972, 1953 by PRENTICE-HALL, INC.,
Englewood Cliffs, New Jersey

Printed in the United States of America

10 9 8 7 6 5 4 3 2 1

ISBN: 0-13-893842-3

Library of Congress Catalog Card No.:
73-172677

Prentice-Hall International, Inc., *London*
Prentice-Hall of Australia, Pty, Ltd., *Sydney*
Prentice-Hall of Canada, Ltd., *Toronto*
Prentice-Hall of India Private Limited, *New Delhi*
Prentice-Hall of Japan, Inc., *Tokyo*

DEDICATION

To my mother, Emily,
for whom this book is a realization
of a faith,
and to my father, John DeWitt,
for whom it would have been
had he lived.

—R. T. DeW.

REVISION DEDICATION

To Dr. Lewis Maiden
and
Dr. Leota Maiden
for their encouragement,
advice, and invaluable help
in preparing this book.
—K. D.

CONSULTANTS

Archery and Shuffleboard. Mrs. Frances Moore Prater, McMinnville, Tennessee.

Badminton. Dr. Duane R. Slaughter, Head, Department of Health and Physical Education, David Lipscomb College.

Bowling, Mr. Gaius M. Bruce, Doctoral Candidate, George Peabody College.

Conditioning. Dr. Leon Garrett, Head, Department of Health and Physical Education, George Peabody College.

Gymnastics and Tumbling. Thomas E. Hanvey, Associate Professor of Health and Physical Education, David Lipscomb College.

Golf and Tennis. Mr. Eugene Boyce, Professor of Health and Physical Education, David Lipscomb College.

Handball. Dr. Glen Reeder, Professor of Health and Physical Education, George Peabody College.

Ice Hockey. Ken Murphey, Former Professional Hockey Player.

Soccer. Mr. Tom Gannis, Coach, Nashville Rangers.

Speedball. Mrs. Connie Koenig, Instructor of Physical Education, George Peabody Demonstration School.

Swimming. Dr. Helen B. Watson, Head, Department of Health and Physical Education for Women, University of Tennessee.

Table Tennis. Mr. John White, Southern Regional Tournament Director, U.S. Table Tennis Association.

Track and Field. Mr. Dean Hayes, Track Coach, Middle Tennessee State University.

Volleyball. Dr. Ed Welch, Department of Physical Education, West Virginia Institute of Technology.

Wrestling. Mr. Joe Drennan, Wrestling Coach, Ryan High School, Nashville, Tennessee.

contents

preface

Dr. R. T. DeWitt's book, *Teaching Individual and Team Sports,* has been a leader in the field of physical education since its first printing in 1953. My purpose in revising this valuable book is to keep it in circulation by bringing it up to date. In individual and team sports, terminology has changed somewhat, and methods of teaching have improved. The revision has attempted to follow Dr. DeWitt's style and format by devoting one chapter to each of twenty-four sports. Chapters on conditioning, fencing, field hockey, skiing, and touch football help to modernize the book. It is the author's hope that these changes will increase its usefulness.

For convenience, each chapter, with the exception of the one on conditioning, has been subdivided so that the background, basic skills, teaching procedure, and skill tests will always be found in the same sequence. As a further aid to the teacher and sports enthusiast, at the end of each chapter there are discussion questions, definition of terms, and a bibliography.

It is hoped that the sections on teaching procedure and skill tests will prove helpful to teachers who are interested in these aspects of individual and team sports. The writer believes in the objective testing of students' skills as opposed to incomplete judgments based on guesswork. One of the chief aims of the original book was to improve the methods of judging achievement, with the hope that the teacher's testing and grading would exemplify that sense of "fair play" required of sports participants.

ACKNOWLEDGMENTS

I would like to thank the many people who have helped make this book possible. Special thanks go to Mrs. Joyce Simmons and Mrs. Anne Zentz for typing the manuscript; President Athens Clay Pullias, Vice-President Willard Collins, and Dean Mack Wayne Craig of David Lipscomb College; my wife Diane for her sympathy and understanding; Miss Virginia Alexander for her invaluable help with the art work; Dr. Duane R. Slaughter, Head of the Department of Health and Physical Education, David Lipscomb College; and Dr. Glen Reeder, George Peabody College.

K. D.

Teaching
INDIVIDUAL
and
TEAM SPORTS

archery

1

BACKGROUND

Archery is one of the oldest sports known to mankind. It is difficult to determine when it began or what group of people was responsible for its origin. Some historians are of the opinion that archery is 25,000 years old, but others say that it cannot possibly have existed for more than 6,000 years. Regardless of when the sport originated, indications are that it was practiced among most of the peoples of the world. Since many of them were entirely cut off from the others, it would seem that archery was developed independently by different groups. It is assumed that early man tried propelling a shaft through the air by the whip of a wooden stave because he was looking for a method of killing and injuring at greater distances than that at which the sling and spear were effective.

Archery was employed for two specific purposes by early man: to secure food and to protect himself from his enemies. Because warfare gets more attention from historians than methods of securing food, it is rather easy to trace the use of archery in warfare as it developed through the years. The people of Egypt were among the first to realize that the bow hurled an object a greater distance than any means previously used in warfare. As a result, they secretly supplied their troops with bows and arrows and required diligent practice until the men could hurl a small shaft more than 100 yards. Soon after the Egyptian soldiers learned how to use the bow and arrow, they engaged in a victorious war with Persia. After this new weapon proved so effective, they waged further successful warfare on other nations.

It is thought that archery was employed in warfare by the Egyptians, Greeks, Turks, Japanese, English, and French, in that order. The American Indian used archery to a great extent, but because his equipment was extremely crude, it is questionable whether he ever became as proficient in the sport as tales about him would lead us to believe. The Indians were such efficient stalkers that they approached close enough to game (or enemies) for even their crude weapons to be quite effective.

The English fought many wars with the bow and arrow and developed marksmanship to an extremely high degree. Much of England's ability to wage victorious war is credited to this one factor.

Many types of archery equipment have been developed through the years. The bow used by the Egyptians so successfully was between 4½ and 5 feet in length. The arrows measured from 24 to 32 inches long and were tipped with bronze.

The Turks and Greeks are said to have preferred a short C bow—that is, it looked like the letter C when unbraced. They also used a bow approximately 6 feet long. Some of the bows used by African tribes were 6 feet long or longer. The bow of the American Indian was rather short. The English originally used a bow 4½ to 5 feet in length, but it became more successful when increased to 6 feet. African Pygmies used a 3-foot bow, and the Japanese employed one 6 to 7 feet long. The Mongolians and the French are known to have used the crossbow.

The Battle of Crécy was won by the English, with longbows, against the French, using crossbows. The longbow proved to be more nearly accurate at medium and long range, and much faster. The English, with their longbows, could loose six arrows to only one from the French crossbow. By standing shoulder to shoulder, with bows held vertically, the English could send a forest of arrows. The French had to stand 5 to 6 feet apart with their crossbows. Moreover, crossbows were frequently getting out of order, and took longer to reload and shoot.

Records indicate that archery was first recognized and organized as a sport during the seventeenth century. In 1673 a group of archers met in

Yorkshire, England and originated the ancient Scorton Arrow contest. A small silver arrow was specified as the prize to the winner. The contest still exists and, of course, is the oldest continuous archery tournament. King Charles II of England recognized archery as a sport in 1676. The rulers of European countries gave their approval to the sport, and it has flourished since the seventeenth century.

The "Society Royal Toxophilite," designed to advance archery, came into being in England in 1790. In 1844 the Grand National came into existence and sponsored, that year and since, the national championships.

Even though some people in America had been participating in archery since white men first arrived on the North American continent, it was not until 1828 that serious consideration was given to it. In that year, a group organized under the name of United Bowmen of Philadelphia. The group continued to develop the sport until it disbanded in 1859.

The National Association of Archers, formed in 1879, and later renamed the National Archery Association, is the governing body of the sport. The first tournament was held the year the organization was formed, and since that time others have been conducted annually.

The National Field Archery Association, which is separate from the NAA, was founded in 1939. The Professional Archers Association (PAA) was formed in 1961; its members compete for merchandise and cash prizes.

The international organization, officially titled Federation Internationale de Tir a l'Arc, is commonly called FITA. In 1931 FITA's first tournament was held in Poland. Although archery was recognized as a demonstration sport in the Olympic Games in 1908 and 1920, great effort by many individuals and organizations was needed to have archery gold medal competition included in the 1972 Games. The NAA now differentiates between amateur and professional archers in order to field an Olympic team.

Archery is one of the most interesting and challenging sports known today. It is an ideal out-of-doors life-time recreation. Though developing the basic skills is easy, it is extremely difficult to achieve a high level of competency. Aiming, although simple, is different from that used with firearms, and therefore seems to be a great challenge. When the archer finally begins to hit the bull's-eye often, he feels a sense of achievement. The terminology used in archery is different from that of any other sport. The equipment and environment associated with it are of legendary character, and this serves as a romantic motivation to many people. Although most archers engage in target shooting, the number of field archers is growing. Other uses of archery include hunting, fishing, clout shooting, flight shooting, and archery golf.

TACKLE

bows

Early bows were made from innumerable kinds of wood. The Indians used the best kind that could be found on their hunting ground. Those in the territory now known as Tennessee used Osage orange and red cedar. Oregon or Washington yew, Osage orange, and Tennessee cedar were generally rated the best bow woods; other woods used included hickory, bamboo, ironwood, black locust, and sassafras. Bows made from one piece of wood were called *self bows*. The English, utilizing their international trade, preferred Spanish yew. A bow stave of Spanish yew was worth ten English elm staves.

Most of the modern bows are made of wood laminated with fiberglass. The fiberglass gives the bow greater cast (shooting distance), and the wood causes a smoother release (less vibration). Practically all composite bows today are of some form of the working recurve. A serviceable and economical bow to use in schools and camps is a recurve bow made completely of fiberglass (Figure 1-1).

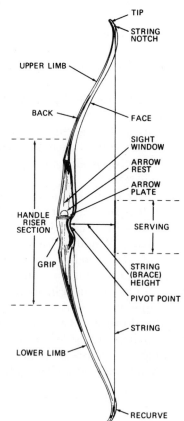

FIGURE 1-1 *Recurve Bow* (From Donald W. Campbell, *Archery*. © 1971, Prentice-Hall, Inc. Reproduced by permisson of the publisher.)

The earlier bow strings were made of hemp, were single-looped and tied to the bow with a timber hitch knot. Most archers today use dacron, double-looped, nylon-serviced strings. These strings may be easily made using a board and nail jig.

arrows

The most common arrow wood is Port Orford cedar, found in the coastal areas of Oregon and Washington. Alaskan cedar and Sitka spruce are good, as are other conifers. The American Indians frequently used maple-leaved viburnum.

For good scores the quality of the arrows is more important than the quality of the bow; therefore, an archer should use the best arrows he can afford (Figure 1-2). The spine (stiffness) of the arrows should be matched

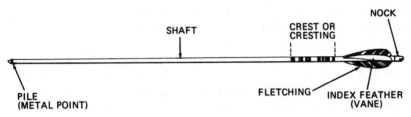

FIGURE 1-2 *Target Arrow* (From Donald W. Campbell, *Archery,* © 1971, Prentice-Hall, Inc. Reproduced by permission of the publisher.)

to the weight of the bow. Most of the better archers now use fiberglass or aluminum shafts.

target

The target used in target shooting is 48 inches in diameter; it usually has a reinforced center and is covered with burlap. It is supported on a tripod with the center of the bull's-eye 51 inches (1963 rule change) from the ground. The distance from the target depends upon the type of round being shot and upon which part of the round is being shot at the particular moment. The distance may be from 20 to 100 yards. In field archery the target distances vary from 15 to 80 yards with 6, 12, 18, and 24-inch targets.

BASIC SKILLS

Shooting an arrow is very simple because all that is necessary is to pull back the string and let it go. However, it is not easily accomplished because there are so many steps that must be done correctly and in the *same* manner on each and every shot to achieve any degree of accuracy. At the moment of release, a very high level of coordination is needed to control the body and the bow. Throughout the learning period and all practice sessions and competition, the keyword is *consistency*!

Before shooting, each student should be provided with an arm guard, glove or tab, arrows to match his arm length and weight of his bow, and, if possible, a quiver. This protective equipment *must* be worn each time he shoots.

bracing the bow

There are three methods of stringing the bow: the push-pull, the step-through, and a mechanical stringing device. The step-through method is not recommended for recurve bows because of the possibility of twisting the lower limb against the ankle. This disadvantage is eliminated if an ankle strap with a loop behind the heel is used, as this loop will allow the entire bow to turn when under pressure.

Before bracing, the archer should place the lower loop of the string completely in the lower nock, push the upper loop up toward the upper nock, and the string on the face or belly side of the bow. In the push-pull method, the archer stands with the toes pointing straight ahead and his weight on both feet. The handle is held in the left hand, and the lower nock is placed on the inside of the left instep; the bow should not be pushed against the ground. The thumb and forefinger of the right hand should be placed on the back of the bow, with the fingers toward the nock (Figure 1-3). Students should be cautioned not to place fingers between

FIGURE 1-3 *Bracing the Bow* (Reproduced from Don Cash Seaton, Irene A. Clayton, Howard C. Leibee, and Lloyd L. Messersmith, *Physical Education Handbook,* 5th ed. © 1969, Prentice-Hall, Inc., adapted from Donna Mae Miller and Katherine L. Ley, *Individual and Team Sports for Women.* © 1955, Prentice-Hall, Inc., by permission of the publisher.)

the string and the face of the bow in case the hand should slip off the back. As the left hand pulls up, the *heel* of the right hand should push forward as the thumb and forefinger manipulate the string into the nock. Before tension on the bow is slowly released, the student should check, by feel, that both sides of the loop are in the nock. The archer should look straight ahead as the bow is pushed to the side, to prevent the bow tip from hitting his head if the hand should slip off the bow.

After the bow is strung, the distance between the string and the handle (bracing height) should be checked carefully so that it is the same at all times. Different heights will produce a different thrust to the arrow.

To unstring the bow, the reverse procedure is used. Before bending the bow the archer should place his right forefinger against the loop on the belly side; and when the string is slack, the finger should pull the string toward the handle, slowly releasing the tension on the bow. If the student has difficulty using the left hand and the left foot, he should try using the right hand and the right foot.

stance

The body should be held in a relaxed upright position, one foot on each side of the shooting line, with the head turned toward the target. Imaginary lines drawn through the shoulders, hips, and the end of the toes should point toward the center of the target.

grip

The left thumb and forefinger should be around the handle, with the thumb on top of the fingertip, and the other fingers relaxed. The thumb and fingers should have no pressure on the sides of the bow. The base of the thumb should be on the pivot point of the handle, so the bow will not torque, or turn, as the arrow is released. The grip should be *exactly* the same on each shot.

nocking the arrow

With the string between the arm and the body, the archer holds the bow parallel to the ground with the left arm. The arrow is held by the nock in the right hand with the fingers pointing toward the crest and then the arrow is placed across and on top of the bow with the cock feather up. The arrow nock is placed on the string at a 90-degree angle opposite the arrow rest. Some prefer the nocking point $\frac{1}{8}$ to $\frac{1}{4}$ inch above the

90-degree angle. The nock should fit tight enough to remain in place but loose enough to come off if the string is lightly tapped. After nocking the arrow, the first three fingers of the drawing hand are placed on the string, the forefinger above the arrow nock and the middle and ring finger below the nock. The thumb and little finger are relaxed toward the palm. The string should be in the groove of the first joint of the finger. Each finger should have equal pressure on it during the draw and hold; at times there may be a "lazy" ring finger.

draw

The bow arm is raised to shooting position, the fingers are placed on the string, and the drawing hand should come straight back to the anchor point. The fingers serve as "dead hooks" on the string, the back of the hand is flat, and the wrist is straight. The right elbow should move back with the muscular power coming from the shoulder and upper back between the shoulder blades. The shoulders move down and back, and the shoulder blades move toward each other. The bow arm should remain steady with emphasis on the pull rather than on the push of the draw. The bow arm elbow should be rotated down and back so the arm would move parallel to the ground if it were bent; this position will prevent the string from hitting the elbow on release.

anchor

The anchor serves as the rear sight for the arrow and must not vary if the arrows are to score consistently. The drawing hand should be under

FIGURE 1-4 *Drawing the Bow*
(From Donald W. Campbell, *Archery.*
© 1971, Prentice-Hall, Inc. Reproduced by permission of the publisher.)

the jaw bone with the string touching the center of the chin and the tip of the nose (Figure 1-4). The drawing arm should be in a straight line with the arrow, with the forearm close to the shoulder. The muscular force should still be coming from the upper back and not from the fingers. The bow arm should be in the same position as in the draw—the left elbow rotated down and back, the left shoulder down and back, and the wrist straight. The shoulders, hips, feet, and arrow should be lined up with the center of the target. The body should be erect, and the weight on both feet.

In field archery and hunting, the high anchor is usually used. The drawing hand comes to the cheek bone with the forefinger anchored at the corner of the mouth. The head has a slight cant so the string will not hit the end of the nose on release.

hold and aim

The steady anchor and full draw must be maintained to prevent creeping, which will cause the arrow to go low. There are three methods of aiming: instinctive, or barebow, point-of-aim, and bowsight. In the barebow method, both eyes are focused on the target, and the elevation of the bow arm is controlled by kinesthetic sense. In the point-of-aim method, the end of the arrow is lined up with some mark on the ground. The shorter the range the closer the mark will be to the archer. This method has the psychological disadvantage of not looking at the place where the arrow should hit.

Nearly all target archers use a mechanical sight in aiming. The simplest sights are nothing more than a strip of tape on the back of the bow with a large-headed pin to the left of the bow. The position of the pin for each distance must be determined by trial and error. The greater the distance from the target, the lower the pin will be. As the range is shortened, the pin moves up.

When the students have learned the fundamentals well enough that they are grouping their arrows, they are ready to start using the sight. If adjustments in the position of the pin must be made, the pin should be moved in the direction of the error. If the arrows are low, the pin is lowered. It is easier if two different colored pins are used as this adjustment is being made. The first pin is left in its original position, and the second is placed in the estimated new position.

The left eye is closed, and the right eye looks to the right of the bow string and to the left of the bow through the sight to the center of the target. The head of the pin is placed in the exact center of the gold circle and is held there until the arm settles down and the pin is steady on the target (Figure 1-5).

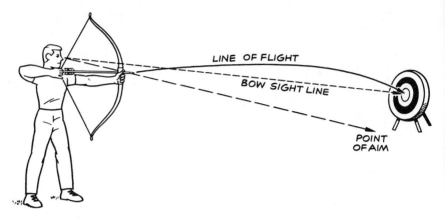

FIGURE 1-5 *Aiming the Arrow*

release

When the aim is steady, the fingers of the drawing hand relax, and the string rolls off the fingers. No effort should be made to straighten the fingers; the bow does the work. The bow arm should not push the bow toward the target, but should hold the bow steady as it pushes the arrow forward and returns to its position before the draw.

follow-through

If the archer has kept the proper muscular tension between the shoulder blades, the drawing hand should automatically move back along the neck. This is a recoil action that is *allowed* to happen, not *caused* to happen by jerking the hand backwards. The bow arm maintains its shooting position. After releasing the string, the archer should hold the shooting position for at least five seconds. This follow-through or after-hold prevents the arms from being dropped too soon. It also gives the archer an opportunity to check his fundamentals so he is aware of what errors he is making.

retrieving the arrows

The arrows should be pulled out of the target or ground at the same angle at which they entered. If the feathers are embedded in the target or under the grass, the arrows should be pulled out by the points.

scoring

In target archery, six arrows are shot in an end, but in field archery only four arrows are shot. In regular target shooting the 5-ring target face is used with the values of 9, 7, 5, 3, 1 recorded. In FITA competition, the 10-ring face is used, and the values are (gold) 10, 9, (red) 8, 7, (blue) 6, 5, (black) 4, 3, (white) 2, 1. In field archery the values are 5 and 3.

If an arrow cuts two colors, the higher value is recorded. If an arrow penetrates, passes through, or rebounds from the target, seven points is the score for that arrow if the range is 60 yards or less and five points if the distance is beyond 60 yards. If the arrow hits the target outside the white ring, that arrow is considered as a miss and is so scored.

STANDARD ARCHERY ROUNDS

American (men and women) 30 arrows at 60, 50, and 40 yards
York (men) 70 arrows at 100 yards; 48 at 80 yards; 24 at 60 yards
Columbia (women) 24 arrows at 50, 40, and 30 yards
Clout 36 arrows at 180 yards (men) and 120 yards (women) using a 48-foot target lying flat on the ground.

Men's FITA	122 cm. face	36 arrows at 90, 70 meters
	80 cm. face	36 arrows at 50, 30 meters
Women's FITA	122 cm. face	36 arrows at 70, 60 meters
	80 cm. face	36 arrows at 50, 30 meters

SAFETY

The bow is a powerful weapon with a great penetrating force. Students must realize this fact from the beginning. Archery is a safe sport if all the safety rules are closely followed. These rules are designed to protect the archer, other archers in the area, and the archery equipment. All students should learn these rules first, and the teacher should strictly enforce them at all times.

1. Before shooting, each archer should carefully check all of his equipment, looking for frayed strings or servings, nocking points, cracked arrows and loose fletchings. Cracked arrows should be broken in two pieces so they cannot be shot.

2. All archers should use the same shooting line, and the targets may be placed at different distances if desired.

3. No arrow is nocked until the archer is on the shooting line. All arrows are "quivered" until the shooting signal.

4. The field captain or teacher should signal with a whistle. One blast signals to start shooting; two blasts mean to cease fire immedi-

ately; one blast after cease-fire means to retrieve the arrows. The double whistle can be used as an emergency signal if someone starts to walk across the range.

5.   All archers should shoot at the same time, step back from the line when finished, and, on the signal, retrieve the arrows at the same time. The archers should approach the target from the side and pull the arrows from the side of the target. At no time should they stand in front of the target while pulling the arrows.

6.   Before shooting at any target, the archer should look beyond it to be sure that there is no one in the area. The arrow should not be shot up a hill in such a manner that if it misses the target, it will go over the crest, where the archer cannot see a clear field.

TEACHING PROCEDURES

Although there is no one order in which the material must be presented, the following is suggested for a class of beginners:

1.   The teacher should outline the course to the students, including the materials to be covered, procedures in handling the equipment, safety rules, and the grading or evaluation method used. Special emphasis must be placed on the safety rules throughout the course.

2.   The students should learn the parts of the bow and arrow, and these terms should be used throughout the course.

3.   The teacher demonstrates how to string and unstring the bow, and then the students practice doing so.

4.   The students learn how to use arm guards and gloves or tabs.

5.   The teacher should demonstrate target shooting, stressing the seven basic fundamentals of shooting: stance, nock, draw, anchor, hold and aim, release, and follow-through.

6.   The students practice the fundamentals by mimetics, stressing correct body positions and contraction of the upper back muscles.

7.   The students practice stance, nock, draw, anchor, hold and aim, and then come down to starting position. Stress should be put on the correct movement patterns.

8.   The teacher should watch each person, in turn, release his first arrow. If he is shooting well enough, he shoots the remainder of his arrows as the teacher is checking the others.

9.   The teacher should teach the proper method of retrieving the arrows from the target and from the ground. If any arrows are lost in the grass, the criss-cross hunting system should be used. All stu-

dents should help look for lost arrows to save time.

10.   As the students continue to shoot additional ends, the teacher should continually assist the students to eliminate their errors. Those that complete their end first should practice their mimetics until all movements are accurate.

11.   The "buddy system" may be used to check each other's skills and form while practicing mimetics or shooting.

12.   When the students are grouping their arrows, the use of the tape-and-pin bow sight should be used.

13.   When the students are hitting the target, the scoring procedures should be taught, and each student should keep his own scores. Scoring as in a tournament should be included sometime during the course.

14.   In future class sessions various distances and methods of shooting should be used to add interest and competition as the students' skills increase.

SKILL TESTS

Archery lends itself well to testing. An excellent criterion of whether a person is a good archer is the score he makes while shooting. The scores, shooting form, and the scores on a written exam should determine the final grade in the classes in which a grade for each student is recorded.

daily scores

After the members of the class have become reasonably proficient, a cumulative score for each archer is kept. Because all students will not shoot the same number of arrows during the course, the average score per arrow shot or per end may be figured. Based upon a graduated scale, skill grades may be determined for each student.

shooting form

A checklist including all of the shooting techniques may be used to evaluate each student's shooting form. If this checklist is used two or three times, it will help the student to know and then strengthen his weak points as the course progresses.

tournaments

An informal tournament may be conducted at the conclusion of the course and the students ranked according to their total scores.

written test

A written test may be given to determine how well the students know and understand the material covered during the entire course.

DEFINITION OF TERMS

Addressing the Target. The stance or position in which the archer is ready to shoot. The body is turned so that it is parallel to the line of flight of the arrow, with the head turned toward the target.

Anchor Point. A very definite point on the chin contacted by the index finger and string. In general, it is the point to which the drawing hand is brought as a part of the act of aiming.

Arm Guard. A piece of leather or some other material worn on the bow wrist and forearm to serve as protection from the bowstring.

Arrow Plate. A piece of hard substance different from that of which the bow is made, set in the bow where the arrow is supposed to cross to prevent wear.

Arrow Rest. A projection just above the bow handle on which the arrow may rest.

Arrow Stand. A rack in which arrows are stored. The term can also have reference to a ground quiver.

Back of the Bow. The part of the bow that is on the opposite side from the string.

Belly of the Bow. The inside of the bow; the part toward the string; also called the face.

Bow Arm. The arm used to hold the bow in the act of shooting.

Bowman. A person who participates in archery.

Bowyer. A person who makes archery equipment.

Brace. The act of stringing a bow.

Bracing Height. The distance between the bowstring and the handle.

Broadhead. A flat piece of steel with sharp edges fitted on the end of the arrow. *Broadhead* and *broad arrow* are often used interchangeably. A hunting arrow.

Cast. The flight distance a bow can shoot.

Clout Shooting. A round in which the archers shoot at a 48-foot target, which is lying flat on the ground. Women shoot at 120 or 140 yards and men at 180 yards.

Cock Feather. The one feather of an arrow that is at a right angle to the nock.

Composite Bow. A bow made of several layers, usually of wood and fiberglass.

Creep. A forward movement of the string hand before the release, which causes the arrow to go low.

Crest. The colored stripes of the arrow just below the feathers, used for identification.

Draw. The act of pulling the string back to the anchor point preliminary to aiming and release.

Elevation. The angle or height of the bow arm when in the act of shooting.

End. Shooting six arrows; a scoring unit.

Eye. The loop at the end of the bowstring.

Face. A new term for belly. It also refers to the scoring area of the front of the target.

Field Captain. The person in charge of a tournament.

Finger Tab. A flat piece of leather used to protect the fingers from the string friction.

FITA. Federation Internationale de Tir a l'Arc. The round used in international competition.

Fletch. To glue feathers on the arrow.

Fletcher. A person who glues feather to arrows. Historically, an arrow maker.

Fletching. A feather on the arrow.

Flight Arrow. An arrow that is especially constructed to make it lighter and less resistant to the air for the purpose of achieving greater distances on shots.

Flight Shooting. Competition in which the archers shoot for distance instead of hitting a target.

Footed Arrow. One that has a piece of hardwood spliced on the pile end to make it stronger.

Handle. The thick mid-section of the bow, where the bow hand grips the bow.

Head. The metal point, pile, or tip of the arrow.

Hen Feathers. The two feathers on an arrow that are not at right angles to the nock.

Hit. The arrow striking the target face for a score; hitting the skirt is not a hit.

Hold. To keep the bow at full draw while aiming before releasing.

Lady Paramount. The woman who is in charge of a tournament for women; more often *field captain* is used now.

Limbs. The parts of the bow that extend away from the handle.

Loose. To release the string while shooting.

Nock. A groove cut in the end of an arrow or on the tips of the bow into which the string is placed.

Nocking Point. A place on the string, usually marked, at which the arrow nock is fitted preliminary to drawing.

Overbowed. Using a bow that is too strong for the archer.

Overdrawn. The act of drawing so far that the arrow point comes within the face or belly of the bow, a dangerous procedure.

Pile. The point, tip, or head of an arrow.

Point of Aim. A point or spot at which one aims the end of the arrow in order to hit the target.

Quiver. A container in which the arrows are carried; may be a belt, shoulder, or ground quiver.

Range. The place of shooting or the distance being shot.

Recurve Bow. A bow with limbs that curve to the back near the tip.

Round. The term applied to the specifications of the number of arrows shot and the distances to be used in a specific tournament.

Self Arrow. An arrow made wholly of a single piece of wood.

Serving. The wrapping of a bowstring with a smaller thread to prevent wear at that point.

Shaft. The main body of an arrow.

Shaftment. The part of the arrow from the crest to the nock.

Shooting Line. The line the archer straddles when target shooting. In field archery the archer stands with both feet behind the shooting line.

Sight. An adjustable device on the upper limb of the bow to aid the archer in aiming; it is lined up with the center of the target.

Skirt. The part of the target face on the outside of the white circle; also called the petticoat or apron.

Spine. The springiness or stiffness of an arrow which should be matched to the weight of the bow.

Tackle. Archery equipment.
Target Face. The part of the target on which an arrow may hit for score.
Tassel. The bundle of pieces of yarn for the purpose of wiping arrows.
Timber. Called before shooting in field archery to warn other archers in the area.
Vane. The feather of an arrow, usually made of plastic.
Weight. The force, in terms of pounds, necessary to draw a bowstring the length of the arrow. Unless otherwise marked, it is measured at a 28-inch draw.

DISCUSSION QUESTIONS

1. How did the use of the bow and arrow develop?
2. How has archery figured in the early history of various countries?
3. Name the different types of bows.
4. Why is safety important in archery? Cite specific safety measures.
5. What is the American Round? the FITA?
6. How should a class be organized for teaching?
7. What is meant by the terms (a) nock, (b) serving, (c) end, (d) round?
8. Of what different materials are bows made? Arrows?

BIBLIOGRAPHY

Athletic Institute, *Archery Fundamentals.* Chicago: The Athletic Institute, 1949.

Barrett, Jean, *Archery.* Pacific Palisades, California: Goodyear Publishing Company, 1969.

Elmer, Robert P., *Archery.* Philadelphia: Pennsylvania Publishing Company, 1906.

Gordon, Paul H., *The New Archery.* New York: Appleton-Century-Crofts, 1939.

Klann, Margaret L., *Target Archery.* Reading, Massachusetts: Addison-Wesley Publishing Company, Inc., 1970.

Lambert, Arthur W., Jr., *Modern Archery.* New York: A. S. Barnes & Company, 1929.

Menke, Frank G., *The New Encyclopedia of Sports.* New York: A. S. Barnes & Company, 1947.

Miller, Myrtle K., *Archery Training Guide.* (rev. ed.) Upper Saddle River, New Jersey (Roxbury, Vermont): Teela-Wooket Archery Camp, 1964.

National Archery Association, *The Archer's Handbook.* Ronks, Pennsylvania: National Archery Association, 1966.

Price, Frank W., ed., et al., *Colliers Encyclopedia.* Vol. 2. New York: P. F. Collier and Son Corporation, 1949.

Reichart, Natalee, and Keasy, Gilman, *Modern Methods in Archery.* New York: A. S. Barnes & Company, 1936.

Shane, Adolph, *Archery Tackle.* Peoria, Illinois: The Manual Arts Press, 1936.

badminton

BACKGROUND

The game of badminton was originally played in India and for centuries was known as *poona*. English army officers first learned about it in the middle of the nineteenth century and liked it so well they played it on their return to England in 1871. As other people saw the game, many became interested and started playing also. In 1873 at a party given by the Duke of Beaufort in his country home known as Badminton near Gloucestershire, England, the game of *poona* was played extensively. In telling about it later, the participants described it as "the game at Badminton." So associated did the game become with the name Badminton that the new title stuck, and so it is known today.

The same rules that guided the game in India were used in England until 1887. They were, to some extent, confusing and contradictory. More

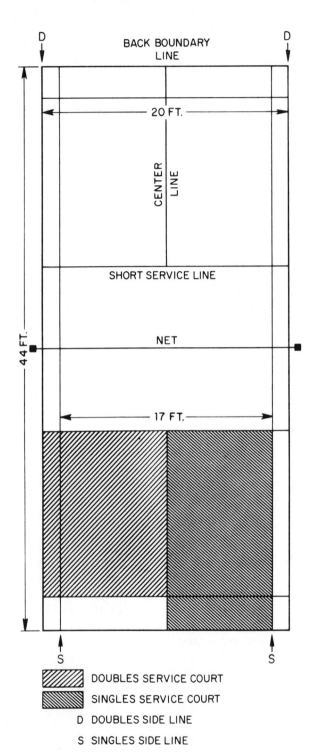

DOUBLES SERVICE COURT

SINGLES SERVICE COURT

D DOUBLES SIDE LINE

S SINGLES SIDE LINE

18

and more players began to realize the need for a complete revision. A group of badminton enthusiasts formed the Bath Badminton Club for the chief purpose of adjusting these rules to the newest ideas advanced by the English players and to standardize them for common usage. The rules drawn up in 1887 have remained virtually unchanged to the present time. In 1895, the Badminton Association of England was formed to take over the authority of the Bath club. This latter group is responsible for the only changes since that time, and they have been minor. The game quickly spread to Canada, the United States, and Australia.

The first championship tournament for men in England, though not considered official, was held in 1897. The next year, a tournament was held for women. The first official championships took place in 1904, and they have been conducted several times since.

The game gained phenomenal popularity in a comparatively short time. There were more than 9,000 badminton clubs in the British Isles just after World War II. Recently, tennis enthusiasts have taken to the game as well as people interested in other sports, and a count now would show vastly more clubs than were in existence in 1945.

Americans began playing the game enthusiastically in the late 1920s, and in recent years standard play facilities in the homes of the moderately well-to-do have included a badminton court, usually in the yard (Figure 2-1). However, outdoor play is not as satisfactory as the indoor game, since only a slight breeze will adversely affect the flight of the lightweight bird.

Badminton championships were conducted by the American Badminton Association (ABA) from 1937 to 1942 and resumed again in 1947. The ABA is the governing body for badminton in the United States. It is possible to become affiliated with this organization by either club or individual membership. Membership includes subscription to the ABA publication, *Badminton, U.S.A.*, which contains news items and other articles of interest to badminton players.

BASIC SKILLS

Badminton is a game that varies from slow, steady, cautious activity to fast and furious action. The bird, or shuttlecock, does not react like a ball because it is built to be air resistant, to turn immediately after the stroke, and to advance base first. The resistance causes it to lose speed rapidly and to drop suddenly. The player has the thrill of hitting the bird extremely hard, with confidence that it is not likely to go out of bounds. He is challenged also to acquire the skill necessary to control this object whether it be traveling rapidly close to the beginning of its flight or slowly toward the end.

the grip

Most badminton players use slightly different forehand and backhand grips when making the basic strokes. The basic forehand grip for a right-handed player is taken by holding the racket face perpendicular to the floor and gripping the handle in the right hand with the butt of the handle touching the heel of the hand. The "V" formed by the thumb and index finger should be on top or slightly toward the forehand face of the racket. The handle should run diagonally across the palm of the hand with the index finger slightly separated from the other fingers. All fingers and the thumb should be wrapped around the racket handle (Figure 2-2).

FIGURE 2-2 *Forehand Grip* (From Don Cash Seaton, Irene A. Clayton, Howard C. Leibee, and Lloyd L. Messersmith, *Physical Education Handbook*, 5th ed. © 1969, Prentice-Hall, Inc. Reproduced by permission of the publisher.)

In order to avoid fatigue, the player should hold the racket loosely, but firm enough to control it as the bird is contacted during a rally.

Starting from the forehand grip, the basic backhand grip is taken by moving the thumb up the backhand side of the racket handle with either the inside or "meaty" surface of the thumb exerting pressure on it. The index finger is moved down to contact the middle finger. These movements result in a slight rotation of the racket handle to the right (Figure 2-3).

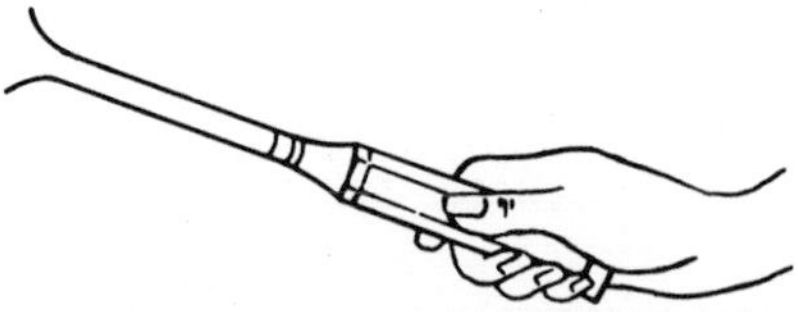

FIGURE 2-3 *Backhand Grip* (From Don Cash Seaton, Irene A. Clayton, Howard C. Leibee, and Lloyd L. Messersmith, *Physical Education Handbook*, 5th ed. © 1969, Prentice-Hall, Inc. Reproduced by permission of the publisher.)

wrist movement

Wrist movement, or hand rotation, is very important in badminton. On the forehand stroke, the racket is brought to the ready position with the hand completely supinated. When a stroke is to be made, the arm moves so as to bring the racket in proximity to the bird. The hand then quickly pronates, causing the racket face to move quickly and with much force to the bird. Many strokes are made with a minimum of arm movement but with much wrist movement (Figure 2-4).

FIGURE 2-4 *Playing Position* (From Barry C. Pelton, *Badminton.* © 1971, Prentice-Hall, Inc. Reproduced by permission of the publisher.)

serving

The forehand grip is preferable in serving. In making a serve, the head of the racket must be lower than the serving hand, and the bird must be below the waist when it is struck. To put it simply, a serve must be underhand. The basic motion is wrist movement, so there must be flexibility and strength in that particular part of the forearm. In making a serve, the player should place his feet from 12 to 18 inches apart, with the left foot (assuming the serve is made with the right hand) slightly farther forward than the right. It should be pointed out here that some instructors teach the service with the right foot forward because they believe that the server is in a better position for quick returns to the backhand. The bird is held at its base between the thumb and index finger of the left hand with the base pointing downward. It is held slightly above the waist. As the racket starts through its underhand arc, the bird is released so that the racket can hit it (Figure 2-5). The serving force may be slight, barely causing the

FIGURE 2-5 *The Serve* (From Barry C. Pelton, *Badminton*.
© 1971, Prentice-Hall, Inc. Reproduced by permission of the
publisher.)

bird to get into the service court, or it may be great, putting the bird well
back in the court. When the serve is underway, the player should take a
strategic position near the center of the court, well balanced and ready to
move in any direction to assure a successful return. It is wise for a player
to vary the speed and direction of his serve. He should also learn more
than one position in which to serve in order to confuse the opponent.

forehand and backhand

The development of good forehand and backhand strokes will be of great help in acquiring balance, rhythm, and power.

The forehand is employed when the bird is returned to the player's right. His left foot and shoulder should be near the net and his right foot back. He should be in balance, with his weight principally on the right foot, shifting to the left when the stroke is made, and with his knees bent slightly. The bird should be hit when it is directly in front of the body. Eyes should be on it constantly. On the forehand or on almost any other shot, the racket should be brought through a stroke smoothly and, just before the bird is hit, the hand should pronate, bringing the racket through even faster. Power comes in a strong wrist movement (Figure 2-6).

FIGURE 2-6 *Forehand Stroke* (From Barry C. Pelton, *Badminton.* © 1971, Prentice-Hall, Inc. Reproduced by permission of the publisher.)

The backhand is executed by turning the body ⅜ of a turn to the left from a position facing the net. By looking over the right shoulder, the player should watch the bird as it approaches. The correct backhand grip is taken, the hand is pronated, the elbow is flexed, and the shoulder is rotated inward. As the bird nears the contact area, the shoulder rotates outward, the elbow extends, and the hand supinates forcefully. This movement is accompanied by shifting the weight from the left to the right foot and rotating the trunk to the right (Figure 2-7).

FIGURE 2-7 *Backhand Stroke* (From Barry C. Pelton, *Badminton.* © 1971, Prentice-Hall, Inc. Reproduced by permission of the publisher.)

Correct forehand and backhand stroking comes with practice, and much time should be spent on it. A good grip is important, as is a relaxed hand that still has firmness.

Both the forehand and backhand may be executed with the contact of the bird being made in the overhand, sidearm, or underhand position. The type of stroke will be determined by the height of the bird at contact, but the basic forehand or backhand movement will be similar at each of the three contact points.

the clear

By using either the forehand or backhand, a player can effect what is known as the "clear." It is employed to direct the bird to the back of the opponent's court high enough to go over his head. It should be directed to the baseline of the opponent, who then must take the bird as it is falling. A clear shot may be made cross-court to the opposite corner, but it is best to direct the bird down one side or the other, depending on where the shot originated. Beginning badminton players usually rally by hitting a series of clears.

the net shot, or hair pin

The net shot requires very little power and is executed by a wrist and forearm movement. It can be played from almost any stance or body position although it is best to step toward the bird with the foot on the racket-hand side as it is played. The bird should be placed just over the net. If it crosses the net too high, the player is setting up a kill shot for his opponent rather than causing the opponent to set up one for him.

the drop shot

A drop shot is sometimes defined as any shot that causes the bird to drop quickly after crossing the net. The term is more commonly used to describe an overhand stroke that starts fast but, by a lessening of power at the last second, drops the bird just over the net. The shot may be made at a distance from the net or up close. Usually it is made when the opponent is back, expecting a smash or a clear.

the drive

A drive is a hard stroke in which the racket and the bird travel fast in a horizontal line. It is best to direct the bird either to an unoccupied part of the court or directly toward the opponent. The flight of the bird may be either straight down-court or cross-court.

the smash

The smash is a very hard downward stroke from a forehand, which sends the bird in a straight line to any part of the opponent's court. It is essential to hit a hard shot in order to give speed to the flight of the bird. A slow bird allows the opponent to get in position to return it.

If the player is right-handed, his left foot is forward, with the other far enough away to make a good balance. The bird is contacted at a point where the player is reaching to his limit overhead. The racket face should be in advance of the right shoulder. As the racket is brought forward, the player may need to twist to the left to put maximum power into the shot.

The left foot may step forward as the shot is made to facilitate additional power.

game strategy

Between two players of equal skill, the winner will be the one who takes advantage of his opponent's weaknesses. A capable badminton player sends the bird to the spot most difficult for his opponent to reach. He strokes frequently to different parts of the court, making sure to maintain irregularity in his procedure in order to keep his opponent guessing about his next move. The player should also play the bird in such a way that his opponent will be likely to set it up for him. The opponent's weaknesses should be determined as soon as possible, and shots should be played to them.

A badminton player has difficulty hitting a bird that comes close to his body. In most cases, the bird should be hit extremely fast to make it difficult for the opponent to see and to hit. Birds should also be hit where the opponent least expects them. A player should avoid giving away his intentions.

After making a stroke, a player should return to a position from which it will be easiest to get to any shot that may follow. He should stand at this spot, feet apart, knees slightly bent, ready to move in any direction quickly.

TEACHING PROCEDURES

It is important that there be enough equipment for the entire class to play the game. Minimum equipment for the best results is a racket for each student and a bird for every two. A badminton class should be limited in size so there will be four students, certainly not more than five, for every available court. The average school will not have more than three courts available either inside or out, so class size should be limited from twelve to fifteen students. In any practice session the net should always be an obstacle to shots.

It would be unfortunate to exclude the sport of badminton from the physical education program because classes would be too large. To cope with this situation, a large class might be divided into smaller groups, with each participating in a different sport. Since dual sports appear to be supplied less adequately with equipment, such a procedure might be tried with several such sports. A rotation could be effected, giving each student the opportunity to engage in all the sports before the school term is over.

When the teacher meets the class for the first time, a brief background of the activity should be given, covering its origin as well as its present status. A brief demonstration of the game should be conducted, along with a running account of rules involved and the various shots made. Before the first class ends, each student should have had a chance to swing a racket and hit a bird a few times. It is necessary to provide the opportunity for him to learn the reaction of the racket and bird as early as possible so that he can begin to enjoy playing the game.

To get the pupils in a position for hitting the birds, each one should be handed a racket, with half the class on one side of the nets and half on the other. It works satisfactorily in the practice sessions to have as many as six to a court as long as care is exercised that players are not hit by the rackets of other players. During the first three or four class meetings, the players should do nothing more than hit the bird in an attempt to get it back over the net. The service technique may be taught because it is a good way to begin the stroking. Instruction in this particular skill should begin early.

After it is apparent that the students have learned the reaction of the rackets and the birds, the teacher should begin teaching the various strokes. Though this may be done in any order desired, it is suggested that it be the same as that used in the discussion of strokes in this chapter. By the time the class has been meeting two weeks, the students should be allowed to play short games up to 7 points. When the skills have been practiced three weeks, the students should be allowed to play full 15-point games frequently. The teacher may pass among the players and make criticisms and corrections as the play proceeds.

It is possible to do a reasonably effective job of teaching badminton to large classes with limited space and insufficient equipment. A publication developed through the Lifetime Sports Education Project of the American Association for Health, Physical Education and Recreation makes many valuable suggestions for such teaching. It is entitled *Ideas for Badminton Instruction* and may be ordered from the AAHPER.

game modification

The cost of the better badminton rackets and the tournament quality feather birds makes badminton a rather expensive sport. For schools, it is desirable to use less expensive rackets and nylon shuttlecocks or birds. A word of caution is in order here. Use rackets that are comparable in weight to the more expensive rackets and nylon shuttlecocks that come close to meeting the standards for bird flight as set forth in the official badminton rules of the International Badminton Federation. Rackets that are too heavy and birds that are either too slow or too fast in flight make it impossible to teach the skills of the game properly.

SKILL TESTS

clear test

Mark a regulation badminton court as shown in Figure 2-8.

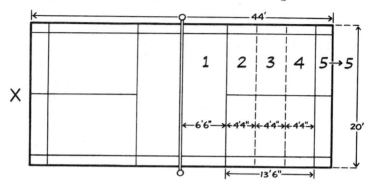

FIGURE 2-8 *Badminton Court*

ADMINISTRATION OF THE TEST. The player stands behind the baseline as indicated by the "X" in the diagram. From this position both the forehand and backhand clear test are taken.

1. Forehand clear test: From the correct position on the court, the student places the bird on the *forehand face* of the racket, tosses it overhead, and strokes a *forehand clear* as far as possible.
2. Backhand clear test: From the correct position on the court the student places the bird on the *forehand face* of the racket, tosses it overhead, and strokes a *backhand clear* as far as possible.

SCORING. Each player is given seven trials on the forehand and seven trials on the backhand. The best five of each of these seven trials is the player's score. As indicated in the diagram, the deeper the clear is hit, the higher the score, to a maximum of 5. To be scored, a bird must fall within the doubles court or the sidelines extended. A bird falling on a restraining line is given the higher value of the line in question.

Other tests to establish grades may include the low serve test, the high serve test, and the wall volley test. These tests are described in the publication *Ideas for Badminton Instruction* and other publications listed in the bibliography.

DEFINITION OF TERMS

Backhand. A stroke made when the shoulder of the arm making the stroke is toward the net and the back of the hand and back of the racket are forward.

Bird. See Shuttle.

Clear. A stroke directed over the head of the opponent and to the back of his court.

Doubles. A game in which a team of two players plays against a team of two others.

Doubles Service Court. A space 13′×10′ from which the bird is put in play in doubles.

Down the Line. A stroke made aiming the bird down the side line.

Drive. Any hard horizontal stroke that sends the bird straight, hard, and low over the net.

Drop. A shot that causes the bird to go low over the net and fall immediately after crossing.

Fault. Any play that causes a rally to be lost.

Forehand. Any shot taken when the shoulder of the arm making the shot is away from the net and the front of both hand and racket are toward the net.

Game. A point in competition when a side has reached 15 or some other predetermined number of points.

Handicap. The spotting of a certain number of points.

Inning. A term at service. The time during which a player or team holds service.

In side. Serving side.

Kill. A hard shot that the opponent fails to return.

Left Half Court. The part of the court on the left side of the center line as a player faces the net.

Let. A situation that allows a rally to be replayed.

Match. Best two out of three games.

Rally. Continual stroking of a bird back and forth across the net until the point is completely played.

Return. Any stroke other than a serve that gets the bird legally across the net.

Right Half Court. The part of the court on the right side of the center line as the net is faced.

Server. The person putting the bird into play.

Service-over. The change of serve from one side or team to the other.

Service. The act of putting the bird into play.

Set It Up. Any upward stroking that puts the bird in the air in such a position that the opponent can hit it down.

Setting the Game. When the game ties at 13–13, the receiver, who is also the first to make 13 points, has the choice of setting the game at 5 points, making the total points necessary to win 18, or ending it at 15 points. If the game ties at 14 points, the receiver has the choice of ending the game at 15 points or setting it at 3 points. If the game is set at 3 points, a total of 17 will be required to win.

Shuttle, Shuttlecock, Bird. An object made of cork and feathers that is propelled in the game of badminton. Shuttlecocks are also made of nylon or other synthetic materials.

Singles. Game played by two people only, one on either side of the net.

Singles Service Court. A space 15′6″×8′6″ from which the bird is put into play.

Sling or Carry. A term indicating that the shuttle is carried on the racket. It is illegal.

Smash. A hard downward stroke that sends the bird straight over the net and fast downward.

Stroke. The act of hitting the bird with the racket.

DISCUSSION QUESTIONS

1. How did badminton get its name?
2. What organization first began to standardize the rules?
3. Why is badminton different from the usual tennis type of game?
4. Describe a good basic grip.
5. What is the "clear" shot?
6. Give five points you consider important in game strategy.
7. How would you teach a group badminton during the first class period?
8. How can you test skills in badminton?

BIBLIOGRAPHY

books

Cummings, Parke, *The Dictionary of Sports*. New York: A. S. Barnes & Company, 1949.

Davidson, Ken, and Gustavson, Lea, *Winning Badminton*. New York: Ronald Press, 1953.

Fisher, Herbert L., *How to Play Badminton*. Minneapolis: Burgess Publishing Company, 1939.

Industrial Recreation Association, *Standard Sports Areas*. Chicago: Industrial Recreation Association, 1944.

Jackson, Carl H., and Swan, Lester H., *Better Badminton*. New York: A. S. Barnes & Company, 1939.

Ketchum, Leon, *Badminton*. Chicago: A Chicago Park District Publication, 1937.

Mitchell, E. D., *Sports for Recreation*. New York: A. S. Barnes & Company, 1952.

Poole, James, *Badminton*. Pacific Palisades, California: Goodyear Publishing Company, 1969.

Rogers, Wynn, *Advanced Badminton*. Dubuque, Iowa: William C. Brown Company, 1970.

Tunis, John R., *Lawn Games*. New York: A. S. Barnes & Company, 1943.

Varner, Margaret, *Badminton*. Dubuque, Iowa: William C. Brown Company, 1966.

————, *Sports for the Fun of It*. New York: A. S. Barnes & Company, 1940.

Yocom, Rachael B., and Hunsaker, H. B., *Individual Sports for Men and Women*. New York: A. S. Barnes and Company, 1947.

periodicals and guides

Badminton U.S.A., Official publication of the American Badminton Association. Grace Devlin, Dolfield Road, Owing Mills, Maryland.

Ideas for Badminton Instruction, Lifetime Sports Education Project, American Association for Health, Physical Education, and Recreation. 1201 Sixteenth Street, N. W., Washington, D. C., 1967.

baseball

3

BACKGROUND

The early history of the game of baseball is not authenticated. Little was written about it during its evolutionary days, and any statement of how it developed must be based on circumstantial evidence and much assumption. The game of cricket, the basic pattern of which is like baseball, has been played for centuries in England. It accompanied the early settlers to this continent, where it was played in one form or another. Parents had little time for games, but the children participated in cricket or some modification of the sport. It may be assumed that the equipment they used was of a makeshift variety, since it is reasonably certain that it was not secured in any quantity from England.

The old game of rounders is an activity frequently mentioned as one of the stages through which baseball passed before reaching its present form. In playing the first games of rounders, children probably used old cricket balls and cricket bats, but instead of wickets to which cricket players ran, they used stakes driven into the ground. The stakes may or may not have been set in a diamond or square pattern. There had to be someone to pitch the ball, someone to catch it, and, of course, a batter between the two. A good guess would be that there was little if any defensive organization. The boys probably were scattered out in the field, hoping they would be where a ball might come after being hit.

For a player to be put out, he had to be "plugged," which meant being hit with a thrown ball while running between stakes. It is of interest to note that "plugging" lasted as late as the early 1840s. It is understandable that "plugging" made it unnecessary to have men specifically designated to play at the different stakes.

As children played the game more and more, the secondhand equipment supplied by parents wore out, and it was necessary to devise makeshift balls and bats. Thus strings wrapped around a solid core of a rock or a piece of wood formed the first baseball, and a stick cut from a hickory or ash sapling was probably the first bat.

As the popularity of the game increased, problems that developed were ironed out. A beginning was made on some systematic rules, and flat stones replaced the stakes to decrease hazards.

Many forms of baseball were tried, some of which still exist in children's play today. These forms involved changes in the number and location of bases rather than in rules. At first, there was only one base or stake; later, there were two, three, and finally four. The game was called at various times "One Eyed Cat," "Two Eyed Cat," "Town Ball," and the "New York Game." The rules are obscure. It is certain that the players used the cricket type of scoring. It is also highly possible that many cricket rules were employed.

In all probability each town or center had its own playing rules, and only in later years, when inter-town competition began, was there any thought that rules should be unified. It is assumed that the bats, even though they were hickory saplings, had a flat surface similar to the cricket bat. The scoring for a long time probably was done as in cricket; when a team reached a certain number of runs, it was declared the winner. If there ever were "playing periods," they were probably agreed upon in advance. It is also believed that the number of players was gradually reduced.

No one knows exactly when the name of baseball became attached to the game. Some unreliable evidence suggests that it came into use during the early 1830s, after stones had been substituted for stakes. Physical-education historians say that as early as 1825 "baseball" was played in the Round Hill School at Northampton, Massachusetts.

The history of baseball from 1825 through the next 20 years is a matter of stormy debate. Many think that Abner Doubleday first conceived the diamond-shaped field that is used today and that he was the sponsor of the first game played at Cooperstown, New York, in 1839. Other sources say that Doubleday probably never played baseball and that it was a flourishing game long before 1839. Evidence already cited in this discussion bears out this latter statement.

Another story believed by many is that a baseball diagram similar to the diamond of today was laid out by Alexander Cartwright in 1845, and tried in a game in 1846 at Hoboken, New Jersey. "Plugging" is supposed to have been used in this game and retained in the rules for several years afterwards.

In contrast to the obscure early history of the game, what follows is reasonably well substantiated.

The group interested in baseball in the New York area did much work on the rules and on the diagram for the playing field. They set up a "baseball" diagram in 1842 that listed home plate as the striker's box. The distances between bases in the order they were run were 48, 60, 72, and 82 feet. The last place to which the player was to run, making a score if he got there safely, was slightly to the left of home plate. It is significant that these rules and the diagrams were formulated by a group of adults. Even though it was still primarily a boys' game, men were also playing it. As a direct result of adult interest in the sport, the first baseball club in the history of the game was formed in 1845 in New York. It was called the Knickerbocker Baseball Club. Another set of rules was drawn up during the winter of 1845–46; these more nearly approached the present-day rules and served as a standard by which the game could be played. The bases were now an equal distance apart and 21 hands, or innings, had to be played for a complete game.

In the first recorded game under these new rules, the New York Nine defeated the Knickerbockers 23-1 in four innings. The first baseball uniforms were worn by the Knickerbockers in a practice game in 1849. In the second recorded game between two organized ball clubs, the Knickerbockers met the Washington Baseball Club in 1851 and won in extra innings, 22–20. In a return game, won by the Knickerbockers, the first box score in the history of baseball was kept by one of the players.

It was inevitable that baseball players should organize. In March of 1858, 25 clubs met, elected officers, and further standardized the rules. This organization lasted until the early 1870s, when professional baseball became popular.

The first game to which admission was charged was played July 20, 1858. The fee was required for the rental of the playing field, and a total of $750 was paid by 1,500 spectators.

Colleges began to play the game in the late 1850s. Williams College played Amherst in July, 1859, in the first recorded game, and lost, 66–32. By the 1860s, baseball was being played by Bowdoin, Dartmouth, Harvard, Princeton, and Yale.

By this time the game was creating so much interest that the Excelsiors of Brooklyn made the first baseball tour in 1860, played six games, and won them all. The Cincinnati Red Stockings, who had organized in 1866, began paying their players in 1869. The salaries ranged from $600 to $1,400 for an eight-month season. They toured the country from March 15 to November 15, winning 55 games and tying one. The winning streak was finally broken by the Brooklyn Atlantics, who beat the Red Stockings 8-7 in an extra inning.

The National Association of Professional Baseball Players was organized in 1871. Clubs that belonged to this organization included Boston, Chicago, Cleveland, Philadelphia, and Troy. Along with the games at this time, however, there was considerable drinking, gambling, and general corruption. The situation had become so serious by 1875 that baseball was threatened with extinction. William A. Hulbert and A. G. Spaulding, both of whom had a great interest in the game, wanted to lift it to a respectable position. As a result the National League of Professional Baseball was formed, and in 1900 the American League was organized. There were several minor leagues in 1887, including the California, Eastern,

FIGURE 3-1   *Baseball Field*

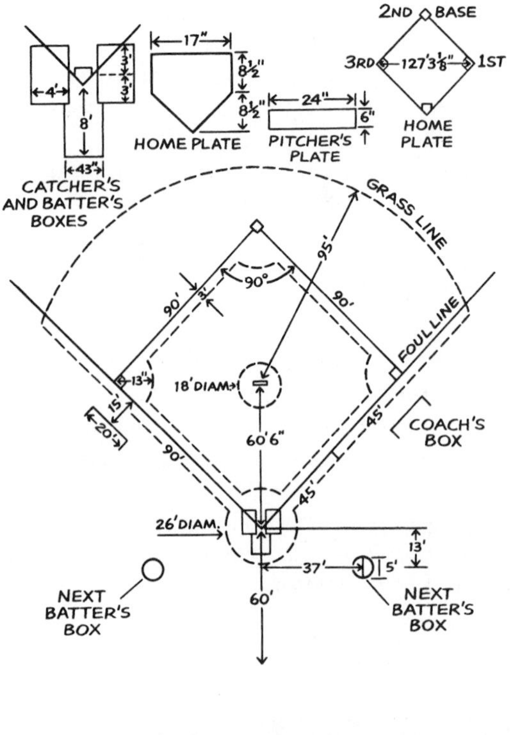

International, New England, Northwestern, Ohio State, Southern, and Western leagues.

In 1903 the two major leagues and the minor groups banded together to form "Organized Baseball" and were ruled by the National Commission. During all this time equipment was being added to the game and the size of the diamond was standardized (Figure 3-1). The game has remained virtually unchanged since 1920.

BASIC SKILLS

Baseball requires extreme concentration and alertness. Much of the time during a game the player is inactive. He is in his defensive position waiting for a ball to be hit to him or thrown to him in a play for the baserunner. When anything happens in baseball, it usually happens in a hurry, and the man involved in the play must be ready to move and perform whatever skill is necessary. When the team is at bat, the situation is much the same. In that phase of the game, the player is either sitting in the dugout, batting, or running bases, and the job of concentration is still a problem. The teacher of baseball will have trouble developing the habit of concentration in the beginning player. As a player's skill improves, the problem of concentration will in most cases take care of itself.

throwing

It is essential that the good ballplayer learn all the skills, but it is particularly important that he learn to throw well. A ball may be thrown varying distances and from many positions. Each throw may differ from the others to some degree. However, for the average throw of from 80 to 125 feet, there are certain basic fundamentals that in some ways apply to every throw. The ball should be held in the hand with the first two fingers placed over the top of it and spread comfortably. The thumb is placed underneath the ball opposite the fingers. At the release the ball should roll off the ends of the two fingers in order to put reverse, or back spin, on it. This results in a more nearly straight, accurate flight.

The stance is extremely important in an accurate throw. The left shoulder should be toward the target as the preparation is made, assuming the player is right-handed. This means that the lateral line of the feet should be in line with the target and that the body actually should be facing at a right angle to the target. The weight should be equally distributed on both feet. The feet should be spread apart to about the width of the shoulders or some other comfortable distance. The arm goes up then back, forward, and down, forming a fairly well-defined circle. As the arm goes back, the weight first shifts temporarily to the right, or back, foot. As the arm continues its circle, the left leg is extended in the direction of the target. As the arm is brought to the upper arc, the weight shifts to the left foot until, at the time of release, the weight is completely on it, and the body is moving forward. The arm comes down in a follow-through across the body, relaxing as it slows down. Balance is regained immediately by bringing up the right foot and distributing body weight evenly on both feet.

Throwing requires much practice. The ball must be thrown literally thousands and thousands of times over different distances in many different circumstances until it becomes a well-defined habit. The mind of a baseball player must be free to concentrate on the strategy of the game, and it can be free only when throwing is a habit.

catching

It is necessary to consider protection for the player's hand before discussing the mechanics of catching. Because the bare hand is unable to withstand the punishment of catching, and because balls can be caught less accurately in the bare hand, protection is necessary. The protection will be either a mitt or a glove, large enough to aid in trapping the ball but not so large and cumbersome that the ball is difficult to retrieve and throw. The glove should be comfortable and must fit well. The type of hand protection depends in a large measure on the position of the player. The catcher and first baseman use mitts; others use gloves. The size of the first baseman's mitt is specified by rule. Outfielders and pitchers use larger gloves.

The catch in baseball is basically the same as the catch of any ball in any game. The catcher moves into the line of flight of the ball and reaches out with his gloved hand, the open side of the glove toward the ball. Just before the ball gets to the glove, the hand starts to move back. As contact is made, the glove continues back, gradually bringing the ball to a stop. Here is a formula that will be of help in having the glove in the correct position to catch a directly oncoming ball: if the ball is above the waist, fingers up and thumb to right; below the waist, fingers down and thumb to left; to the right, fingers out and thumb down; to the left, fingers out and thumb up. If the ball is extremely far to either the right or the left, this formula will not work.

Because throws must often be made immediately after a catch, preparation for the throw should begin during the catch. As the ball is contacted and slowed down, the player should start positioning his feet for the throw. As the glove slows down at the end of the catch, the right hand should reach into the glove and take the ball for the throw.

Moving baseballs will approach the potential receiver in a variety of ways. They may be fly balls, line drives, or ground balls. In any case, and especially for ground balls, it is a good rule to keep the eye on the ball until it is safely in the glove. The receiver should be relaxed and never "fight" the ball by pushing at it.

pitching

It has been estimated that from 60 to 75 percent of the defense is good pitching. The percentages are open to question, but everyone agrees that pitching is extremely important.

The way a ball curves, some of its speed, and its other actions are in a large part dependent on the way it is held and how it leaves the hand. Since the seams present a friction surface, it is advisable to place the fingers either on and in line with them or across them. Except for one pitch, which involves the thumb and three or four fingers, the grip is taken with the index and second fingers plus the thumb. It has been said that a pitcher could do a better job if he did not have the third and fourth fingers.

The grip should be just tight enough to be firm, and it is fundamentally the same for almost all the deliveries. Other factors governing the flight of the ball in most pitches are the action of the wrist and the release.

The pitcher's stance is made by placing the right foot in contact with the rubber and the left foot slightly back of it. Just prior to any delivery movement, the arms are hanging down by the sides. They then move forward and return down. The right arm moves back in what is called the back swing. At the end of the back swing, the arm moves down and forward and comes to rest in the glove. This preliminary movement is known as a pumping motion. As the back swing is being completed, a slight pivot is made on the right foot so that the pitcher faces third base. As the ball and hands meet at the glove, the left leg is raised, and all the weight is placed on the right foot. The ball is kept hidden by the glove and hand so that the batter will not know what pitch is coming. While the leg is up, the right arm starts describing an arc down and back. The shoulders are thrown back as the arm describes the circle. As the arm gets its height in the circle and begins the forward motion, the weight is gradually moved from the right foot to the left, which is now stretching out toward the target. As the arm goes forward, it is bent at the elbow. At a point about even with the head and slightly back, the elbow slows up and allows the forearm to move on faster. The wrist breaks forward an instant before the ball leaves the hand.

After the ball leaves the hand, body weight shifts completely to the left foot, which has been planted slightly off-center. The right foot then comes up even with or slightly in front of the left foot, the weight is distributed evenly, and the pitcher is set for a possible hit ball in his direction. During this movement of the right foot, the arm follows through down across the body as if it were pulling down a shade.

It is important to any pitch, and particularly to the fast ball pitcher, that the weight and power of the body be behind it. Power and weight are put into a delivery by a series of coordinated movements. When the body is back, the left leg up, and the arm ready to start its forward movement, the pitcher is like a tightly coiled spring ready to be turned loose. The body movement is then from that position to one leaning in the direction of the target, and it should be very fast.

The curve ball actually begins when the arm is about at the ear on its last forward movement. The wrist and hand turn in toward the head so that, as the arm completes the movement, the ball leaves the finger from the side. A good curve is one that breaks quickly just before it crosses the plate.

hitting

Hitting is the chief offensive weapon. Successful hitting requires timing, power, and the ability to diagnose the pitches. It is essential that a batter also be able to relax at the plate to the extent that he will not be psychologically "tied up."

THE STANCE. The batter should stand near the back of the batter's box with his legs in line with the pitcher. His feet should be at least the width of his shoulders apart with much of his weight on the right, or rear, foot. The bat is held in the hands with the left hand on the bottom and the right hand immediately above and touching it. The grip is firm but not too tight. The bat is held back, up, and ready to swing. The left arm is almost straight, the right elbow points to the ground, and the arms are well away from the body. The batter looks over the left shoulder. This bat position is taken as soon as the pitcher starts his delivery. The head is up facing the pitcher, with the eyes on the ball from the moment the pitcher steps on the rubber. During the swing the bat should reach just across the plate.

THE STRIDE. As the batter anticipates the release of the ball, the body moves forward, and the left leg steps about 6 inches toward the pitcher. The batter's strides should be short and, normally, straight ahead, since it is very difficult to step in any other direction on a fast ball pitcher. The step should be completed at the time of contact with the ball. This move allows body weight to be a factor in the force that is applied.

THE SWING. The swing starts at a time when the batter sees that it is a good pitch, and he thinks he can make contact with it. The bat should go forward in a horizontal, or level, swing. Just prior to this swing, the batter should have followed the ball and started judgment on it as soon as the pitcher released it. He should continue to look at it until he has either hit or missed it. The spin of the ball will indicate to the alert batter whether the pitch is a curve or a fast ball.

The wrists should precede the bat around until an instant prior to the contact. They should then "break," which means they should begin an additional snap, which causes the bat to move around much faster than the actual swing is bringing it. There are those who believe the major share of power is in the wrist action. The flight of the bat should be gradually stopped in the follow-through, and the batter should recover his balance and, if he hit the ball, proceed to first base. The batter should keep false motions and wiggling of the bat at a minimum. They are of no benefit whatsoever.

BUNTING. There come times during the course of a baseball game when it is offensively important to advance a man at the possible sacrifice of an out. Well-laid bunts, however, will frequently result not only in a man's advancing but in the batter also getting on base. If a batter intends to bunt, he should never give a hint of that intention. He should stand at the plate as if he were going to swing away. When the pitcher gets ready to release the ball, the batter very quickly brings his feet side by side in the batter's box even with the plate, faces the pitcher, and slides his right hand up the bat about half way. Some coaches prefer, instead of moving the feet side by side squarely toward the batter, to pivot the feet on the heels in a 90-degree angle, since there is less motion and less chance of giving away the intention. The bat is horizontal, well in front of the batter, and the thickest portion of it is directly over the plate. Effort should be made to bunt the ball low so that it will roll along the ground. Where the ball is directed depends on where the base runner is, where the pitch is thrown, and where the defense is playing.

A drag bunt, usually performed by left-handers, is made for the chief purpose of getting on base. The word "drag" has reference to the act of dragging the ball down the first base line. The bat is extended behind the batter to contact the ball while the batter actually begins a stride to first base.

fielding

This phase of the game is included here as an addition to the section of this chapter on catching. Catching the ball is the act of stopping and gaining control of it. Fielding a ball includes the act of catching and, further, of playing it correctly after it is caught. The good defensive man makes preparation for throwing as he is catching. Prior to any play, the defensive baseball player must know the number of outs, the tendency of the batter, the men on base, and any characteristics they may have. On the basis of this knowledge, he must decide in advance what he will do if the batter hits to him. His movements must be relaxed and unhurried, but at the same time definite and positive.

FLY BALL. At the crack of the bat, all men on the field must begin a careful judgment of the direction of the ball. It takes but a moment to determine where it is going, and the men in that general vicinity should move toward it. Assuming the ball is going high into the outfield, it has not gone too far in its flight when it is clearly determined who should field it. If it is clearly in a fielder's territory, this man quickly should judge its probable landing area and move there. As he takes his place beneath the ball, his eyes should be on it, and his feet comfortably apart so that he can move in any direction. The outfielder should attempt to catch every fly ball in a position from which a throw can be made.

LINE DRIVE. A line drive is a hard-hit ball that remains in the air until it passes the infield, but is too high to be caught by an infielder. The fielder must be ready for a line drive at all times and, if one comes his way, must attempt a catch. The fielder must move quickly and, in most cases, snag it with one hand. Line drives often catch runners off base, and an alert fielder can sometimes start a double play.

HARD GROUND BALL. In fielding a hard ground ball, the man should move quickly to get his body in front of the ball. It is extremely important that he remain relaxed and that he keep his eye on it until it goes into his glove. If the ball is low, he should be in front of it, feet apart and knees bent. If it bounces high, he must take it any way he can, except that the fingers of his glove should be up. As soon as the ball is safely in his glove, he begins a throw to the correct base. The throw must be hard, accurate, and fast but not too hurried.

SLOW GROUND BALL. The fielder must move up on a slowly bounding ball. If he waits for it to get to him, it may give the runner the time he needs to reach first base. As the fielder approaches the ball, he stops and sets just before it gets to him. As he catches it, he takes a throwing position. The fielding is then effected just as with the other type of grounder.

POSITION PLAY

The different positions require varying anatomical and physiological characteristics as well as specific duties and skills. When a player is deciding what position he prefers to play, he should study the requirements and duties of each, analyze himself as best he can, and determine at which he may be most efficient. Generally, the infield requires fast, alert, and quick-reacting men; the outfield needs fast men, but not necessarily those with the quickest reactions. Height is an advantage in some positions, whereas weight is more important in others.

catcher

The catcher works continually in a very tiring job. He is the spark plug of the defensive play, being a guide for a major portion of it. An outstanding catcher can inspire confidence in a team and keep play at a high level.

The catcher should have a strong, reasonably heavy build and at least medium height; he should have big hands and a live arm. He should be endowed with a great deal of endurance. He should be able to catch any kind of pitch, be oblivious to the bat movement, be expert at catching pop ups, and be able to throw accurately with speed to any base.

The catcher is the brains of the defense. He has many jobs to perform and must be alert to the characteristics of the opponents and the game's progress. He signals every pitch on the basis of his judgment of the batter's ability. He must know the number of outs, the bases occupied, and keep his team informed at all times of changes that take place or plays to make in specific situations.

When the pitcher is in the act of pitching, the catcher gets ready for the ball by going to a full knee-bend with mitt up, open side toward the pitcher as a target. The right hand is kept closed to protect the fingers but in readiness to open and cover the ball the instant it lodges in the mitt. He stands immediately behind the plate and close to the batter. He should be in readiness at all times to go high for a ball or to drop low to stop a low ball. Because a catcher may have to throw immediately in order to retire a baserunner, he should be able to throw with a shoulder-and-arm motion, and with a very minimum of body movement.

Because it is the catcher's job to determine the type of pitch to be delivered each time, he must have a way to impart this information to the pitcher. He uses signals, and they are generally made while he is crouched. A certain number of fingers means a certain type of delivery. The signals can be decided upon between the two men, but the infielders should have knowledge of the signs being used. It is important that the signals be given in such a way as not to be seen by the opponents, particularly a runner at second base.

A skillful, alert, confident, and intelligent catcher can do much toward making his team defensively strong.

pitcher

Although there have been notable exceptions to this rule, most good pitchers have live arms. A pitcher should be strong, be in good physical condition, and have an alert mind, courage, and poise. The effective pitcher will have natural throwing ability and free pitching-arm movement. A pitcher who can hit well and can field is a valuable asset to a ball club, though these attributes are of secondary importance.

He should most certainly have control of his delivery and should have mastery over a variety of deliveries, including a fast ball, a sharp-breaking curve, and an effective change-of-pace. He should work on his delivery so that the pattern of motion for all will be much the same.

The pitcher should make every pitch count. It is well to get the batter on the defensive as soon as possible; in order to do this, the first pitch should be a strike. The pitcher's control should allow him to play for the batter's weakness. He should try to get the batter to swing at pitches over the corners, since these will be hit with much less force and accuracy if they are hit at all. He should vary the type of pitched balls from fast ones to curves and change-of-pace, and never allow a batter to get set for any particular pitch.

The pitcher must be alert to all situations as they develop on the diamond. He must assist in holding runners on base. He must finish a delivery ready to field a base. He must back up the various bases on throws from the outfield.

He must frequently play first base when the first baseman has to field the ball. The pitcher must see much of what goes on around him. He must see the batter and the catcher, and must be alert to movements of the men on base and his own fielders. He should also check change of positions for left- or right-handed batters.

The general pattern of delivery should be the same in all cases. The factors that make for a fast ball, a curve, or a change-of-pace are the ways the ball is gripped and the way it leaves the hand.

THE FAST BALL.   The most important pitch for the young pitcher to master is the fast ball. A fast ball does not mean overpowering speed, which is a natural skill. Many pitchers capable of throwing hard never seem to fool a batter with their quickness because the ball travels in a straight line. To master the fast ball, the pitcher must have control of it and the ability to make it move.

The grip is the first fundamental to be learned. The ball should be held so the fingers of the throwing hand make the best contact on the seams of the ball. The grip ordinarily will depend upon the individual pitcher, and he should experiment until he finds the one that is most efficient for him. Many pitchers hold the ball with the first two fingers on top and across the seams at their widest part. The thumb is underneath and the third finger along the side of the ball. Other pitchers grip the ball with the first two fingers along the seams at their narrowest part.

THE CURVE BALL. The initial grip and arm action for throwing the curve ball should be identical with that of a fast ball, so the pitcher does not give away the pitch before it is delivered. As the windup is started and the ball lifted over the head, the fingers slide parallel to the seam, so the second finger has good contact along a seam. It usually is gripped more tightly with the second finger, while the index finger merely acts as a guide.

Some pitchers shift their middle and index fingers until the middle finger is on the curved part of the seam. Others turn the hand from the back of the ball to the outside so the curved part of the seam is inside the hand and then place the middle finger along the seam. The middle and index fingers are close together, and the thumb is flat on the ball.

As the pitching arm is brought forward and the ball is about to be released, the wrist is snapped inward. This snapping of the wrist is very important, since it causes the ball to spin faster and the curve to break sharply. The wrist must be relaxed for the pitcher to get the proper wrist snap and to utilize the entire length of his fingers. There is a downward pull as the ball comes off the surface of the middle finger and rolls over the index finger. The pitcher should be striving for all possible downward rotation on the curve, since this is what makes the ball hard to hit. A shortened stride helps the pitcher to get more break on the ball since it is easier for the arm to follow through in a downward direction. The pitcher should feel that his hand has inscribed a circle beginning where the throwing arm started forward and ending at his opposite knee.

THE CHANGE-OF-PACE. The change-of-pace is delivered with the same body and arm action as the fast ball, but it travels more slowly. In throwing the change-of-pace, some pitchers grip the ball as they normally do for their fast ball, but they jam the ball farther back into the thumb and index finger, taking the fingertips off the ball as it is released. The ball is pushed forward off the middle joints of the two fingers. To slow the ball more, the pitcher should "pull" the hand down, like pulling down a window shade.

This pitch can be thrown by another method in which the ball is gripped loosely, well back in the palm of the hand, and then delivered with very little pressure by the fingers. Usually three fingers are placed on top of the ball when this method is used.

infielders

Certain phases of a baseball game are handled in generally the same manner by each infielder, or call for teamwork on the part of two or more infielders. When a fly ball is barely out of the infield, it should be handled by the outfielder if he can get to the ball and calls for the play, since a man running toward a ball can more accurately judge it than a man backing up to it. The infielder nearest to the ball should call for it if he can make the play, since the outfielder may be too deep to make the catch.

Ground balls are handled by a fielder in balance and nearly in a position to throw. The infielder should run up to a ground ball instead of waiting for it to get to him. He must be alert to the position of baserunners and must always check for base touching. He must think ahead about the play to be made in any situation. He should know from the catcher's signals the type of delivery to be made, since this will have some effect on the course of the ball if hit by the batter.

There are three defensive positions infielders may take, depending upon the plays that are expected. The first is deep, which is a normal position, with players several yards outside the base lines. This position is assumed when the bases are empty. The next is moderate, with the infielders a few feet outside the base lines, when the bases are partly occupied and a bunt is expected. The third is close, with the infielders in line with the bases, when the bases are loaded or there is a man on third about to score. If a double play is anticipated, the shortstop and the second baseman will play a few steps closer to second base.

FIRST BASEMAN.   It is the job of the first baseman not only to make putouts at the base after others have fielded and thrown to him, but also to act as a fielder just as any other infielder. Although he will not get as many chances to field a batted ball as the other infielders, he assumes as much responsibility for those that come his way. In fact, if there ever comes a time when he must decide whether to protect the base or field a ball in his area, he is obligated to choose the latter. The pitcher will generally take over his base for him.

The first baseman should be tall, angular, and agile. He should be able not only to field batted balls but also to catch any kind of throw from the other players. He should play near enough to the base that no great effort will be required for him to be on the base for a put-out. Since the baserunner has the right-of-way on the base, it is necessary for any baseman, and particularly the first baseman, to place his foot toward the side of the base and not directly on top of it. His body should lie out of and away from the area immediately above it. Prior to the time a thrown ball reaches him, he should stand just inside the diamond with his heels against the base. If the throw is good, he places the pivot foot, which is generally the right, on the base just as he gets ready to make the stretch. If the throw is to the right, his left foot is the pivot foot; if to the left, his right foot becomes the pivot foot. He should reach out and make every effort to contact the ball at the earliest possible moment. The chief reason for reaching out for a ball is to make it reach its destination more quickly.

The first baseman must learn to catch with one hand. Since he is forced to stay in one spot, he must often reach with his left hand to a position that his right hand cannot get. Should the baseman have to leave the immediate area of the base in order to field a ball, the pitcher will cover the base for him. Since the pitcher will be in motion toward and across the base, it is necessary that the ball be thrown as accurately as possible. It should be thrown shoulder high and with the necessary lead in order that it may be easily caught.

When a runner is on first base, it is necessary that the baseman play close to or even on the base so that he can be there if the pitcher makes an effort to throw the runner out. The baseman stays in the immediate area of the base until the pitcher starts an actual delivery. He then moves quickly to his fielding position. If the batter is a left-handed hitter, the baseman plays closer to first than when the batter is right-handed. He should also handle cut-offs from right and center field near the mound.

SECOND BASEMAN. The average second baseman is of medium weight and height. There are, however, good second basemen who are either short or tall. Regardless of height, it is of prime importance that he be fast, a sure fielder of any kind of ball, and able to throw hard and accurately from any position. He should be mentally alert and a good diagnostician of impending situations. He should be a good pivot man who has the movements necessary for the double plays. He should vary his position from right to left, depending on whether the man at bat is left- or right-handed. He must be able not only to throw hard and straight but also to throw easily with a wrist snap to the shortstop covering second.

The second baseman backs up the shortstop on plays at second or rundowns between second and third. He acts as a relay man on a throw from right center or right field. If a runner is caught off first and is then trapped between first and second, he acts as one of the men effecting the run-down. The second baseman should try for all balls hit to the right of second base. He should cover second after every pitched ball has passed the batsman if first is occupied. He should back up the first baseman if he is attempting to field a ball.

He should work hard in developing skills in the double play. How to take the ball, pivot, and throw should be second nature to him.

On receiving any ball, the second baseman makes an effort to get directly in front of it and be ready or getting ready to throw when the ball reaches him. He should at all times have a clear understanding with the shortstop on certain basic plays as to just what each will do in relation to the other.

SHORTSTOP. Almost without exception, the shortstop is either of medium height and weight or short. His reaction time is very fast; he can catch any type of throw well or field any ball hit into his area. He must have an exceptionally good throwing arm and must be able to get a throw off quickly and accurately. He must be exceptionally fast on his feet and be able to think in quickly developing situations. He should try for all balls hit low enough for him in the area to the left of second base.

When he is assisting on a double play, he should be able to toss the ball to the second baseman immediately after catching it without changing from the position in which he caught it.

He should team up with the pitcher and have a pre-arranged signal in order to catch a runner off second base. He should have an understanding with the second baseman as to who covers the base in specific situations. He acts as the relay man on left-center field and left field throw-ins. He backs up the second baseman on throws to that base and acts as the cut-off man when the situation calls for it.

The shortstop covers third on throws from left field to home plate. The third baseman serves as cut-off man on this play.

THIRD BASEMAN. The third baseman should have practically the same qualities as the shortstop. He should have quick movements and reactions. He is closer to the batter and has less time to respond to a hard-hit ball than any of the other infielders. He must be mentally alert and be able to anticipate plays, particularly bunts, since many bunts are attempted down the third base line.

If the third baseman gets a slow bunt in his direction, he should rush at it fast and pick it up in his bare hand, if it has stopped rolling. If the ball is still rolling, he should use his glove to field it. The throw should be made underhand.

The third baseman is the cut-off man when the situation calls for it. He should charge all balls and get any he can reach to his left, but if he cannot field the ball, he must hustle back to third when men are on base. He should never retreat into the shortstop position.

INFIELD PRACTICE. The following six rounds are standard procedures for infield practice, in which the ball is hit to the first player listed and then thrown around the infield as indicated by the bases or plate:

Round 1 (to first base; ball hit directly at each man)
1. 3B–1B–C–3B–2B–1B–C
2. SS–1B–C–SS–3B–C
3. 2B–1B–C–2B–3B–C

4. 1B–SS–1B–C
5. C–1B–SS–C

Round 2

Same as first round except hit the ball to infielder's left.

Round 3 (double play: ball hit infielder's left)
1. 3B–2B–1B–C–3B–C
2. SS–2B–1B–C–SS–C
3. 2B–SS–1B–C–2B–C
4. 1B–SS–1B–C
5. C–SS–1B–C

Round 4

Same as third round except hit the ball to infielder's right.

Round 5 (to first base: ball hit to infielder's right)
Same as Round 1 and 2

Round 6

The ball is hit slowly to each infielder, and the throw is made to first base as he charges-in. The infielder continues off the field to complete infield practice.

In order to complete the above fielding routine in ten minutes, which is usually allotted for pre-game infield and outfield practice, the coach uses at least three baseballs. This allows for balls getting by the defense. The coach should try to keep two balls in play; hitting a second ball previously hit completes a cycle.

outfielders

The outfielder, to play his position best, must be fast with a strong arm. He should be able to throw far and accurately. His value to his team can be enhanced greatly if he is a good hitter. Many coaches place this ability above fielding for outfielders, since it is believed that if a man is a good hitter, the fielding ability can be developed.

In choosing men for the three positions, it is necessary to place them according to specific abilities. The right fielder should have a strong throwing arm. He is frequently called on to throw faster, more accurately, and, many times, farther than any of the other fielders. This is the throw to third for a runner who left first on a long fly ball to right field or on a single to right.

The center fielder must be the fastest of the three because he covers the most territory and must take more put-outs than the others.

The left fielder should also have a good arm, and he should be fast and able to field ground balls well.

The outfielders back up the bases directly in front of them or another base if there is a chance for a ball to come into their territory. In fielding a fly ball, the outfielder should regulate his speed so that he can get under the ball before it reaches him in order that he may get better set for the throw. In blocking a ground ball, he should place his right knee just above the ground and form a pocket with his legs.

During batting practice prior to the game, the fielder should study each of his opponents in order to determine where he hits, generally. The outfielder, just as other players, should determine in advance where he will throw the ball if it comes his way. The ball should be thrown in advance of a runner. It should hit the ground about ten feet in front of the baseman and bounce to him. If two outfielders are about to catch a ball simultaneously, the one most nearly in position to throw in the necessary direction should be the one to make the catch. An outfielder must never hold a ball; it should be thrown to the infield immediately.

When a right-handed batter is up, the outfielders play to the left. For a left-hander, they play to the right.

In practice, outfielders should do much running while getting in a position to catch the ball so that they will have the practice of catching fly balls on the move. If the ball is hit behind them, they should practice taking their eyes off the ball, running to where it will probably come down, and then looking up and catching it. They should practice long, accurate throws frequently and should do a lot of running.

GAME STRATEGY

Baseball is a highly complicated game requiring mental concentration and alertness. Much thought must be given to the strong and weak points of the opposing team, and plans made accordingly. Things that should be known before a game are the type of pitching the other team has, and the speed, alertness, and hitting and throwing ability of each opponent. The skill of the catcher will determine how much base stealing will be attempted, even though most bases are stolen on the pitcher. Whether the pitcher throws with the right or left arm may determine who will be in the lineup to face him. During the game, many situations will arise requiring decisions that will have to be made with an eye toward winning. If these decisions are made soundly and carefully, the chances of winning are better. There will be times when a player must make a quick decision. His value to the team is greater if he can think fast and accurately.

offensive strategy

Offensive strategy involves batting and base running. There are so many different possibilities that only a few points, based on the beliefs of the writer, can be discussed.

In hitting, it is of greater importance to hit line drives than to attempt a home run every time at bat. The batter's primary goal should be to meet the ball squarely. Most power hitters swing too hard, and this affects their timing and balance, leading to frequent strikeouts. The good hitters use a moderately hard, smooth, and basically level swing, featuring good wrist action. This type of swing will produce line drives and power hits, the ultimates in the batting art.

The batting order is highly important, and it is generally considered good policy to place the four best hitters at the top of the batting order. The first man up should have good speed and the ability to get on base. The second man in the batting order should be a good left-handed hitter, who has speed and can bunt, with the ability to hit behind the runner. The third man should be the best average hitter on the team, and the fourth man in particular should be the long-ball "clutch" hitter. On down the batting order the next-best hitter is the next batter until the end, where the weakest hitter, generally the pitcher, comes up. It is advisable, however, to put a better-than-average hitter somewhere among the last five men in the batting order so that the end will not be too weak. The number seven hitter will have many opportunities to drive in runs.

Offense is highly important, and frequently a good hitter who is a poorer fielder than a teammate will be chosen to play a certain position. When at the plate, the batter should be ready for each pitch; if the ball is in the strike zone, he should swing at it. Certain circumstances may call for a change in this procedure, but generally this should be the policy. When the count is three balls and no strikes, the general practice is to take the next pitch in the hope that it will be a ball. The writer takes a different and highly controversial stand. When the count is three and nothing, the pitcher does not want to walk the man and generally throws a "fat" pitch across the plate. If the batter is a good hitter, he should be able to make solid contact with the pitch.

The batter becomes a base runner the moment he hits a fair ball, or the moment a third strike is missed or dropped by the catcher, provided first base is unoccupied and there are fewer than two outs. With two outs, the batter may run to first base, even if it is occupied.

The batter should run out all fairly hit balls, even though it appears that he will be a sure out. Defenses have been known to miss the easiest kind of ground balls and pop flies. The base runner should never loaf, since this is a sign of a lazy ballplayer.

After the runner is on first base, he should take his lead by sliding his feet, rather than stepping out or crossing over. This will enable him to return quickly, if necessary. When the pitcher has started his delivery, a longer lead may be safely taken in order to get a better start toward second in case the batter hits the ball.

The base runner should develop the habit of standing with his left foot touching the inside edge of the base when he receives the sign, which usually comes from the third base coaching box. He must be aware of runners ahead of him, the score, outs, inning, and outfielders' depths. Knowledge of the outfielders' positioning, speed, and throwing ability will help a runner decide how far he can advance on a hit, whether he should tag up on a fly ball, and how far to move off the base on an outfield fly. Each time the runner returns to his base he should look for a signal from the coach.

When a runner comes into a base on a force play, it is best if he slides. At second on the double play, he should slide for two reasons: first, to upset the pivot man; and second, for his own protection, since the pivot man is throwing down the base line. If it is not a force play and there is every indication that the play will be close, the runner should slide. He can slide in one of two ways, head first or feet first. The head first slide is not recommended because of the danger involved. The position of the baseman determines on which side of the base to slide. If the baseman is on the left, the runner should slide to the right; if on the right, to the left. When going into a slide, the runner throws his feet toward and turns his body to the side toward which he is sliding. The bottom leg is thrown out away from the base while the top leg hooks the base. Practice on sliding should first be done in a sawdust pit and later tried on the base line.

A base runner should always remember the shortest distance between two points is a straight line, and he should not waste valuable time and steps when circling the bases. He should touch the infield corner of the base in stride, using either the left or right foot. The important thing is to hit the base in stride.

When rounding first, it is advisable to run without watching the ball until the base is reached. Once there, the runner should try to locate the ball and listen to the first base coach for instructions.

When making the turn, the runner should not be afraid to take a few extra steps. Some coaches teach their players to go about a third of the way toward second. This places extra pressure on the outfielders and, if the ball is bobbled, the runner is able to advance to second.

The runner should develop the habit of rounding the base hard, always being ready to take the extra base if the opportunity presents itself. On a hit to right, the he should not round the base quite as far, since the right fielder may throw behind him. Of course, if the batter knows he can make two bases, or if the coach is pointing toward second, he should continue without hesitation.

This procedure also applies to high flies behind the infield; a hard run and a good turn will enable the runner to make second if the ball drops in. The batter must be careful not to overtake a runner already on first base, as he will be out automatically. A similar precaution should be taken on long outfield flies, as the runner already on base may tag up in order to advance.

The coach should advise the batter on such plays. In some cases, however, the nature of the play will make it impossible for him to give any more definite information than "round the base." Here the runner must use his own judgment, make his turn, and proceed according to his running ability, the fielder's throwing ability, the score, the outs, and the inning.

defensive strategy

Much of defensive strategy has been discussed under the play of the various positions. This section will be devoted to the general aspects of defense applying to all positions. It is impossible to lay down a set of rules to be followed at all times, since the nature of the particular situation might justify another defensive measure. As far as possible, the following points should be used as a guide in defensive baseball:

1. All defensive men must be in the correct position at all times.

2. Each player should plan in advance what he is to do with the ball when it comes to him.

3. Base runners should be kept, when possible, from getting in a position to score. These positions are generally considered to be second and third base.

4. The ball should be thrown around as little as possible. Every throw makes an error possible.

5. Do not attempt impossible plays.

6. Play the ball in advance of the base runner.

7. If first and third are occupied and the batter is a good hitter, deliberately walk him in order to pitch to a weaker hitter and set up a situation for a double play or a force play at any base.

TEACHING PROCEDURE

The practice sessions in baseball should start at least six weeks prior to the first game. The catchers and pitchers need to begin work first, because they must be in the best physical condition and because the development of their skills and their understanding of the game must be even greater than that of the other players. These men should be coached exclusively for a week, with the major portion of their time spent in throwing, catching, and running. A part of the time may be given to discussions of game defense and how these two positions figure so strongly in the final result of the game.

At the end of a week, the other men are called out to practice, and this second week is spent in much the same procedure as that used with the pitchers and catchers during their first week. Gradually added during the latter part of this week are pepper, shagging fly balls, and more strenuous running. An important problem a coach must face every day during the season, but particularly during the first week, is the tendency for a boy to throw hard before he is ready. During the first week, the coach should spend much time stressing the values of condition and warm-up, particularly of the throwing arm. He should set a hard and fast rule to govern a gradual warm-up of the throwing arm in each daily session of pregame practice.

During the third week, practice should be well under way on all phases of the game. Daily sessions should include everything previously practiced plus sliding, base running, and batting. At the end of the fourth week, there should be a practice game in which all the men should be given a chance to perform under game pressure. During the last two weeks prior to the first scheduled game, there should be another practice game to make a final check of the men.

teaching drills for throwing and catching

The skills involved should be demonstrated and discussed. The group should then divide into two lines. In each line the men should be standing side by side and facing the men in the other line. Every man should be equipped with a glove, and there should be one baseball for every two men. The two lines should be about 30 feet apart, and the throwing should go on between pairs of men, one in each line. After a period of catching a straight, well-directed ball, the receiver will profit by being thrown ground balls. As catching skills are improved, further practice can be gained by putting the men around the bases and having a type of infield practice in which they may catch all kinds of balls.

batting practice

There are two basic and time-tested ways to practice batting. Pepper is used principally to develop an eye for the ball and coordination of movement. Four, five, or six men form a semicircle facing a man who is to do the hitting. The first man tosses a ball in the direction of the hitter, and it is hit to another man, who tosses it back. This procedure continues around the semicircle. After a certain number of hits, the batter is replaced by one of the men in the semicircle.

The second method is more like a real game. All the men number off for their batting order. The first man goes to the plate and the others to the field in the various positions. A pitcher, throwing fairly good pitches, gives the batter something to hit. The fielders get the practice of playing the batted balls. After a certain number of swings, the second man in order comes to bat, and the previous batter takes his place in the field.

Both these methods of batting practice are used extensively. Some coaches use nothing else, even for total team practice, after the season is several weeks old. There is one great disadvantage: only one man at a time gets batting practice, and, in the field, the other men are standing idle except when balls are hit to them. One way to solve this problem is have only four men in the outfield to take the ball off the bat, while other fielders are at their positions receiving fungos. Players who are standing around can also play pepper, or work on sliding or other phases of the game.

When the season gets under way, practice sessions should consist principally of batting practice. One phase of the game generally neglected in batting practice is base running. It would be a simple matter to put some of the batters on base so that both the base runner and the defensive men might get that necessary practice.

As the season goes along, time should be spent in polishing up ragged playing edges on certain skills and in instilling baseball sense into the team.

rules for players[1]

1. No player should walk after a ball.
2. All players, except pitchers, run from their positions to dugout.
3. A player keeps the bat off his shoulder.
4. Never throw behind the runner.

[1] This set of rules has been handed down from coaches to players for many years. The origin is unknown to the writer.

5. The player who keeps his head up will never have to hold it down.

6. A player should never alibi.

7. The batter should run out all fair hit balls.

8. A player should never quit.

9. Don't be a faultfinder.

10. A pitcher without physical and mental control is lost.

SKILL TESTS

Baseball lends itself well to testing. There are very definite skills involved; by placing a point evaluation on each skill, it is very simple to arrive at a score that indicates one player's ability as compared with another's. In activity classes that are a part of the regular physical–education program, it is necessary to assign grades, and more reliability can be placed in objective testing than in subjective judgment. By careful planning and organization, it is possible to test a class of twenty-five or thirty in not more than two days. When a boy has mastered the skill objectives in any single skill test, he should be credited with one point for each objective.

fielding ground balls

In this test the boy is placed in the shortstop position. His job is to field five batted balls and throw them to first. The phases of the throw he will be checked on are as follows:

1. Playing the ball correctly (running up on slow one, waiting for fast one)—1 point

2. Getting in front of the ball and reasonably low—1 point

3. Fingers down on low ball, up on high one—1 point

4. Recovering in position to throw—1 point

5. Making hard throw to first—1 point

6. Making accurate throw to first—1 point

The man hitting the ball to the fielder tries to vary the hits so as to include a fast one, a slow one, one to the left, and one to the right. The same man should hit to all the fielders in order to eliminate the factor of variation present when more than one person does the hitting.

fielding fly balls

In this test each boy is given the opportunity of catching and throwing fly balls. One man does all the hitting, and the man nearest the ball will be called upon to take it. He is given six points if he catches the ball and throws it home hard and accurately. Two points may be subtracted for a poor, slow throw. If the boy fails to catch the ball but fields it well for the throw, he may be given two points.

batting

A batter is thrown five strikes. He hits them as best he can. The emphasis is on power, as can be seen by the scoring table. The same man does the pitching to all the batters. The other men in the class are in the field in regulation defensive positions. The instructor judges all hits and records the points. The scoring is as follows:

1. Long fly ball over the outfield—6 points
2. Any hit—5 points
3. Caught fly ball to outfield—4 points
4. Any fast ball to infield—3 points
5. Slow roller to infield—2 points
6. Foul or infield fly—1 point
7. Foul tip, strike, etc.—0 points

base running

Each man is timed on running the bases. He starts at home plate and circles the bases in proper order. His score is the number of seconds it takes him to cover the distance.

SOFTBALL

Softball is included in this chapter on baseball for two reasons: softball grew out of baseball, and most of the playing skills and strategy are the same. However, to avoid duplication, only those phases of the game that differ from baseball will be discussed here.

There are a number of conjectures as to how softball originated. One group maintains that several years ago baseball players wanted some sort of similar activity which could be played indoors during the cold winter months. Indoor space was limited, so they devised different equipment that would be usable in small quarters. After these players had devised a larger ball and a smaller bat and had worked on basic skills, they formulated some rules for playing the game. It did not prove popular at that time and was considered only a substitute for the regular game of baseball.

According to other versions, the Y.M.C.A., the Y.W.C.A., public schools, and other organizations modified the game of baseball for use indoors. Later, a game called "playground ball" was devised for use on smaller areas out of doors. Canada was the scene of much development of playground ball during the late 1920s. About 1930, two Chicago men, Leo Fischer and M. J. Pauley, began working on a type of outdoor ball, using a larger ball and smaller space. They carried on this development and in 1933 sponsored a tournament in connection with the Chicago World's Fair.

At the same time Fischer and Pauley were working with the game in Chicago, the National Recreation Association had been developing playground ball and had created considerable enthusiasm for the sport in several of the larger cities.

The name "softball" remained dominant, although the ball used was not soft, and it is now the accepted name. During the 1933 tournament, it was found that nearly all the teams entered played under different rules. It was deemed practical to unify the rules.

The Amateur Softball Association was founded in 1933 and proceeded to formulate a set of rules and standardize the size of the diamond (Figure 3-2). The game grew rapidly for two reasons. First, it was quite popular;

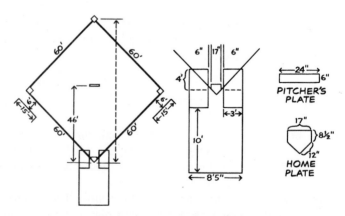

FIGURE 3-2   *Softball Field*

and second, there were men with time on their hands during the depression years who wanted such a team game.

differences between softball and baseball

1. The playing area is smaller.
2. The pitcher must pitch underhand.
3. The base runner must remain in contact with the base until after the ball leaves the pitcher's hand.
4. The bat is shorter, smaller in diameter, and lighter.
5. The ball is larger and heavier, being 12 inches in diameter and weighing from 6 to 6¾ ounces.
6. Seven innings constitute an official game.
7. The pitcher is not considered in pitching position until the catcher is in position to receive the pitch.

Except for pitching, the skills and playing strategy involved are almost identical to baseball and need not be repeated. It is advisable to use the drills and coaching points listed for baseball in teaching softball.

DEFINITION OF TERMS

Balk. The act of a pitcher in failing to make a delivery he has started.

Battery. Pitcher and catcher. Hence they are each other's battery-mates.

Batting Average. Number of hits divided by times at bat.

Big Hop. A ground ball that takes a big bounce.

Bull Pen. A section down the first and third base foul lines, in foul territory, where the pitchers and players may warm up to be ready to go in the game.

Called Strike. A pitch that is called a strike by the umpire, even though the batter made no attempt to hit the ball.

Coaches. Assistants to the manager.

Control. Ability to get the ball in the strike zone close to where the pitcher wants to throw it.

Curve. A ball thrown by the pitcher that curves as it reaches the plate.

Cut-off Play. When an outfielder is throwing the ball toward home plate, the first or third baseman catches it with the idea of throwing out a runner trying to advance or of keeping a runner from advancing.

Double Header. Two games to be played the same afternoon or evening.

Double Play. A play in which two base runners are put out.

Dugout. The players' bench for each team on the first and third base foul lines.

Error. A hit ball that should have been fielded, according to the official scorer, but is dropped or missed by a fielder.

Fast Ball. A hard, straight ball thrown by the pitcher.

Fly Ball. A ball that is hit high into the air.

Force Play. A force occurs when the fielder throws out a base runner instead of the batter.

Foul Ball. A ground or fly ball that is hit to the right or to the left of the playing field.

Foul Tip. A pitched ball that the batter touches with the bat, causing it to go behind him.

Full Count. When the batter has three balls and two strikes on him.

Hit. A ball hit by the batter that cannot be reached by a fielder or that, if reached by the fielder, cannot be returned in time to throw the batter or preceeding base runner out.

Home Run. A ball hit by the batter far enough away that it allows him to circle the bases without being put out; hit out of the ball park.

Inning. Each team having batted and made three outs.

Knuckle Ball. A ball that is thrown off the knuckles of two fingers.

Line drive. A hard-hit ball that travels in a line and not very high.

Manager. The man employed by the owners to run the ball club.

Mound. The rise in the center of the diamond where the pitcher's plate is located.

Out of Play. A ball hit by the batter in foul territory that cannot be reached by a fielder.

Pepper. A type of drill used in practice in which a player bats a ball thrown to him back to the player who threw it or to a person next to him. Three to six players take turns throwing to the batter and catching the ball.

Pick-off Play. A play in which an attempt is made to throw out a runner who is playing too far off the base.

Pinch Hitter. A substitute put in to hit for a regular player.

Rosin bag. A mesh bag of powdered resin that is used by the pitcher to dry his hands between pitches.

Sacrifice Bunt. A ball hit by the batter to advance a base runner and be put out himself. This is not counted a time at bat.

Screw Ball. A ball that breaks down and to the right when pitched by a right-hander.

Shagging. Running after and catching a fly ball as a part of practice.

Shoe-string Catch. A catch of a fly ball just above the ground.

Single. A safely hit ball that allows the runner to reach first base.

Slow Ball. A pitch that the pitcher lets up on in speed in order to fool the batter. This pitch is often called "change-of-pace."

Squeeze Play. A form of hit-and-run play in which, when there is a runner on third base and not more than one out, the batter bunts a pitched ball previously designated by signal, and the runner starts for home plate as soon as the pitcher makes his motion to pitch.

Steal. A base runner makes a break for the next base as the pitcher starts to throw to the batter, and reaches this base without being put out.

Strike Out. A pitcher is given credit for a strike-out when he throws a third strike at which the batter either swings and misses or does not swing.

Triple. The batter is able to reach third base on a hit.

Triple Play. A play in which three base runners are put out on the same play.

Two-base Hit. A fair-hit ball that enables the batter to get to second base.

Walk. The batter is allowed to take his position on first base when the pitcher throws him four balls.

Wild Pitch. A pitched ball that the catcher cannot reach.

Wind-up. The motion the pitcher goes through before making his pitch.

DISCUSSION QUESTIONS

1. Trace the development of baseball.
2. What part did the following people play in the development of the game: Alexander Cartwright? Abner Doubleday? A. G. Spaulding?
3. Name two qualities essential for a boy to be a good baseball player. For what reasons are they essential?
4. Describe the movement of the hand in correctly catching a ball.
5. How important is good pitching in baseball?
6. How should the shortstop field a fast ground ball?
7. Do anatomical and physiological characteristics need to be considered in choosing players for certain positions? Why?
8. Analyze the job of the first baseman.
9. List some points on offensive strategy.
10. What should be the characteristics of the first four batters?
11. Why and how did softball develop?
12. What are the essential differences between softball and baseball?

BIBLIOGRAPHY

Allen, Ethan, *Major League Baseball.* New York: The Macmillan Company, 1938.

Barbour, Ralph Henry, *How to Play Better Baseball.* New York: Appleton-Century-Crofts, 1935.

Brandt, Bill, *Do You Know Your Baseball?* New York: A. S. Barnes & Company, 1947.

Chapman, Charles E., and Severied, Henry L., *Play Ball.* New York: Harper & Row, Publishers, 1941.

Cochrane, G. S., *Baseball—The Fan's Game.* New York: Funk and Wagnalls Company, Inc., 1939.

Coombs, John W., *Baseball: Individual Play and Team Strategy.* Englewood Cliffs, N.J.: Prentice-Hall, Inc., 1951.

Dugan, Ken, *How to Organize and Coach Winning Baseball.* Englewood Cliffs, N.J.: Parker Publishing Company, 1971.

Grayson, H., *They Played the Game.* New York: A. S. Barnes & Company, 1944.

Hughes, W. L., and Williams, J. F., *Sports—Their Organization and Administration*, pp. 353–359. New York: A. S. Barnes & Company, 1944.

Litwhiler, Danny, *Baseball Coach's Guide to Drills and Skills.* Englewood Cliffs, N.J.: Prentice-Hall, Inc., 1963.

basketball

4

BACKGROUND

Late in the nineteenth century, the leadership in the Young Men's Christian Association suddenly became aware that attendance and membership in their organization were declining. Looking into the situation, they found that the formal types of activities, such as gymnastics, tumbling, drills, and dumbbell exercises, were gradually becoming less attractive to the general membership. Seeking a remedy for this growing lack of interest, Dr. Luther Gulick, superintendent of the physical training department of the Y.M.C.A. Training School in Springfield, Massachusetts, commissioned one of his teachers, James A. Naismith, to devise a game that could be played indoors in the evening. Dr. Naismith had already been thinking about such a game, and when this assignment was made, he set about the task in earnest.

In the initial planning, it was to be a game that middle-aged men could play. It could not be rough. Dr. Naismith found that all team games employed a ball; and in those he had witnessed, roughness occurred when an opponent attempted to impede the progress of the player who was advancing the ball. He had to find a way to employ a ball and yet prevent the roughness. He also had to determine what type of goal would be used.

As a result of all these basic considerations, Dr. Naismith devised the game of basketball. In his original game, he did not allow the man in possession of the ball to advance it. He placed a penalty on any sort of bodily contact. Seven men made up a team. The goal was a horizontal ring placed on the wall over the heads of the players, through which the ball had to be thrown in an arch from above. In so placing the goal, he eliminated the factor of force. Thus the game of basketball was born in 1891, and the first official game was played on January 20, 1892.

At first, it was played by the men for whom it was intended. But very soon boys became interested in it and virtually took it over. Many who played it at first were looked upon by the rougher type of boys as sissies, since it embodied little or none of the characteristic roughness of other games of the time. As the years passed, it became somewhat rougher, no longer set apart in the minds of some as an "easy" game to play.

As the game grew older, many experiments were tried in an effort to improve the play. From the original seven required for a team, the number was changed to eight, to nine, and eventually to the present team of five players. Three playing periods were first provided, each one lasting 20 minutes. Now the high school game is divided into four periods of 8

FIGURE 4-1 *Basketball Court—Optimum Width 50 feet Inside Sidelines*

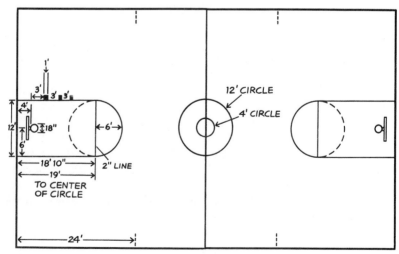

minutes each, and college basketball into two periods of 20 minutes each. Field goals once counted 3 points, and three fouls automatically gave a team 1 point. Now 2 points are awarded for each field goal and 1 point for each successful free throw.

These variations in playing rules were tried at different times by several groups. There was much confusion when teams using different rules played each other. As a result, many organizations (including the Y.M.C.A., the A.A.U., colleges, and high schools) met nearly forty years ago and standardized the rules.

The game is played on a hardwood court approximately 94′×50′. The official court markings are shown in Figure 4–1.

Basketball has become so popular in recent years that more people play it and more people see it played than any other game.

BASIC SKILLS

Basketball requires the use of many skills in rapid succession during the course of a game. It is necessary that they be developed to a high degree of efficiency. It is also necessary that they be performed with some degree of relaxation. There must be controlled muscular contraction, confined to the movements involved in performing the skills, but not interfering with them. As one author has put it in writing of a skill in another sport, the movement should be "liquid."

One must also be able to see more of the playing area than that immediately in front of him. Good peripheral vision enables a player to register movements of opponents and teammates alike in areas he is not facing directly.

Another sight factor necessary for good basketball playing is depth perception—the ability to judge the distance from teammates and the goal. If a player is gifted with these two kinds of vision, he has a better chance of succeeding at the game of basketball.

passing

It is difficult to pick one skill from a game demanding so many different activities and say it is the most important one. However, it may be safe to say that there are no skills more important than passing and shooting. The pass is the principal means by which the players maneuver the ball down the floor to a scoring position and, at the same time, it is one of the chief means by which the opposition is maneuvered out of advantageous defensive positions. The pass generally is considered so important that most defense is devoted not to inhibiting movements of the offense, but to breaking up the passing attack. A basketball team must know how to execute several different types of passes quickly and how to throw them accurately to stationary or moving targets.

Passes should be varied in speed. They should be slow when the receiver is coming toward the passer, hard and fast when the receiver is breaking away, and reasonably fast when there is little movement among players. Accuracy is more important than speed, although a fast pass is essential against strong opponents. Movement of the ball should be fast and constant, and all drills should be directed toward this end.

There is no easy way to develop passing skill. Practice and drills, day after day, are necessary. The drills should simulate game conditions as nearly as possible. The good passer develops accuracy through constant drilling and hard work.

TWO-HAND CHEST PASS.   This pass in all probability is regarded as the basic pass in basketball. It is easy to get off and usually accompanies the rapid movement of the ball such as found in a pattern attack. It should not be used for long passes, but it is effective if the distance does not exceed 20 feet. In making the pass, the player should hold the ball in his hands in what is called the 10-point touch—that is, with the fingers and thumbs, not the palms, in contact with the ball. The ball is held just in front of the chest, about 6 inches away from the body, with both arms equally flexed. When the pass is to be made, the ball is released with a snap of the wrist, elbows, and fingers, to produce a reverse spinning motion as the thumbs are snapped under and through. A player should not, under any circumstances, drop the arms and then bring them back up to give greater acceleration to the movement. This is a dead giveaway that the pass is coming and prepares the defensive player to stop it. In making the pass from a stationary position, the player should be in a slight crouch, head up, feet placed where he feels the balance is best. If he makes the pass while in motion, no particular body position is required as long as he is balanced.

BASEBALL PASS.   This pass is used for both short and long distances but preferably for the latter during a fast break. It can be executed during a jump to increase the initial height of the ball, but it is best started while both feet are firmly planted on the floor. It is similar to the overhand baseball throw. The left foot is placed forward in the direction the ball is to go. The ball is held firmly in the right hand, with its weight resting on both fingers and palm. The pass actually begins in front of the chest. It goes back by the face to a near extension of the arm back of the head. From this point, the arm and the hand push the ball forward in an upper arc. Again the hand should be kept directly under the ball so that it leaves the fingers with bottom spin, which enables it to maintain a more level flight and go straight to the target.

HOOK PASS.   This formerly was one of the favorite passes in the game. The hook pass is still excellent to initiate the fast break following a rebound from the defensive board. It is an effective pass when a player is closely pressed by an opponent. The ball is held in the hand, with the fingers spread. The passer should have the left side of his body to his immediate opponent as he goes into the air, if he is passing right-handed. The pass starts from a crouch position and traces an arc out and away from the body, up, and finally over the head, in the lateral line of the body. As he starts this motion, the passer should jump high into the air quickly in such a way as to catch the guard out of timing with him so that he will not go up at the same time. As the pass is made over the head with the motion of the right arm, the left hand is released and brought high for protection.

BOUNCE PASS.   The bounce is frequently utilized as a deceptive measure to get the ball to a man who is closely guarded. A bounce made when the opponent expects an air pass is frequently successful. The bounce may be made by one or two hands, since this makes little difference, but some sort of preliminary fake should be made. It is important that the ball does not hit the floor too far away from the receiver. This error will result in the ball "floating" after the bounce, and it can be easily intercepted.

catching

A pass receiver should learn to catch a basketball thrown at any speed in such a manner as to gain control of it and be ready to pass it again quickly and accurately. Basically, a pass is caught by meeting it with the arms fully extended and coming back with it, gradually slowing it to a complete stop. As more accurate timing is developed, it is not necessary to extend the arms quite all the way out or to slow the ball so gradually. The ball can be caught with one hand, but more accurately and surely with both. After the beginner learns to catch a pass while standing, some practice should be conducted in which he will have an opportunity to catch while in motion. Later, he should learn to catch and pass a ball in the air before he touches the floor.

shooting

Since the final score is indicated by points, and points are made by shooting, it follows that skill in shooting is exceedingly important. A team may pass well, dribble well, and play alert ball; but if the men cannot shoot, they cannot win the ball game. There are many ways of shooting and many positions a player may find himself in when making a shot. Most basketball players fall into certain types of shooting and perfect their particular styles to a fine degree. This is well, but a player should also practice a variety of shots from several different positions so that if the opportunity presents itself for a particular kind of shot, he will be capable of making it.

Shooting must be allotted a large portion of time in every practice session. Shooting practice should be conducted under conditions that approximate as nearly as possible those of a real game. Very seldom, even in set shots, will a player have plenty of time in which to shoot. The majority of shots will be attempted while he is moving and while under pressure from an opponent. After the fundamental movements of each shot have been mastered, the game situation should be used in the drill.

Two-Hand Set Shot. This is fundamentally the same as the two-hand chest pass described earlier. The real difference is direction. In the shot for a basket, the ball should be sent in a high arc toward the goal. Unless otherwise stated on a specific shot, the aim should be toward the rim of the basket and not the backboard. As in the case of the chest pass, no preliminary motions should be made to indicate the time of shooting. This particular shot at one time was the most frequently employed in the game of basketball, but because of developments in recent years its use has declined.

One-Hand Jump Shot. This versatile shot may be taken from any position on the court, but with best results from within 20 feet. It may be taken from a stationary position or on the run after terminating a dribble. It has several advantages over the two-hand set shot in that it can be executed faster, with more accuracy, and it is more difficult for the defense.

In executing the shot, the ball is held in both hands and carried high overhead, with the shooting hand on the back of the ball and the fingers well spread. As the ball is moved into shooting position, the shooter should jump straight into the air and concentrate on the target. If the shooter is right-handed, the left hand holds the ball, and at the peak of the jump, the right hand and wrist propel the ball toward the goal. The follow-through is with the right hand and arm as the shooter propels the ball off the left hand. The ball is shot with the elbow as straight as possible, as this position will get the ball higher into the air and make it more difficult for the opponent to block the shot.

When moving into the shot from a dribble, the shooter stops completely and jumps straight into the air. If this is done correctly, he will land exactly where he took off.

If the shooter wants to execute the jump shot starting with his back to the basket, he should turn his body and face to the basket as he jumps. If he is closely guarded and wants to get off a jump shot, he should fake and shoot or drive quickly, stop, and shoot. This maneuver will leave the defensive man guessing and always a half-step or a step behind.

LAY-UP SHOT. The lay-up shot is the short one-handed shot that is taken from in front of or to the side of the basket. It is used by the player who drives, passes, and cuts for a return pass or, in general, by any player who has the opportunity to shoot while moving close to and toward the basket.

The shooter jumps off the left foot, if the shot is taken from the right side, and carries the ball up high with both hands, the right hand being on the back of the ball with the fingers well spread. The ball is cushioned on the five fingers and does not rest on the palm or heel of the hand. The shooter springs off the ball of the left foot and drives the right knee high into the air. The body is extended, reaching as high as possible, with the eyes fixed on a spot about 18 inches above the basket where the shooter will "lay" the ball. When the peak of the jump is reached, the left hand is taken off the front of the ball, which is placed softly on the target with the right hand, the ball being under fingertip control. The follow-through is as high as possible, with the eyes fixed on the target until it passes from view. The shooter lands on both feet and quickly returns to the court.

The spring for the high jump comes from the player's left leg when shooting right-handed and vice versa. The ball of the left foot should hit the floor hard; added momentum is obtained by driving the right knee hard and high into the air.

It is recommended that all lay-ups be taken by banking the ball off the backboard. If the shooter is coming in directly in front of the basket, he should take a step to the side, then in toward the basket again, and shoot the ball off the board into the basket.

Players should learn to shoot naturally with the left hand as well as with the right. The shot should be taken with the hand opposite the defensive man; in this way, the player protects the ball with his body.

TIP-IN. One of the chief methods of scoring in modern basketball is to control the rebound and tip the ball into the goal. In order to perform this shot effectively, the player must predict which way the ball is most likely to rebound, get high in the air, and by using one hand, contact it in such a way as to direct it to a spot on the backboard similar to where the shooter would place a lay-up shot. A slight snap of the wrist will propel the ball back into the air again. Jumping ability, fingertip control, and relaxation in the air are very important. Fingertip control can be developed by tipping the ball up against the backboard time and time again.

PIVOT SHOT. The pivot shot is taken when the player finds himself within 15 feet of the basket (foul line distance) with his back to it. It is a common shot for those playing center, but it is also a valuable type of shot for anyone playing basketball.

The shooter stands with his back to the basket, from 6 to 10 feet away from it, holding the ball at the fundamental position, and with his feet well spread and in line. To shoot with the right hand, the shooter pushes off with the right foot, pivots on the left, jumps into the air, and lands with the feet in line facing the basket. The weight should be forward, and the shooter should be ready to go into action immediately. The shot is made exactly as the one-handed set shot except for the body action.

As soon as the shooter knows he wants to shoot, he should fake one way with the ball, head, or head and shoulders, and then go the opposite way for the shot. He should locate the target, pivot, place the right hand behind the ball, and hold it there with the left hand. As the shooter faces the basket, he should carry the ball past his right ear and shoot as he would a one-hand set shot. He should let the ball go and follow through with the right hand and arm straight toward the basket.

Hook Shot. The hook shot is a difficult one to master, but very effective for a player who moves into the pivot position with his back to the basket. It is effective because it is very hard to defend against. It is usually taken within 15 feet of the basket, and it is a short, accurate shot.

The hook shot is executed by the shooter starting with his back to the basket. To shoot with the right hand, he carries the ball in both hands, pushes off the right foot, and pivots on the left. The left hand is taken off the ball and the elbow is carried high in a bent position as the body pivots around to face the basket. With his right elbow straight, the shooter propels the ball with the right hand and wrist in an arc over the top of the head. The body pivots around as the arm follows through, so that the shooter lands on both feet facing the basket—ready to rebound, if necessary.

pivoting

The pivot is a highly important skill employed by the man with the ball to enable him to make some bodily movement without actually walking. It is the one way he has of maneuvering, other than walking or running, to prevent the defense from tying him up into a jump ball. Basically, the pivot involves keeping one foot firmly planted on the floor in such a way as to limit all movement to a turn. The other foot can move in any direction that is clear and can touch and be taken from the floor as many times as the player chooses. The body should be kept reasonably low and in balance.

There will come many times in a game when the player must stop the dribble or catch a ball while he is in the air and stop by placing both feet on the floor. If he must move about during the time he has come to a stop and prior to the time he gets rid of the ball, certain rules govern which foot may be moved. If the player lands in stride, the back foot is the pivot foot. If he lands with both legs even, either may be used, provided they land simultaneously. If they land in a one-two count, the first to strike the floor is the pivot foot.

If the time allotted to the pivot in the practice schedule is any indication, most coaches do not consider it of much importance. The coach who neglects the pivot is failing to develop a highly important skill.

dribbling

The dribble is the only way a player may move from one part of the court to another while in possession of the ball. It becomes necessary many times during a game to seek a more advantageous position from which to shoot or pass to another player. The dribble should be equally well-performed with either hand, and practice should be toward that end. The basic position for the dribble is a slight crouch, feet apart, and head up. The arm and hand movement should remain always fluid. The ball should be contacted with the fingers long before it reaches its highest point. If a dribble is to be continued, the ball must never be brought to a rest in the hand. This is called palming the ball and will result in a turnover to the other team. In advancing a ball down the floor, it is best to use at least a waist-high dribble. In close front court play in nearly all situations, the low dribble should be used because it is harder to break up. In either type of dribble, it is important that the dribbler be able to "feel" the direction of the ball so that he can look ahead of him to see the other players and find a possible receiver or a lane through which he may pass.

OFFENSE

Basketball has always demanded good physical condition in its players, but in the modern version of the game this demand has increased tremendously. In any offense, whether it features the fast break or not, there must be movement on the part of all five players. The type of offense to be used depends to some extent on the ability of the players who make up the team.

fast break

The object in the fast break is to get the ball down the floor before the defense has a chance to set itself up. Primarily the fast break is based on good rebounding, passing, and dribbling on the run.

This type of offense, which demands the consistent application of rapid and disciplined movements, should be carefully planned and practiced. It should create a high number of 3-on-2 and 2-on-1 situations, which should increase the probability of getting the second and third shots.

A fast break can get under way from any defense, but it works more effectively from a zone, since the position of the men remains relatively constant. A team composed of fast men is well-fitted for this kind of offense, since their speed will give them an advantage over a slower team.

The organized fast break involves mastery of the following phases:

1. *The outlet pass.* Players are instructed to execute the outlet pass to one of the assigned areas using the hook or baseball pass.

2. *Reception of outlet pass.* The outlet pass should be made to the area shown in Figure 4–2. The short sideline area is the best for the outlet pass.

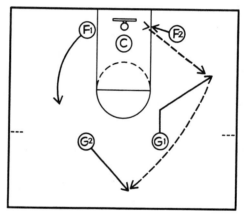

FIGURE 4-2 *The Outlet Pass and Centering the Ball*

3. *Centering the ball.* After the ball has been received in the side area, it should be centered as shown in Figure 4–2.

4. *Filling the lanes.* When the ball has been centered, the lanes should be filled on both sides of the ball.

5. *Trailer.* The use of a man following behind the breaking offense will provide defensive balance should a counter-break occur. The trailer is usually the player who took the initial rebound and made the outlet pass.

6. *Full stop at foul line.* The middleman who is handling the ball

should come to a full stop at the foul line, unless he is able to split the defense. This maneuver eliminates the possibility of offensive charging and permits the ball to be passed to the open man, since the defense is outnumbered.

The middleman has the alternatives of passing to either of his team-mates on the sidelines, executing a jump shot from the foul line, splitting the defense, or setting up the trailer.

pattern offense

This type of offense is usually attacking a man-to-man defense. The offense may take the form of pattern or free-lance movement consisting of screening techniques and use of cutters. Numerous systems have been used to exploit individual defensive weaknesses. When a team has an offense built around its guards, the attack usually consists of screening toward and away from the ball, screening by the forwards—which increases the opportunities for the give-and-go maneuvers—driving, and outside scoring opportunities. Pivot attacks to exploit tall players may take the form of a single low or high post, or a double low or high post. A five-man, shuffle-type offense is employed by a team without a superstar in order to distribute scoring and to provide a disciplined pattern of attack. Regardless of the system employed, constant movement of the ball, cutting, screening, and floor balance are required.

zone offense

The zone attack varies with the type of defense used by the opponent and the weakness of the personnel. As a general rule, a 1-3-1 offensive alignment is used against even zone formations (2-3, 2-1-2) and a 2-1-2 offensive alignment against odd zone formations (1-3-1, 1-2-2). A zone pattern offense should employ maximum movement of the ball and players, with men breaking toward the ball from behind the zone. This is an excellent way to exploit zone weaknesses.

jump ball plays

There are approximately a dozen jump ball situations in each game, making this an extremely important phase. A team should spend some time developing plays for each jump ball situation. Most teams use the diamond or box formation, with the basic man-to-man defensive princi-ples dictating the position of a player in relation to his opponent. In the *clock method,* the circle is assumed to be a clock face, with 12 o'clock directly ahead, 6 behind, and 3 and 3 to the left and right. The number called indicates the direction of the tip, should it be controlled. Figure 4–3 shows the clock method being used from a diamond formation. The *rotation method* is used from the box formation in which a player gives a signal which indicates the direction each player should rotate (Figure 4–4).

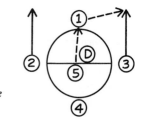

FIGURE 4-3   *Clock Method of the Jump Ball Play*

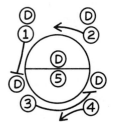

FIGURE 4-4   *Rotation Method of the Jump Ball Play*

DEFENSE

Defense in basketball is still of tremendous importance, in spite of the fact that scoring is exceedingly high. In a general way, although it will vary in different situations, the defensive stance is one of good balance. The body is in a slight crouch, with the feet apart and arms extended in readiness for blocking passes. If the man being guarded has the ball, the defensive player stands more erect than he would if he did not have it. The defensive player must at all times be able to move in any direction. This can be done by keeping generally in the stance already described. If the offensive man starts moving, the defense must stay with him. In moving with him, the player should shuffle his feet but never cross them, unless the man has taken a sprint across the floor, and it is necessary to keep up with him. If a dribbler is moving down the court, the defender should get between him and the center of the court and bear him out to the side, making sure, of course, not to push him.

The defensive player should stay between his man and the basket. He should make constant use of peripheral vision while doing his job. He should see not only the man whom he is guarding but others as well, and he should observe the progress of the ball in order to be alert to what move he may have to make next. Good defensive players talk to each other to keep alert to situations or to warn of impending movements. The defense should be alert to fakes and pivots, for it is quite easy to get in a disadvantageous position. When the offensive player gets away a shot, the defensive player immediately becomes a rebound man and should turn, face the basket, and make an effort to take the ball off the board.

All offenses must be played through some sort of defense. The defensive team must prevent scoring by the offense, and the type of defense and its effectiveness determine in a large measure the final result of the game. The defense may effectively prevent scoring by intercepting passes, by blocking attempts at field goals, by forcing the passer to make inaccurate and ineffective passes, or by forcing the offense to shoot from a greater distance away from the basket. In any case, each individual is an important cog in any defensive setup, and his alertness, speed, and aggressiveness contribute materially to the effectiveness of whatever style of defense is used. Skills of the individual players may be the deciding factor in choosing the type of defense. Players who can shift direction quickly, are in top physical condition, are fast, and can anticipate an opponent's movements are prime material for the man-to-man defense. With a group of slower players who can still be depended on to defend a certain area, the zone defense is preferable. Players who are screened easily should be used in zone defense.

man-to-man defense

The man-to-man defense is commonly used as a basic defense by most college teams and by many teams on the high school level. This defense has many advantages over the other types. As far as the individual is concerned, another contest is going on besides the ball game itself. He is pitted against an opponent and charged with the responsibility of preventing him from shooting, passing, or moving about the floor effectively. Generally this other man is charged with the same responsibility when he is on the defense, and when the game is over, one of these two will emerge the victor. Another advantage of this type of defense is that the coach delegates responsibility, and individual defensive failures are more easily spotted and corrected. The man-to-man defense allows play over the entire floor when it is necessary to attempt to secure control of the ball.

There are some obvious weaknesses in the man-to-man defense. Because the men are constantly moving and changing directions, often at full speed, it is important that they be in top physical condition. Because of the reasonably close play of both men in each of the five pairs, it is possible to utilize screen plays much more effectively.

A few playing hints can be given to the individual who must operate in the man-to-man defense. He should be in top physical condition. He should never cross-step upcourt. He should always stay between his man and the basket. He should continually be aggressive. He should keep up a continual chatter, particularly to his own men, warning of impending moves and possibilities.

To the coach who utilizes the man-to-man defense, some points are worth mentioning here. The entire squad should be kept in top physical condition. Each player should be impressed with the importance of his assignment so that he will take pride in doing a good defensive job. The opponent should be studied in advance so that the defensive assignments may be made more accurately on the basis of height and variations of ability. Use some other type of defense occasionally in practice sessions so that if it ever becomes necessary to change, the players will know what to do.

zone defense

The zone defense is held in high regard by many coaches, especially in the high schools. Its advantages are few but important. It is not so taxing on the stamina of the individual player as other defenses, and this is an important factor when coaching at the high school level. Zones should be utilized on the small court, where they can be defended adequately. A man-to-man defense on such a floor would result in close play and a great deal of fouling. If a coach has a team susceptible to screens in a man-to-man defense, it may be necessary to utilize the zone system.

The disadvantages are that a zone defense does not designate responsibility to specific men, there is no provision for playing outside of designated areas, and there is always the possibility that two or more offensive men will overload one area.

In the zone defense, each player is assigned a specific area to cover. The assignment zones may vary according to the situation, but generally the forwards cover each side of the court away from the end line, and the guards cover each side of the court nearer the end lines. The center may vary his position in three ways. He may be under the basket (1-3), around the free throw line (2-1-2), or out and even with the forwards (3-2). His movements will, in a large measure, depend upon where the offense is concentrating its attack. Each player should understand clearly the limits of his zone and feel a responsibility for any man who enters it. He should not be so aggressive that he retains responsibility for a man after he leaves his zone.

full-court pressing defense

This type of defense is utilized by many teams late in the game when they are behind in score. As soon as a team loses the ball downcourt and goes on defense, instead of running back to its own court, it picks up the offense, man-to-man. Since the team being pressed is not usually prepared, such a defense is confusing and the defensive team has a good chance of recovering the ball. Some teams employ the pressing defense quite effectively throughout the entire game.

"boxing out" on the rebound

One way to keep a team from getting possession of the ball after a shot is to keep the players from the vicinity where the rebound is most likely to go. In man-to-man or 2-1-2 zone defenses, there is generally a triangle of players around the basket, composed of three pairs of players. Each pair consists of a defensive man on the inside (nearer the goal) and an offensive man on the outside. When a shot is made, the defensive men hold their positions, thus preventing the offensive men from moving in. As soon as the ball contacts the rim or the board, the men turn quickly and move upward to take the rebound, getting there ahead of the men who were "boxed out."

Players who have a tendency to play too far under the basket may be "boxed in" so that they cannot get a wide rebound.

TEACHING PROCEDURE

Basketball is a fast and vigorous sport, requiring top physical condition. The participants should, as in any sport, be screened by a medical examination. Anyone with an organic deficiency that excessive activity may affect should not be allowed to play. The one skill used more than any other is running, and much time should be devoted to it. Calisthenics are of minor importance; only stretching and limbering-up activities should be included. Heavy calisthenics may have a tendency to tighten up the muscles. For a few days prior to formal practice, the players should be assigned to running and jogging outdoors. By the time practice gets underway, they will be in good shape. Volleyball may be used to develop tip-in ability. Rope skipping strengthens legs for the jumping that is so necessary.

Every practice should include running, stretching, and limbering-up exercises, shooting of all types, passing, dribbling, and work on both offensive and defensive plays. During the first week, there need not be any team play, but during the second week, a scrimmage should be held to determine individual weaknesses so that plans may be made for correcting them subsequently. After about two weeks, there should be some scrimmaging regularly in addition to all the other activities listed. Intra-squad play should be used for the purpose of practicing basic skills under game conditions, perfecting plays, polishing defense, and improving physical condition. As a part of learning basketball, the players should become acquainted with the rules during the course of a practice and through the study of rules in a players' handbook.

It is important that there be no idleness during a practice except for rest. There should be several baskets and backboards so that more players will have the opportunity to practice the various shots.

If basketball is part of a physical education course, the time generally is limited to 30 minutes—certainly not more than 40 minutes—and the class usually meets three times a week. For the first three weeks, the time should be allotted carefully to include as many skills as possible during each 30 or 40 minutes. A skeleton allotment might consist of 5 minutes for warm-up exercises, 10 minutes for shooting, 10 minutes for passing and catching, 5 minutes for dribbling, and 10 minutes for floor-play fundamentals such as pivoting and guarding. As time passes, it will be possible to reduce the allotment for some of the activities and include practice for offensive plays and defensive work, and finally a scrimmage. Game situations should be provided in the interscholastic or the intramural program.

organizing class for pass drills

There should be at least half as many basketballs as there are players on the squad. In passing practice, this will allow two players to pass a ball between themselves, and there will be no loss of time in waiting for others to finish using the ball. To have five basketballs among ten players is at least five times more efficient than to have one basketball among the same number. At first, in learning the basic movements involved in passing and catching, the squad should be placed in lines so that the coach may better see them. Later, when catching and passing while standing still have become habits, some movement should be added to approximate the game situation.

dribble drill

This particular drill is the only one that requires a basketball for every player. However, since most schools will not have that much equipment, the illustrations are based on one basketball for every two players. When learning the basic dribble, the players should remain stationary, all the dribblers in a line on one side facing their partners, who are in another line waiting their turn. After the skill has been learned to the point where it can be performed fairly well, the players should be allowed to move around objects while dribbling.

Because of overcrowded class conditions, lack of enough play space, or a combination of both, it becomes necessary frequently to conduct practices, scrimmages, and sometimes intramural contests in a greatly modified manner. The chief modification is to play one-goal basketball. Any number of players up to five may be used on a team. All the players in the game will have as a goal the same basket. The game may be played in half court, with two games in progress at the same time. If the gymnasium has two cross courts, there would be six goals. In such a case, there could be six games, with a total of sixty players participating. The rules are the same as for regulation basketball with two exceptions: there is only one goal, and if the defensive team gets the rebound, the ball must be taken out of bounds away from the goal to simulate bringing it upcourt.

Another game from which must fun may be had when there are only a few players present is "21." It is a shooting game only and can be used to increase skill and add interest to shooting drills. Each man in turn shoots from beyond the free throw circle, gets the rebound, and takes 1 lay-up shot. The long shot, if made, counts 2, the lay-up 1. The player shoots again in his turn. The first man to score 21 is the winner.

SKILL TESTS

pivot pass test

This is a test to determine ability to pass accurately, quickly, and hard after a pivot. It is performed during the time period of 20 seconds. The player stands back of the free throw line facing the goal, with the ball held ready to throw. At the signal "Go," he throws the ball hard toward the backboard. When it rebounds to him, he grasps it, pivots completely, and throws up again. This is continued for the entire 20 seconds. The score is the number of times the ball hits the backboard during that time. If he misses the backboard or hits the rim in such a way as to deflect the ball, he must run, get it, return to the throwing spot, and continue. This puts a heavy premium on accuracy. The test can be varied by throwing to a wall or by eliminating the pivot. It has one disadvantage in that the player may become dizzy from the pivoting. A fairly good score is 11.

dribbling test

The dribbling test emphasizes speed, good ball handling, and maneuverability during the dribble. Six chairs are placed at intervals of 8 feet over a distance of 50 feet. The start should be conveniently placed at an end boundary line and the chairs set in a line straight down the floor. It is 10 feet from the start to the first chair and 8 feet from chair to chair. The run should be made in a figure eight. The score is the number of seconds it takes to dribble the entire distance up and back. If the ball hits one of the chairs or is kicked so that it is deflected out on the floor, the player should go get it, bring it back to the point of the error, and continue. A good score is 10.

shooting test

An attempt is made in this test to simulate a game situation by hurrying the shooting. A time limit of 30 seconds is placed on the test. The player stands back of the free throw line facing the basket, with ball in hand. At the signal "Go," he shoots. After the ball leaves his hand, he can cross the line to retrieve it. If he makes the basket, he is credited with 2 points, and he goes back to the free throw line and shoots again. If he misses, he retrieves the ball and attempts one lay-up shot. If he makes it, he is credited with 1 point. In any case, after the lay-up attempt, he goes back to the free throw line to try another long shot. Some players have made as many as 16 points on this test, but the average score will be between 6 and 10.

combination running, dribbling, and shooting test

An attempt is made to combine these three skills into a semblance of a game situation. Time will be a factor, and all three skills will be performed, but there will be no defensive opposition. The test begins on one end line at the signal "Go." The player dribbles the length of the court, shoots until he makes a basket, runs back to the goal under which he started, shoots until he makes it, then returns to the other goal, shoots until he makes it, retrieves the ball, and goes to the end line there. The time elapsed, in seconds, is his score.

free-throw test

This is an optional test involving shooting skill. A set number of free throws should be attempted (25 is suggested), and the score is the number of free throws made. This test takes as much time as any of the others, if not more, and is suggested only as another possibility.

DEFINITION OF TERMS

Air Dribble. Tossing the ball into the air during a dribble or batting it into the air and touching it before it strikes the floor.

Back Court. That part of the playing area from the center court line to the opponent's goal.

Basket. A ring 18 inches inside diameter and attached to the backboard, with a suspended cord-net, through which players attempt to shoot the ball.

Blocking. Personal contact that slows the progress of an opponent who does not have the ball.

Charging. Personal contact against body of an opponent by the player with the ball.

Crip Shot. An attempt to make a goal by jumping from the floor close under the basket and laying the ball up with one hand.

Defense. The team that does not have the ball in its possession.

Double Foul. A situation in which two opponents commit personal fouls against each other at the same time.

Dribble. Bouncing, throwing, batting, or rolling the ball and touching it again before any other player touches it.

Field Goal. Score from the court during play. It counts 2 points.

Foul. An infraction of the rules resulting in the awarding of one or more free throws to an opponent.

Free Throw. A chance to score one point from a position behind the free throw line without being guarded.

Front Court. The part of the playing area between the center court line and the end line of the team's own basket or goal.

Holding. Personal contact with an opponent that interferes with his movement.

Intermission. The rest period between the first and the last half.

Jump Ball. A ball tossed up between two opposing players by an official.

Multiple Foul. The commission of personal fouls against the same opponent at the same time by two or more teammates.

Offense. The team that has the ball in its possession.

Out of Bounds. A ball that touches the floor or a person outside the boundary lines or the supports or back of a backboard.

Own Basket. The basket into which a team is trying to score.

Pass. Movement of the ball caused by a player in control—a way of advancing the ball to another player.

Personal Foul. One that involves contact with an opponent when the ball is in play.

Pivot. The act of a player's moving while holding the ball—one foot must stay in contact with the floor.

Referee. One of the officials to govern play according to the rules.

Scorer. An official who records points scored, substitutes, fouls committed, and other pertinent statistics.

Screen. The legal action of a player in preventing or delaying an opponent from reaching a certain position.

Shooting. An attempt to put the ball through the goal.

Side Lines. The boundaries on the long sides of the court.

Substitute. A player who takes the place of another player during a game.

Technical Foul. A foul occurring while play is suspended, or one that does not involve player contact.

Time-out. A period provided in the rules during which a player may request rest or discussion of strategy.

Timer. A person who keeps the official playing time by using a controlled clock.

Traveling. When a player in possession of the ball progresses illegally in any direction.

Umpire. One of the officials to govern play according to the rules.

Violation. A rule infraction that does not involve a foul.

DISCUSSION QUESTIONS

1. What were Dr. Naismith's basic considerations when he was devising the game of basketball?

2. What were the first basketball rules?
3. What are the advantages of utilizing peripheral vision?
4. Name the two basketball skills considered to be the most important. Why are they so considered?
5. Why is it better to pass straight and hard?
6. Name two passes and explain when each should be used.
7. Why should a player know more than one type of shot?
8. Describe a good dribble.
9. Why has basketball speeded up so much in recent years?
10. Describe the fast break and list its advantages.
11. Describe the pattern play offense and list its advantages and disadvantages.
12. What may individuals do in a game while on the defense that will help break up the play of the other team?
13. Name some points a defensive man should remember in doing his best job.
14. Name some advantages and disadvantages of the man-to-man system of defense.
15. Name some advantages and disadvantages of the zone defense.

BIBLIOGRAPHY

Bee, Clair, *The Basketball Library,* 4 vols. New York: A. S. Barnes & Company, 1942.

Dean, Everett S., *Progressive Basketball.* Englewood Cliffs, N.J.: Prentice-Hall, Inc., 1946.

Dintiman, George B., and Barrow, Loyd M., *A Comprehensive Manual of Physical Education Activities for Men.* New York: Appleton-Century-Crofts, 1970.

Healey, William A., *Coaching and Managing High School Basketball.* Danville, Illinois: Interstate Printing Company, 1942.

Hobson, Howard A., *Basketball Illustrated.* New York: A. S. Barnes & Company, 1947.

Holman, Nathan, *Championship Basketball.* Chicago: Littleton Technical Library, 1942.

Hughes, William L., *The Book of Major Sports.* New York: A. S. Barnes & Company, 1938.

———, and Williams, Jesse Feiring, *Sports—Their Organization and Administration.* New York: A. S. Barnes & Company, 1944.

Mitchell, Elmer D., *Sports for Recreation.* New York: A. S. Barnes & Company, 1952.

Murphy, Charles C., *Basketball.* New York: A. S. Barnes & Company, 1939.

Naismith, James, *Basketball, Its Origin and Development*. New York: Association Press, 1941.

National Federation, *Official Basketball Rules*, latest edition. Chicago: National Federation of State High School Athletic Associations.

Rupp, Adolph F., *Championship Basketball*. Englewood Cliffs, N.J.: Prentice-Hall, Inc., 1948.

U.S. Naval Institute, *Basketball*. New York: A. S. Barnes & Company, 1943.

Wilkes, Glenn, *Basketball Coach's Complete Handbook*. Englewood Cliffs, N.J.: Prentice-Hall, Inc., 1962.

Wooden, John R., *Practical Modern Basketball*. New York: The Ronald Press Company, 1966.

bowling

5

The actual origin of bowling can be only a guess, but it is believed that sometime during or prior to the seventh century A.D. a game known as *bowles* or *bowling on the green* came into existence in Italy. It did not gain large popularity there and consequently had no effect on the development later of the same game in other countries.

The object used to knock down pins in the early development of the game was oblong in shape. This probably was due to the fact that round stones could not be obtained, and it was necessary to use those as near to roundness as possible. This adaptation helps to explain the shape of the object employed in the game of bowles today.

The game has been known for centuries in some form or other in many countries of the world. Bowles has been played in England for at least

83

seven centuries. Ninepins is probably of Dutch origin, having been popular in Holland for a long time. The game was known as *carreau* in France for hundreds of years. Curling, introduced to Scotland by the Flemish immigrants more than 300 years ago, is an adaptation of bowling on the ice, and currently enjoys much popularity in Canada. The game has carried many names and has been played in many forms. Among them are kaylies, quilles, skittles, and cloish. Some of them were played with cans, but most used pins similar to those of today.

The history of bowling in England is interesting. Many of the kings played it but finally curbed it for one of two reasons: first, the game was used by many as a gambling device and, as a result, a decree forbade it; later, when started again, it developed such a following and took the people away from archery that Edward III banned it.

When archery was replaced by gunpowder, the ban was lifted, and the people began bowling again. Sir Francis Drake became one of the game's chief proponents.

As played in America today, it is probably descended from the old game of ninepins, which was played originally by the Dutch, Germans, and Swiss. In its early history, the alley was a bed of clay or cinders. As the game developed, a board 12 inches or more in width was substituted. The nine pins were set up in three rows of three each. The board platform was from three to four feet in width.

The Dutch probably had most to do with the initial interest in bowling in America. Everywhere they settled, the game was played and greatly enjoyed. Washington Irving's story of Rip van Winkle, set in the Catskill Mountains, has much to say about the game.

It was not long, however, as with many sports that attract the attention of men, before gambling began to be associated with it. Finally, it became generally known, just as it had in England, as a gambling device, and both Connecticut and New York legislated against it. In other states the ordinary decent business or working men became disgusted with the way it was being used and refused to participate in it. It is said that our present game of tenpins came as a result of adding another pin to circumvent the law that forbade the game of ninepins.

Many people interested in bowling began a move to legitimize it. As a result, the National Bowling Association was formed in 1875. However both this organization and the American Amateur Bowling Association, formed in 1890, failed to correct the corrupted condition of the game. Finally in 1895, in Beethoven Hall in New York, the American Bowling Congress, generally known as the ABC, was formed. Under the guidance of this organization, bowling has grown steadily.

The first National Championship was held in 1901, when 41 teams of 5 men each participated. Today there are more than 40,000,000 bowlers in the United States. About 1,000,000 people of all ages took up bowling for the first time in 1970. It is the most popular participant sport in this country, and is also believed to be the fastest growing game.

BASIC SKILLS

Bowling is played by rolling an 8- to 16-pound ball down a level, smooth maple and pine alley 63 feet long in an attempt to knock down all 10 pins located at the opposite end from which the ball is started. The best bowler is the one who can knock down the most pins in the specified number of opportunities. Various methods of delivering and of directing the ball to a definite part of the triangular arrangement of pins are considered the likeliest to knock down the most pins. These methods are the essential considerations in the discussion of basic skills.

There are modifications of the game of bowling, such as duckpins, in which smaller pins and balls are employed. The fundamentals are much the same for all games of this type. This discussion is therefore confined to bowling.

the grip

The ball rolled down the alley to knock over the pins at the other end may not exceed 16 pounds in weight, nor be greater than 27 inches in circumference. It should be uniformly balanced. The method by which this ball is held is called the grip.

A bowling ball has either two or three holes for fingers. It may be necessary for a person to try both the three-fingered and the two-fingered grip in order to decide which he prefers. However, the three-fingered grip is recommended for beginners. In any case, regardless of grip, a ball must fit the fingers as nearly perfectly as possible in order to assure maximum comfort, consistency, and safety, as well as good scoring (Figure 5–1).

FIGURE 5-1 *The Finger Grip* (From Lou Bellisimo and Larry L. Neal, *Bowling.* © 1971, Prentice-Hall, Inc. Reproduced by permission of the publisher.)

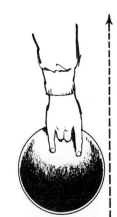

In determining whether a ball fits the fingers, the thumb should be checked first. When the thumb is placed in the hole as far as possible, it should be reasonably loose, but the fingers should still make contact with the ball on all sides. None of the fingers should fit so tightly that release is difficult. When in doubt whether a proper fit has been attained, looseness is to be given the greater consideration. The span of a bowling ball is the distance between the nearer edge of the thumb hole and the finger holes. The distance should be such that the second finger will fit into its hole up to the second joint without cramping the hand. The third finger should be inserted the same way as the second. When gripping a ball, the fingers not inserted in holes should be spread evenly, yet comfortably and in such a manner that each finger may exert some force in guiding the ball.

In gripping the ball, the thumb should not be completely buried in the hole, but about three-fourths of the way in. This position allows an easy release and assures a smooth continuity of motion, which is very important. Every finger plays a part in the delivery of the ball. By practice and experimentation, the function of each can be determined and better bowling ability attained.

the stance

The stance in bowling is extremely important. It is the basis for all forward movement and should be carefully considered. There usually is a distance of 21 feet behind the foul line in which the approach may be made. Where the bowler takes his initial stance will depend in large measure on whether he uses the three, four, or five-step delivery. Most accomplished bowlers prefer the four-step approach, since its rhythmic nature appears best suited for imparting proper speed to the ball without causing a loss of balance at the time of delivery.

The bowler should take his stance at the distance he prefers. His body should be erect, and he should be facing the pins squarely. The feet may

FIGURE 5-2 *Four-Step Delivery* (From Don Cash Seaton, Irene A. Clayton, Howard C. Leibee, and Lloyd L. Messersmith, *Physical Education Handbook*, 5th ed. © 1969, Prentice-Hall, Inc. Reproduced by permission of the publisher.)

be slightly spread or together, depending upon his comfort. It is important that the weight be distributed evenly on both feet. Assuming that the bowler is right-handed, the weight of the ball should rest squarely on the left hand at slightly lower than chest level, and in front of the right hip. The right hand at this moment should grip the ball but not bear any of its weight.

the approach

THREE-STEP APPROACH.   This approach is not recommended because it involves, in the main, only the force employed by the arm and body. Momentum counts but slightly if at all. Since some beginners may wish to try the three-step approach, it will be explained briefly. The left foot leads off, and the ball goes forward. The right foot steps, and the ball goes back. Then, as the left foot moves forward to the foul line, the ball is brought forward and released. There is little speed forward and much arm movement.

FOUR-STEP APPROACH.   In any approach, footwork is extremely important. Everything else being equal, footwork is the key to good bowling. Correct footwork combined with effective arm movement can make for a smooth, accurate delivery.

The steps should be in a fairly fast walk, not a run. The last step should be made so there will be room for a short slide that will stop just behind the foul line. The steps should be taken so the left foot reaches the foul line just as the ball is ready for release. Every effort should be made to effect a smooth approach. The knees should be bent slightly as the steps are being taken, and the bowler should be relaxed. The body should be bent forward slightly, and the approach made in a straight line (Figure 5–2).

In making the four-step approach, the right foot steps forward, and the ball is pushed outward on the first step. At the bottom of the back swing, the left foot passes the right as it moves forward. When the ball

reaches the top of the back swing, the right foot again steps forward. The left foot and the ball now move forward at the same time. The left foot is placed before the ball completes its forward motion, and as the slide is made, the ball is released.

FIVE-STEP APPROACH. There is little difference between the four and the five-step approach other than the additional step. The start of the five-step approach is made from slightly farther back, and the steps are a little shorter and quicker. The arm movements are the same as in the four-step approach, except that they are timed somewhat differently. A little practice will quickly indicate the difference.

the delivery

The delivery is the act of releasing the ball. There are several types of releases, depending on what the bowler wants the ball to do. In any case, however, it leaves the hand during the time the slide is being made toward the foul line. There are essentially four deliveries, each of which gives a particular motion or direction to the ball. They are known as the back-up, the curve, the hook, and the straight ball.

The back-up is seldom used because it is difficult to execute and because, even when rolled correctly, it is not so effective as the hook or the curve. The back-up is a way of rolling the ball so that it curves to the right for a right-handed bowler. The fingers impart a clockwise spin as it is released.

The hook and the curve are so similar in method that both will be considered under the title of curve ball delivery.

STRAIGHT BALL DELIVERY. In this delivery, the fingers grip the ball so that the palm is up and in the direction the ball is to go. The release should be made in such a way as to cause the roll of the ball to go straight toward the pins. It should have no side roll at all. The straight ball is easier to throw with accuracy, but it is not so effective as either the hook or the curve. Opinion is sharply divided among bowling experts on whether beginners should master the straight ball before learning to throw the curve or the back-up. The author recommends that beginners who aspire to higher bowling scores start throwing the hook ball initially.

CURVE BALL DELIVERY. Curving the ball makes it go among the pins at a much more advantageous angle than is possible with a straight ball. The spin imparted by the bowler to the ball is in turn imparted to the pins. A counterclockwise motion is given to the hand as the ball begins to leave it. The thumb releases the ball first and finally the fingers. Instead of having a forward rolling motion, the ball slides forward but actually is revolving sideways in a counterclockwise movement. It is considered expert bowling to be able to roll a curve accurately.

aiming

One of the factors involved in accurate aiming and bowling is the speed of delivery. Aim and control of the ball can be mastered only by the bowler being reasonably relaxed and by concentrating carefully on each delivery. The ball should have some speed on it, but it should be gauged in such a way as not to impair its control. The spinning effect that a properly delivered ball imparts to the pins is lost if it has too much momentum. One speed is most effective for each style of delivery, and the bowler should experiment until he finds that best suited to him.

Either one or both of two points may be used in aiming. One is the point between pins 1 and 3, commonly referred to as the "one-three pocket." It is the contention of some authorities that if the ball is supposed to go there, that is where it should be aimed. The other point is a spot on the alley, determined by practice, that the ball should cross in its journey to the target. In this delivery, one would ignore the pins almost completely and expect the ball, if placed so as to cross the spot accurately, to proceed to the pins. Some bowlers use both points in their aiming. They look directly at a spot halfway up the alley and by peripheral, or split, vision see both the near spot and the head pin.

There are good bowlers who use both methods, so one may suggest that each player use that which he feels is best for him. In any case, the bowler should practice his approach and delivery until they near perfection and then concentrate on learning how best to aim.

A strong factor in aiming is the "speed" of the alley. Some alleys are even and smooth-surfaced, whereas others are relatively rough, although the difference in surfaces is small because of ABC alley surface specifications. Normally, there is much less resistance on the smooth alley, and the ball is not slowed down so rapidly as on the rough. Curves are not so effective on the smooth as on the rougher and slower alley. The bowler should roll the ball several times over the alley in order to determine how fast it is, so that he can aim and roll accurately.

It is suggested that the beginning bowler roll a hook ball toward the head pin, attempting to place it between pins 1 and 3.

scoring the game

A bowling game consists of 10 frames. In each frame a maximum of two balls may be rolled. Should there be no strikes, the bowler would roll a total of twenty times in a game. If he should roll a strike, he would roll no more in that frame but would put an X in the little square in the upper right-hand corner of the scoring box for that frame. After the next two rolls, he would add the 10 made on the strike to the score on the next two rolls and then place the total in the frame where the strike was made.

If on the other two throws the bowler had another strike and three other pins, his score in the frame would be 23.

A sample of a score sheet is shown in Figure 5–3.

The number of the frame is shown under each. The score made during each frame is indicated by the numbers with the square. Strikes are indicated by an X in the upper right-hand corner. A single line in the small square indicates a spare. The numbers on top indicate the number of pins knocked down on each roll in each frame.

In the first frame the bowler knocked down 8 pins on the first ball and none on the second. His score thus far was 8. In the second frame he hit 5 and then 4 pins on his two rolls, bringing his total to 17. In the third frame he knocked down all 10 pins on the two rolls. This is called a spare and allows the bowler not only the 10 pins but, in addition, the pins made

FRAME	1	2	3	4	5	6	7	8	9	10	Total
JONES	8	17	32	39	59	74	79	88	103	111	111

Score made
on each roll... 8,0 5,4 5,5 5,2 10 7,3 5,0 9,0 6,4 5,3

FIGURE 5-3 *Score Sheet*

on the next roll. At the time the spare is made, no score is shown in that particular frame. A mark is placed in the upper right-hand corner to indicate that a spare was made. On the next roll the bowler knocked down 5 pins. The 17 made up to the second frame, the 10 on the spare, and the 5 on the first roll after the spare are added together. The total, 32, appears in the third frame. On the second roll after the spare, 2 pins were knocked down. These 2 and the 5 are added to the 32, and the resulting 39 is placed in the fourth frame.

In the fifth frame the bowler made a strike—that is, he knocked down all the pins on one roll. An X is placed in the upper right-hand corner to indicate what happened. The bowler gets whatever he makes on the next two rolls added to the strike. He rolled 7 and 3, which is shown over the sixth frame. The 10 pins are added to the 10 of the strike and also to the 39 in the fourth frame to total 59 for the fifth frame. On the next roll after the spare the bowler hit 5 pins. These are added to the spare and to the 59, which gives him a total of 74. He knocked down 5 pins in the seventh frame. These were added to the 74, making 79. He hit 9 pins in the eighth frame, for a total of 88. A spare was made in the ninth frame. It was indicated in the corner, and on the next roll 5 pins were knocked down. The sum of 88 plus 10 (the spare) plus 5 is 103, which appears in the ninth frame. A total of 8 pins were hit in the tenth. These added to 103 make a total game score of 111.

bowling hints

1. There must be a maximum amount of "sameness" in all deliveries: the feet should make the same movements; the arms should make the same moves; the hand and fingers should be placed in the same position and move the same each time. The bowler should also try to use the same ball.

2. The ball should be delivered smoothly with a natural movement of the arm.

3. The delivery should be practiced so that it is as nearly automatic as possible.

4. The ball should be rolled, not thrown.

5. The ball must not be rolled too fast or too slowly. It must have the right amount of speed and the right amount and angle of rotation. A speed somewhere between the two extremes, depending upon the physical condition of the bowler and the alley surface, should be found.

6. A straight-arm delivery should be used. The position of the hand remains the same throughout the delivery. There should be no attempt to drive or snap the ball or add motion by twisting the wrist.

7. Generally, the ball should start its roll on the right side of the alley about ten boards in from the gutter.

8. The arm should follow through after each delivery.

9. The successful bowler must relax.

10. There is no substitute for frequent practice.

team play

Most bowling is done informally, with two or more people going to an alley and bowling one or more games. There are, however, many bowling leagues organized throughout the country, each of which is composed of several teams of five players. These leagues operate in various types of recreation programs and are extremely competitive in nature and highly enjoyable to the participants.

A team is made up of four or five of the best bowlers in a particular organization who can bowl well under competitive pressure. League matches are usually scored by a point system: one point for each game won of the three games bowled and a fourth point awarded to the team with the highest pin fall for the three games. The games are bowled on adjoining alleys. Each team bowls a complete frame on one alley and then switches the alley with the other team. This continues during the entire match.

A group of five players will vary in ability and also in temperament. How well each bowls under pressure is an important factor. In making out the bowling order, the best-scoring bowler who also is good under pressure should be placed in the last spot.

The second-best bowler should bowl first to enable a team to get a good start. The weakest bowler should be placed in the third position, and the other two bowl in the second and fourth positions.

TEACHING PROCEDURE

It is best always to do all bowling instruction at a regulation alley. However, most schools are not equipped with alleys and are not located near a commercial alley. Even if one happens to be nearby, the cost is often prohibitive for the school or the individuals involved. It may be possible, if a school is located conveniently, to take the class to a commercial alley at a time during the day when few people are bowling and teach at little or no cost.

In the majority of schools, where no bowling alleys are available, it is still possible to teach bowling. It may be done in a series of steps:

1. In a gymnasium mark off with chalk, or tape, several alleys. Line up the students and teach them the approaches—particularly the four-step approach—without the bowling ball.

2. After the movements have been mastered, the students may be equipped with softballs and allowed to roll them down the marked-off alleys.

3. After this skill has been practiced a while, they may use as a target a variety of objects arranged in the same placement as bowling pins should be. These may be paper cups, foot-long two-by-fours, paper milk cartons, or similar objects.

4. If funds are available, light plastic pins, a small net to keep the pins from scattering, and a lightweight, hollow plastic ball may be purchased for use in a gymnasium.

5. As a culmination of the activity, the class should be taken to a local alley and allowed at least one day of regulation bowling with on-the-spot correction and instruction in fundamentals.

SKILL TESTS

It is difficult to test bowling because some of the skills involved defy separation from the total process. If these skills or phases are separated, the only judgment that can be made is, at best, subjective. On the other hand, since the number of pins knocked down by a bowler is a good indication of his ability, the game score or scores may easily be used for testing purposes. Since the teacher may choose to use both methods, the means of testing are described here.

The Grip. The person's grip is observed, and a point is given for each correct detail of the position of the ball in the hand, and of thumb and finger positions.

The Approach. The bowler is allowed to bowl five times. Points may be given for excellence in starting position, speed, position of body, position of head, the slide, timing, smoothness, and consistency.

The Delivery. Upon bowling five times, the player is checked and given points for the position of the head at the release, the movement of the body at the release, the speed of the ball and the final placement of the ball.

The Bowling Score. The score a bowler makes in a group of games is a fairly accurate indication of his ability. As a test, he may be allowed to bowl three, four, or five games, and either the average or the total score may be used to indicate his ability. More than one game should be rolled because a superior bowler may be off form or a weak bowler can be "hot" at the time he takes the test.

DEFINITION OF TERMS

Alley. A smooth wood strip 63 feet long and 41 or 43 inches wide, usually made of maple and pine, on which the game is played.

Alley Man. A person who is in some way connected with bowling—such as owner, employee, instructor, or stockholder of a bowling alley.

Approach. The term used to describe the movements that take place from the stance to the foul line.

Baby Split. A situation that occurs when eight pins are knocked down in one roll, leaving a combination still standing of pins 2 and 7 or pins 3 and 10.

Back-up. A reverse hook.

Ball. A composition or hard rubber sphere not exceeding 27 inches in circumference or 16 pounds in weight with which the pins are struck.

Blow. The failure of an attempt to spare, not counting splits.

Board. One of the strips of wood, usually maple or pine, from which an alley is built.

Body English. Movement of body made after ball leaves fingers.

Break. Failure to strike or spare on two rolls.

Brooklyn. A ball that, on the roll, hits the left side of the head pin.

Chalk. Substance used to rub on the hands and fingers for the purpose of drying them.

Cherry. The act of knocking down the front one of two pins necessary for a spare.

Cross-over. Same as Brooklyn.

Curve. Path of a ball that rolls toward the right gutter and then back to the one-three pocket. For a left-handed bowler, the path is toward the gutter and back to the one-two pocket.

Dead Ball. A ball in some way affected by an outside force or by something else that is not the fault of the bowler. It is played over.

Dead Wood. Any pin that has been knocked over.

Delivery. The act of releasing the ball on its way to the pins.

Double. Two successive strikes.

Double Wood. A situation in which a pin is left standing immediately behind another.

Error. Same as blow.

Follow-through. The continuation of body movement after the ball is released.

Foul. An infraction of the rules involving stepping or reaching over the boundary lines. Any pins knocked over do not count.

Foul Line. A line across the alley placed there to show the limit of the approach.

Frame. One of ten parts into which each game is divided.

Full Hit. The act of hitting a pin in the center.

Grip. The method of holding the ball for delivery.

Gutter. A rounded groove approximately 9 inches wide, one of which is located on each side of the alley.

Head Pin. The pin nearest the bowler.

High. Same as full hit.

Hold. The act of gripping the ball.

Hook. A roll that curves from the right side into the one-three or the one-two pocket. Same as curve except that the break is sharper and faster.

House Ball. A ball furnished by the particular alley or firm.

Interference. The act of a spectator or another bowler in affecting adversely the roll of a participant.

Kick-back. The outside edge of the two alleys.

League. A group of teams bowling against each other according to a predetermined schedule.

Leaves. The pins standing after a roll.

Loft. The act of elevating the ball at the delivery in such a way as to cause it to drop onto the alley rather than to roll out smoothly.

Mixer. A ball that spins into the pins in such a way as to knock them against one another.

Open Frame. One of the ten parts of a game in which there is no mark indicating a spare or a strike.

Pin. Object at which the ball is rolled.

Pit. The space at the end of the alley into which the pins usually go when knocked over.

Pitching. The act of throwing instead of delivering correctly a bowling ball.

Pocket. Space between pins 1 and 3 and pins 1 and 2.

Rebound. The act of the ball bouncing off the rear cushions and back among the pins.

Return. The concave pathway over which bowling balls are returned.

Roll. The movement of the ball from the bowler down the alley.

Runway. Space from the foul line back, which must be at least 15 feet in length.

Slow Alley. One not highly polished and somewhat rough, on which a ball will curve more effectively.

Span. The space or distance between the hole for the thumb and the one for the second finger.

Spare. The act of knocking down the remaining pins on the second roll.

Spiller. A ball that effectively scatters the pins.

Spin. Same as mixer.

Split. An arrangement of the pins made by the first roll in which there is a distance at least the width of a bowling ball between two of the pins still standing.

Spot. The position designated for a pin to stand. It may also be the place on the alley on which the ball is placed at the beginning of a roll.

Stance. The position taken prior to the approach.

Straight Ball. One that travels straight down the alley.

Strike. The act of knocking down all ten pins on the first ball.

Tap. A roll that appears to be perfect, yet fails to effect a strike.

Thin Hit. The act of hitting a pin barely on its outside edge.

Three Hundred. A perfect game of twelve strikes.

Turkey. Three successive strikes.

Wood. A pin.

Working Ball. A mixer or spinner.

DISCUSSION QUESTIONS

1. How did bowling begin?
2. By what names has bowling been known?
3. How did the game of tenpins develop in America?
4. What is the object of bowling?
5. Describe the grip.
6. Name two types of approach. Describe them.
7. How is a bowling ball aimed?
8. What is meant by the terms strike, spare, frame, and span?
9. List a group of hints one might give a bowler to improve his game.
10. How would you teach bowling if you did not have an alley at school?

BIBLIOGRAPHY

American Bowling Congress, *Playing Rules, 1970–71 Season.* Milwaukee: American Bowling Congress, 1970.

Bellisimo, Lou, *The Bowler's Manual.* Englewood Cliffs, N.J.: Prentice-Hall, Inc., 1965.

Casady, Donald, and Liba, Marie, *Beginning Bowling.* Belmont, California: Wadsworth Publishing Company, 1965.

Fait, Hollis F.; Shaw, John H.; and Ley, Katherine, *A Manual of Physical Education Activities.* 3d ed. Philadelphia: W. B. Saunders Company, 1967.

Falcaro, Joe, and Goodman, Murray, *Bowling.* New York: A. S. Barnes & Company, 1940.

———, *Bowling for All.* New York: A. S. Barnes & Company, 1943.

Lifetime Sports Foundation. *Gymnasium Bowling Program.* Washington: Lifetime Sports Foundation, 1964.

————, *Teaching Lifetime Sports Skills.* Washington: U. S. Government Printing Office, 1966.

Mitchell, E. D., *Sports for Recreation.* New York: A. S. Barnes & Company, 1952.

Seaton, Don Cash; Clayton, Irene A.; Tiebee, Howard C.; and Messersmith, Loyd L., *Physical Education Handbook.* Englewood Cliffs, N.J.: Prentice-Hall, Inc., 1969.

Showers, Norman E., *Bowling.* Pacific Palisades, California: Goodyear Publishing Company, Inc., 1969.

Stanley, D. K., and Waglow, J. F., *Physical Education Activities Handbook.* Boston: Allyn and Bacon, Inc., 1969.

conditioning

6

BACKGROUND

The term "physical conditioning" refers to a program of activity designed to improve such factors as strength, endurance, flexibility, and coordination. The objectives vary according to individual needs. For the athlete, conditioning may lead to improved performance in a particular sport. To the average high school or college student, it may provide for improved performance in intramurals or in recreational activities. For the middle-aged man or woman, a program of physical conditioning may very well be one method of improving general health and the health of the cardiovascular system in particular. It may also provide a method of weight control, and a positive outlook that comes from being physically fit.

This chapter should serve as a guide for anyone who is interested in achieving a state of improved physical fitness and then maintaining that level. Suggestions for initiating a training program, methods of training, and the beneficial effects of exercise will also be discussed.

STARTING A TRAINING PROGRAM

Regardless of one's objective in undertaking a program of physical conditioning, certain common sense precautions should be observed. The first of these is a complete medical examination.

For those individuals under thirty years of age who have had an examination within one year and were told that nothing was wrong with them, any type of exercise is appropriate.

A person from thirty to forty years of age and apparently well should have had a complete examination within three months prior to starting an exercise program. For people in this group, there need be no restrictions for exercise, provided the examination did not reveal any physical problems.

For individuals over forty the same examination should be administered with the addition of an exercise electrocardiogram. Reasonable caution should be followed for this group in the selection of, and participation in, strenuous activities.

A word of advice to those people who have the responsibility of planning and supervising a training program. Always follow the instructions of an examining physician concerning a prospective exercise participant. In many cases the physician may suggest a limited program for a period of time prior to strenuous activities.

PRACTICAL SUGGESTIONS FOR TRAINING

Once the suggested guidelines pertaining to medical examinations have been met and the individual has been declared physically capable of exercising, some practical matters should be considered. These include such factors as exercise uniform, frequency of exercise, best time to exercise, length of exercise period, intensity of exercise, type of training program, diet and exercise, seasonal exercise, and complications or physical impairments resulting from exercise. These will be considered in sequential order.

uniform

There need be no special uniform for a conditioning program. However, consideration should be given to comfortable, loose fitting clothing. This may be shorts and shirt, or a sweatsuit can also be used. Rubberized suits that tend to increase perspiration during exercise are of little value to the development of physical fitness. Of particular concern should be the selection of appropriate footwear. Shoes should be comfortable, have relatively thick soles, and provide some ankle support. There is particular need for this type of shoe at the beginning of an exercise program.

frequency

The frequency of exercise is largely dependent on the individual's objective. If the training program is for the development of fitness for athletic competition and time is a factor, workouts should take place five or six days per week. If the objective is not preparation for competition, less frequent workouts will develop fitness. The person who elects to train three or four times each week should do so with the understanding that getting "fit" will require a longer period of time. Experience has shown that periods of exercise conducted two days per week, for example on Monday and Friday, produce some muscular soreness. There is evidence that fitness is not maintained with only two weekly workouts unless they are inordinately strenuous. For these reasons, three training sessions per week appear to be a minimum standard.

length of exercise period

The length of the exercise period, like the frequency, is dictated by the individual's objective and certain other factors. Again, as in the matter of frequency, if preparation for vigorous competition is the purpose of training, one to one and a half hours will be required daily. The young, healthy boy or girl should reach a high level of physical fitness within three or four weeks of daily training sessions of this length. This, of course, assumes the training program to be a sound, progressive one that is structured for this particular purpose.

For the person who is not training for athletic competition and wants to improve his level of physical fitness, a lesser amount of time may be required. Frequently this type of person will find it virtually impossible to spend an hour and a half away from his business or profession. He should not be excluded from participation in training sessions because of the time factor. A program that requires thirty minutes per day, on a five-day basis, can produce a favorable change in physical fitness. Suggestions for programs of this type will be presented later in this chapter.

Students enrolled in physical education classes are usually restricted to thirty or forty minutes for a class period. If the conditioning program is being conducted in a school setting, it obviously must conform to this period of time. A well-planned and organized program can produce changes in fitness in youngsters even if given this limitation.

best time to exercise

Traditionally, those who are involved or have been involved in competitive athletics believe the late afternoon is the appropriate time for physical conditioning. In reality, the best time for a workout is an individual matter. Certain guidelines should be followed in setting the time. It is probably better not to exercise strenuously immediately after a substantial meal. The time selected for exercise should be one that can be followed on a regular basis with a minimal amount of interference. Some people find early morning a convenient time while others prefer just before retiring for the night. Many business and professional people exercise during their lunch hour. Any time that can be made a regular and systematic part of the day's activities seems appropriate.

intensity of exercise

There are two methods by which the intensity of exercise can be altered. The first of these is changing the speed of the activity. Generally speaking, exercise or activities that are executed rapidly require a greater output of energy. For example, running 100 yards at a slow speed is not nearly so exhausting as running the same distance at maximum speed. Likewise, calisthenic-type exercises may be more demanding if executed at a very rapid pace.

The second method consists of extending the duration of the activity. Obviously, exercises that are continued over a longer period of time require a greater expenditure of energy. With these two concepts in mind, it is possible for the participant to change, at will, the intensity of a training session.

type of training program

The types of physical conditioning methods available are almost too numerous to mention. For this reason only a partial listing is included here with a brief description of each. The training methods are not listed in any particular order of preference or importance. More detailed explanations appear at the conclusion of the chapter.

Weight training. This probably is one of the oldest methods of physical training. It involves the use of barbells and dumbbells.

Usually the objective in this type of training is the improvement of strength and/or physique.

Isometric exercises. This method probably had its beginning with the system of "Dynamic Tension" advocated by Charles Atlas. More recently it has been used by a variety of athletic teams as a means of improving muscle strength.

Calisthenics. This method is characterized by a series of free exercises in combination to form the main part of a workout. Calisthenic-type activities may be employed to exercise almost any muscle group or groups.

Interval training. This training technique utilizes activities that produce an increase in pulse rate followed by a decrease. An example of this method would be short runs at near maximum speed followed by jogging and/or walking.

Endurance training. Training of this type includes jogging and/or running for prolonged periods of time. As the name implies, this method is important in the development of endurance, particularly cardio-respiratory endurance.

Combination activities. This program of physical activity utilizes two or more training techniques, for example, circuit training (explained on page 93), calisthenics, and weight training.

STRUCTURE OF A CONDITIONING PROGRAM

A typical conditioning program should be divided into three phases: a warm-up, an intensive workout, and a cool-down or recovery phase.

Warm-up. The warm-up should cover approximately ten minutes. Activities should include bending and stretching, walking, and slow jogging of sufficient intensity to produce sweating and a pulse rate of 100–120 beats per minute. The primary purpose of these activities is to prepare the body for more strenuous exertion. A general warm-up is of particular importance in a conditioning program for adults. For younger people the value is reflected in reduced damage to muscles that can occur during sudden strenuous movements. The warm-up should be a part of any type conditioning program.

Intensive workout. Following the relatively slow warm-up, the various systems of the body should be ready for the more strenuous activities. Efforts that are near maximal should be a part of this phase of conditioning. The duration of this phase should cover approximately two-thirds to three-fourths of the total exercise time for each session. An hour's workout should provide for forty to forty-five minutes of relatively strenuous activity. A pulse rate that is 80 to 90 percent of one's maximum rate should be attained several times during interval-type training. During activities such as weight training, the heavier lifting should be accomplished during the intensive workout phase. However, pulse rates during weight training and isometric training probably will not reach the aforementioned percentage of maximal rate.

Recovery phase. After the more strenuous workout, a period of time of at least five minutes should be devoted to walking or to moderately strenuous exercises. The recovery phase is of particular importance in training programs for adults. Just as the body needs preparation for strenuous activity, a recovery period is necessary for returning the body systems to near pre-exercise levels. Longer recovery periods are indicated if the workout has been unusually strenuous.

diet and exercise

Almost without exception, authorities are in agreement that no special diet is necessary during physical conditioning programs. The balanced diet advocated by expert nutritionists for the American population contains all the nutrients the body needs. Therefore, additional meals or dietary supplements are not required for a person participating in a conditioning program.

seasonal exercise

The conditioned person should be able to work out in any type of weather. Emphasis should be placed on the term "conditioned." If an individual is healthy and possesses a reasonable level of physical fitness, cold weather should not be a deterrent to exercise. For the person who is not fit, a period of acclimation to temperature extremes is important. One should dress appropriately for workouts in either temperature extreme.

complications or physical impairments

A certain amount of muscular soreness may normally result from participation in a conditioning program. This is particularly true for those who are just starting an exercise program. This soreness is usually temporary and disappears within a few days without complications. Soreness of this type should not prevent a person's continued participation.

Of a more serious nature are the so-called "charley horses" or muscle pulls, which cause fairly severe pain during movement of the affected part. Rest usually will clear up these types of impairments, and the person can then return to his regular routine. Frequently, another type of activity can be substituted, and participation can be continued without interruption. An example might be replacing running with a program of swimming.

Joint involvement—ankle, knee, or shoulder—may require complete rest and the attention of a physician. It is not unusual for soreness and swelling to occur in the ankles and knees during the initial stages of conditioning. These problems are more common among those who have not exercised on a regular basis. Previous injury to a joint may be aggravated by exercise. Most of these problems are correctable and should not keep a person from his conditioning program for any extended period of time.

ADVANTAGE OF PHYSICAL FITNESS

It is important to keep exercise in its proper perspective from the very beginning of a conditioning program. There is no guarantee that it is a panacea for all of man's physical and mental ailments. Research does not support any claim for increased longevity as a result of exercise. There are, however, scientifically proven advantages of living a physically active life from childhood to old age. Some of these are listed here.

The feeling of well-being that comes from being physically fit, though difficult to measure, is an important outcome of physical conditioning. Statements from participants in exercise programs speak of a more positive outlook, increased energy for the day's routine, and a feeling that they are "on top of the world." This result cannot be discounted and is one of the truly beneficial aspects of physical conditioning.

Improved performance of the heart in conditioned people is probably the most significant physiological aspect of regular exercise. The resting pulse rate of a trained individual decreases, reflecting a stronger contraction of the heart and a more forceful expulsion of blood with each contraction. The truly conditioned person may have a resting pulse rate of 40 beats per minute as compared to the average 72 to 78 beats.

Increased work capacity of the physically fit person is obvious. While the maximal heart rates of the conditioned and the unconditioned persons may be essentially the same, the conditioned person will have accomplished significantly more work when his maximal rate is reached.

Numerous studies have shown a relationship between cardiovascular fitness and protection from coronary heart disease. Active railroad section workers, London bus conductors, postmen, and Israeli communal workers have all had a decreased incidence of myocardial infarctions (heart attacks) when compared with their less active counterparts. Additionally, when these active people had infarctions, they were less likely to die than the more sedentary individuals. Many physicians and scientific investigators believe that regular and systematic exercise may provide one method of protection against coronary heart disease, a leading cause of death in the United States.

A variety of studies have reported conflicting results of exercise on such factors as serum cholesterol, triglycerides, and other lipids (fats). Medical opinion generally indicates that lower levels of fats in the blood is a desirable objective, but it should be noted that this alone will not ensure cardiovascular health. There is also general agreement that strenuous exercise, when accompanied with a loss in body weight, can reduce the levels of circulating fats. It should be emphasized that the exercise must be strenuous and in most cases there must be a weight loss in the individual.

Regular exercise has also produced a reduction in the resting blood pressure of individuals. It has been suggested that a decrease in peripheral resistance, caused by increased vascularization of muscles, may be the reason for the pressure reduction. The type and intensity of the exercise is an important factor in this blood pressure reduction.

Studies have been conducted that suggest an improved collateral circulation in the heart of the conditioned individual. These are not conclusive at this point, but this could very well be one of the most important effects of exercise.

Finally, improved strength and muscle tone are recognized benefits of exercise. Tremendous gains in individual strength have resulted from well-planned programs. An improved general appearance is associated with good muscle tone. This improvement is frequently associated with a change in body composition; i.e. an increase in muscle tissue with a reduction of fat tissue. This would suggest that regular exercise is an excellent method of maintaining a more desirable body weight. This result is particularly important to a nation in which many people are classified as obese.

EXAMPLES OF TRAINING PROGRAMS

weight training

General statements.   Certain guidelines should be followed in setting up a training program with weights.

1. The beginning lifter should use a weight that he can control at all times.

2. A lifter should not hold his breath while straining to lift a weight.

3. Most effective results are usually obtained with workouts every other day.

4. A lifter should attempt to complete a minimum of six repetitions of each exercise. Three sets of these repetitions should be completed during each workout for maximal strength development.

Training program.

1. Warm-up exercises—use light weights—five minutes
2. Two-arm military press
3. Two-arm curl
4. Flat footed squats—do not exceed 90-degree knee bend
5. Two-arm pull-over on bench
6. Rowing exercise
7. Bench press
8. Reverse curl
9. Dead lift
10. Sit-ups—bent knee position with ten-pound weight behind neck

circuit training

General statements. A training circuit may be set up either indoors or outdoors. An effort should be made to include a variety of activities in the circuit. The intensity of the training using the circuit may be increased by:

1. Increasing the number of repetitions at each station.
2. Increasing the number of stations in the circuit.
3. Increasing the number of times the circuit is completed.
4. Attempting to decrease the time required to complete the circuit.

Training program—11 station circuit

Station 1—Warm-up activities

Station 2—30 step-ups on 16–18 inch bench

Station 3—35 bent leg sit-ups

Station 4—30 push-ups

Station 5—30 burpees

Station 6—Run in place 200 steps

Station 7—Jump and reach 15 repetitions

Station 8—Side straddle hop, 75 repetitions

Station 9—Chin-ups, 5 repetitions

Station 10—Parallel bar dips, 10 repetitions

Station 11—Coordination hops, 30 repetitions

interval training

General statements. Interval training probably provides one of the most effective means of improving cardiorespiratory fitness. The person undertaking interval training should have been exercising for several days; several weeks is necessary for adults.

Training program—30 minutes

1. Warm-up activities—10 minutes

Walk—1 minute

Jog—1 minute, 140–50 steps/minute

2. Run—1 minute, 180–200 steps/minute

Walk, jog, run in this order until five of these cycles have been completed (15 minutes).

3. Recovery—5 minutes of walking or slow jogging

DEFINITION OF TERMS

Aerobic. Requiring the presence of oxygen.

Anaerobic. Occurring in the absence of oxygen.

Athlete's Heart. A dilated heart resulting from overstrenuous exertion; it is no longer believed to exist.

Atrophy. A wasting of tissue, usually as a result of a lack of use: applies to muscle tissue.

Blood Pressure. The force with which the blood distends the walls of the blood vessels.

Calorie. The amount of heat required to raise the temperature of one gram of water 1-degree C., beginning at 15-degrees C.

Cardiac. Pertaining to the heart.

Cardiac Output. The volume of blood pumped by the ventricles of the heart in one minute.

Cardiotachometer. An instrument that provides a continuous record of heart rate.

Coronary Blood Vessels. The vessels that supply the heart with blood.

Crest Load. The largest work load that the body can carry and still maintain a balance between oxygen intake and oxygen requirement.

Electrocardiogram. A record of the spread of excitation through the heart during the cardiac cycle.

Ergometer. An apparatus used to measure the work output of an individual— usually a stationary bicycle.

Fatigue. A diminished capacity for work caused by the effects of previous work.

Heart Sounds. Sounds produced by closure of valves in the heart.

Homeostasis. Equilibrium of the internal environment of the body.

Hypertension. An abnormal increase in the resting arterial blood pressure.

Hypertrophy. An increase in the size of a tissue or organ in the body.

Isometric Contraction. A contraction that does not produce a shortening of the muscle.

Normal Load. A light or moderate work load.

Overload. A heavy work load where the oxygen supply is inadequate to meet the demands.

Oxygen Debt. The amount of oxygen required following exercise to reverse the anaerobic reactions of the exercise period.

Pulse. The distention of the arterial walls caused by the expulsion of blood from the heart.

Sphygmomanometer. An instrument used to measure arterial blood pressure.

Stroke Volume. The volume of blood ejected by each ventricle during contraction.

Treadmill. An instrument with a continuous moving belt that can be operated at various speeds and elevations.

Work Load. The intensity of work.

BIBLIOGRAPHY

books

Astrand, Per-Plof, and Radahl, Kaare, *Textbook of Work Physiology.* New York: McGraw-Hill Book Company, 1970.

Casady, Donald R.; Mapes, Donald F.; and Alley, Louis E., *Handbook of Physical Fitness Activities.* New York: The MacMillan Company, 1965.

Cooper, Kenneth H., *The New Aerobics.* New York: M. Evans and Company, Inc., A Bantam Book, 1970.

de Vries, Herbert A., *Physiology of Exercise.* Dubuque, Iowa: William C. Brown Company, 1969.

Morehouse, Lawrence E., and Miller, Augustus F., *Physiology of Exercise.* Saint Louis: The C. V. Mosby Company, 1967.

journals

Brozek, Josef, "Body Composition." *Science* 134, 29 September 1961, pp. 920–30.

Campbell, Maurice, "The Mortality Rate from Heart Disease." *American Heart Journal* 68, July 1964, pp. 1–2.

Eckstein, Richard W., "Effect of Exercise and Coronary Artery Narrowing on Coronary Collateral Circulation." *Circulation Research* 5, May 1957, pp. 230–35.

Fox, Samuel H., and Skinner, James S., "Physical Activity and Cardiovascular Health." *The American Journal of Cardiology* 45, December 1964, pp. 731–46.

Garrett, H. Leon; Pangle, Roy V.; and Mann, George V., "Physical Conditioning and Coronary Risk Factors." *Journal of Chronic Diseases* 5 (1966), p. 899.

Golding, Lawrence A., "Effect of Physical Training upon Total Serum Cholesterol Levels." *The Research Quarterly* 32, December 1961, pp. 449–506.

Hein, Fred V., "The Contributions of Physical Activity to Physical Health." *The Research Quarterly* 31, May 1960, pp. 263–85.

Montoye, Henry J., "Summary of Research on the Relationship of Exercise to Heart Disease." *The Journal of Sports Medicine and Physical Fitness* 2, March 1962, pp. 35–43.

White, Paul Dudley, "Health and Sickness in Middle Age," *Journal of Health, Physical Education and Recreation* 31, October 1960, pp. 21–22.

gymnastics and tumbling

7

BACKGROUND

The original meaning of the word *gymnastics* was, according to several sources, "to train in athletic exercises." The term was first used in early Greece and applied to forms of athletic activities such as running, jumping, throwing the javelin, and wrestling. Over the span of several hundred years, the term *gymnastics* has come to mean a specific type of exercise, not particularly gamelike in nature. In this chapter, it refers to tumbling as well as to activities on the horse, the rings, the bars, and trampoline.

In all probability, the gymnastic skills we know today were first practiced by the Romans and included the skill of mounting and dismounting a horse. Gymnastics was stressed during the Middle Ages, when knights vaulted and climbed ladders, ropes, and poles as part of their physical training. They also built human pyramids for the purpose of getting men to the top of walls and towers.

Toward the end of the eighteenth century gymnastics attracted the attention of certain people important in the field of physical education. These men can be divided into two clearly defined groups: those looking for activities with educational value, and those searching for exercises that would develop strength, skill, endurance, and national unity.

One of these individuals was Johann Friedrich Guts-Muths (1759–1839), who taught at the Schnepfenthal Educational Institute in Germany for fifty years. He is known as the grandfather of gymnastics in Germany. He wrote *Gymnastik für die Jugend,* in which he listed and described many gymnastic and recreational activities for children. Among these were listed the climbing of mats, ropes, and rope ladders; balancing, swinging, and many stunts. He believed that exercises should be enjoyable and should aim to strengthen and harmonize the body and the mind.

Gerhard Ulrich Vieth (1763–1836) had much to say about gymnastics in his *Encyklopadie der Leibesübungen.* He wanted schools to promote gymnastics and to place less emphasis on intellectual attainment. He particularly liked such activities as walking, climbing, jumping, and vaulting. He described in detail many of his vaulting exercises.

Johann Pestalozzi (1746–1827), along with his other educational contributions, is considered the father of calisthenics and free exercises, and did much to promote gymnastics and play in the schools.

Friedrich Jahn (1778–1852), was interested in developing German national unity for the purpose of defeating Napoleon, and did more to develop the field of gymnastics than any other individual. He started by taking boys and young men into the country and practicing gymnastic exercises. He proved extremely popular because of his enthusiasm, skill, personality, and storytelling ability. As time went on, the groups increased in size until as many as 500 went with him each day. From these he picked the best leaders, and they in turn taught others. Besides tumbling stunts, he introduced new types of apparatus, such as the parallel bars, the high bar, jumping standards, the side horse, balance beams, and vaulting bucks and standards. Jahn's groups were called Turnerbunds and the members were known as Turners. The societies numbered in the hundreds. His influence was so great that much of the apparatus he invented is still in use, and there are many Turner societies functioning today.

In this chapter no attempt is made to cover gymnastics completely or in minute detail. It is written to give to the beginner instruction in some basic and intermediate movements in tumbling, vaulting, parallel bars, horizontal bar, rings, side horse, and trampoline.

Adequate safety precautions are of utmost importance in the gymnastics program. Safety devices such as the overhead belt, the hand belt, and the wrist safety straps are described below. The hand spotting method with lowered equipment may also be used for teaching new stunts.

OVERHEAD SPOTTING BELT. The overhead spotting belt consists of a single pulley and a double pulley attached to an overhead beam or to the ceiling. A double rope passes through the double pulley, with one rope going downward where it is attached to the safety belt. The other rope passes horizontally overhead and through the single pulley on the opposite side. The spotter grasps the double strand of rope that hangs from the double pulley and can support the performer by pulling downward.

THE HAND BELT. The hand belt is a regular safety belt with ropes attached to each side. Spotters stationed at the sides of the performer can grasp the ropes and provide the necessary support by lifting upward.

BASIC SKILLS

tumbling

FORWARD ROLL. The performer should assume a squat position, with his hands on the mat a shoulder's width apart, and arms outside the knees. The legs extend slightly and push, the arms bend at the elbows, and the body is lowered toward the mat. The performer pushes forward with the feet and contacts the mat with the back of the head and shoulders, not the top of the head. At this point he reaches forward and completes the roll by grasping his shins and pulling the heels close to the buttocks in a tuck position. He follows through by bringing head and shoulders forward and rising to a standing position. The forward roll may begin from a standing position after it has been mastered from the squat position (Figure 7–1).

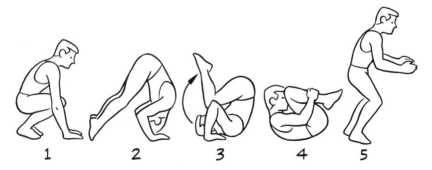

FIGURE 7-1 *Forward Roll*

BACKWARD ROLL. The tumbler should assume a squat position, with his hands on the mat and arms outside the knees. He extends his legs slightly and pushes backward. As the buttocks contact the mat, the chin moves forward on the chest. The knees remain close to the chest, and the hands move above the shoulders in a palm-upward position. As the roll progresses, the hands contact the mat and push to relieve strain on the neck. The performer must keep the hips high, extend the legs, and land on the feet. The backward roll may begin from a standing position after it has been mastered from the squat position (Figure 7–2).

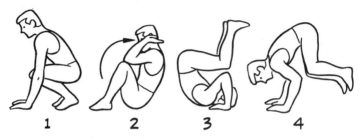

FIGURE 7-2   *Backward Roll*

STANDING DIVE ROLL.   The dive roll is similar to the regular forward roll except that the tumbler gives a push with both feet from a standing position, and the body is suspended in air for a moment longer. The arms must flex sharply at the elbow to absorb the shock of landing as contact is made with the mat. From this point on the technique of the dive roll is the same as the forward roll. The running dive roll may follow. It differs from the standing dive roll in that the performer runs, takes a short, low hurdle, and starts from both feet. The remainder of the roll is the same (Figure 7–3).

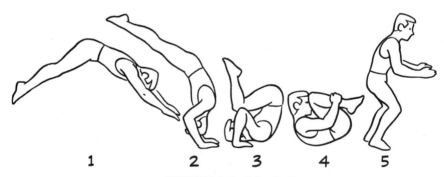

FIGURE 7-3   *Dive Roll*

HEADSTAND.   From a standing position on the mat, the performer reaches down and places the hands forward about a shoulder's width apart, with the front portion of the head beyond the hands so that a line drawn between the hands and from head to hands would form an equilateral triangle. He should push off the mat with the feet, walk the hips forward to a position over the head, press downward on the mat with the hands, slowly lift the legs one at a time from the mat, and straighten them as they move over the head. As the balance point is reached, the feet and legs must be kept straight and together, with the toes pointed (Figure 7–4).

FIGURE 7-4 *Head Stand*

CARTWHEEL.   The cartwheel begins from a standing position. The side that is most natural to the performer should determine how he faces down the mat. He bends sideways and places the near hand outward from the foot in the middle of the mat. At the same time, he pushes off with the forward leg and kicks the rear leg sideways over the head, allowing the weight to shift to the other hand during the sideward progression of the body. He keeps his head up and eyes on the middle of the mat and between the hands. As the movement of the body progresses beyond the sideward handstand position, the legs are kept wide apart in their sideward progress toward a landing on the mat. Upon landing, the forward leg first receives the body weight, and the trailing leg reaches outward. The outward reach of the leg has a pulling effect and is most effective in bringing the body to a graceful standing position. The tumbler should land with the head turned in the same direction the cartwheel is moving. If he encounters trouble in learning the cartwheel, he should try it from the other side.

HANDSTAND.   The performer bends forward and places his hands on the mat about a shoulder's width apart with the fingers pointing forward and spread apart for a wide base of support. He should position the shoulders over the hands with head up, and eyes focused forward on the mat. One leg (the left) should rest in a flexed position underneath the body, and the other leg should be stretched backward and fully extended.

At this point the right leg is thrown backward and overhead. The left leg pushes off the mat simultaneously and joins the right leg overhead in a handstand position. Pressing hard on the finger tips while extending the head backward will help to prevent an overbalance. An underbalance may be corrected by moving the chin forward toward the chest and by shifting the weight to the heel of the hand.

After the skill has been practiced with the assistance of a spotter, the individual may use the wall to aid him in mastering the handstand. When using the wall method, the performer should place his hands on the mat at a position near the wall which will enable him to push cautiously away from it with one foot to a free handstand. He should never duck his head, but always keep it and the neck extended, and eyes upward.

CHEST ROLL. From a handstand position, the tumbler quickly flexes the arms and lowers the chest to the mat. In an arched position, the body rolls from the chest, to the abdomen, to the hips, and to the thighs. The feet are held upward as an extra precaution against injuring the toes on the mat. The upper body rolls upward to a straight-arm position as the roll is completed.

KIP UP. The performer begins the kip up from a sitting position; he rolls backward and brings the legs close to the chest in a tight pike. Once a tight pike has been assumed, the hips drop forward. After they have dropped slightly forward, the kipping action begins. The legs are extended vigorously upward and outward and then downward and underneath the body to a landing position. This movement is accompanied by a simultaneous forceful extension of the elbows and a push off the mat with the hands. Ideally, the tumbler should strive to keep his hips up with the back arched and allow the feet and legs to be pulled underneath the body rather than to permit the hips to sag so that he lands in a squat position. It will be difficult for the beginner to avoid the squat position and bent legs during the first attempts, but with practice he will be able

FIGURE 7-5 *Kip up*

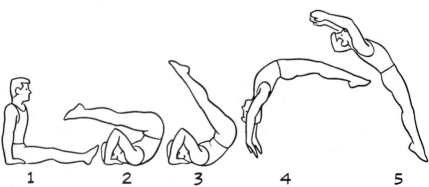

1   2   3   4   5

to execute the move with good form in which the legs are kept straight during the kipping action. The landing should be made with the back arched and arms overhead (Figure 7–5).

HEADSPRING. The headspring should start with a short run and low hurdle in which the tumbler lands on both feet. Without losing momentum, he then bends immediately forward, places his hands and the front part of the head on the mat, the head slightly ahead of the hands. He extends the knees and pushes off from his feet. The hips must ride forward until they are over and beyond the head position while the feet and legs are held downward, causing the body to assume a pike. When the hips reach an overbalance and as the body starts to fall off balance, the hips and legs are extended forcefully as described in the kip up, while the shoulders and arms push forcefully on the mat. The back is kept arched while feet and legs continue the circling motion and are drawn under the body, to the landing position with the hands overhead.

SKIP STEP. The skip step is a very important skill which must be learned before the performer can progress to the more advanced tumbling skills. It starts with a run and a skip on the right foot, while the left foot is held up and slightly forward. The arms are raised to an overhead position. There is a slight forward lean, the weight then shifts to the left foot, and the arms move downward toward the mat. The skip step is a basic mandatory skill and must be learned by all who desire to tumble (Figure 7–6).

FIGURE 7-6 *Skip Step*   1   2

FRONT HANDSPRING. The tumbler must begin the handspring with the skip step and with the arms in an overhead position. He then bends downward and places the hands on the mat in front of the feet and about a shoulder's width apart, with the arms absolutely straight. The left leg pushes hard off the mat, and the right leg is thrown powerfully overhead.

The shoulders and arms give a simultaneous push. As the right leg travels overhead, the left leg joins it, and the circular motion of the legs continues overhead. The performer must attempt to keep his hips up high (arched back) and pull his feet and legs underneath his body for a landing. Several rules are listed below that the tumbler must observe if he is to learn this skill in the minimum of time (Figure 7–7):

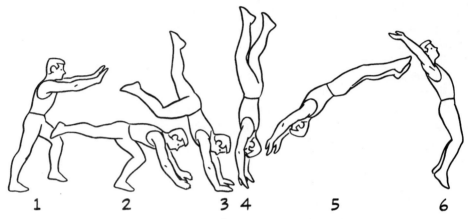

FIGURE 7-7   *Front Handspring*

1.   During the skip step be sure to incline the body forward and place the hands well in advance of the feet.

2.   Do not let the shoulders ride forward to a position beyond the placement of the hands. Shoulders directly over the hands is a good rule to follow.

3.   Keep arms straight and push with the shoulders and hands.

4.   Do not duck the head.

5.   Upon landing, keep hips high, head up, and pull feet and legs underneath the body.

ROUNDOFF.   The roundoff must be learned properly by anyone who aspires to become proficient in the art of tumbling. The performer begins the roundoff with a run and skip step on the right foot while lifting the left foot up and placing it slightly forward. There is a slight forward lean of the body, and the arms are raised to a position about even with the head. As the weight shifts to the left leg, the body bends downward, and the left hand with fingers pointing to the left is first placed on the mat, followed by the right hand with the wrist rotated inward toward the left hand and fingers pointing also to the left. The shoulders must be kept square, and the hands in the center of the mat in order to keep the shoulders from twisting to the left and causing the hands to be placed left of center. As the hands contact the mat, the left leg pushes forcefully off the mat. The body makes a quarter turn while the right leg is kept straight and extended powerfully overhead. As the legs reach the handstand position, there is another quarter twist of the hips which enables the body to complete a half turn. The legs then snap downward, the shoulders extend, and the fingers and hands push hard against the mat as the legs are drawn underneath the body. The latter portion of the twisting action causes the tumbler to land facing the opposite direction from which the roundoff began (Figure 7–8).

FIGURE 7-8 *The Roundoff*

Listed below are a few suggestions which should enable the beginner to establish proper techniques in learning this skill:

1. Raise the arms overhead during the skip step, but keep the body inclined forward.

2. Reach, but do not overreach, when placing the hands on the mat.

3. Rotate wrists to the left when placing the hands. Proper positioning of the hands is necessary to give the proper twist to the body. Let the weight shift from the near arm to the far arm as the legs circle overhead.

4. Keep legs absolutely straight as they move overhead and beyond the perpendicular line of gravity.

5. Push forcefully with the shoulders and arms during the kickdown movement of the legs.

BACK HANDSPRING.   The back handspring, or flip-flop, begins with the performer in a standing position, his arms stretched forward at shoulder height with palms downward. The move begins with a downward and backward swing of the arms and a bending of the knees to a sitting position (like sitting back in a chair). The back should be kept straight and vertical. At a point where the tumbler would fall off balance backward, he throws the arms powerfully upward and backward toward the mat, and also forces the head backward along with the movement of the arms. Simultaneously the feet push away from the mat, the knee joints extend, and the hips thrust vigorously upward, giving the body an arched appearance. As the arms stretch backward and make contact with the mat, there is a slight pause as the weight of the body settles on the shoulders and arms. This slight pause permits the trailing hips and legs to move to an arched handstand position. The shoulders then extend, and the hands push off the mat. At this point the trunk and hips flex, the legs are snapped downward, and the feet are pulled well underneath the body as they make contact with the mat (Figure 7–9).

FIGURE 7-9   *Back Handspring*

Listed below are some important things the beginner should observe as he attempts to learn this maneuver:

1.   Be sure to keep the arms straight. Swing them downward and as far backward as they will extend during the sitting phase.

2.   Avoid the tendency to lean forward during the sitting movement. Sit in a chair to establish the correct sitting position.

3.   As the arms move upward, they must move backward, with emphasis on the backward movement. This follow-through helps

pull the chest and shoulders backward in order that the hands may contact the mat at a point where after a slight pause, the snapdown to it can occur.

4. The head must move straight backward. Never attempt to look over the shoulder.

FRONT SOMERSAULT. The front somersault is a forward roll performed in the air. It begins with a running low hurdle in which the performer lands on both feet with knees slightly flexed. The knees then extend quickly and very forcefully; the arms are lifted forward and upward. The trunk flexes, and the hips force upward and overhead. The arms reach forward and grasp the shins in a momentary tight tuck position as the body rolls in the air. The tumbler then releases the tuck and extends the legs and trunk as the body descends to a landing position on the mat (Figure 7–10).

FIGURE 7-10 *Front Somersault*

TUCK BACK SOMERSAULT. There are three guiding principles to successful performance of the back somersault: arms up, knees up, and head back. The tumbler begins the stunt with a vigorous jump in which the arms are thrust upward and overhead in a stretching motion. This upward motion provides a transfer of energy from the arms to the body and helps to lift it into the air. As it leaves the mat, the hips and knees flex and move the legs upward toward the hands. The arms reach forward, grasp the shins, and pull the legs into the chest in a tight tuck as the head is extended forcefully backward. The body then completes the rotary motion, the tuck is released, and the tumbler makes the landing in a standing position (Figure 7–11).

1   2   3   4   5

FIGURE 7-11   *Tuck Back Somersault*

still rings

SAFETY.   The ring event requires strong shoulders and arms, and since the entire weight of the body is supported by the hands, a powerful grip is mandatory. To help a performer build the strength needed to work the rings, a list of progressively arranged exercises has been provided. Spotting is more difficult when the rings are at competition height. For this reason it is suggested that they be lowered to about shoulder level at first and then raised to higher levels as more skill is acquired and body strength increases. Some additional safety measures follow:

1.   The ring equipment such as cable, straps, and attachments should be checked periodically for weakness.

2.   Sufficient padding underneath the rings must be provided. The eight-inch landing pad will make a good landing surface if available.

3.   Many ring routines impose a great burden on the shoulders. The abrupt pull at the bottom of certain swinging moves may also cause the performer's grip to be torn from the rings. Adequate spotting, therefore, is very important.

4.   Chalk should be available to keep the hands from slipping.

STRAIGHT-BODY INVERTED HANG.   From a straight-body hang, the performer should swing the feet and legs backward and then forward. With arms straight, he presses downward on the rings. Keeping the head forward, he gradually extends to a straight-body inverted hang, the arms tight at the sides. In order to minimize wavering and vacillation of the body, the gymnast should press the arms tightly to the sides. He should pull the head slightly backward and allow the body to assume a slight arch (Figure 7–12).

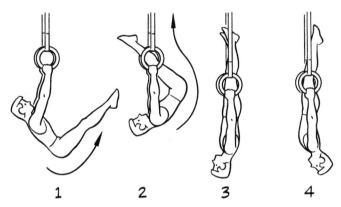

FIGURE 7-12 *Straight Body Inverted Hang*

INVERTED PIKE HANG.   The performer assumes a straight-body inverted hang. He then brings the head forward and moves the thighs downward toward the face to a pike position.

SKIN THE CAT.   From the inverted pike hang, the performer moves the hips and legs through the arms and backward through the rings as far as possible. Cautiously, in order to prevent shoulder strain, he should extend the hips and legs and stretch the legs downward toward the floor. When the body reaches the end of this extension, he forces the hips upward and back between the arms to the original inverted pike hang.

BIRD'S NEST.   From a straight-body hang, the performer swings the legs backward, then forward and upward, and places the insteps in the rings. He turns the hands so that the palms will be outward, making it easier to place the instep in the center of the rings. He then rolls backward and forces the knees and hips through the arms. Finally, he arches the back and finishes in a hanging position with the abdomen toward the mat.

PENDULUM SWING.   The performer begins the swing by bringing the legs forward to a pike position. They then relax, drop, and swing backward with the body assuming an arched position. They then swing forward. The body assumes a slight pike, and as the legs pass the vertical hand position, the arms pull and the legs whip upward. The pull with the arms serves to elevate the body at the peak of the forward swing. The body then swings backward.

STRADDLE CUT-OFF BACKWARD.   From a straight-arm hang, the gymnast swings his legs backward, then forward and upward. As they swing upward, they should be in a straddle position, with the arms pressing downward on the rings. As the legs rise upward toward the arms, he pulls hard with the arms, throws the head back, and releases the rings. The body continues its rotary motion to a landing position on the feet (Figure 7–13).

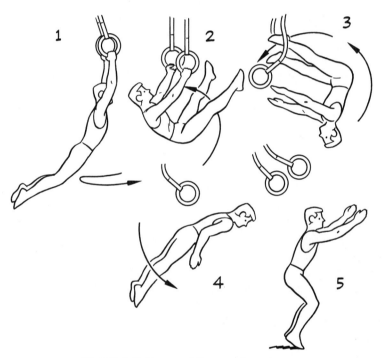

FIGURE 7-13   *Straddle Cutoff Backward*

PRESS TO A SHOULDER BALANCE.   The gymnast begins with an L seat. He bends the arms and leans forward, keeps the legs straight, and forces the hips backward overhead to a pike position, with the shoulders above and in front of the rings. Then he lowers the shoulders between the rings, and continues to bring the feet and legs overhead to a shoulder balance on the rings (Figure 7–14).

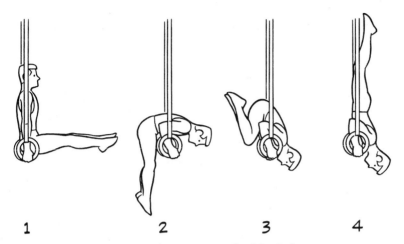

1   2   3   4

FIGURE 7-14   *Press to a Shoulder Balance*

KIP.   From a hanging position on the rings, the performer swings the feet upward between the cables, with the legs in an open pike. Next he drops the legs toward the chest to a tight inverted pike. The moment the tight pike is reached, there is a powerful upward and outward extension of the legs which lifts the hips upward about level with the rings. The leg extension is accompanied by vigorous pull with the arms in which the performer forces his head and shoulders forward over the rings. The arms then force downward on the rings, and the performer comes to a straight-arm support as the legs complete their downward swing.

DISLOCATE.   The dislocate is a skill which precedes many important moves in ring competition and must therefore be learned well by anyone who aspires to work the rings. From a straight-body inverted hang, the gymnast drops the legs quickly toward the chest to an inverted pike hang. They then recoil out of the pike, the body extends, the head is pulled backward, and the arms are pushed out to the side. It is very important that the arms press downward as they push the rings sideward because this action raises the shoulders between the rings. The shoulders then rotate, the arms are kept straight, and the rings are pushed forward in front of the face. The dislocate is completed as the body swings downward to a hang. As it swings downward, there is a hard jerk as the weight of the body settles on the shoulder girdle and hands. For this reason the shoulders and arms apply a downward pressure on the rings, and the hands grip the rings firmly to absorb the shock received by them at the depth of the downswing (Figure 7–15).

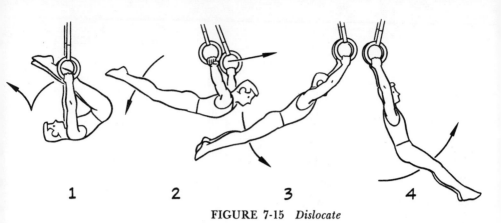

FIGURE 7-15 *Dislocate*

SHOOT TO SHOULDER STAND.   The shoot to shoulder stand should begin
with the performer bringing his legs forward from a straight-body hang.
He next swings them backward, then forward. As they pass the vertical
position underneath the rings, they are swung forcefully upward in a
pike. His arms then bend and pull the shoulders up toward the rings,
while the feet and legs continue to rise upward between the cables. At
this point the legs drive upward, the head is pulled backward, and the
hands shift from a hanging grasp below the rings to a supporting grip
above them. The body then assumes a slightly arched position and comes
to rest in a shoulder stand position between the rings.

INLOCATE.   The performer starts the inlocate from a straight-body
inverted hang, with the legs extended upward, and outward. They fall
downward, and the body assumes a slight pike. As the legs swing backward and pass the vertical position underneath the rings, the body experiences a momentary arch, which is followed by a vigorous hip lift and a
downward press of the arms. The hips then roll overhead and between
the arms to an inverted hang. The performer should be instructed to
tense the arm and shoulder muscles to absorb the jerk that results when
he drops to the inverted position (Figure 7–16).

FIGURE 7-16 *Inlocate*

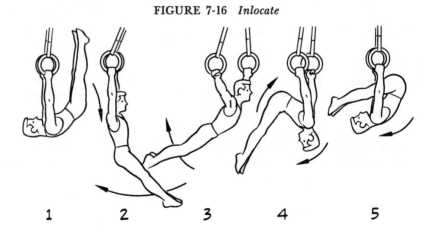

Front Uprise. This move can begin from a pendulum swing or from an inverted hang. Here, however, we shall use an inverted hang. The body of the gymnast falls forward, downward, and then backward. The legs swing forward, and as they pass the vertical position, the legs and hips lift vigorously upward while the arms pull forcefully on the rings. This upward lift of the legs transfers a great amount of weight upward. The arms then immediately press downward, and the body straightens. At this point, the performer forces the head and shoulders quickly forward over the rings, and drops his legs forward. The arms straighten and he finishes in a straight-arm support (Figure 7–17).

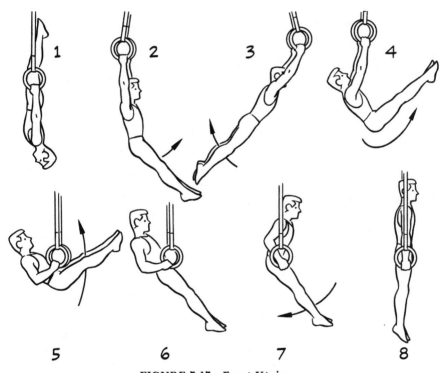

FIGURE 7-17 *Front Uprise*

Press to a Handstand. From a support half lever, the performer flexes his arms and moves his hips backward and upward, with his eyes focused on the mats below. The beginner should be cautioned to flex the arms only enough to form a right angle between the upper arm and the forearm. If they bend more than this, the shoulders drop so low that pressing out is very difficult for the beginner. The performer continues to move his hips between the cables and overhead, raises his legs, and as his body begins to straighten, he extends his arms, and presses to a straight-arm handstand in the rings.

parallel bars

SAFETY. The following suggestions are made to ensure the gymnast's safety on the bars:

1. Make sure bars are properly tightened.

2. Place adequate mats around and under the parallel bars.

3. Apply chalk to the hands to keep them from slipping off the bars.

4. Adjust bars to low height while teaching beginning skills.

5. Use one or more spotters in all beginning moves. The spotters must take the precaution to spot with their hands underneath the bars rather than between the performer and the bars. They should also be cautious to keep their head out of the way of swinging arms and should support the performer by lifting the hips, by grasping the upper and lower arm, or in other instances by grasping and lifting the sides of the individual.

DIPS. An exercise recommended for development of the shoulders and arms in preparation for parallel bars is the dip. This is performed from a straight-arm support by bending the arms, lowering the body to the bars, and then pressing up to a straight-arm support. After building up strength through this exercise, the student may attempt the swinging dip.

STRADDLE TRAVEL. The performer starts from a straddle or cross seat position with hands on the bars in front of the legs. The arms must be kept straight throughout this move. He leans forward with the weight shifting to the hands, and swings the legs backward. The legs close together as he swings forward between the bars. The body is piked on the front end of the swing, and the legs are separated and come to a straddle rest position on the bars (Figure 7–18).

FIGURE 7-18 *Straddle Travel*

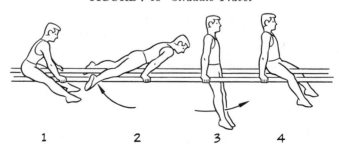

1   2   3   4

FRONT DISMOUNT. From a straight-arm support, the performer swings both legs forward and upward between the bars, and then leans forward and swings backward (high swing), keeping the weight centered over the hands and shoulders. When the feet reach the top of their backward swing, the left hand pushes away from the left bar and forces the body over the right bar. The left hand is transferred to the right bar, and the right hand releases its grip and extends out to the side. The performer then dismounts to the mat with the left hand grasping the left bar and the right hand extended sideward.

REAR DISMOUNT. From a straight-arm support, the gymnast swings his legs forward and upward. The body pikes, and the legs swing forward and over the left bar. The right hand simultaneously pushes away from the right bar and moves the body to the left and over the bar. The left hand also releases the left bar, which is then grasped by the right hand as the performer drops to the mat.

FORWARD ROLL TO UPPER ARM HANG. From a straddle seat position with hands in front of the body, the gymnast rolls forward, forcing the hips upward and the head downward. He then places the elbows out to the side and allows the weight to settle on the upper arms. (This outward movement of the elbows is required in order to prevent the shoulders and head from falling through the bar). As the hips roll over the head, the chin moves forward, the legs are placed together, and the hands release the bar and move forward to regrasp the bar in front. The body continues to roll forward, and the performer finishes the exercise in an upper arm hang.

SHOULDER BALANCE. The shoulder balance starts from a straddle or cross seat position. The performer rocks forward and moves the elbows to the side. The hips are forced upward as the weight of the body comes to a momentary balance on the upper arms, the feet and legs are brought together, and the legs are gradually extended overhead to a shoulder balance position. The body should be slightly arched, the head kept up, and toes pointed (Figure 7–19).

FIGURE 7-19 *Shoulder Balance*

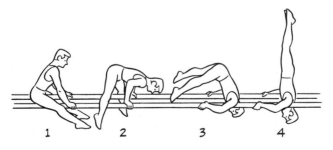

1   2   3   4

BACKWARD STRADDLE SHOULDER ROLL. From a straddle seat the performer grasps the bars to the rear of the body. He then rolls backward with his elbows well out to the side. As the shoulders receive the weight, the arms press downward on the bars, the hips are forced upward, and the legs reach backward and over the head. As the body begins to roll backward, the hands release the bars, reach over the shoulders, and regrasp the bars in front of the body. The performer then settles to a straddle seat as the roll is completed.

BACK UPRISE. This skill requires that the parallel bars be adjusted to a height that will permit the performer's feet to clear the mats underneath. The bars should be at shoulder height.

From an upper arm hang, the performer flexes the hips, presses down on the bars with the hands and arms, and extends the legs upward and outward. At the peak of the forward extension, the body begins to swing backward. As the hips swing backward, the burden on the arms increases, and the hands and arms press vigorously against the bars in order to keep the arms from being drawn outward, which would cause the body to be lowered somewhat between the bars. As the legs reach the peak of the backswing, there should be a forceful lift by the heels and hips. The arms simultaneously press downward on the bar and then pull the body forward to a straight-arm support (Figure 7–20).

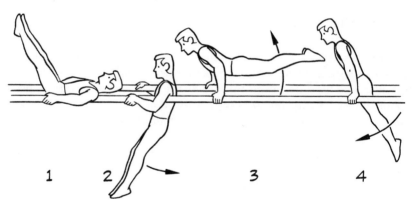

1   2   3   4

FIGURE 7-20 *Back Uprise*

FRONT UPRISE. From an upper arm hang, the gymnast's body pikes, the legs swing forward and upward, and then they swing backward. This movement is followed by a forward swing. As the legs reach the peak of this motion, the arms and hands press hard and pull forward on the bars. At the same time the legs lift vigorously upward to a pike position. This motion of the legs is transferred to the body, providing a lifting effect.

The hips thrust forward, and the body comes to rest in a straight arm support (Figure 7–21).

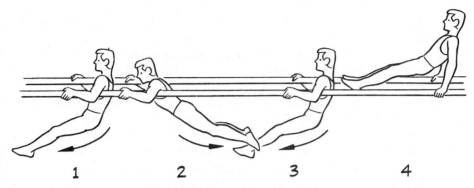

FIGURE 7-21   *Front Uprise*

UPPER ARM KIP.   From an upper arm hang with arms pressed against the bars, the performer lifts the legs forward and overhead, and the body assumes a balanced inverted pike position with the weight resting on the shoulders. At this point the hips are allowed to drop off balance forward, and the legs extend vigorously upward, outward, and downward. The hands and arms press hard against the bars, the arms extend at the elbow joints, and the performer finishes the move in a straight-arm support

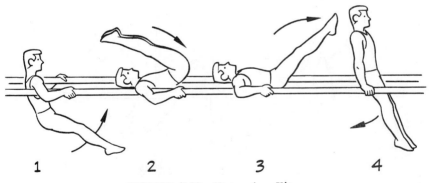

FIGURE 7-22   *Upper Arm Kip*

(Figure 7–22). A good preliminary exercise and safety measure for this skill is to have the performer spread the legs and assume a straddle seat position during the first attempts.

PRESS HANDSTAND.   The handstand begins from an L seat or half lever. The performer bends his arms at the elbows and gradually lowers his body forward, forces the hips backward overhead, and keeps his head up with eyes focused on the mat below. Slowly he extends the legs overhead with feet and legs together and toes pointed. He must strive to assume a straight body rather than an arched position. The line of gravity should pass from the back of the heels down across the buttocks, through the shoulder blades, and finally bisect the hands.

The student should learn the handstand on the floor and then practice it on the low parallel bars, gradually making higher adjustments and always facing outward, before attempting to perform at regulation height. When learning the handstand on the low parallel bars, the performer should be taught how to lower to a shoulder stand in order to present a hand fall in case of an overbalance when the bars are moved to a higher position and the handstand is attempted with the body facing inward.

UNDER BAR CAST.   From a straight-arm support the performer begins to fall backward between the bars. The arms remain straight, and the legs are raised to a pike position. At the bottom of the swing below the bars, the legs move in close to the chest in a tight pike position. An upswing of the body accompanied by a vigorous upward and forward extension of the legs follows from the pike position. Simultaneously the hands pull forcefully on the bars and release their grip. The arms then move upward between and over the bars to make the catch in an upper arm hang. The performer should strive to catch the bar with the hips and legs above the bar (Figure 7–23).

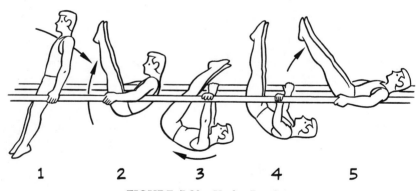

FIGURE 7-23   *Under Bar Cast*

SWING TO HANDSTAND.   No person should attempt the swing to the handstand until he has mastered the kick up to the handstand both on the floor and the low parallel bars.

The swing to the handstand begins from a straight-arm support on the bars. The legs lift forward and upward to a slightly piked position. The performer then leans forward at the shoulders and swings his legs backward. They continue backward and overhead. The arms remain straight and push against the bars as the handstand position is reached. The performer should strive to maintain a straight-body handstand as described in the press handstand.

horizontal bar

Horizontal bar work calls for more giant swings and circles around the bar than any other event. Consequently, the wear on the hands is greater, and the gymnast must take precautions to keep his hands in good condition. Relaxing the grip on the bar at intervals when a tight grip is not necessary will not only protect the hands but will also help the gymnast to perform the moves more efficiently.

SAFETY.

1. Inspect equipment regularly. Check the floor plates, cables, and turnbuckles. Inspect the pulleys, beam clamps, and ropes for overhead spotting devices. Use rope of fine quality and replace it immediately if it becomes worn or frayed.

2. Provide enough mats to insure adequate padding. The eight-inch foam rubber crash pad is an excellent shock absorber and should be used in teaching beginning moves. It should also be used in performing the more risky dismounts or wherever there is a great deal of stress on the feet or the ankle and knee joints.

3. Even though a performer has mastered a skill or routine it is always best to use at least one spotter. Teach all students the importance of spotting and how to spot. Use chalk on the hands to help prevent slipping from the bar.

4. Use the adjustable horizontal bar in teaching elementary skills, and lower it when necessary. The low position of the bar makes spotting easier and more effective. The height of the bar should be increased gradually with the progression of skills.

5. Remove any hazardous objects, and do not permit any balls in the area.

6. All gymnastic skills should follow definite progressions. This is particularly true with regard to the horizontal bar. Skills should be learned progressively, and a person must not be permitted to advance to a move that is beyond his ability or for which he is not prepared.

7. Either the lampwick or leather type of palm guard should be

worn, and shorter workouts should be planned to help prevent friction and tearing of the hands.

8. Remove excess chalk from the bar with fine sandpaper or emery cloth.

9. Always use the proper grip for each stunt. Never use the reverse grip when the regular grip should be used, or vice versa.

10. Several safety devices are used in teaching the more advanced horizontal bar skills, such as the wrist strap, bar safety swivel, and others. The overhead safety belt, however, is the most effective safety device that can be used in teaching advanced skills.

It is suggested that the horizontal bar be moved to a lower position for teaching most of the fundamental skills. This will make it easier to hand-spot as well as reduce the risk of greater injury to the performer in the event he should fall from the bar. Swinging moves, however, where the body is in a fully extended position, will require that the bar be raised to keep the feet from dragging.

FRONT SUPPORT. The performer should stand in front of the bar and grasp it with a regular grip. He should jump upward, pull with the arms to a front rest position on the bar with the weight of the body supported on the hands and upper thighs.

SKIN THE CAT. This stunt begins with the performer in a standing position in front of the bar with his hands in a regular grip. He jumps upward and brings the legs between the arms and the bar. He next moves the legs through the arms, extends the body, and stretches the legs downward toward the mat. Finally he pulls upward, moves the hips and legs back through the arms, and then comes to a standing position.

HIP SWING UP. From a standing position in front of the bar and with the hands in a regular grip, the performer jumps upward and immediately raises the legs up and back over the bar. The body is now in a pike

FIGURE 7-24 *Hip Swing Up*

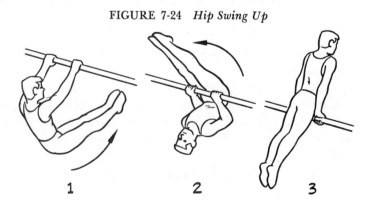

1   2   3

position with the hips and lower abdomen in contact with the bar. As the legs swing upward, the arms bend and pull against the bar. The performer continues to pull with the arms, circles the bar, and finishes in a front support position (Figure 7–24).

SINGLE-KNEE CIRCLE FORWARD. The performer starts from a single-knee support on top of the bar, with one leg placed between the arms, the knee hooked over the bar, hips elevated, and arms straight. Both hands assume a reverse grip. He begins the fall with the head up, shoulders and head stretched forward to increase the radius of the circle. The arms must remain straight and the head must not duck. As he nears the bottom of the circle, the body pikes very quickly and continues to rise upward. The arms bend, and the head and shoulders are forced forward as the body approaches the top of the bar. The arms straighten again as the body returns to the single-knee support position on top of the bar.

SINGLE-KNEE CIRCLE BACKWARD. This stunt begins with the performer in a sitting position, the bar resting in the middle of the crotch, the forward leg between the arms, and the other leg extended backward. The hands assume a regular grip. The circle is begun with a backward push which causes the body to fall backward and away from the bar. The head and shoulders remain forward, and the forward leg slides over the bar until the bend of the knee is reached. At this point the head is thrown backward; the rear leg reaches backward, and then swings forward and upward around the bar as the body falls downward. The arms are bent as the body nears the completion of the circle but straighten to give support as the performer comes to a rest position on top of the bar.

REAR VAULT DISMOUNT. The performer starts in a front support position, leans slightly over the bar, and swings his legs backward and upward. As they reach the height of the bar, he turns to the right and brings them up sharply to a pike position. The arms then pull the body forward until the weight is centered over the bar. The right arm releases its grip, and the support shifts momentarily to the left arm and then releases as the body passes over the bar in a pike position. The performer executes a quarter turn to the right and lands with the right hand on the bar and the right side of the body toward it.

FORWARD SEAT CIRCLE. This move begins from a sitting position on the bar with the hands in a reverse grip. The head tilts slightly backward and the hips rise until the bar is just behind the heels. The gymnast then falls forward and downward, moves his legs forward until the bar is behind the upper thighs, and keeps his thighs close to the chest in a pike position. The arms pull hard at the bottom of the circle. He completes the circle and finishes in a pike sitting position on the bar. The legs will probably be bent during first attempts but they should be kept straight as more experience is obtained (Figure 7–25).

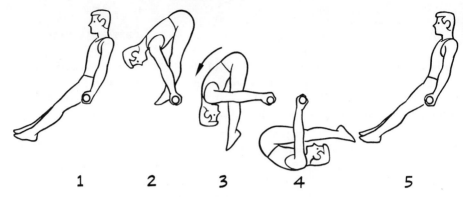

FIGURE 7-25 *Forward Seat Circle*

STRADDLE SOLE CIRCLE BACKWARD. From a front rest on the bar with a regular grip, the performer leans forward, elevates his hips rapidly, and brings his legs forward to a pike position, legs straddling the bar. The soles of the feet are placed on the bar outside the hands. He then falls off balance backward, keeping his legs straight and his hips as high as possible, and lengthens the radius of the body by bringing the chest close to the thighs. The circle continues around and under the bar. On the upswing the body is shortened by bending the arms and shifting the grip to the top of the bar. It is permissible for the performer to bend his legs slightly in the beginning stages as he approaches the top of the bar. The arms pull hard during the circular motion around the bar. The performer flexes his arms and legs slightly and forces his shoulders forward as the body completes the circle position on top of the bar.

THE CAST. The performer jumps up and catches the bar in a regular grip with a slight forward swing. The body passes under the bar on the backswing, and the legs then extend, giving the body a momentary arched appearance. At the end of the backward swing and as the forward swing begins, the chest is pulled toward the bar, the legs are raised, and the instep is brought close to the bar. The arms then straighten, the legs extend away from the bar, and the body assumes a straight position, after which it swings backward (Figure 7–26).

FIGURE 7-26 *The Cast*

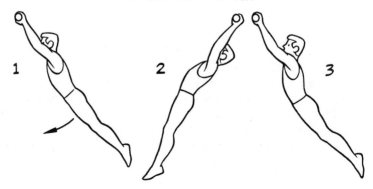

SWINGING HALF TURN. The described cast above is followed by a backswing. As the body swings forward, the legs lift forcefully upward. At the height of the forward swing, the hips lift upward, and the head and shoulders turn to the left. The right hand releases its grip, reaches across the left hand, and grasps the bar in a regular grip. The performer now has a mixed grip. The feet and legs are held closely together during the turn with the toes pointed.

KIP. The gymnast performs the cast as previously described and lets his body swing forward with a slight arch at the end of the swing. At this

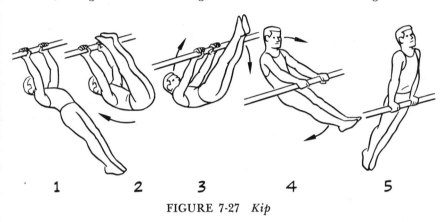

1   **2**   **3**   **4**   **5**

FIGURE 7-27 *Kip*

point and not before, he brings his insteps up sharply to the bar and holds momentarily, allowing his hips to swing backward. At the end of the backswing, he extends his legs upward, outward, and downward while pulling forcefully with his arms. As his body swings upward, he should shift his hands to the top of the bar and move his shoulders forward over it. The performer should finish in a straight-arm support. (Figure 7–27).

BACKWARD UPRISE. The gymnast starts with a mixed grip. He performs a high forward cast, and at the end of the backswing he lifts with

4   **5**   **6**

his heels, pikes with his hips, and pulls forcefully with his arms to a front support on top of the bar. He should make an effort to push his shoulders well forward as the support position is reached. The arms usually will bend during the first attempts but will straighten with practice.

REVERSE KIP. This move should first be performed on the low bar. The performer starts with the cast. After the cast and backswing, the body swings forward. As the body swings backward, the feet and legs are raised rapidly between the arms in a tight pike. At the peak of the backswing, the performer presses down on the bar and extends his legs straight upward. When he reaches the peak of this upward extension, his hips drop through his arms, and his legs flex rapidly toward the chest as his body assumes a tight pike position at the bottom of the swing. As the body swings forward, the hands press downward on the bar, the head and shoulders are forced backward, and the legs are extended backward—all in one simultaneous motion. The grip is shifted to the top of the bar as the performer rises to an L seat. He should lean to utilize the rebound of the bar and pull forcefully with his arms as his body assumes a tight pike (Figure 7–28).

FIGURE 7-28 *Reverse Kip*

HALF GIANT SWING.   The half giant begins with a front rest position. From this, the performer swings his legs backward and upward as his arms push his body backward away from the bar. During the downswing which follows the backward cast, the body should be straight, without an arch, and the head should be centered over the body. As the body swings forward, the legs swing sharply upward and over the bar in a pike position, and the hands shift rapidly to the top of the bar. The move is finished in a front support position. A quick shift of the wrists during the upswing over the bar places the hands between the chest and the bar and will prevent a painful flopping of the chest or abdomen across the bar during the learning process (Figure 7–29).

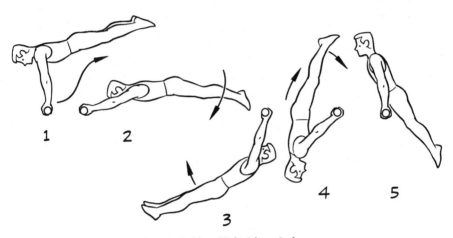

FIGURE 7-29   *Half Giant Swing*

FORWARD OR REVERSE GRIP GIANT SWING.   From a front support on the bar with a reverse grip, the performer bends his arms and leans well over the bar. The legs then extend forcefully backward overhead, the arms extend vigorously at the elbow joint and push to a straight body handstand on top of the bar with the head raised. As the body begins to fall forward, the head drops forward between the arms, and the body swings forward and downward. The body then swings underneath the bar and begins its upswing on the back side of the bar. The head is then raised, and the arms—absolutely straight—press downward and pull forward, pulling the head and shoulders over the top of the bar. The hips lift at the same time, and the body assumes a piked position as the circle continues toward the top of the bar. As the body approaches the handstand position, the legs extend, and the body again assumes a straight-body handstand on top of the bar. Caution should be exercised to keep the shoulders from moving too far over the bar. If this happens, the rest of the body cannot catch up and the performer will flop over the bar.

After a degree of confidence is gained, the performer may continue the forward giants by again dropping the head forward between the arms and following the same procedure as the handstand position on top of the bar is reached.

BACKWARD OR OVERGRIP GIANT SWING. The performer begins with a cast backward from a front support to a temporary handstand on top of the bar. He keeps his body straight on the downswing with eyes focused on the bar, which will bend during the downswing. As the body swings under the bar, the legs move upward to a pike position. The bar rebounds slightly upward, helping to lift the body. The performer should take advantage of this rebound and pull with his arms. The head should be pulled backward, the hands should shift to the top of the bar, and the body should assume a straight position. The performer then moves his head forward to a normal position and passes over the bar in a straight body handstand position. If another giant swing is desired, he simply continues over the bar, stretches his body, and continues on around the bar.

It is always good for the beginning gymnast to learn how to come to a front rest from a giant swing. This is done by pulling the head and shoulders forward over the bar and lowering the body to a rest position.

side horse

Suggestions for working the side horse:

1. The shoulders should be extended, and the body should be kept straight in all support positions.

2. The arms must be kept absolutely straight at the elbow joint.

3. The hips should swing with the legs in the leg circle movements on the side horse. In double-leg circles, the performer should stretch the hips outward in an effort to gain a wide range of movement in the swing away from the horse.

4. The performer should push away hard from the pommels before releasing his grip in order to allow one or both legs to pass between the pommel and the hand.

5. Scissor movements swing sideways in pendulum fashion with the legs close to the knees.

HALF LEG CIRCLE MOUNT (*right leg half circle counterclockwise*). This mount begins with the performer facing the right end of the horse, his left hand on the right pommel and his right hand on the top. He jumps from both feet, leans slightly to the left, straightens the left arm simultaneously and swings the legs and hips to the right. The right arm pushes hard off the right end as the right leg is raised above the horse. The right hip then turns inward. As the body swings to the left, the right hand is replaced on the end of the horse with the fingers pointing slightly backward.

Half Leg Circle Forward from Front Support (*right leg half circle counterclockwise*).   From a front support position, the performer's body swings to the right, the right leg swinging high above the horse. At the same time the weight shifts slightly over the left arm. The right arm pushes off the pommel, and the right hip turns inward as the right leg swings downward to the front side of the horse. The legs and hips swing downward to the left, the right hand regrasps the pommel, and the body swings through the straddle support where the crotch contacts the left arm. The legs continue in a follow-through and swing upward to the left.

Half Leg Circle Backward from Front Support (*right leg half circle clockwise*).   This move begins from a front support with the performer's legs and hips swinging to the right. The right leg swings high to the right, and the left leg follows. The weight shifts slightly to the left arm. At the peak of the swing to the right, the hips turn inward. The legs then swing downward to the left, the right hand regrasps the pommel, and the body swings to the left. The hips and legs, especially the left leg, continue to swing high to the left so that the right leg can pass underneath. The left arm pushes off the pommel, and the weight shifts to the right arm. The body swings downward, the left hand regrasps the pommel, and the body comes to rest in the front support position.

Double Leg Half Circle Forward (*counterclockwise*).   From a front support the performer swings both legs to the right and raises them over the horse. The right arm pushes off the pommel, and the weight shifts somewhat toward the left arm. The hips extend, and the performer attempts to stretch his body as his legs pass over the horse. The right hand quickly regrasps the pommel with the arms straight. At the same time, the performer leans backward with his head and shoulders and finishes in a rear support. The legs continue to swing to the left.

Full Leg Undercart Circle from a Rear Support (*right leg counterclockwise*).   The performer starts from a rear support, swings his hips and legs forcefully to the left, and shifts his weight slightly to the right arm. At this point the body assumes a pike, and the left hand pushes forcefully off the pommel as the legs lift upward. The left hip turns slightly inward, making it easier for the right leg to pass under the left leg and over the horse. The hips extend during the downswing, and the left hand quickly grasps the pommel. The body swings to the right through the straddle support and continues in a high swing. The weight shifts slightly to the left arm. The performer leans backward from the shoulders, and the right leg passes over the top of the horse and swings downward to the left. Here it joins the left leg in a rear support.

BACKWARD SCISSOR. The performer begins the backward scissor with a swing to the right in a straddle support, with his right leg over the front and his left leg on the back of the horse. Both legs swing high to the right with the hips slightly piked, and the shoulders shift slightly over the left pommel. The right hand pushes forcefully off the pommel as the feet and legs move upward. At the peak of the hip lift, the left leg is lifted high and passed underneath during the scissor. The left leg then moves forward, and the right leg passes backward over the horse. The body then extends and swings downward in pendulum fashion, with the right hand grasping the pommel.

FORWARD SCISSOR. The gymnast begins this scissor in a straddle support, with his right leg in front and his left leg over the back of the horse. The hips and legs swing high to the left. The left hand pushes off the pommel, and the shoulders shift a little to the right. At the peak of the leg swing, the hips turn downward with the left leg passing over the right. The body extends, and the left hand regrasps the pommel, with the left leg in front and the right leg back of the horse. The performer keeps his legs close to the horse and quickly regrasps the pommel with a straight arm as he completes the scissor.

side horse vaulting

Side horse vaulting differs from the more difficult long horse vaulting in that the vaults are performed across the horse rather than along its length. Many of the cross horse vaults such as the straddle vault, squat vault, stoop vault, cartwheel and handspring are readily adaptable to the long horse and should be considered as preliminaries to long horse vaulting.

Spotters should be maintained in both takeoff and landing positions in many of these vaults. The duty of the spotter on the takeoff side is usually that of lifting the vaulter from the thighs or hips. The spotter on the landing side should be ready to lift by the upper arm, pull the performer over the horse, and guide him to a safe landing.

SQUAT VAULT. The gymnast begins the vault with a running low hurdle and lands on the Reuther board on the balls of both feet. As the feet leave the board, he brings the hands forward with arms straight to make contact with the top of the horse. The arms force downward and push away from it, and the knees are brought upward to the chest. The tuck is maintained for a moment of free flight, and an effort should be made to keep the back as straight as possible and the hips from rising too high as the feet are drawn upward to the tuck position. At this point, the legs drop downward, the body straightens, and the arms and head lift upward. As the body drops toward the mat, the arms are dropped to the sides, and the ankles, knees, and hips flex as contact is made with the mat to absorb the shock of landing. Gymnasts should observe this method of landing when performing dismounts from the various pieces of apparatus. In preliminary exercises, the performer should jump to a squat position on the horse with the feet resting between the pommels. Then he should rise to a standing position and jump to the mat (Figure 7–30).

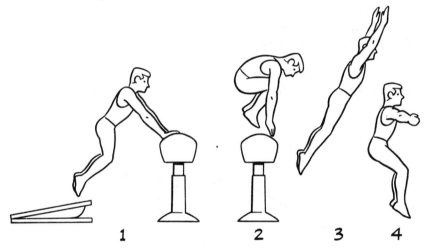

FIGURE 7-30 *Squat Vault*

STRADDLE VAULT.   The technique for the straddle vault is the same as for the squat vault except that the performer spreads his legs in a straddle position, with the knees straight and the toes pointed. He must keep his head and chest up as the hands push away from the horse. To lead up to the full straddle vault, the vaulter jumps to a straddle position on top of the horse with his legs straight. He then rises to a standing position and jumps to the mat (Figure 7–31).

FIGURE 7-31 *Straddle Vault*

FLANK VAULT.   The flank vault begins with a takeoff similar to that of the squat vault. The gymnast follows the takeoff by a sharp hip-lifting movement in an upward direction, which causes the body to pike. As his hands contact the horse, there is an immediate sideward and upward motion of the legs. One hand is removed from the horse and forced upward, and the hips extend from the pike to a straight or slightly arched body position. The hand in contact with the horse pushes against it as the gymnast's body passes over. The dismount is made facing away from the horse.

STOOP VAULT.   The takeoff for the stoop vault is the same as for the squat vault. The vaulter must keep his arms straight as they contact the horse. The stoop, however, employs greater hip lift as well as a piking action of the hips and legs. The legs are flexed forward between the arms and the horse in a tight pike as the hands push away from the horse. The body rises upward because of the vigorous push with the hands. The performer should then attempt to straighten his body just before landing on the mat (Figure 7–32).

FIGURE 7-32   *Stoop Vault*

NECKSPRING.   The neckspring should begin from a standing position. The performer places both hands on the horse, jumps upward, and forces the hips backward and overhead as the body assumes a pike position. He then ducks his head and rolls the hips forward with the feet and legs held downward. The back of the neck and shoulders make contact with the top of the horse, the body resting on the shoulders in the pike position. The center of gravity is then displaced by allowing the hips to fall forward. The legs extend forcefully, and the hands push hard against the horse. The landing is made with the head slightly back and the body facing away from the horse (Figure 7–33).

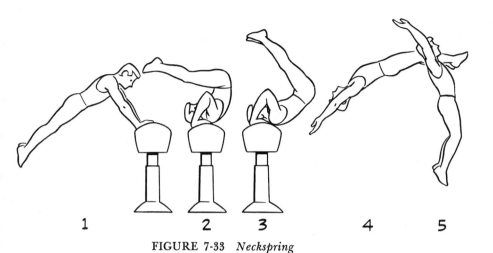

FIGURE 7-33 *Neckspring*

It is most important that the leg extension be delayed until the hips drop far enough forward to displace the center of gravity. After learning the mechanics of the neckspring from a standing position, the performer may use a run and hurdle.

CARTWHEEL.   This is a more advanced vault and requires a fast running approach and hurdle. The performer extends the legs forcefully

FIGURE 7-34 *Cartwheel*

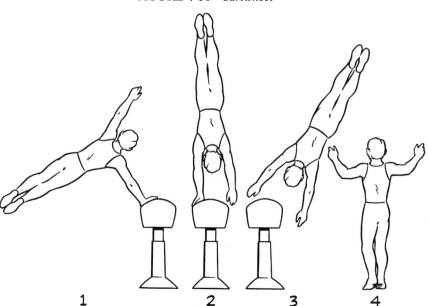

from the Reuther board. During the pre-flight they lift high in an over-head direction, and the hips make a quarter turn as the body rises upward. One hand is placed on the near or takeoff side of the horse and the other hand on the far side. The arms are kept straight upon hand contact with the horse, and the shoulders extend as the weight shifts from the near arm to the far arm. This action provides the rebound and after-flight from the horse. The body should be kept straight with feet and legs together, toes pointed, and the head up as it moves laterally over the horse. The feet and legs should be guided to a sideward landing position. The vaulter can accomplish a balanced landing by forcing the feet and legs outward in a lateral direction to counter the tendency of the feet to fall too far underneath the body (Figure 7–34). Before attempting a cart-wheel vault, the gymnast must be able to perform a cartwheel on the floor.

HANDSPRING. The handspring is also an advanced vault requiring a great deal of pre-flight, which in turn calls for a fast run and hurdle. As the feet of the performer contact the takeoff board, there is a vigorous lifting of the feet and legs in an overhead direction. The takeoff should be high enough to permit the body to be straightened during pre-flight and to descend on the horse and make hand contact from an almost vertical position. Upon contact with the horse, the vaulter must keep his arms absolutely straight and his head up. The shoulders then extend, and the body recoils from the straight-arm position. The gymnast lands with his back toward the horse. Hips and knees must be flexed to absorb the shock of landing (Figure 7–35).

FIGURE 7-35 *Handspring*

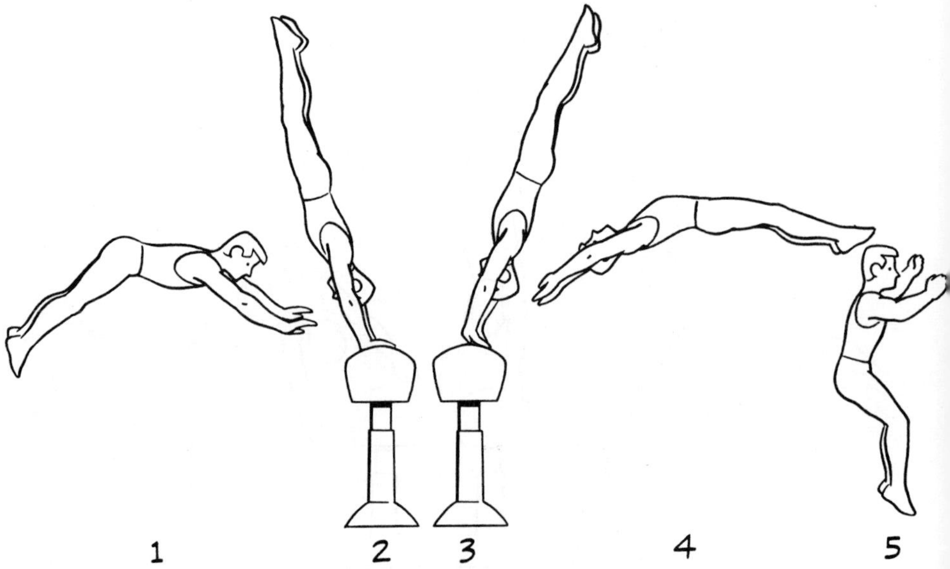

1   2   3   4   5

trampoline

Trampolining develops a great sense of coordination, relocation (awareness of body position while in the air), timing, body control, courage, and self-confidence. It can help the gymnast in various tumbling skills and it is an excellent means for teaching the tumbler how to twist. The trampoline can be used to teach diving, and recent studies show that trampoline activities can be helpful in treating the mentally retarded.

The trampoline is a great source of fun, relaxation, and pleasure. Many youngsters have become interested in gymnastics and have become fine gymnasts as a result of the inspiration they received from learning trampoline skills.

SAFETY. Trampolining is potentially dangerous, but so are football, diving, skiing, and many other sports. Listed below are a number of safety rules that those who engage in this activity should carefully observe.

1. Students should be instructed in folding and unfolding the trampoline. To avoid injury, those handling it must exert a backward pressure on the frame during the folding action until the tension is released. Because of the danger of the frame flying over and severely injuring someone, it is imperative that this precaution be observed.

2. Students should know the proper way to get on and off the trampoline. One hand and one foot should be placed on the frame while getting off. The beginner should never bounce from the bed to the floor.

3. The art of "killing the bounce" by flexing the knees as the feet make contact with the bed should be taught. This will prevent the performer from being bounced out of the bed if he should land in an off balance position.

4. Teach students to stay in the middle of the bed and to focus their eyes on the frame pads at the end of the trampoline, not on their feet.

5. Insist that students follow a progressively arranged order of skills while learning to use the trampoline. Fundamental skills must be mastered before moving on to more advanced activities. Allow no one to bypass essential fundamentals and attempt skills beyond his ability or for which he is unprepared.

6. Low bouncing should be encouraged. High bouncing by the novice or beginner is more difficult to control and therefore dangerous.

7. Provide frame pads, and keep them securely fastened and in place at all times.

8. Provide at least four spotters, one at each end and each side. Never permit students to practice alone.

9. Horseplay is inappropriate. The trampoline is sometimes used for clown acts, but those who participate are experts in trampoline skills.

THE FEET BOUNCE. The performer begins the feet bounce from a stance on the trampoline with his feet a comfortable distance apart. To start the bounce, he swings his arms upward and backward in a circular motion and raises his body on the toes. The arms swing downward, the hips and knees flex, and the heels settle down and make contact with the bed. The arms again swing forward, and as they pass the vertical line bisecting the center of gravity, the toes and balls of the feet press downward on the bed, the knees and hips extend, the arms lift, and the body rises upward with feet and legs together and toes pointed in coordination with the rebound from the bed. The body descends, and just before the feet contact the bed, the legs separate to a comfortable landing stance. The arms then whip downward and help the body weight depress the bed. The bed rebounds, and the body is again projected upward.

HALF PIROUETTE. The half pirouette is a half turn on the long axis of the body. In other words, the gymnast performs a half twist with the body in a vertical position. He starts from a regular bounce. Upon rebounding from the bed, he lifts the arms above his head, which turns to the left, as the upper body and hips twist to the left. Then he drops his legs to a vertical position. The body continues to turn. The half pirouette is completed, and the landing is made facing in the opposite direction from the starting position.

FULL PIROUETTE. The technique for performing the full pirouette is basically the same as in the half pirouette. In the full pirouette, however, the body completes a full turn instead of a half turn, and the performer keeps his head fixed in the direction of the turn as the twist is completed.

TUCK BOUNCE. The performer starts with a regular bounce. As the body rebounds upward from the bed, the back is kept straight, the knees are drawn to the chest, and the hands grasp the shins to hold the legs to the chest in a tuck position. At the peak of the upward flight, the legs are released, and the performer lands in a vertical standing position.

PIKE STRADDLE TOE TOUCH. The gymnast starts with a bounce. At the height of it he raises his legs to a straddle pike, and leans forward from the waist. The arms reach forward, and the hands touch the toes. The legs then extend quickly underneath the body to the regular landing position.

SEAT DROP. Beginning with a regular bounce, the body rises upward, and the legs are brought to a pike position. The performer lands in the bed with his head erect and body straight but inclined slightly backward. At the same moment, the hands also contact the bed, landing at the sides and slightly behind the hips. It is important that the hands and the whole posterior surface of the legs from the heels to the buttocks land simultaneously on the bed. As the bed rebounds, the performer presses on it with his hands and drops his legs under his body to a standing position.

HANDS AND KNEE DROP. The performer starts with a regular bounce. He raises the hips slightly during the ascent, and keeps his head erect with eyes forward on the bed. As he descends, the legs bend and are drawn underneath the hips for a landing on the hands and knees. The body then rebounds, the head and shoulders are raised, and the legs are straightened for the landing position on the feet.

KNEE DROP. After the gymnast makes a vertical takeoff, the back remains straight, and the legs bend as his body drops back toward the bed. Upon contact with the bed, the back must remain straight or very slightly flexed to prevent a painful forward tilting of the pelvis. The arms are dropped sideward and down, the toes are pointed, and the landing is made on the knees—the knees and top of the feet contacting the bed simultaneously. As the body rebounds, the arms swing upward, and the legs are straightened in preparation for landing.

FRONT DROP FROM HANDS AND KNEES. A good preliminary for teaching this skill is to lie prone on the bed and reach forward with head up and hands and forearms in contact with the bed. After this exercise has shown the landing position, the student should start on his hands and knees, take a few bounces, and as the body leaves the bed, straighten the body, raise the head and shoulders, and reach forward with arms slightly bent. The body should land flat.

FRONT DROP. The performer begins with a regular bounce. As the body ascends, the hips are forced slightly upward, the legs are raised backward, and the trunk and upper body are lowered until the body assumes a horizontal position. The palms, forearms, chest, abdomen, and thighs should make simultaneous contact with the bed. The performer pushes down with his hands as the trampoline rebounds, raises the head, and pulls the feet under the body to a standing position. He should be cautioned always to drop his forearms and hands so they will make contact with the bed at a position below the chest. The arms should never be raised above the head. Failure to observe this precaution may cause a painful exposure of the nose and face upon landing. The landing should always be made in the center of the bed. To avoid back injury, the performer should move over to the side of the bed, where a spotter can push downward on the back if the lower legs rise too high, or lift upward on the thighs in case they are not high enough. If he does not raise his legs high enough, the performer should be instructed to draw his legs underneath his body and land on the hands and knees. This will keep him from landing on his thighs and falling forward on his face.

BACK DROP. Upon rebounding, the performer leans slightly backward and raises the legs forward and upward as the body rises from the bed. He lands on the lower back and buttocks with arms at his sides. The chin should be lowered to the chest and held in this position to keep the head from flying backward and straining the neck muscles as the body contacts the bed. As the bed rebounds, the legs are extended, forcing the hips upward. The landing is made with the body in a slightly arched position.

BACKWARD SOMERSAULT (*layout*). On takeoff from the bed, the arms stretch upward. As the body rises from the trampoline, the chest thrusts upward and the hips lift forward and upward. The head remains back, and the eyes focus on the bed as the body rotates to the head-down position. The gymnast should make an effort to maintain the layout position from takeoff until just before the landing. An almost vertical takeoff is important. The revolution is accomplished by the upward thrust of the hips and chest and by pulling backward with the head, arms, and shoulders.

CODY. The cody begins with a front drop in which most of the body weight lands on the hips and thighs. As the bed rebounds, the somersault is started by pushing from the bed with the hands and by pulling backward with the head, arms, and shoulders. The knees are raised to the chest, and the arms grasp the shins to pull them into a tight tuck. The rotary movement of the body continues, and the performer opens out of the tuck and lands in a standing position.

TEACHING PROCEDURE

A course in gymnastics should aim toward the development of strength, agility, neuromuscular coordination, and general good health. More specifically, however, the objectives include the development of strength in the muscles of the shoulders, back, arms, chest, and abdomen. In addition, gymnastics improves the posture and increases agility, flexibility, coordination, and balance. Gymnastics requires a great deal of mental prowess and develops such qualities as alertness, courage, and precision. Since split second timing is required in most gymnastic moves, the gymnast develops the ability to think quickly. The nature of gymnastics promotes such character traits as self-confidence, perseverance, self-discipline, and responsibility.

Because of the complicated maneuvers involved in gymnastics, and the danger that accompanies every phase of these activities, the ideal class should number no more than ten. This enables the instructor to give individual attention to each student and see that he is adequately spotted on each exercise. Not every class is ideal, however, and the instructor probably will find himself with many more than ten students. Every effort should be made to limit the class to not more than thirty students.

An example is given here of the organization for a class of thirty. Two situations are quite obvious: first, if all thirty students are kept on one activity, there probably will not be enough equipment available to keep all of them busy at one time; second, if the class is divided into groups to work on different activities, assistants will be needed.

This pattern is set for three groups of ten, with one group tumbling, one on the high bar and the horse, and one on the parallel bars. A student leader is required for each group. The instructor will work with the leaders prior to the class, reviewing the fundamentals of the stunts to be performed and the necessary spotting. Because of the risk involved, a trained gymnast should be present to spot the student at every practice session. Everyone should be taught to spot. As the class proceeds, the teacher serves as a supervisor over all the groups. A new skill is given to the students each day after they have had time to practice what they have already learned. Each group spends an equal amount of time each day on each of the various activities.

CLASS ORGANIZATION

Activities			*Time*
1. Preclass conference with student leaders			9: 30– 9: 45
2. Roll call			9: 45– 9: 46
3. Calisthenics			9: 46– 9: 51

FIRST DAY

Tumbling	Vaulting	Parallel bars	
Group I	Group II	Group III	9: 51– 9: 59
Group III	Group I	Group II	9: 59–10: 07
Group II	Group III	Group I	10: 07–10: 15

SECOND DAY

Horizontal Bar	Side Horse and Trampoline	Rings
Group I	Group II	Group III
Group III	Group I	Group II
Group II	Group III	Group I

In teaching gymnastics, it is important that the skills be demonstrated correctly and that the instructor analyze each stunt thoroughly. The leader should check each student carefully each time he performs and provide adequate safety precautions. After a student finishes an activity, his faults and skills should be pointed out and suggestions made for improvement.

SKILL TESTS

The best measure of whether a student has achieved the objectives set for the course is to test him on his ability to perform the activities that have been presented to him. A student should be given one point for any stunt creditably executed. A list of these activities may be made up on a check sheet. When a student performs properly, a check is placed by his name. Any time a student achieves the skill, he should get credit for it.

At the end of a course, every student should have been given an opportunity to practice, perform, and be checked on all the activities taught. His score will be the number of check marks or the number of points he has received. A frequency distribution can be constructed from the scores and grades established in that way.

DEFINITION OF TERMS

Apparatus. Equipment used for gymnastics.

Approach. The way in which a performer moves to where he will begin a gymnastic stunt.

A.A.U. Amateur Athletic Union of the United States.

A.A.H.P.E.R. American Association for Health, Physical Education and Recreation.

Arch. A curved body position in which the body describes an arc.

Baroni (Brandy). A forward somersault with a half twist in a pike position.

Back Handspring, or Flip-flop. A stunt in which a person assumes a sitting position and throws the arms and head backward. When the hands contact the mat, the performer extends the legs, pushes with the hands, and moves the feet underneath the body to a landing position.

Back Somersault. A complete backward roll of the body in the air.

Backward Roll. The act of pushing backward, tucking, and rolling on a mat until the body makes a complete circle to the feet.

Cast. An extension upward from a piked position, and away from the support position in either a forward or backward direction.

Cartwheel. Sideward movement of the body in which the weight is transferred from one hand to the other while the legs are spread in the air. The arms and legs resemble the spokes of a wheel.

Cody. A trampoline somersault performed from a front drop.

Cut. A move in which the legs pass between the hands and the apparatus.

Dislocate. An extension of the legs and body from a fixed hand position, accompanied by a rotation of the shoulder joint in a backward direction.

Dismount. A gymnastic move used to get off the apparatus.

Dive Roll. A tumbling skill in which the tumbler jumps from both feet, dives forward, lands on the hands, and rolls to the feet.

Double-leg Circle. A movement in which the legs move as a unit in a circular fashion around a point of support.

Flank Vault. A move in which the gymnast jumps over the horse with his side to the apparatus.

F.I.G. Federation of International Gymnastics. This organization makes the rules which govern all international gymnastics.

Forward Roll. A complete turn forward on a mat or supporting surface in a tuck position.

Front Grasp. A grip on the high bar with the palms outward.

Front Somersault. A complete forward turn in the air taking off from the feet and landing on the feet.

Grip. The grasp the gymnast uses in working the apparatus. Grips may be defined as regular or overgrip, reverse, cross, mixed, eagle, and false. This chapter, however, discusses only the regular and reverse grips.

Hurdle. The push off from one foot to a two foot landing. This hurdle is used in vaulting.

Jump. A push off the floor from both feet into the air.

Killing the Bounce. A rapid flexion of the knees by the performer to stop the rebound of the trampoline bed.

Kip. A movement from a hang in which the body pikes, then extends and completes the move in a support position.

Left Circle. A counterclockwise leg circle on the side horse.

Lever. A held position in which the body is horizontal to the floor.

Longitudinal Axis. A line drawn through the body from the top of the head to the soles of the feet.

Mount. A move used to get on the apparatus.

Muscle Up. A pull up on the rings with a false grip to a straight-arm support.

Pike. A body position in which the hip joint is flexed with the legs held perpendicular to the trunk.

Pirouette. A vertical turn about the longitudinal axis of the body.

Press. A handstand movement in which the performer slowly extends the hips and legs overhead while slowly extending the arms.

Reuther Board. A takeoff board which affords a small amount of spring. It is used primarily in vaulting, but it can also be used for mounts on the parallel bars.

Right Circle. A clockwise leg circle on the side horse.

Routine. A sequence of gymnastic or tumbling stunts.

Scissors. A movement of the legs in side horse work that resembles the action of a scissors. One leg moves forward and the other leg moves backward over the horse.

Seat. A position in which the body weight rests on the buttocks and thighs.

Somersault. A complete turn in the air either forward or backward from feet to feet.

Straddle Seat. A sitting position on the parallel bars in which one leg is over one bar and the other leg is over the other bar, the weight resting on the thighs.

Straddle Vault. A leap over the horse with the legs wide apart.

Support. A position in which the weight is supported by the hands with the arms in a straight position. The shoulders should be above the hand position.

Swing. A movement describing an arc while in a hang position.

Swing Up. A swing from a hang to a support position.

Tuck. A position in which the chin moves forward to the chest with the hands grasping the shins and pulling the knees to the chest.

Twist. A turn about the longitudinal axis of the body.

Uprise. A movement from below to above a piece of apparatus. At the end of a forward or backward swing, the body moves from a hang to a support position.

U.S.G.F. United States Gymnastics Federation. This organization is the governing body for gymnastics in the United States.

Vault. A jump over a horse, parallel bars, or horizontal bar in which the hands thrust away from the apparatus.

DISCUSSION QUESTIONS

1. Give a brief history of gymnastics.
2. List some of the values to be derived from participation in gymnastics.
3. Define the following terms: baroni, cast, circle, cody, dislocate, double-leg circle, uprise, and kip.
4. Explain some gymnastic movements and discuss them from the standpoint of the laws of physics.
5. How might a class of thirty students be organized?
6. List some safety precautions that must be provided in teaching gymnastics.

BIBLIOGRAPHY

Bailey, James A., *Gymnastics in the Schools.* Boston: Allyn & Bacon, Inc., 1965.

Farkas, James, *Age Group Gymnastic Workbook.* Tucson, Arizona: United States Gymnastic Federation, 1964.

Frey, Harold J., and Keeney, Charles J., *Elementary Gymnastic Apparatus Skills Illustrated.* New York: The Ronald Press Co., 1964.

Griswold, Larry, *Trampoline Tumbling.* St. Louis, Missouri: Business Collaborators, Inc., 1958.

Hughes, Eric L., *Gymnastics for Men.* New York: The Ronald Press Co., 1966.

Kenney, Chuck, *Trampolining Illustrated.* New York: The Ronald Press Co., 1961.

LaDue, Frank, and Norman, Jim, *Two Seconds of Freedom.* Cedar Rapids, Iowa: Nissen Trampoline Co., 1960.

Laporte, William R., and Renner, Al G., *The Tumbler's Manual.* Englewood Cliffs, N.J.: Prentice-Hall, Inc., 1944.

Loken, Newton C., and Willoughby, R. J., *Complete Book of Gymnastics.* Englewood Cliffs, N.J.: Prentice-Hall, Inc., 1967.

Price, Hartley D., *et al., Gymnastics and Tumbling.* New York: The Ronald Press Co., 1968.

Ryser, Otto E., *A Teacher's Manual for Tumbling and Apparatus Stunts.* Dubuque, Iowa: William C. Brown Co., 1968.

Szypula, George. *Tumbling and Balancing for All.* Dubuque, Iowa: William C. Brown Co., 1957.

United States Gymnastic Federation. *U.S.G.F. Rules* 1965–66. Tucson, Arizona: United States Gymnastic Federation.

fencing

8

BACKGROUND

The original function of fencing, or dueling, was to inflict injury or to kill an enemy. The growth of this sport is a tribute to the progress of civilization. From its beginnings the skills developed were used as a method of war and a device for settling personal disputes. Even though the weapons used in these battles are known, and included the double-edge sword, the ancestor of the modern fencing weapons, little evidence remains on how they were used and what regulations, if any, prevailed. Such bouts certainly were violent and undisciplined, and mixed with wrestling. The tactical maneuvers of each individual were jealously guarded.

Through the years the weapons of fencing reflected the purposes and types of combat prevalent in each era. The armies of the Middle Ages used a two-handed sword for destruction of their foes. The heavier weapons were eventually replaced by light rapiers with sharp points and sharp edges.

When gunpowder was introduced, the sword lost its value in warfare; but the aristocracy continued to use fencing as a method of settling personal disputes. The number of injuries and deaths from duels caused nations around the world to banish the sword as a weapon. The nineteenth century saw fencing rise as a new and acceptable sport of skill and strategy rather than sheer strength. Women became active in it when protective equipment was developed and the techniques of foil fencing were refined.

The French, Hungarian, Spanish, and the Italian are famous schools of fencing. The French deviated from the original Italian school by removing the crossbar, modifying the grip to permit more free finger movement and thus greater maneuverability and deception. Though today fencers use the best features of both schools, the Italian style is still outstanding for its powerful overbearing movements.

Although fencing has not gained the rapid popularity of some other sports in the United States, it has grown steadily in popularity among men and women. Many large cities have fencing clubs with trained fencing masters for the membership. The Amateur Fencer's League of America governs activities in the United States in accord with international rules and in alliance with the Amateur Athletic Union.

VALUE OF FENCING

Fencing as a physical education activity offers physical, mental, moral, and social values on a par with many of our more popular sports in the United States. The physical and mental aspects are unlimited. A good fencer must have developed a neuromuscular pattern that enables him to coordinate reactions and skillful movements in terms of a fraction of a second. He must have the explosive action of a sprinter and the agility and strength that can be developed only through constant practice. Endurance and stamina are necessary for maximum activity in a given bout. Competitions are composed of many bouts for the individual, and only the well-trained are able to finish strongly. Mentally, a fencer needs the tactical intelligence of a general. He must be constantly alert, perceiving the slightest change in his opponent, and instantaneously form a strategy that will enable him to score. In short, it may be said that fencing can develop the utmost in speed, strength, timing, a quick analytical mind, and emotional stability.

Through physical and mental development, the fencer is constantly subjected to exercises of moral and social significance. The sport is associated with a code of behavior held in great esteem. The fencer is indoctrinated with a respect for the rights of his opponent. It is morally significant that a large number of fencers call touches against themselves. An atmosphere of unaffected respect and politeness for one's opponent is common in even the most important meets. It is not unusual for a fencer to award his opponent the winning touch of a championship match. Historically, fencing has been associated with the traditional qualities that make a man both masculine and gentlemanly.

DESCRIPTION

Fencing is a sport in which two individuals engage in hand-to-hand combat with a foil, epee, or sabre (Figure 8–1). The foil is considered the

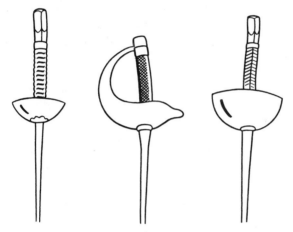

FIGURE 8-1   *Types of Weapons*   (From Don Cash Seaton, Irene A. Clayton, Howard C. Leibee, and Lloyd L. Messersmith, *Physical Education Handbook*, 5th ed. © 1969, Prentice-Hall, Inc. Reproduced by permission of the publisher.)

basic weapon in modern fencing. It is the lightest of all fencing weapons, encouraging good body mechanics through balance and posture control. The foil is a descendant of the practice weapon used when dueling was permitted. It is theoretically a pointed weapon that is used to inflict a puncture wound. The blade, tapered and blunted at the end, is rectangular. To the blade is attached the guard or bell, a 3 or 4-inch cup-shaped metal disc that protects the band.

In modern fencing contestants are protected by padded clothing, a mask, and a blunt tip on the point of the weapon. The objective is to score a touch (hit) against the adversary. The foil and epee are thrusting weapons with which touches can be scored only with the point. The epee is a dueling sword, a modern version of the eighteenth century rapier, which is a heavier and more rigid weapon than the foil. Although the handle is similar to that of the foil, the guard is larger for more adequate hand protection, and the blade is triangular in order to reduce flexibility without greatly increasing weight. The main differences between competition with the foil and the epee are that the entire body is a valid target with the epee, and the foil target is limited to the torso area alone— the arms, legs, and head are foul areas. Hits are scored only according to time differences.

Because of the speed and minuteness of action often involved in scoring, a three-pointed button called *point d'arret* used to be attached to the tip of the epee blade and inked red as often as necessary. When the point caught the jacket, it left ink marks, which aided the judges in establishing the validity of the touch. However, a more modern method of scoring in epee and foil has completely replaced the point d'arret. The use of an electric scoring machine not only removes the doubt of a touch, but also establishes the time sequence of double touches up to one-thirtieth of a second apart.

Most spectacular of the three weapons is the modern version of the broadsword or calvary sabre. The sabre is a thrusting, cutting, and counter-cutting weapon. Consequently, touches may be scored with the point or with either of the cutting edges. In sabre fencing, a cut is a scoring blow made by striking the target with either edge of the weapon; flat hits or grazes do not count. This differs from a scoring thrust made with a tip of the weapon, the only touch awarded in foil and epee. Sabre bouts are still judged in the classical manner, with director and jury, since the scoring machine cannot be used.

Both the foil and the sabre are conventional weapons. Touches are valid on the basis of priority, and a "right of way" is granted by the observance of certain rules. In epee the entire body is the target, and touches are awarded on the basis of first arrival only. Epee fencing, therefore, is the closest to actual dueling, although the cavalry sabre has sometimes been used as a dueling weapon.

the bout

The bout is the contest between the two fencers; it may be official or non-official. Official bouts in foil are fenced in five touches for men, and four for women. In epee and sabre it is also five touches; women do not compete in either of these weapons.

Practice bouts are called free play. In free play, touches must always be acknowledged by the contestant hit, by calling "touched" or "hit." A

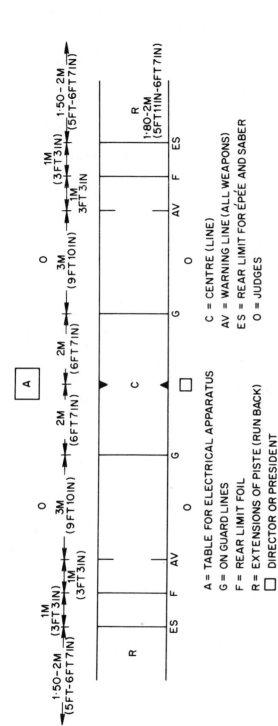

FIGURE 8-2 *The Regulation Piste for All Three Weapons*
(From Amateur Fencing League of America, *Fencing Rules Manual*, p. 17.)

157

foul touch is acknowledged by calling "foul" or rather by calling the part of the body touched, such as "arms" or "mask."

The fencing strip is the part of the floor used for combat. Usually it is linoleum, copper, cork, or rubber, although a gymnasium floor is suitable. The official strip is 40 feet long and between 5 feet, 11 inches and 6 feet, 7 inches wide (Figure 8–2).

The official strip of the Amateur Fencer's League of America is marked by drawing five parallel lines across the width of the strip, each 1 inch wide: (a) the center line dividing the strip in the middle; (b) two on-guard lines, one on each side, drawn at a distance of 2 meters from the center; (c) two warning lines, one on each side, drawn at a distance of 1 meter from the end of the official strip. The on-guard lines indicate where the fencers assume the on-guard position at the start of the bout. The warning lines inform the fencer that he is near the end of the strip.

the mask and costume

Some type of body protector should be worn at all times when an individual is fencing. Fencing jackets are the best since they are made of strong cloth and are designed and reinforced for more adequate protection. Half-jackets are designed for practice and cover little more than half the body. They are very practical for group instruction. The full jacket is the most desirable for women. It is recommended that they wear extra breast protection of steel wire mesh cups with padded material under the jacket.

The fencing mask is made of strong fine wire mesh to protect the head and throat without interfering with visibility. A canvas or nylon bib that covers the throat is attached to the inside of the mask. Sabre masks are padded on the top and sides to shield the fencer from the heavier blows of that weapon. The mask is held on the head with a padded back spring attachment.

The most satisfactory shoe for fencing is leather with flat soles and a bracing strap across the front, although tennis shoes or low heeled rubber-soled shoes are practical for classwork.

BASIC SKILLS

The mastering of the basic skills in fencing cannot be over-emphasized. The body position and movements involved are comparatively artificial and are not natural sports motions such as running and jumping. The careful practice of fundamentals will soon accustom the individual to the unique movements.

The basic fundamentals discussed here are those that apply to foil fencing. Anyone interested in epee or sabre fencing should consult the list of references at the end of this chapter. Generally, the fundamentals for all weapons are quite similar.

All are described as though the fencer is right-handed.

the grip

The handle of the foil is curved slightly and should be grasped with this curve fitting into the palm of the hand. It should be gripped by the thumb and index finger close to the guard (Figure 8–3). The thumb

FIGURE 8-3 *The Foil Grip* (From John H. Shaw, Carl A. Troester, Jr., and Milton A. Gabrielsen, *Individual Sports for Men.* © 1964. Reprinted by permission of Wm. C. Brown Company Publishers, Dubuque, Iowa.)

should be along the top of the handle, with the underside being supported between the first two joints of the index finger. These are the main manipulative fingers,. while the remaining fingers curve around the narrow surface, holding the handle firmly in the palm and flat against the inside of the wrist.

the salute

It is traditional always to salute the opponent before fencing (Figure 8–4). Before putting on the mask, the fencer stands at attention and

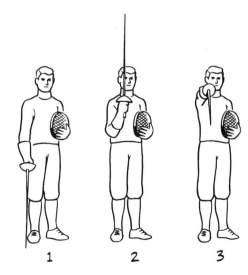

FIGURE 8-4 *The Salute*

smartly raises the guard in front of his face with the blade standing straight up. Then, facing the opponent, he quickly brings the blade down with the arm extended and the point at the floor in the opponent's direction.

the call

The call is a method of informing the opponent of a desire to halt a bout: it is made by stamping the right foot twice.

the guard

The position or stance in which fencers oppose one another is known as the guard. All offensive and defensive movements originate from it. To take the on-guard position, the fencer should assume a position of attention and raise the foil arm-level with the eyes, maintaining a straight line from the shoulder to the point of the foil. He should then bend the foil arm, keeping the elbow free from the body with the point of the foil at eye level, and the forearm almost horizontal. Simultaneously, the left arm is arched to the rear, acting as a counterweight. He should maintain an erect body posture, with the knees flat, directly above the feet. He then should move the right foot forward and place it flat. It should be opposite the left heel and at a distance suitable to the fencer's height. Both knees should remain bent and directly over the middle of the feet. The weight

FIGURE 8-5 *On Guard* (From Don Cash Seaton, Irene A. Clayton, Howard C. Leibee, and Lloyd L. Messersmith, *Physical Education Handbook*, 5th ed. © 1969, Prentice-Hall, Inc. Reproduced by permission of the publisher.)

should be distributed evenly on both feet (Figure 8–5). The proper distance between the feet should be maintained during the advance and return to the guard position after a lunge.

the advance and retreat

The advance is a maneuver that brings the fencer within attacking distance of his opponent. From the guard position, keeping the body erect, he advances the right foot, followed by the left foot at the same relative distance. The movement should be a sliding one with both feet maintaining contact with the floor. The leg remains bent throughout the movement, with the ankle directly beneath the knee. The advance should be a smooth effort, with only a short pace forward being necessary. It is important to maintain the correct length of stance in both the advance and the retreat.

The retreat is a maneuver that takes the fencer out of his opponent's reach. From the guard position, he moves the left foot back, followed by the right foot at its proper distance. Complete immobility of the trunk, which must remain in an upright position, should be maintained in both the advance and the retreat. If correctly executed, ether the advance or retreat will end in a perfect on-guard position.

the lunge

One of the most important single movements in fencing is the lunge, the final foot movement in the attack. Considerable practice is necessary to develop this advantage to the utmost. It is a long and forceful reach with the legs, which takes the weapon to the opponent.

The execution of the lunge combines several simultaneous movements. The front foot is raised from the floor and the whole body is impelled forward. This forward lunge comes primarily from the explosive and forceful straightening and extension of the rear leg. The rear arm is flung down and back so it ends parallel with the rear leg. The body is balanced slightly forward, the forward lean aiding in overcoming the initial inertia. The forward foot arrives on the floor in a position at right angles to the rear foot, which has remained flat. There is no settling or sagging into position. The forward movement is complete. The thigh and lower leg should form a right angle at the knee, in the full lunge, with the front knee over the heel of the foot (Figure 8–6).

FIGURE 8-6 *Lunge* (From Don Cash Seaton, Irene A. Clayton, Howard C. Leibee, and Lloyd L. Messersmith, *Physical Education Handbook*, 5th ed. © 1969, Prentice-Hall, Inc. Reproduced by permission of the publisher.)

To recover from the lunge, there should be a thrust back with the right heel and a pull with the left leg. Simultaneously the left arm is brought upward strongly to its former position, which aids in pulling the body back. The foil arm returns to the guard position.

the simple attacks

The simple attack is an attack made in one movement or an attack made without any previous feint or threat to the opponent's target. There are three main types of simple attack: the *straight thrust,* a direct attack executed only in one line; the *disengage,* an indirect attack started in one line and, by passing under the opponent's blade, finished in another; and the *cutover,* an indirect attack with the blade passing over the opponent's point.

THE STRAIGHT THRUST. The straight thrust is no more than a straight lunge. Since the lunge has already been described, it will not be necessary to discuss the execution of the straight thrust.

In teaching the straight thrust, however, there are certain features that must not be missed. The beginner has a tendency to be timid. He does not drive out in an explosive manner. Rather, he steps or falls into the lunge position. This is much too slow. The following game is a device to help speed the lunge.

One student is on guard at the proper distance from the wall. Another student holds a glove or some other suitable object high against it. Without previous indication, he drops the glove. When this happens, the fencer is supposed to lunge and pin the glove against the wall.

It is no easy task. The fencer will soon learn that if he is not forewarned when the glove will fall, the best way to try to pin it is to extend the arm quickly and drive. Many advanced fencers practice in this manner to speed their lunge.

Another tendency, the opposite of meekness, is to lunge too hard. This results in an overlunge, causing loss of lateral balance, falling forward, or inability to recover quickly. Unfortunately there is no very good teaching device for correcting this tendency.

A very important principle to remember in fencing is that the expert fencer has rigidly disciplined habits. Since habit is paramount to skillful fencing, the instructor must make every effort to teach only correct habits and to prevent the incorrect ones from becoming established. The latter is one of the most difficult tasks in teaching fencing.

THE DISENGAGE. The disengage is a simple, indirect attack involving the passing of the point under the hand or guard of the opponent from a closed to an open line. This is one of the most used and useful of all actions in fencing. To execute a disengagement, the point is passed under the opponent's blade into the opposite line with a progressive movement of the foil arm, followed by a lunge, taking care that the right-of-way has been gained. The foil should be kept close to the opponent's blade.

THE CUTOVER. The cutover is a disengagement made by passing the point over the opponent's blade. To execute it, the blade is raised with the wrist and fingers, retaining contact with the opponent's blade until the opposite line is reached. At this point the arm is extended and a lunge is executed in an attempt to make a touch.

COMPOUND ATTACKS. An attack that is preceded by one or more feints of action is called a compound attack. One that is made up of a feint of disengagement deceiving a simple parry is called a "one-two attack." A "one-two-three attack" is composed of two feints of disengagement. An attack that consists of a feint of disengagement deceiving a counter parry is termed a "double."

ATTACK ON THE BLADE. An attack on the blade involves some type of pressure on the opponent's blade with one of three purposes in mind: to feint or provoke a reaction, to invite an attack, or to open a closed line.

The *beat* is a sharp decisive blow made on the middle part of the opposing blade. It is executed primarily with a compression of the thumb and index finger.

The *pressure* is a pressure against the middle part of the opponent's blade. If the opponent returns it, a sudden release may provoke a reaction and open a line.

The *glide* is an attack executed by gliding the blade along the opponent's blade as the thrust is completed.

The *pressure glide* is a sideways and forward pressure on the opponent's blade. As the foil arm is extending, the blade is pressed on the blade of the opponent.

An *attack taking the blade* is an action upon the opposing blade with the object of warding off the point and at the same time dominating the opponent's blade. The opponent's blade is forced out of line by controlling the blade while attacking. Care should be taken to execute controlled resistance on the blade in order to avoid carrying the point out of line and to insure the completion of the movement before the attack is delivered. The blade may be taken in three ways:

The opposition is progressive in the line of engagement much like the glide. This must be a simple attack, with emphasis in opposing the opponent's blade during the lunge.

The bind seeks to control the opposing blade by carrying it from a high to a low line, and vice versa. The strong part of the blade is placed against the weak part of the opponent's blade. The fencer will semicircle the point and simultaneously slide forward on the opponent's blade. This will place the opponent's point low and out of line.

The envelopment brings the opponent's blade back to the line in which it was previously situated, both points describing a complete circle. It is followed immediately by a slide forward on the opponent's blade.

COUNTER ATTACKS. A counter attack involves the use of time and is executed against the opposing offensive. It can be used if an opponent is attacking slowly and has not taken the right of way. A time thrust is an action best used on a compound attack, blocking out the final movement. A stop thrust checks a slow offensive at the beginning and will score before the original attack. In both actions, the counter is the rapid extension of the foil arm before the opponent has gained the right-of-way or before a compound attack must be parried. The touch landing first is counted.

SECONDARY MOVEMENTS. These are attacks that are meant to be parried so that the return attack can be capitalized upon for a successful counter-return. The redoubled is a renewal of the attack against an opponent who has parried and failed to riposte or against an opponent who has retreated to avoid a hit. The replacement is an offensive action executed without rising from the lunge. This can occur only when the opposing parry is not followed by a riposte.

DEFENSIVE MOVEMENTS. The parry is the fencer's defensive action for diverting the attacker's blade. Its object is to use just enough deflecting motion to protect the threatened area. By overprotecting and moving the foil hand too far, a new target opening may be created. A simple parry deflects the attacking blade, leaving it outside the line in which it was delivered. A counter parry deflects the blade to the opposite line of attack. Whether simple or counter, a parry may be executed in two different ways: in the opposition parry the blade is diverted by pressure without losing contact; the beat parry is a crisp blow on the opponent's blade with an immediate return to position.

There are eight standard parries—two defending each of the four sections of the target. The parries of four, six, seven, and two should be mastered first. They tend to be the stronger, more natural movements, and keep the point of the foil more in line with the target.

Parry of four defends the high inside line of the target. It is executed by moving the foil hand to the left with the elbow remaining stationary and the foil tip pointing toward the target. The pommel will be off the wrist to the left.

Parry of six defends the high outside line of the target. It is performed by moving the foil hand to the right with the elbow remaining stationary and the foil tip pointing toward the target. The pommel will be moved to the wrist quickly.

Parry of seven defends the low inside line of the target. It is executed by dropping the tip of the foil in a clockwise semicircle. The foil points to the opponent's knee with the palm of the hand facing upward.

Parry of two defends the low outside line of the target. It is executed by dropping the tip of the foil in a counterclockwise semicircle. The foil points to the opponent's knee with the palm of the hand facing downward.

The parries of one, three, five and eight are weak and awkward compared to the other four. They are useful for variety but should be attempted only by advanced fencers.

Parry of one defends the high inside line of the target. It is executed by keeping the forearm horizontal and the elbow to the right as the hand, palm downward, and drops the point of the foil lower than the hand. The foil points toward the opponent's feet.

Parry of three defends the high outside line of the target. It is executed by moving the foil to the right, palm downward, with the point of the foil higher than the hand.

Parry of five defends the low inside line of the target. It is executed by moving the hand to the left, palm downward and lower than the elbow. The point of the foil is higher than the hand.

Parry of eight defends the low outside line of the target. It is executed by moving the hand to the right, palm upward, with the point of the foil lower than the hand and pointing to the opponent's knee.

A counter, or circle parry to deflect the blade to the opposite line of attack involves more finger movement than the simple parries. It can be used for variety and to confuse the opponent. A counter parry on a high line of the target is executed by dropping the tip of the foil under the attacking blade and circling the blade out to the opposite line. A counter parry on a low line of the target is executed by moving the foil tip over the attacking blade and circling it out to the opposite line.

Riposte. A riposte is a return attack, or the sequel to a successful parry. The defense assumes the offense immediately after the parry by extending and threatening the target as quickly as possible. The riposte has the right-of-way over a second attack by the original attacker, providing there is no hesitation. The riposte can be either a simple or compound attack.

Playing Strategy. The fencers are usually placed on guard either in or out of distance. When in distance, they are at the interval where the lunge of one will reach the other. When out of distance an advance is necessary to come within lunging reach. Distance varies with the fencer, and each seeks to have the other take his own.

When in distance, the fencers may fence in or out of engagement. In engagement means that each fencer closes either the inside or outside line, and crosses his blade with that of the opponent. When out of distance, the opponents fence out of engagement, usually assuming an outside guard.

Fencers often seek to vary distance by moving in and out, attacking with simple lunges as well as preceding a lunge with advances. These changes disturb the opposing fencer's ability to estimate the distance from which he can expect an attack to be launched.

Initial feints, by the rapid and smooth extension of the blade with the point threatening the target, often draw a parry that can be deceived. A movement against the blade often causes the defender to parry, thus opening his defense and target for attack. Occasionally a stamping of the front foot aids the feint with the weapon, although this is more often dramatic than effective.[1]

[1]Don Cash Seaton, et al., *Physical Education Handbook*, 5th ed. (Englewood Cliffs, N.J.: Prentice-Hall, Inc., 1969), 150-51.

TEACHING PROCEDURE

The instructor may give a short and inspiring history of fencing to help develop interest and a proper attitude for new experiences in a combative sport. At the beginning of a unit an explanation of safety precautions, fencing equipment, and demonstrations is essential. Basic exercises and novelty games are helpful in developing strength and agility and in releasing tensions often present.

It is usually best to bring the class close to the instructor in an informal semicircle for demonstrations. For executions and practice, the line formation, with an even number of lines, should be used. If the area is small, it may be necessary to stagger the lines so that no one stands directly behind another. In either case, when pairing off, alternate lines about-face and those opposite each other fence together. Later, positions should be shifted so that a variety of partners are fenced. This type of organization will be assumed throughout, except where otherwise designated.

Before the class practices a certain skill, the teacher should demonstrate and explain its use in a bout. Basic skills of the guard position, grip, advance, lunge, and recovery should be stressed for form, agility, and effectiveness. The salute and call should be taught early to add dignity and courtesy to informal practice.

Emphasis on the basic parries of six and four gives a fencer confidence to work against simple attacks. These should be emphasized early in the teaching procedure. The addition of riposte skills encourages agility and alertness and increases practice pleasure. Each fencer practices skills against an opponent, first on the teacher's command and later in bouting sessions. Early bouting is encouraged to break tedious but necessary drills. Selected films and demonstration bouts help maintain interest.

As students progress, attacks on the blade, compound attacks, and counter parries are introduced. Bouting and officiating should encourage students to participate with community fencing groups.

SKILL TESTS

Evaluation in fencing classes is complicated by the numerous parts contained in a single skill. An effective evaluative plan should consider the student's knowledge and understanding of rules of bouting, safety, and officiating, and his skills. The student's ability to fence effectively should reflect his skill development.

It is desirable to evaluate a student's progress and skill individually. A rating scale may be developed for each skill taught. For example, the teacher may wish to evaluate several separate skills of: (1) guard position, (2) advance, (3) retreat, (4) advance and lunge, (5) cutover lunge, (6) disengage lunge, (7) parry of four, (8) parry of six, and (9) riposte.

Aside from the simple execution of the above skills, the teacher may evaluate their execution considering the student's (1) ability to advance, retreat, and lunge in good form with accurate judgment of distance, and (2) his ability to execute attacks and parries with precision and speed.

Rating scales used by student officials are helpful in evaluation of general fencing ability. Tournament play in a round robin pool may be arranged so each participant evaluates all other members of the class on fencing ability and strategy.

The complete picture of the student's progress includes a written examination covering the rules, history, and safety of the sport.

DEFINITION OF TERMS

Advance. A forward movement of the body toward the opponent.

Attack. A forward movement of the body and weapon that attempts to touch the opponent's target.

Attack on the Blade. Beat, pressure, and glide attacks used to deviate the defensive point.

Breaking Ground. Retreating out of distance with both feet.

Bout. A contest between two individuals.

Change of Engagement. Attacks composed of one or more feints.

Covered. A position of the foil that closes the line of engagement.

Cut-over. A disengagement made by passing over the opponent's blade.

Development. The combined actions of the arm extension and the lunge.

Disengagement. The movement of the weapon from the line of engagement into the opposite line.

Double. An attack deceiving a counter parry.

Engagement. The crossing of the blades.

False Attack. An attack that is not intended to score.

Feint. A movement of the blade meant to resemble an attack in order to draw a reaction from the opponent.

Lines. The theoretical division of the target corresponding to the fencing position.

Mask. A wire mesh face protector.

Match. A contest between two teams with any one or more weapons and consisting of a series of bouts.

Pass. A touch that does not hit properly.

Phrase. A period in a bout when there is no cessation of action.

Pool. A group of individuals or teams competing on a round-robin basis.

Retreat. To step back, open the distance; opposite of advance.

Riposte. The offensive action after a successful defense.

Simple Attack. An attack made with one movement, either direct or indirect.

Strip. Place on mat where a fencing bout takes place.

Touch. A hit on the target that would puncture or wound if the weapons were pointed.

Tournament. A series of competitions in one or more weapons, organized as individuals or team events or both.

Uncovered. A position in which the line of engagement is not closed.

DISCUSSION QUESTIONS

1. What physical and social values may be derived from participating in fencing?
2. Discuss the differences among the weapons used in fencing.
3. Explain the difference between simple and compound attack.
4. What safety precautions are necessary in conducting a fencing class?
5. What are the offensive movements in fencing?
6. What are some exercises for learning the offensive movements in fencing?
7. What are the various defensive movements that may be employed?
8. Discuss evaluative procedures for a class of beginning fencers.
9. How can interest in fencing be motivated?
10. Discuss the meaning of using attack on the blade.

BIBLIOGRAPHY

Bower, Muriel, and Mori, Torao, *Fencing.* Dubuque, Iowa: William C. Brown Company, 1966.

de Capriles, José R., ed., *Fencing Rules and Manual.* Massachusetts: Iteffernan Press, Inc., 1968.

Castello, Hugo, and Castello, J. M., *Fencing.* New York: The Ronald Press Company, 1962.

Castello, J. M., *Theory and Practice of Fencing.* New York: Charles Scribner's Sons, 1961.

Garret, Maxwell R., *Fencing*. New York: Sterling Publishing Company, Inc., 1961.

Miller, Kenneth D., *Physical Education Activities for College Men and Women*. Dubuque, Iowa: William C. Brown Company, 1963.

Mitchell, Elmer D., *Sports for Recreation*. New York: The Ronald Press Company, 1952.

Palffy, Alpar J., *Sword and Masque*. Philadelphia: F. A. Davis Company, 1968.

Shaw, John H., Troester, Carl A., and Gabrielsen, M. Alexander, *Individual Sports for Men*. Dubuque, Iowa: William C. Brown Company, 1964.

Sports Illustrated Book of Fencing. Philadelphia: J. B. Lippincott Company, 1961.

Vince, Joseph, *Fencing*. New York: The Ronald Press Company, 1962.

field hockey

9

BACKGROUND

The exact origin of field hockey is not known, but it is believed to be the oldest stick and ball game. There is reason to believe that a crude form of hockey was played by the ancient Greeks, Romans, and Persians as early as 500 B.C. The sport was forbidden in England because it interfered with the practice of archery, which was the basis of national defense.

The word *hockey* is the anglicized version of *hoquet*—French for the curved shepherd's stick that was used to play a game that was popular in Europe during the Middle Ages.

The modern game was developed in England about the middle of the nineteenth century, and it has since spread to many countries. In those days players never used a definite marked-out striking circle, but the rules stated that no goal could be scored if the ball were hit from a distance of more than 15 yards from the nearest goalpost. In 1833 the famous Wimbledon Club was formed; this was a landmark in the progress of the game. A few years later hockey clubs for men and women sprang up throughout England. The real birth of modern field hockey came with the formation of the Hockey Association in 1886 and the adoption of the striking circle. Interest in the game spread quickly throughout England.

At the beginning of the twentieth century, field hockey became even more popular, making headway not only in Europe but also in New Zealand, Africa, India, Australia, Japan, and Canada. In 1901 Constance Applebee, a member of the British College of Physical Education, introduced field hockey in the United States through a demonstration at the Harvard College of Physical Education. In 1908 the game was so widespread that it was included in the Olympic Games for men only.

In 1922 the United States Field Hockey Association was formed in Philadelphia to encourage hockey for women. The association worked to unite the players throughout the country, and to make the rules and equipment uniform. This organization has been very active in helping schools, colleges, and clubs promote the game. Hockey has become very popular in New York and Connecticut in recent years, with teams often going on tours. The sport has taken its place in the physical education programs of junior and senior high schools, private schools, and colleges.

Field hockey is one of the few truly amateur games in the world today; there are no professional teams. The international governing bodies are the International Hockey Board, comprised of England, Scotland, Ireland and Wales; and the Federation Internationale de Hockey, which has approximately thirty countries in its membership, including the United States.

Today the leading countries in this sport are India, England, the Netherlands, Germany, and Pakistan. Field hockey has the distinction of being the national game of India, which has dominated every Olympic competition.

DESCRIPTION OF THE GAME

Field hockey is played on a grass field 100 yards long and 60 yards wide (Figure 9–1). The goals are 7 feet high and 12 feet wide. The game is played by two teams of eleven players: five forwards, three halfbacks, two fullbacks, and a goalkeeper. Each team attempts to advance a ball toward the opponent's goal and to hit it between the goalposts with a curved stick. A goal counts one point. The game starts and restarts after each goal with a bully on the center line, taken by the two center forward players. Regulation playing time is two 30-minute halves with a 10-minute rest period between them. Playing time is sometimes shortened for school

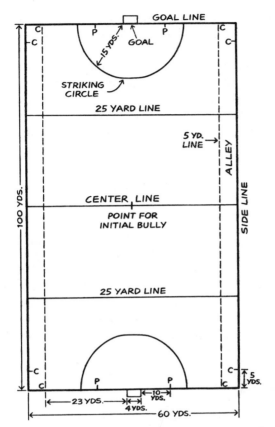

FIGURE 9-1   *A Regulation Field for Field Hockey*

teams. Time out is permitted only in case of injury, and no substitutes are allowed.

The general strategy for field hockey is similar to soccer. The principal difference is that no obstruction is allowed in field hockey because of the danger involved. To place one's body in a position to block an opponent and the ball is forbidden, since the sticks are relatively heavy and are used for hard striking. If a player were permitted to defend the ball with the body, the game would become quite hazardous. The goalkeeper wears heavy pads and is the only one allowed to kick the ball or stop it with the foot. All players, however, may stop the ball with the hand.

If the defenders hit the ball over the goal line intentionally or commit a foul within the striking circle, a penalty corner is taken. The ball is placed 10 yards from the goal post. This is also called a short corner. In the case of other fouls, a free hit is awarded to the offender's opposing team on the spot where the infraction occurred. When the ball goes over the side line, an opponent of the player who last touched it rolls it in by hand.

There is one umpire for each half of the field. The umpire refrains from enforcing a penalty if he believes that to enforce it would give an advantage to the offending team.

The offside rule is similar to that in soccer except that three opponents are required to place a player onside if he is ahead of the ball and in the attacking half of the field.

BASIC SKILLS

grip

The heel of the stick is set on the ground with the toe turned up. The left hand grips the top of the handle. The right hand is placed just below the left with the fingers of both hands curled around the stick. The V formed by the thumb and index finger of each hand is directly in alignment with the toe of the club. The grip is firm, but not tensed. This is the fundamental position for all strokes. The right hand will adjust and readjust itself up and down on the stick according to the stroke that is used.

carrying position

When the stick is not in use, it is carried comfortably across the body in a position ready for quick and immediate use. The left hand retains its normal correct grip with the toe of the stick pointed upward. The right hand makes a hook by facing the palm forward and supporting the stick at approximately its midpoint. Thus the stick rests easily across the front of the body, parallel to the ground and out of the way of runners, the flat part of the head facing in the direction of the runner, ready to drop quickly to the ground to intercept or play the ball.

dribble

The dribble is a method of controlling the ball while advancing it by a series of short taps with the flat side of the stick while the player is running. The ball should be kept close enough to the dribbler so that he can control it. As running speed increases, the strokes should be played stronger (Figure 9–2).

In performing the dribble, the player should relax the arms, holding the left arm away from the body with the left shoulder slightly in

FIGURE 9-2 *The Dribble* (Adapted from Maryhelen Vannier and Hally Beth Poindexter, *Individual and Team Sports for Girls and Women.* © 1960, W.B. Saunders Company, by permission of the publisher.)

advance, and the right hand gripping several inches below the left. The stick is held perpendicular to the ground, and the impetus given to the strokes in the dribble is principally a wrist action.

In dribbling on the run, the player should maintain the ball slightly to the right front of the right foot, to prevent running into or kicking the ball.

driving

"Driving" is passing or shooting with an increased application of power in order to cover distance rapidly or to force the ball past a defender. The drive is performed by the player placing both hands together at the top of the stick as for the dribble. In the execution of a straight drive, the left shoulder points in the direction the ball is expected to travel. Even for the hardest shots, it is not necessary to raise the stick more than slightly above the waist. After the impact of the blade on the ball, the already firm wrists tighten abruptly so as to insure a short follow-through and to prevent a foul. As in all forceful hitting patterns, there is a transfer of weight from the rear to the forward foot. The left drive is almost identical with the straight drive except for the position of the ball, which is closer to the left foot. The angle of the blade's contact and the direction of the stick's swing send the ball in the chosen direction.

In order to drive to the right, the player must contact the ball to the outside of, or even slightly behind, the right foot. The stick is swung behind the back as the body twists from the hips toward the right; body weight is on the forward right foot for the resumption of a run. This is an exacting stroke for beginners to master.

The player should remember that in all well-executed drives the player's left shoulder must point toward the direction desired for the path of the ball.

push pass

The push pass is used when there is not sufficient time to execute a drive. It is usually employed for short and more accurate passing. The body should be crouched and the pass made with either foot forward. The right hand should be well down the stick to execute a quick pass. The stick faces the direction of the pass and pushes the ball. There is no backswing. When this pass is smoothly and skillfully executed, it has accuracy and power and can be easily received by a teammate.

flick

The flick is a shot made with the face of the stick in contact with the ball and with no backswing. It is performed by the wrist and arm action of pushing the club head behind the ball and flicking the ball into the air to a teammate. The follow-through movement of the stick, in the direction of the flick, is important to execute this stroke successfully.

scoop

The scoop is a slow pass that can be used effectively as a dodge, a short pass, or even a shot for a goal. The ball is lifted into the air, as the name implies. The right hand moves at least halfway down the stick, and the toe of the blade is inserted under the ball as the right hand lifts while the

FIGURE 9-3 *The Scoop* (Adapted from Maryhelen Vannier and Hally Beth Poindexter, *Individual and Team Sports for Girls and Women.* © 1960, W.B. Saunders Company, by permission of the publisher.)

left hand pulls the handle downward (Figure 9–3). This action lifts and projects the ball forward, often over the stick of the opponent who is about to tackle the ball carrier. He is then in a position to continue on with the ball, leaving the tackler in a pursuing position.

fielding

The ball may be stopped with the stick or the hands. (Stopping with the feet tends to be inaccurate.) Stopping with the hands is likely to be dangerous and often causes the player to violate the rule of "advancing the ball." This leaves the stick as the best method for stopping the ball. It is often the quickest stop to use because the player's stick is ready to play the ball immediately thereafter. The player places his body directly in front of the oncoming ball with one foot or both feet behind the stick. The right hand slides down the handle about five inches. The tip of the blade faces down toward the ball in order to trap it between the ground and the blade. As it is stopped, the hands should relax their grip slightly, giving with the ball to deaden the hit so that it will stop rather than pop over the blade.

tackling

Tackling is a means of getting the ball away from an opponent. All tackles should be made in such a way that a foul is not committed. Learning the fundamental requisites of each tackle, attaining proper distance relationship with an opponent, and concentrating attention on the ball, can lead to very effective tackling. All players should constantly be aware of the total playing situation at any particular moment, including the approximate positions of both offensive and defensive players. This knowledge will result in continued possession of the ball and its advancement toward the opponent's goal.

A straight tackle is made on the stick side of an approaching opponent when the ball is off that player's stick. The tackler places the stick against the ball without backswing as in stopping or fielding. It is held there as the opponent overruns the ball. The tackler is then ready to execute a dribble or pass.

The circular tackle is made by the player on the non-stick side of the opponent who is dribbling the ball. The tackler runs alongside the dribbler, circles in front of him, and taps the ball away as it comes off the stick.

The left-hand lunge is made when the tackler is on the stick side of the dribbling opponent. He runs along the side of the dribbler with his stick in the carrying position. Keeping his left hand at the top of the stick, he releases his right hand, throwing the stick to his own left as he lunges and places his club head directly and firmly in front of the forward-moving ball. The action will either stop the ball or push it back. If the lunge is successful, the tackler immediately turns left, places his right hand back on the stick and starts to dribble away. If the lunge is unsuccessful and he fails to stop the ball, he should run to catch up and continue the lunge.

The jab is made from either side of the opponent. The tackler reaches toward the ball making several jabs at it, trying to spoil its intended progress. This is a one-handed stroke made with either hand at the top of the stick and can be played from either side of the player with the ball.

dodging

Dodging is an effective method of avoiding an oncoming tackler. To execute an oncoming dodge, the player must dribble the ball close to the forward foot and make short passes. If the ball is dribbled too far out in front of the player, or if a long pass is attempted, the ball is easily picked up by an attacking player.

RIGHT DODGE. A right dodge is made by a player who passes to his own right or to the non-stick side of the tackler and then runs to the left to regain possession of the ball. He then should pass to a teammate to avoid the tackler who may try to tackle back.

LEFT DODGE. In performing the left dodge the dribbler should keep the ball on his stick side. He then takes the ball downfield to the opponent's left. Just before the ball reaches the opponent, the dribbler steps to the left, quickly pulls the ball directly to the left only a few inches, and then again quickly taps the ball forward. This maneuver requires skill and accurate timing.

TRIANGULAR PASS. In this situation as the dribbler approaches the attacker, he passes diagonally forward either right or left to a teammate. The teammate in turn passes back to the dribbler, who already has run around and to the rear of the attacker to meet the ball again. This is one of the most fundamental and most used plays on the hockey field.

the bully

The bully is the play used to start or restart a game of hockey. One player from each team will take the bully. They face each other in the center of the field with their feet astride the center line. Each player must face the side lines squarely. The ball is placed on the line between them (Figure 9–4). They cannot move their feet until the bully is completed. The bully is started with each player alternately striking the ground with the heel of the stick on his own side of the ball, and then striking the opponent's stick above the ball three consecutive times. With the third meeting of sticks above the ball, the bully is completed, and players are free to move into playing or attacking areas. After the sticks are hit for

FIGURE 9-4 *The Bully* (Adapted from Maryhelen Vannier and Hally Beth Poindexter, *Individual and Team Sports for Girls and Women.* © 1960, W.B. Saunders Company, by permission of the publisher.)

the third time, the ball is hooked back out of reach of an opponent by inverting the toe of the stick, and from this position of the ball a pass is made to a teammate.

The bully is used to:

1. Start the game at the beginning, after half time, and after a goal has been scored.
2. Restart the game after the ball has gone over the end line off the attacker's stick.
3. Restart the game when the ball has gone over the end line off the sticks of two opponents simultaneously.
4. Restart the game after a penalty bully.
5. Restart the game after a simultaneous foul by two opponents.[1]

penalty bully

This is a bully given for a foul committed by the defensive team:

1. That prevented a certain goal from being scored.
2. That is a willful breach of the rules.
3. That is part of a pattern of deliberate or repeated fouling.[2]

The penalty bully is taken 5 yards out from the center of the goal line

[1]Don Cash Seaton, et al., *Physical Education Handbook*, 5th ed. (Englewood Cliffs, N.J.: Prentice-Hall, Inc., 1969), 160.
[2]*Ibid.*, p. 161.

by the player who fouled and any player chosen by the attacking team. All other players, including the goalkeeper, if he is not the participating defensive member, are placed beyond the 25-yard line and must remain there, not taking part in the game until the penalty bully is over. The penalty bully will result in one of the following situations:

1.   A goal is awarded to the attacking team, and the penalty bully is completed when:
   (a)   The ball goes between the goalposts off the stick of either player.
   (b)   The defender commits a foul.
2.   There is no score, the penalty bully is completed, and the game is restarted with a bully in the center of the 25-yard line when:
   (a)   The ball goes outside the circle.
   (b)   The attacker hits the ball over the goal line but not between the goalposts.
   (c)   The attacker fouls.
3.   The penalty bully is repeated when:
   (a)   The defender hits the ball over the goal line but not between the goalposts.
   (b)   The ball goes out of the circle or over the goal line off the sticks of the two opponents simultaneously.
   (c)   There is an improper bully or a double foul.
   (d)   Any other player interferes.[3]

roll-in

When a ball goes out of bounds, it is taken by a player on the team opposite the last one touching it. The roll-in is executed by a player who

FIGURE 9-5 *The Roll-in* (Adapted from Maryhelen Vannier and Hally Beth Poindexter, *Individual and Team Sports for Girls and Women.* © 1960, W.B. Saunders Company, by permission of the publisher.)

is outside the side boundaries. Usually the halfback takes the roll-in, holding the stick in one hand and the ball in the other. The ball is rolled onto

[3]*Ibid.*, p. 161.

the field of play, as in bowling. It must contact the ground within 3 feet of the side lines, and it must not be thrown or bounced. The player rolling the ball in may not play it again until it has been touched by another player. The other players may enter the alley as soon as the ball crosses the outside line (Figure 9–5).

corner

This formation is awarded as an advantage to the attacking team and has two variations:

1. *Long Corner.* Sometimes called only a *corner*, it is awarded when the ball is unintentionally sent over the goal line, not between the goal posts, off the stick of a defender. The ball is placed 5 yards from the corner on either the goal line or side line, on the side of the goal where the ball went out.
2. *Short Corner.* This is sometimes called a penalty corner, and it is awarded when:
    (a) The ball goes over the goal line without any attempt being made to keep it on the field.
    (b) The defense fouls in the circle.

The ball is placed not less than 10 yards from the nearer goal post on either side of the goal on the end line. The attacking team may choose on which side the penalty corner will be taken.[4]

corner play

Usually the wing of the attacking team takes the hit for the corner. The other forwards station themselves around the circle, stick and feet just outside the circle line. The halfback backs up the forwards.

The defending team's six players are stationed with their feet and sticks behind the goal line. Each player is opposite the stick of the person he is to cover. The five forwards of the defending team remain at the 25-yard line.

No player may be nearer than 5 yards to the player taking the hits. As soon as the ball is hit, these players may move. Other defending players may not be nearer than the 25-yard line, which they cannot cross until the ball has been touched by a player other than the hitter, or it has come out of the circle.

The wing usually passes to one of the other forwards. No player may

[4]*Ibid.*, p. 161.

shoot for the goal unless the ball has been stopped on the ground or has touched the stick or person of a defender.

To execute an excellent corner, the wing hits hard, but the ball stays on the ground and does not bounce. The forward executes a good stop and a quick shot at the goal.

free hit

When a foul is committed, a free hit is given to the opposite team, except when a foul is committed by the defense inside the circle. When a free hit is awarded in the circle, the ball may be placed anywhere inside the circle and is usually played by a back.

For a free hit outside the circle, the ball is placed on the spot where the foul occurred and is put into play by the defensive player in whose area the foul occurred. All other players must be 5 yards away. The ball must be motionless. The player taking the free hit can use any legal stroke, but after taking the free hit cannot play the ball again until it has been touched by another player. A free hit play should be made quickly before the opposing team can get set to meet it.

goalkeeping

The goalkeeper has many more skills to learn and acquire than any of the other players. He must be able not only to execute good stickwork, but to stop the ball with feet, legs, and hands. The goalie has the privilege of kicking the ball and may stop it with the flat hand but cannot bat it.

The goalie should take a position in front of the goal line, never on it. The goal line is an imaginary line from goalpost to goalpost with an extending semicircle about one yard out on the field. The goalie faces the attacking field with feet together and knees bent in readiness to shift to left or right. The feet or legs should be used to stop and clear the ball. The stick is used to clear only in an emergency. To clear is to get the ball out of area of the goal. The ball should be cleared with the inside of the foot and passed out to a back. At times the goalie has little time to clear. High-kicked balls in the path of onrushing forwards should be discouraged.

Should a forward dribble toward the goal alone, the goalie can rush out to meet the attacker as he enters the striker's circle. If a shot is going to miss the goal, the goalie should not touch it, but permit it to go over the end line.

TEAM STRATEGY

offensive play

The forward line players generally carry the brunt of the attack, although aggressive halfbacks are frequently in a position to score. All forwards should be expert dribblers, skilled and deceptive passers in either direction, and effective tacklers. Forwards should have a strong sense of position spacing on the field so as to avoid confusing teammates by being in the wrong area. Every forward line player should employ techniques of drawing that require dribbling in the direction in which the ball is not to be hit. Players should keep the ball until an attempted tackle is being initiated, otherwise a back on the opposing team is left free to disrupt subsequent play.

The *center forward* should be especially proficient in bullying in order to gain immediate advantage each time play is initiated at the center line. This position requires that a player move constantly in varying directions in order to evade the opposing center halfback and keep in the center of the field. Positions of other forward line players are generally assumed in relationship to the center forward.

The *inner forwards* should possess superior stick skill and be able to utilize varied passes effectively. A primary duty of the inners, other than shooting for the goal, is to direct the ball to the wings for advancement down the less crowded sides of the field.

The *wing forwards* should be exceptionally efficient dribblers and runners. The wings are seldom in a scoring position and usually center the ball near the 25-yard line with a pass directed ahead of the inners. There are times, however, when a speedy wing may elude a backfielder and maneuver into position for a scoring drive. Wing players must display unusual self-control in staying in position and must not be tempted to enter into play on the ball instead of remaining in the alleys where their performance is more effective. Wings must be able to drive powerfully and accurately both when dribbling at full speed and when taking corner hits.

defensive play

The backs should understand the theory of and be adept in guarding, or *marking* the opposing forward line players. The center halfback guards the center forward, the left halfback marks or guards the right wing, the right halfback marks the left wing, the left fullback guards the right inner, and the right fullback marks the left inner. Whenever possible, marking or guarding should be done from a position between the opponent and the goal and on the stick side where it is possible to reach the ball ahead of the other player.

Backfield players are responsible for disrupting the reception and execution of passes, stopping shots at the goal cage, and tackling aggressively. These players should anticipate and diagnose plays or shots and should move into action quickly either by threatening a tackle or by moving into a position that is favorable for intercepting a pass.

Both the left and the right halfbacks have the job of initiating play through roll-ins and free hits in their respective sections of the field. The center halfback is responsible for taking free hits in the center of the field.

In addition to marking closely, backfield players should be skilled at covering, interchanging, and backing up. These techniques are used in the diagonal system of defense that assures that at all times at least one player other than the goalkeeper remains between the attacking opponents and the goal.

Covering is a situation in which a defending player moves into position to intercept and to cover his own half of the field more adequately. Sometimes fullbacks and wing halfbacks play in a deeper defensive position in order to guard spaces through which a long pass may be directed.

Interchanging is a technique used when a player is unable to recover position after marking, backing up, or tackling unsuccessfully. A teammate moves to assume the responsibilities temporarily. Often all backfield players are affected by the initial interchange and must assume different position assignments. Beginners should learn to play their own position well, while advanced players should master the techniques of interchanging and covering. This is used largely when the forwards have moved down to, or behind the 25-yard line as the remaining defensive players cover to stop the advance.

Backing up is a maneuver by the backfield players used when teammates have set up a forward line in aggressive motion and when marking can be suspended. The fullback on the side of the field where play is not being directed should remain in a covering position between the goal and any attackers. The halfbacks play in a diagonal line and should follow closely behind their forward teammates in readiness to return a pass that has followed an opponent's successful tackle. These return passes should be directed to the center forward or the inners when retrieved in the vicinity of the 25-yard line, since it is less difficult to score from a central position. Wing players should be prepared to recover clearing drives that are near the goal line and to back up on the sides of the circle.

TEACHING PROCEDURE

Since students learn primarily by doing, class meetings should be active ones. Begin with dribbling relays, followed by hitting, first from a stationary and then a running position. Stickwork relays and simple games will make the learning of basic techniques easier, faster, and more enjoyable. Straight, zigzag, stopping and starting, circling to the right then to the left are formations suggested.

Practice in passing relays to both the right and the left while on the run and receiving the ball should follow the dribbling relays. Players should work in pairs for this, changing positions as they move up- and then downfield.

Each new skill presented should be demonstrated, analyzed, and then practiced. Demonstration by experts on film may be shown to give students a basic understanding of what the game is all about. After viewing the film, the class should review the skills already taught before advancing to more difficult ones. Films are excellent in teaching the duties of the forward line players and those of their defensive teammates.

Figure 9–6 shows a drill that may be used to develop the skills of passing and tackling. Both the Os and the Xs move as a unit. If the Xs can

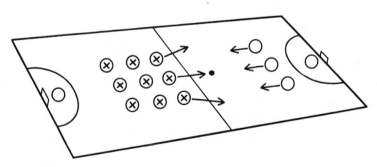

FIGURE 9-6 *Drill Formation for Passing and Tackling* (Adapted from Maryhelen Vannier and Hally Beth Poindexter, *Individual and Team Sports for Girls and Women.* © 1960, W.B. Saunders Company, by permission of the publisher.)

retain possession of the ball, they are to shoot for a goal when in the striking circle, and the Os are to do the same if they gain control and can successfully dribble the ball downfield.

Player positions and their duties should be stressed before actual play begins. This can be done by giving a chalk or magnetized board talk followed by having each team member stand in his chosen player position. The five forwards of one team stand on their side of the line facing the opposing forward line team. Next the defensive players from each team take their positions. It is a good idea to start the game with a bully, first by the wings on one side of the field and then the other, next by the inners, and finally by the centers. Every time the players get into groups the teacher should stop the game, re-stress positioning, and have each one stand where he can check his own position and see for himself if his team really is grouped together. Teach marking as soon as the class gains skill in moving the ball successfully up and down the field. Those individuals not playing in the game should be practicing skills on the sidelines so that they may gain mastery of the many techniques of the game.

SKILL TESTS

There are several tests that give an indication of ability in certain phases of the game. The results of these combined with a written test are adequate to establish grades.

running—dribbling test

Each student dribbles around obstacles over a set distance, and the score is the number of seconds elapsing from the time he starts until he returns.

ball control test

On a signal, each student dribbles forward to the left of the foul line until he reaches the restraining line, where he shoots the ball to the right of the first obstacle and runs around to the left of it to recover the ball. He then dribbles around the second obstacle, turns to the right to recover the ball, and then drives it back over the starting line (Figure 9–7).

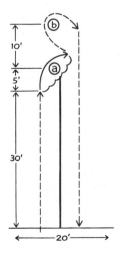

FIGURE 9-7 *Field Markings for the Ball Control Skill Test* (Adapted from Maryhelen Vannier and Hally Beth Poindexter, *Individual and Team Sports for Girls and Women.* © 1960, W.B. Saunders Company, by permission of the publisher.)

DEFINITION OF TERMS

Advancing. Moving the ball to one's advantage with any part of the body.

Alley. Area of the field between the side line and the 5-yard or alley line.

Backing Up. The assistance rendered by the backs to their own forwards.

Bully. Play used to start or restart the game. Opposing players alternately strike the ground and each other's stick three times before touching the ball.

Corner. The method of putting the ball back in play after the defending team has hit the ball over the end line, or made a foul in the circle.

Covering. Defensive anticipatory position much nearer the defending goal than the play (as opposed to marking). Usually refers to a fullback.

Dodge. Play used to evade an opponent while maintaining control of the ball.

Dribble. A series of short strokes used to move the ball downfield.

Drive. A forceful stroke used for shooting, clearing, and passing.

Fielding. Controlling an approaching ball before it is passed or played.

Flick. A wrist stroke in which the ball is lifted for close shooting or passing.

Foul. Infringement of rules, which results in a free hit, short corner, or penalty bully.

Long Corner. The play awarded to the attack after the ball goes over the end line unintentionally, off the stick of the defense. Stroke used in attempting to take the ball from an opponent.

Marking. Defensive position in which the player stays close to his opponent.

Off-side. The foul committed by a player receiving the ball while in an illegal defense.

Penalty Bully. Penalty following a serious breach of rules by the defense in the circle.

Roll-in. Method of putting the ball in play after it has gone over the sideline.

Scoop. Stroke without backswing in which the ball is lifted slightly with the toe of the stick.

Short Corner. The play awarded to the attack for a foul made by the defense inside the circle or when the defense intentionally hits the ball over the end line.

Stick Side. The player's right side. So called because the stick meets the ball on that side of the body.

Striking Circle. The goal-shooting area; the curved line that encloses it.

DISCUSSION QUESTIONS

1. Explain the following defensive tactics: (a) covering, (b) marking, (c) interchanging, and (d) intercepting.
2. Define the specific duties of a goalkeeper.
3. Describe the following: (a) the dribble, (b) the scoop, (c) the bully, and (d) the roll-in.
4. Explain the dodge and its use in the game.
5. Describe the difference between a long and a short corner.

BIBLIOGRAPHY

Delano, Anne Lee, *Field Hockey*. Dubuque, Iowa: William C. Brown Company, 1967.

Division for Girls' and Women's Sports, *Field Hockey—Lacrosse Guide*. Washington, D. C.: American Association for Health, Physical Education and Recreation.

Humiston, Dorothy, and Michel, Dorothy, *Fundamentals of Sports for Girls and Women*. New York: The Ronald Press Company, 1965.

Menke, Frank G., *The Encyclopedia of Sports*. New York: A. S. Barnes and Company, 1969.

Meyer, Margaret, and Schwarz, Marguerite, *Team Sports for Girls and Women*. Philadelphia: W. B. Saunders Company, 1965.

Mitchell, Elmer D., *Sports for Recreation*. New York: The Ronald Press, 1952.

The National Council of the Young Men's Christian Association of Canada, *Athletic Handbook*. Toronto: 1968.

Seaton, Don Cash; Clayton, Irene A.; Leibee, Howard C.; and Messersmith, Lloyd, *Physical Education Handbook*, 5th ed. Englewood Cliffs, N.J.: Prentice-Hall, Inc., 1969.

golf

10

BACKGROUND

There is some disagreement concerning the actual beginning of golf. A farfetched idea has the shepherds of 3,000 years ago knocking pebbles around with their crooked sticks. There are those who, because of a picture showing a native of Holland leaning against a stick, believe that the game originated in that country. The subsequent inactivity of Holland in the history of golf does not give credence to this theory.

The only positive evidence of the origin of the game places it in Scotland. There is a record of golf being played there as early as the fifteenth century, and it probably was played long before it became a matter of record. Golf became so popular in the middle of the fifteenth century that an official act of Parliament in 1457 forbade it because it took the people away from the practice of archery.

King James IV tried the game once and became so interested that he ignored the ban and continued to play. When the people found out, they started playing golf again, and the law against it was never enforced. Mary, Queen of Scots, also took up the game. It is believed that she is responsible for the term *caddie* as applied to the boys who chase the golf balls, because of the cadets who assisted her.

The famous St. Andrews course came into existence in 1754. Its name was changed to The Royal and Ancient Golf Club in 1834. Other clubs established were the Royal Blackheath Club in 1608, the Edinburgh Burgess Golfing Society in 1735, the Honourable Company of Edinburgh Golfers—now at Muerfield Links—in 1744, and the Aberdeen Golf Club in 1770.

These early organizations consisted of people interested in the game who joined together to promote and enjoy it. There were no clubhouses, nor were there any courses as we know them today. Golf was generally played over pieces of ground that linked tillable land to the seashore.

Because of a need for uniformity, a group met in 1754 at the St. Andrews Golf Club and drew up a set of rules to govern the game. Some of the rules then formulated apply to it today.

Golf courses were established in England in the middle of the nineteenth century. Two of the first courses were the Royal North Devon and the Royal Liverpool.

It is a good guess that the first object propelled by a golf stick was a stone or a rounded piece of wood. The first ball designed specifically for golf was a small, thin leather bag stuffed very tightly with feathers and sewn up. In 1848, a gutta-percha ball was used in place of the feather-stuffed ball because it could be hit farther and more accurately. The rubber-core ball came into use in 1902 and has been employed, with certain improvements, ever since.

The "Father of American Golf" is believed to have been John G. Reid. He had a set of golf clubs and balls delivered to him from Scotland and introduced the game on February 22, 1888, to a group of men in Yonkers. This led to the establishment of the St. Andrews Golf Club of Yonkers on November 14, 1888. Reid served as its president for nine years.

Women first began to be associated with the game when two ladies participated in a mixed foursome on March 30, 1889, at the new golf course of Yonkers.

The first United States open tournament was at the St. Andrews Club, in 1894. It was a match play tournament, and the next year it was changed to medal play.

As happens in most sports, groups felt the need to associate for the purpose of standardizing rules. A meeting was held on December 22, 1894. This group formed what was later to be known as the United States

Golf Association, which became the controlling body for amateur golf. More than 1,000 clubs are associated with the organization.

Throughout most of its history, golf was a game for the few in the upper economic levels of society. Today, people in nearly every walk of life play golf. This is probably the result of a tournament held in 1913 at Brookline, Massachusetts, when a young American and former *caddie*, Francis Ouimet, beat two of England's best golfers. The story of Ouimet appealed to people in such a way that interest in golf increased from that day on.

BASIC SKILLS

Contrary to the opinion of those who have never tried the game, golf requires many integrated skills. There is much to be learned regarding the stance and the basic swing. There is a difference between the method one would use to hit a drive, make an approach shot, or hit a ball in a sand trap. Golf presents a challenge to the beginner, who learns immediately that the game is not as easy as it appears. Though there can be, with regular practice, a steady improvement in skills, there will be times when even the veteran golfer will do many things wrong. Speed of swing, accuracy in movement, relaxation, coordination, sound judgment, and endurance are only a few of the factors that are necessary to successful golf. Probably more than in any other sport, the real guides to success in golf, above and beyond those factors already mentioned, are good instruction and practice. Many hours must be spent on each phase of the game in order to approach perfection, though a fair game can be developed in the normal recreation time of the average businessman.

In modern golf, the basic grip and the power put into the swing are about the same for most shots. The construction of the club determines how far the ball will travel. There are, however, a few shots about which this is not true, and they will be discussed separately. Generally, the longer the shot to be made, the more perpendicular the face of the club and the longer the shaft.

In order for a person to become skilled in the various shots, consideration must be given to the grip, the address, and the hand and wrist movement.

the grip

The way in which a club is held is important because the grip must be able to transfer the power of the body and wrist to the club. How a person improves in golf depends very much upon his ability to do the same thing every time. Therefore, the grip should be taken correctly at the outset and practiced until it is performed correctly each time a club is picked up. For most strokes, the club is gripped near the top of the shaft by the left hand. To begin a grip correctly, the golfer places the club head on the ground. Assuming the golfer is right-handed, the left hand is placed on the shaft with the left forefinger making contact with the shaft between the first and second joints. The club then rests diagonally across the palm of the left hand with the end of the club shaft ending just beyond the heel of the left hand. The palm of the left hand must be kept in contact with the club shaft. The fingers should be wrapped around the shaft with the thumb pointing straight down the shaft slightly to the right of center, so that the "V" formed by the thumb and forefinger should point to the right shoulder.

The right hand is then placed below the left, with the center of the palm resting over the thumb of the left hand. The right hand grips the club primarily with the fingers. The thumb of the right hand is slightly to the left of center, ending just below the forefinger. The little finger of the right hand overlaps the index finger of the left hand if the overlapping grip is used. Many golfers prefer the interlocking grip, with the little finger of the right hand interlocking with the forefinger of the left hand. The "V" formed by the right thumb and forefinger should also point toward the right shoulder (Figure 10–1).

ADDRESS POSITIONS

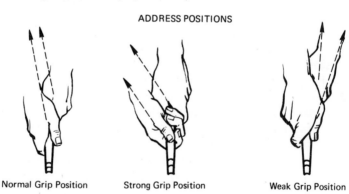

Normal Grip Position   Strong Grip Position   Weak Grip Position

FIGURE 10-1 *The Grip* (From Gary Wiren, *Golf.* © 1971, Prentice-Hall, Inc. Reproduced by permission of the publisher.)

the stance, or address

The stance discussed will be the square, or basic stance. There are variations, some of which will be pointed out at the end of this discussion. Positions of feet, legs, shoulders, head, and arms are all important in the swing, and each must be carefully considered. The feet should be firmly set on the turf about 18 inches apart. It is suggested that they be about as wide apart as the shoulders. Their position should be comfortable and provide body balance. Too great a width can interfere with the effectiveness of the pivot. The knees are flexed just enough to allow for relaxation and movement, but they should not be bent. The trunk should face the ball and should be flexed at the hips to allow the arms freedom of movement when swinging. The head should face the ball directly. The golfer should not "reach" for the ball, but should step to get the correct distance from it (Figure 10–2). "Reaching" tends to create an

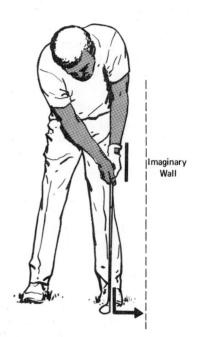

Imaginary Wall

FIGURE 10-2 *The Stance* (From Gary Wiren, *Golf*. © 1971, Prentice-Hall, Inc. Reproduced by permission of the publisher.)

awkward stance and results in an inaccurate swing. The ball should be directly in front of the center line of the body or just enough to the left to allow the club shaft, when addressing the ball, to come from the body at a 90-degree angle to a line from toe to toe.

The beginning golfer should make all his shots for distance from this stance until he has a very smooth swing and hits a good, solid drive. After this point is reached, he may begin to study variations of the swing and try them for effectiveness. The closed stance is made by dropping the right foot slightly back. This stance may enable easier pivoting and as a result allow more power in the swing. The open stance is made by dropping the left foot back about 3 inches from the line of flight. This may cause a desired slice, and it is a better position for short iron shots and for pitch and chip shots.

There is always a requirement for consistency in the stance. The player should assume a good stance every time an address is made. With minor exceptions, he should make sure that his body position is the same at the contact of the ball on a swing as it is at the address.

the hand and wrist movement

Wrists must be strong and flexible since the power of the body and the shoulders is transferred through them. The wrists also serve to develop some power on the break. If done properly and timed correctly, this will double the distance possible by arm and shoulder power alone. Well-coordinated movement requires much practice. Wrist movement is brought about by cocking, or flexing, the wrists in such a way on the backswing that the thumb is much nearer the elbow than it is in a normal position. On the downswing, the wrists begin to straighten, or snap, when they are about waist-high. This causes the club head to move much faster than the normal swing of the arms could make it move.

The fingers and hands should be flexible enough to make any movement required by the swing or the snap, but in general, they should not move to any great extent.

the clubs

Another factor in golf that contributes greatly to success is the correct selection of a club with which to execute a shot. The following list indicates a fairly complete set of clubs and the distances one may expect on well-executed shots:

Woods:	No. 1	driver	225 to 300 yards plus
	No. 2*	brassie	200 to 275 yards plus
	No. 3	spoon	180 to 240 yards plus
	No. 4	spoon	170 to 215 yards plus
Irons:	No. 2		160 to 180 yards
	No. 3*		150 to 170 yards
	No. 4		140 to 160 yards
	No. 5*		130 to 150 yards
	No. 6		120 to 140 yards
	No. 7*		
	No. 8		From 20 to 110 yards depending
	No. 9*		on type of shot
	Putter*		
	Wedge		

*These clubs are suggested for the beginner.

The lower the number of the club, the longer the handle and the more perpendicular the club face. The greater slanting of the club face—a characteristic of the clubs with higher numbers, such as 7, 8, and 9—gives loft and backspin to the ball and results in less distance. The choice of which club to use on a stroke depends upon the distance to be achieved, the obstacles such as traps and hills to be surmounted, and the action one wants from the ball after it hits the ground—a roll or a quick stop.

the swing

A golf swing is rather like the movement of a wagon wheel. The golfer's head represents the hub. As a wheel spins on its axle, the hub makes no vertical or horizontal motion. Likewise, in a golf swing the head should make a minimum of motion. However a good swing may be made even if the head moves slightly in the line of flight. The arms and the golf club represent one of the spokes of a wheel, and circle evenly about the head in such a manner as to cause the club head to return to the ball on the downswing exactly as it left it on the upswing. The main difference in motion between the two is that the spoke is attached directly and, if the hub remains stationary, it can do nothing but return directly to the spot from which it left. The club head, in contrast, is not attached directly to the head but is separated by many flexible joints, including hands, wrists, elbows, shoulders, and neck. Coordination of the flexible factors in the swing in such a way as to minimize unnecessary motion and the ability to perform the same each time will ensure that the club head will return to hit the ball at the same spot from which it started.

In making a swing, one assumes what he believes to be good stance in addressing the ball. From there, the golfer starts the backswing. The body weight begins to shift to the right leg, and by the time the backswing is complete, the weight is almost entirely transferred. During this shift, the right leg is straight and the left leg bends slightly at the knee. When the hands reach a position about hip-high during the swing, the wrists flex into the cocked position. Care should be taken that the wrists do not overflex or become wobbly and allow the club head to get off the circular course. During the entire backswing, the left arm is the guide—the main part of the spoke—and should be kept perfectly straight. When the left arm has gone as far as it can without bending at the elbow, the swing stops and the club is immediately started on its return to the ball. When the hands get back to waist height, the wrists begin to snap so that when the club head reaches the ball, the wrists are straight, and the club is in line with the length of the left arm. As the downswing takes place, the body weight gradually changes so that at the moment the ball is contacted, it is evenly distributed between the two legs. On the upswing, after the ball has been hit, the weight is shifted to the left leg by a bending of the right leg and a straightening of the left. The swing does not

FIGURE 10-3 *The Swing* (From Gary Wiren, *Golf.* ©
1971, Prentice-Hall, Inc. Reproduced by permission of the
publisher.)

stop there but goes on through to a point at the end of the backswing
(Figure 10–3).

It is essential that the eyes look constantly at the ball. The head should
be down and as motionless as possible. It is good to insist that the student
of golf complete the swing circle before he looks up to see where the ball
is going. This should prevent him from raising his head too soon.

the approach

The approach is the act of getting up on the green. Even though a
180-yard, No. 2 iron shot may put the ball on a green, this is not termed
an approach. An approach involves a shot of approximately 50 yards or
less, by which the ball is lofted into the air in such a way as to land on
the green and stay fairly close to where it hit. This type of shot is generally made with a short club that has a greatly slanted head. A few
approach shots are made with a No. 3 or 4 iron, though most of them are
made with a No. 6, 7, 8, or 9 iron. Backspin is put on the ball in this type
of shot, and this causes the ball to stop reasonably close to where it hits.
The stance on an approach shot is somewhat different from that used
on the drives and longer iron shots. The feet are closer together, and
because the clubs are shorter and less power is needed, the body is bent
forward at the hips to a greater extent. The swing is not as wide an arc as
that used in longer shots, and less force is put into it.

pitch shot

For a pitch shot, the feet should be within about a foot of the ball and
closer together than for a regular drive. The left foot should be slightly
back from the line of drive to make the stance open. The weight is chiefly

on the left foot but changes rapidly to the right and back to the left as the swing goes through all its points. The arms swing so little that they describe an arc of less than 15 inches at the wrists. The wrists break almost immediately after the start of the swing. The left arm is kept absolutely straight, and the right bends slightly to bring the elbow in to the body. The hip turns to the right at the beginning of the swing. On the downswing, the wrists begin a slight break. They then go on slightly beyond a point above the ball and complete their snap. The body weight shifts almost completely to the left foot, and the club follows through its circle to a point above the horizontal (Figure 10–4).

FIGURE 10-4 *Pitch Shot* (From Gary Wiren, *Golf*. © 1971, Prentice-Hall, Inc. Reproduced by permission of the publisher.)

chip shot

This shot is used at a closer range to the green than the pitch. It is for less distance, so the factors involved in making it are changed accordingly. Briefly stated, the chip is nothing more than a wrist-action swing of the club. The stance is open, the feet are 3 or 4 inches apart, and the knees are flexed. The arms are close to the body, right elbow on hip, and the back is bent only enough for the hands to get to the club. The ball is about 6 inches in front and slightly to the right of the left foot. The center of the hub on this shot is the wrists. In swinging down into the ball, the hands should be moved slightly so that they will be ahead of the ball when contact is made. Since there is only a small arc in the swing, there is very little follow-through, and the club head stays fairly close to the grass.

bunker shot

The bunker shot is a method of getting out of a sand trap. It is different from the ordinary shot because the club head hits the sand behind the ball rather than the ball itself. It is preferable to make the shot with a heavy club, but the beginning golfer who does not have a wide choice of clubs may use another, such as a No. 7, 8, or 9 iron, nearly as well. The club made specifically for the purpose of getting out of sand traps is the sand wedge.

The same stance is taken on the bunker shot as on regular shots except that it is open and the hips are turned slightly to the left. The feet must be firmly placed in the loose sand. The ball is about 12 inches in front of and just inside the left toe. During the address the club head cannot come to rest on or even touch the sand. Because of this, the aim must be at a spot about an inch back of the ball so that sand will be picked up, thus slowing the club head down. The actual shot is made as previously described.

putting

This stroke is a method of applying force to a ball to cause it to roll along a green toward the cup. It is quite different from the other strokes in its excution. Consideration must also be given to the factors that may affect the course of the ball along the grass. It must be remembered that every golfer has his own style of putting. Though a style employed by one golfer may be entirely different from that used by another, both may be equally effective in getting the ball in the cup. The accompanying description is meant only as a guide to start beginners putting effectively. What the player will do later depends upon what he finds most effective for him in successful putting.

The putting grip is slightly different from that used for other strokes. It is more open—that is, the four fingers are farther apart. The index finger of the left hand overlaps the little finger of the right hand in what is known as the reverse grip. The fingers of the right hand grip the club and the left hand has much of the palm in contact with the shaft near the end. The right hand controls the movement of the club and provides much of the force. The club movement is a complete wrist-break movement, and the arms do not swing at all. The stance for putting begins with the feet comfortably apart and the left foot slightly back of a line extending from the ball to the cup. Knees are bent slightly, and most of the body weight is carried by the left foot. The foot position is taken in such a way that the ball is a few inches in front of the feet and nearer the left side than the right. The hips are flexed to give room for the arms to be placed comfortably in front of the body. The club head is placed back of the ball in such a position that it is square with the cup. All movements of the club head should be in line with the direction the ball is to take. The club should not form an arc in the swing but should travel in a straight line about parallel with the green.

The ball should be hit squarely, with no effort made to put any sort of spin on it. The follow-through is of great importance and should be longer than the backstroke.

Every putt should be made with extreme caution and only after a deliberate examination of the green surface for objects that might affect the movement of the ball. In this examination, the golfer also checks the green to determine its slopes and the grain of the grass. Greens are purposely not level, and because gravity will have an effect on the movement of the ball on most parts of the green, these must be checked carefully and allowances must be made. A ball travels faster with the grain of the grass than against it. The shiny side of the grass is with the grain, and if the ball is hit toward it, the stroke should be easier than if against it.

TIPS ON THE GOLF SWING

1. Do not rush the backswing: allow a slight pause at the top of it.

2. Keep grip firm but not rigid.

3. Keep the right elbow close to the side.

4. Keep the left arm straight.

5. Do not separate the hands at the top of the backswing.

6. Keep the head motionless at all times during the swing.

7. Do not allow the body to sway.

8. Do not try to lengthen the arc of the swing unless muscular flexibility, age, weight, and sight give the athletic ability to do so.

9. Shift weight to the back foot on the backswing and then to the left foot on the foreswing.

10. Keep the knee farthest from the target as straight as possible to insure the best rotation of the hips.

11. Keep club head square to the line of flight at impact by keeping the lower hand directly under the upper hand and in a straight line to the ball at the time of impact.

12. Keep the club head in the line of flight as long as possible after the impact.

TYPES OF GOLF COMPETITION

There are two basic types of competition authorized by the rules, match play and stroke play. There are several varieties of play utilizing elements of one or the other of these.

match play

Each hole is a separate competitive unit. The one winning the most holes is the winner of the match. In match play, not all the holes need be played if the man ahead leads by more holes than remain to be played. The name "bye" is given those holes not played.

stroke play

This is a type of competition in which the winner is determined by the number of strokes required to complete a designated number of holes. Any number of golfers may compete.

medal play

Medal play is a form of stroke competition generally utilized for determining the brackets in which to place golfers in an elimination tournament. The lowest scorer is known as the medalist, and all the golfers are arranged in flights according to their scores. This enables golfers to compete with others in their own class.

types of matches

Match play may be divided into combinations such as single, threesome, three-ball, foursome, and four-ball play. Two persons make up a single match. Three persons competing against each other, each playing a single ball, are known as a three-ball match. If one person playing one ball plays against a pair playing a single ball between them, it is known as a threesome. A four-ball match takes place when two persons playing a ball each team up against another couple doing the same. A foursome takes place when two people on the same side play alternately with a single ball against another couple also playing alternately.

TEACHING PROCEDURE

An ideal teaching situation requires enough open space near the school to permit the use of regulation golf balls. "Shag" balls can usually be purchased cheaply from pro shops at golf courses. Two or three hundred of these balls should be provided for practice. For best results a golf class should be restricted to fifteen students or fewer. The first two or three class periods should be devoted to instruction in the fundamental skills of the golf swing with the use of plastic or similar type practice balls. Each student should have at least one iron for practice. The irons provided by the school should be assorted so that the students may exchange clubs from time to time. Whenever possible students should use their own clubs.

During practice sessions students should line up adjacent to each other about 10 feet apart for safety. Each student should then proceed to hit ten balls. After each one has hit that number, the entire group can retrieve their balls and return to continue this type of practice until class time expires. The instructor should move from student to student giving advice. As the class improves their skills, targets may be set up for accuracy practice. Students also should practice on the short game. This can be done by drawing a circle on the field approximately the size of a green, where they can practice chipping and pitching. If the practice area is large enough, the students may also practice with woods. If the area is only large enough for iron shots, arrangements may be made to use woods on a driving range or the practice area on a golf course. The class should have access also to a practice putting green if possible. Near the conclusion of the unit, it would be ideal if the instructor could take the class to a golf course for their first round of golf.

Since most schools do not have sufficient area for the use of regular golf balls and many schools do not have funds to purchase golf equipment, an alternate suggestion is proposed. The school could furnish a few clubs, with the instructor providing some of his old ones, and the students could bring a variety of clubs from home for each class. The school could furnish a few regulation golf balls for putting practice and several dozen soft composition practice balls. Composition balls react to club strokes in much the same way as a golf ball but do not travel far and are comparatively inexpensive. There should be a golf course in the community where the students may test out skills learned during class time. Stance, grip, basic strokes, and other phases of the game can be taught in the class, and the students can play at the local course in the afternoons or on week-ends. Most golf clubs will allow a class undergoing instruction to play at reduced fees. The teacher should make the necessary arrangements with the local group.

class organization

The students should practice in pairs, since part of the training should be the recognition of faults in their partners and the lending of assistance in correcting them. The class is lined up, either in a straight line or in a semicircle, with partners facing each other and their sides turned toward the instructor. The teacher demonstrates a skill, analyzes it, and then allows one of each of the pairs to practice on it at first while the other partner observes. No regulation or practice golf balls are used during the first two or three class meetings, for it is extremely important to have the students concentrate completely on the body movements rather than on the ball.

After the skills of driving are covered thoroughly and the teacher believes fundamental movement has been reasonably well mastered, the students are provided with plastic golf balls and are allowed to hit them, working with partners as before. Such a routine should be employed with all the strokes. Always, during instruction and drill, one of the partners should hit the ball while the other checks him. After several weeks of this basic instruction, some sort of stroking game using the composition balls should be set up so that the class may be allowed to have some experience in what a golf game is like.

The most important phase of a game of golf is a good swing, and much time and effort must be spent with golfers to develop this skill to as high a degree as possible in the time allotted. There are many methods by which a smooth swing may be developed, and the class should have a great deal of practice in each of them.

THE WEIGHTED HANDKERCHIEF SWING. One of the two partners should tie a stone or other heavy object in one corner of his handkerchief. He should then assume a good driving stance and hold the opposite corner of the handkerchief as if he were gripping a club handle. The handkerchief then hangs from the hands in much the same way as a club handle would extend downward. The student should then begin a swing, the path of the hands being the same as it would be for driving a golf ball except that instead of a single backswing and drive, the movement is continuous, like the swing of a pendulum. At first, the hands will get ahead of the line of the weight. The object of the swinging is to do it so smoothly and with such coordination that the extended handkerchief will be in a direct line with the head. When the golfer can do such a drill smoothly, he is ready to proceed to another drill.

THE HELD-CLUB SWING. The right hand should grasp the club shaft near the head and the left hand near the butt. The stance is taken, and the arms are allowed to hang downward from the shoulders. The golfer then begins a pendulum-like swing in the path his hands would take when driving, and this time he emphasizes the rotation of the shoulders. The head should be kept perfectly still.

HOLDING THE HEAD STEADY. It has been emphasized that the golfer's head plays much the same part in the golf swing as the hub plays in the turn of a wheel, and that it should be kept as nearly still as possible. This is very important, and special attention needs to be given to this aspect of the swing. After the student has been given instruction and practice on the swing, he should have his attention called to his head movement. This can be done by having the golfer get in a stance while his partner faces him and steadies his head with an extended hand, palm toward head. In this way the head is held absolutely still while the swing is being made, and the golfer can check his tendency to move his head by feeling the resistance against his partner's hand when the head starts to move away from a set position.

SAFETY FACTORS. Golf can be a dangerous sport. In a large group there is danger both from the club heads during a swing and from golf balls in flight. Class formation and drills should be conducted in such a way as to insure that no students are in the path of swinging clubs or balls in flight. Use of plastic or soft cotton golf balls for driving in restricted areas will increase safety. It will also minimize ball retrieval, so that a major portion of class time may be spent on the skills.

suggested grading methods

1. Written tests that include fundamental techniques, rules, terminology, and golf etiquette.

2. Consideration of interest and general attitude toward the class.

3. Skill tests as suggested below.

SKILL TESTS

If golf is taught as a part of a physical education class, grades will, in all probability, have to be established for each of the students. These should be objective, based on tests that should determine what the participant actually can do in terms of the objectives of the unit on golf. Several tests may be given which, when the results are totaled, should give a fair indication of the student's ability in the game and of how he compares with the other members of the class. These tests should measure the skills involved in such a way that a point value can be established on each competency.

driving

A measure of golfing ability is the distance and accuracy of a drive.
A fairway or open space may be marked off either by lines or stakes. Cross
lines should be drawn 10 yards apart to indicate the distance of the drive.
Since drives should go at least 150 yards, the lines may begin at that point
and continue up to about 280 yards. Lanes should be indicated along the
length of the fairway. The center of the fairway should be 10 yards wide
and designated as Zone 1. There should be a Zone 2 on either side of Zone
1, each 5 yards wide, and a Zone 3 on the outside of each Zone 2, also 5
yards wide. The side zones are marked to indicate how far off-center the
ball hits, so that a golfer may be penalized for a hook, a slice, or an otherwise misdirected drive. If the ball hits in Zone 1, the golfer's score is the
total distance of the drive. If it hits in Zone 2, 10 yards are subtracted
from the score. If it hits in Zone 3, 20 yards are subtracted. If the ball hits
outside Zone 3, 30 yards are subtracted. The golfer gets three attempts to
score on driving. The test should indicate a good drive on the basis of
distance and accuracy (Figure 10–5).

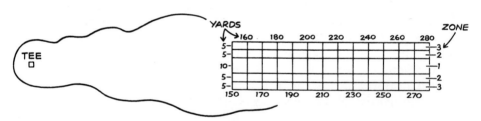

FIGURE 10-5   *Golf Driving Test*

approaching

A series of circles may be marked on the grass. The outside circle
should have a radius of 10 feet and the others radii of 8, 6, 4, and 2 feet
respectively. The inner circle should have a point value of nine and the
others of seven, five, three, and finally one for the outside circle. The

FIGURE 10-6   *Approach Test*

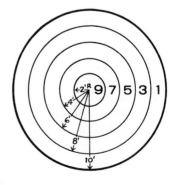

golfer stands at a point 50 feet away from the center of the circles and chips or pitches to the center. His score is the number of points he makes on three approaches (Figure 10–6).

putting

A series of circles similar to those for testing the approach should be set up on a green or a smooth, hard surface for the putt. The center circle should have a radius of 2 inches, and the radii of the other circles should be 6, 10, 14, and 18 inches, in that order. The cup on a green could be the center circle, and the other circles could, of course, surround it. The putter stands at a spot 15 feet away and putts to the circles. His score is the total number of points he makes on three attempts (Figure 10–7).

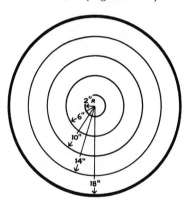

FIGURE 10-7 *Putting Test*

playing a course

If a course is available to the members of the class, they may play eighteen, twenty-seven, thirty-six, or any other number of holes for a score. Since the principal objective of golf is the improvement of the student's ability to play, the score in several holes is a good indication of his ability.

playing a modified course

It is entirely possible that a golf course may not be available to all members of the class. If this is true, a substitute may be used. A hole the size of a cup may be dug at either end of a 100-yard or longer strip of ground. Using cotton or plastic golf balls, the students may play the course by going down and back as many times as the instructor thinks necessary for a valid score. The student's score is the number of strokes he takes to go over the specified number of holes.

DEFINITION OF TERMS

Ace. A hole in one stroke.

Addressing the Ball. The position assumed prior to hitting the ball.

Approach. The shot made from the fairway to the green.

Backswing. The swinging of the club preparatory to the forward drive.

Birdie. The score for a hole played in one stroke under par.

Bogey. The score for a hole played in one stroke above par.

Brassie. The No. 2 wood, so named because it has a brass sole.

Caddie. A boy who assists the player by carrying his clubs and aiding in locating the ball.

Carry. The distance a driven ball travels in the air.

Casual Water. Any temporary water hazard.

Chip Shot. A short approach shot to the green.

Club. An implement used for propelling golf balls.

Course. The area over which golf is played.

Cup. A round hole, $4\frac{1}{4}$ inches in diameter and at least 4 inches deep, located on the green for the ball to fall in.

Disqualification. To remove a player from competition because of an infraction of the rules.

Divot. Turf cut from the fairway by a club head.

Dog-leg. A hole that has a curved fairway leading to it.

Dormie. A term applied to a situation in which the lead of a golfer in match play is equal to the number of holes remaining to be played.

Double Eagle. The score for a hole played in three strokes under par.

Draw. To pull a drive.

Drive. The name applied to the first shot taken for a hole.

Driver. A club that has a long shaft and a wood head. It is used to achieve the greatest carry.

Driving Range. A practice field for driving.

Drop. To roll the ball into the cup.

Dropped Ball. A ball that is dropped by a participant. This is a specific action provided for by the rules in certain situations.

Eagle. A hole completed in two under par.

Even. The situation in which the players have won an equal number of holes.

Face. The front of the club head, which is used to contact the ball.

Fairway. The area between the tee and the putting green.

"Fore". An alarm shouted to warn players who may be in the path of the ball.

Four-ball Match. A match in which partners score their best ball against the best one of two other players.

Green. The smooth area of a golf course, where the putting is done. This area usually extends for 20 yards around the hole.

Grip. The manner of holding the club.

Gross. This term is used in handicap medal play. It is the total score before the handicap is deducted.

Halved. Completing a hole in the same number of strokes as an opponent.

Handicap. A certain score given players, who may subtract this number from the gross score in a handicap tournament.

Hanging Lie. A lie on a downward slope.

Head. Bottom portion of a golf club.

Hole. The cup, located somewhere on the green.

Hole-out. To sink the ball into the cup on the final stroke.

Honor. The right to drive off the tee first, attained by a toss of coin or by having made the smallest number of strokes on the preceding hole.

Hook. A ball that curves to the left when driven by a right-handed golfer.

Iron. A club having an iron head.

Lie. The position of the ball when it stops rolling.

Loft. To stroke a ball very high into the air.

Long Game. The term applied to a player who has the ability to drive consistently for great distance.

Long Iron. An iron with a long shaft; used to get long, low drives.

Match Play. Play where the number of holes won decides the winner.

Medalist. The player with the lowest score on the qualifying rounds.

Medal Play. Competition where the player who has lowest number of strokes for a number of holes specified beforehand is declared the winner.

Mixed Foursome. A female and a male player on each team of a foursome.

Natural Grip. A grip made in such a way that there is no interlocking or overlapping of the fingers. It is commonly called a "baseball grip."

Nassau. A system of scoring based on three points. One point is awarded to the winner of the first nine, one to the winner of the second nine, and one to the winner for the entire eighteen holes.

Out-of-bounds. Ground not prescribed as the golf course, on which play is prohibited.

Par. The number of strokes assigned to each hole required to hole out as determined by a plan of the course.

Penalty. Addition of an extra stroke or strokes to a score.

Pitch Shot. A ball stroked in such a manner as to loft and give it backspin.

Play Through. To pass players who are in front on the course.

Provisional Ball. A second ball played after the first ball is presumed to be lost or out-of-bounds.

Pull. The flight pattern of a ball traveling in a straight line but off to the left of the target for a right-handed player, or off to the right of the target for a left-handed player.

Push. The flight pattern of a ball travelling in a straight line, but off to the right of the target for a right-handed player, or off to the left of the target for a left-handed player.

Putt. To stroke the ball on the green toward the cup.

Putter. A short-shafted club with a straight face, used for putting. A person who putts.

Rough. The unmowed grassy area on either side of the fairway.

Round. Eighteen holes of golf.

Sand-blaster, Sand-wedge. A heavy iron club used to pitch out of sand traps.

Sand trap. An area that has been dug out and filled with sand.

Sink. The act of putting the ball into the cup.

Slice. A ball hit by a right-handed person that curves to the right of a straight line of flight.

Sole. The bottom of the club head.

Tee. A small wooden spike on which the ball is placed for driving. A piece of ground designated as the spot from which to make a drive to the next hole.

Teeing Off. The first shot made when playing for a hole.

Threesome. A group of three players in which one player plays a ball and competes against a pair playing a single ball between them.

Up. A term used to indicate that a player is leading in holes in match play.
Waggle. The movements of the club used for balance before hitting the ball.
Whisker. A type of handicap play in which the player driving nearest to the pin from tee is awarded one point.

DISCUSSION QUESTIONS

1. Discuss the early history of golf.
2. What factors are necessary for execution of the basic skills in golf? Please discuss each factor.
3. What are some of the factors involved in good golf play?
4. What is meant in golf by the term address?
5. Why is wrist-break, or snap, important?
6. What has the shape of a club and the length of its handle to do with the distance and elevation of a shot?
7. Explain a good stance for driving, for putting.

BIBLIOGRAPHY

Americana Corporation, *Encyclopedia Americana,* Vol. 13. New York: Americana Corporation, 1949.

Casper, Billy, *Golf Shotmaking.* Garden City, New York: Doubleday and Company, 1966.

Cummings, Parke, *The Dictionary of Sports.* New York: A. S. Barnes & Company, 1949.

Hogan, Ben, *Power Golf.* New York: A. S. Barnes & Company, 1948.

Jones, Ernest, and Brown, Innis, *Swinging into Golf.* New York: McGraw-Hill Book Company, Inc., 1937.

Middlecoff, Gary, *Master Guide to Golf.* Englewood Cliffs, N.J.: Prentice-Hall, Inc., 1962.

Morrison, Alex. J., *A New Way to Better Golf.* New York: Simon and Schuster, Inc., 1938.

National Golf Foundation, *Golf Lessons.* Chicago: National Golf Foundation, 1965.

Nelson, Byron, *Winning Golf.* New York: A. S. Barnes & Company, 1946.

Nicklaus, Jack, *My 55 Ways to Lower Your Golf Score.* New York: Simon and Shuster, Inc., 1964.

Ouimet, Francis, *The Rules of Golf.* Garden City, New York: Garden City Publishing Company, Inc., 1948.

Player, Gary, *Gary Player's Golf Secrets.* Englewood Cliffs, N.J.: Prentice-Hall, Inc., 1962.

Revolta, Johnny, *Johnny Revolta's Short Cuts to Better Golf.* New York: Thomas Y. Crowell Company, 1949.

Sarazen, Gene, and Snead, Sam, *et al., The Golf Clinic.* Englewood Cliffs, N.J.: Prentice-Hall, Inc., 1949.

Turnesa, Jim, *12 Lessons to Better Golf.* Englewood Cliffs, N.J.: Prentice-Hall, Inc., 1953.

Zaharias, Mildred Didrickson, *Championship Golf.* New York: A. S. Barnes & Company, 1948.

handball

![grey horizontal bar]

11

BACKGROUND

The game of handball originated in Ireland during the tenth century and is believed to have been the basis for the game of tennis. It is assumed that the game originally was played by simply hitting a ball against an outside wall. Later, when the possibilities inherent in four walls were recognized, people started playing handball indoors.

The earliest known name for the game was *fives*, after the five fingers of each hand. Since much of the striking was subsequently done with the palm of the hand, the name evolved quite naturally to the present one, *handball*.

Interest developed in the game about the middle of the nineteenth century when an Irishman named Meham Baggs realized it was possible to put spin on the ball and make it rather difficult for an opponent to return. He became skilled enough to curve the ball in almost any direction he desired. This challenged his opponents to develop the same ability and, as a result, there was a general improvement in the sophistication of the game and an accompanying increase in interest.

There were many great players in Ireland, including John Cavanaugh, David Browning, John Lawler, and Phil Casey. Casey came to America in the 1880s and became a very popular teacher. Handball interest mushroomed as his pupils spread enthusiasm for it, and courts were built or the outside walls of buildings were used. Firemen played the game to get exercise and to help pass the time at the stations.

About 1888, Bernard McQuade moved to America and challenged Casey to a game to determine the champion handball player of America. Casey defeated his fellow Irishman handily and then challenged John Lawler for the world championship. The first man to win eleven games would be declared the champion and the winner of $1,000. The match was arranged in such a way that ten games were to be played in Ireland and, if necessary to determine the champion, eleven in the United States. Casey was losing, 4–6, after the first series of games in Ireland. When the scene of the contest shifted to the smaller American courts, Casey won seven straight games and the title. That match was one of the few professional contests ever held. Handball is generally played only on the amateur level.

Handball rules and courts were standardized by the Amateur Athletic Union (Figure 11–1). In 1897, a tournament was conducted by the A.A.U., and Michael Eagan was crowned the first champion. At this time, handball was primarily played in four-wall courts. As interest developed and four-wall courts became less available, people returned to the one-wall game. It was not long until schools, public recreation places, and private homes had handball courts. The A.A.U. began sponsoring both one-wall and four-wall tournaments. One-wall handball was so popular in New York City that at one time an estimate indicated more than 1,000 courts were in use there.

The game was first played with a hard ball somewhat similar to a modern softball; it was covered with leather and tightly stuffed. Eventually a smaller and much faster hollow rubber ball was adopted, and it still is used today. As the game changed with the advent of the hard rubber ball, players began using gloves to protect their hands and to give better control in placing shots.

Even though handball is more interesting when played using four walls, it is possible to play a challenging one-wall game. Many schools do not have four-wall facilities, but they usually have a smooth wall and playing area free of obstruction so that the game can still be a part of the physical education program.

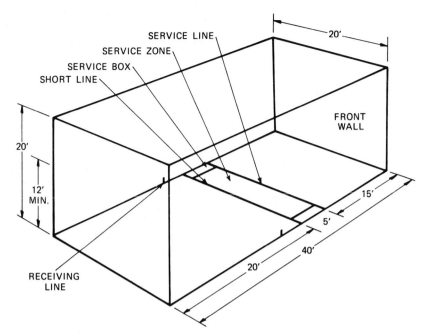

FIGURE 11-1 *Handball Court* (From Richard C. Nelson and Harlan S. Berger, *Handball*, © 1971, Prentice-Hall, Inc. Reproduced by permission of the publisher.)

BASIC SKILLS

Handball is an extremely fast game, employing a great variety of body movements. There are quick stops, turns, and returns; and the ball may be hit in a number of ways. Strategy plays a major role. The game requires considerable energy and top physical condition. It is considered an excellent sport for maintaining good conditioning because it can be played indoors with a minimum expenditure of time.

The rules permit the use of either the hand or the fist, and if a person is to become a successful handball player, he must perfect the skills not only with the right hand but also with the left.

the stance

In order to play a successful game of handball, a player must be in a position from which he can move quickly in any direction, turn his body, and shift his arms so that he can hit the ball with maximum efficiency and control.

Generally, the best court placement for a stance is just back of the short line in the middle of the court, though on many occasions the player will have to play from other initial positions. The handball player faces the front wall, feet about 18 inches apart, with one foot 3 to 4 inches back of the other. The weight of the body is evenly distributed on the feet with slight flexion of both the knee and hip joints. The arms are relaxed, flexed at the elbows, and extended outward in such a way as to cause the hands to be about 12 inches from the hips.

hand position

The position of the fingers and the hand is important in propelling the ball to best advantage. There are three basic placements, depending on what the player is attempting to do with the ball.

CUPPED HAND.   In any hand position, it is important that the fingers be together and the thumb close to the index finger. The cupped hand is employed during most shots. Such placing allows more control of the ball and seems to be more natural than the others. The fingers are flexed slightly so that the hand has a half-moon shape. At contact, the hand and finger muscles contract to give the necessary resistance for changing the flight of the ball and to prevent it from going past the fingers.

FLAT HAND.   The fingers and thumb are perfectly straight, giving a flat surface for contact with the ball. This shot is used to send the ball directly back to the front wall with a minimum of spin. Though spin can be applied with the hand in this position, it is preferable to use the cupped hand for spin shots. The flat hand can be used on all strokes, but it is generally most useful on the underhand stroke from midcourt to the front wall.

FIST.   The fingers are flexed to make a fist. The thumb rests on top of the fist when the hand is in a vertical position, and it is straight. The ball is contacted by the heel of the hand or the backs of the fingers. Such a hand position is used to drive a ball hard and fast, but with less control and accuracy than from the open hand. It is a way to ensure that the ball is low on the wall and stays low on the rebound so that it will be difficult to return.

the serve

This stroke is generally taught at the beginning for two reasons: first, it is the initial skill involved in a game, and second, it is a good basic underhand stroke, which serves as the beginning step in teaching the other strokes. The server stands in the center of the serving area facing the side wall at a slight angle. The feet are approximately 15 inches apart with the body weight evenly distributed on them. The trunk is bent slightly forward. The ball is held about knee-high in the left hand. The ball is dropped, and the right hand comes forward in an easy underhand stroke to contact it as it bounces upward. It is hit to the front wall hard enough so that it returns to a point behind the short line. The ball is now in play.

the underhand stroke

This particular stroke is used more than any other single method of propelling the ball. One of the basic offensive tactics is to keep the ball as low as possible—to allow the ball to drop low before hitting it. A low ball is more difficult for an opponent to see, rebounds faster and harder off the wall, and is easier to place to a particular part of the wall.

The basic position is the same as that in the serve. The arm is extended backward and high, palm down, at the beginning of the shot. As the hand arcs downward, the wrist should be extended prior to contact with the ball and should snap forward for additional force.

On this stroke and all others discussed, there should be some follow-through forward and across the body line.

the side-arm stroke

This particular stroke is used for two basic reasons: the ball has come back to the player at a point about shoulder-high, and it has to be hit by sidearm movement; or, the player desires to send the ball across court to the opposite wall before it gets to the front wall.

On the stroke, the feet are in line with the flight of the ball, the body is slightly crouched, and the arm is brought up parallel to the floor by flexing the elbow and moving the arm backward from the shoulder. The forward movement on the stroke should begin from as far back as possible. The arm is almost straight, there being only a slight bend at the elbow. The ball should be contacted at a point back of or at the shoulder, never beyond it. The hand may be cupped or flat.

the overhand stroke

This stroke is the easiest way to reach a high ball and allows the player to put speed and spin on the ball.

The arm movement is similar to that used in a baseball throw or a football pass. There is also some similarity to the arm movement of a tennis serve.

footwork

From the stance in midcourt back of the short line, the handball player may need to move quickly in any direction. Unless absolutely necessary, he should never turn completely away from the front wall. As a general rule, he should sidestep or back up rather than turn around if a ball is hit deep. This general rule does not apply if the player must cover a great distance rapidly to be sure of playing a shot. A player should make every effort to place himself quickly and become set for the ball, but there are times when he will need to get to a spot so quickly that he must stroke the ball on the move and stop afterward. After a shot is made, the player should move quickly back to the center of the court to be ready for the opponent's return.

strategy

Handball is a game in which there is ample opportunity to utilize a great deal of strategy. Corner shots, crotch shots, hops, placements, and other tactics are employed to give the handball player advantages beyond those of accuracy and strength. In general, he should never find himself falling into a pattern of play. Handball players easily become aware of patterns and adjust their play to take advantage of them. The speed of shots should be varied. Short shots should be mixed with long ones, high ones with low ones, right-hand shots with left-hand ones.

Once the ball is in play, there are many ways in which strategy may be employed. The opponent should be studied, and when a weakness is discovered, it should be exploited. Whenever there is a choice of placing a shot straightaway or cross-corner, it is preferable generally to hit cross-corner. Some shots should be made straightaway in order that the opponent will not begin to expect cross-court shots.

It is effective strategy to hit a few low balls consecutively to draw an opponent upcourt and then to send one high over his head—or to hit some high, long shots to draw him back and then place a low, soft shot in a front corner.

If possible, the ball may be played directly to an opponent who is moving backward. Play a kill every time the opportunity presents itself, and never allow an opponent to get into a position to make his best shot.

TEACHING PROCEDURE

The size of a class should be limited to the number of courts available multiplied by four. If six courts are available, the class size should be twenty-four; if there are two courts, the class limit would be eight. This will enable the players to be active at all times. As a result, every minute of every period can be utilized to the fullest by every student.

Each member of the class should be equipped with gloves. If the school cannot furnish them, each student should bring his own. Any type of cloth or leather glove will be satisfactory for the beginner. The chief objective is to prevent painful swelling of the hands from the repeated impact of the ball.

On the first day of class, the background of the sport should be discussed, along with a very brief explanation of the rules. Two or four students who are fairly skilled in the game can give an exhibition to show what it is like. After this is done, the basic strokes are demonstrated, and the players are assigned specific courts. The entire skill practice should be the stroking of the ball to the front wall by the various methods. It may be carried on in pairs or it may be conducted singly. Modified games should be played during these early sessions. The instructor should go from court to court checking skills and making suggestions for improvement. The students should be encouraged to play between classes, either alone, in singles, cutthroat, or doubles. After a few weeks of skill practice, the class can be broken up into doubles teams and a round robin tournament conducted.

To play one's best game, a player should warm up before playing handball. This can be done in many ways—by jogging, calisthenics, stroking the ball easily, and practicing the fundamental shots.

drills

In order to facilitate learning, there are many drills that may be used during instruction periods. The first two mentioned may be utilized to improve any of the strokes except the serve, depending on where the emphasis is needed.

CLOSE-UP LOW VOLLEY. The player stands about 8 feet from the front wall and volleys the ball, attempting to hit the wall at points less than 3 feet from the floor. Speed is less essential than form and accuracy. The drill may be practiced singly or in pairs.

TIME RALLY. The player stands back of the service line and strokes the ball to the front wall for a designated period of time. The drill may be conducted on either a speed or an accuracy basis. It is best carried out by one person at a time.

TAKING BALL OFF BACK CORNER. The student or a partner throws the ball so that it goes across the back corner, hitting either the back or side wall first. The student then strokes the ball forward to the front wall. This may also be performed off the front corners.

TAKING BALL OFF BACK WALL. This is similar to the above drill except that the ball comes directly off the back wall.

SKILL TESTS

When handball is a part of a physical education program and each student must be assigned a grade, every opportunity should be taken to test him as objectively as possible. Some of the tests available are explained in this section.

service test

The player makes a legal serve. The area back of the short line is chalked off in rectangles. Each rectangle has a value related to its inaccessibility to the receiver. An area near the wall is harder to reach than one out in center court. A low shot near the short line is more difficult to return than one somewhat back. The player serves five times, and his score is the total of the value of the areas his serves fall into (Figure 11–2).

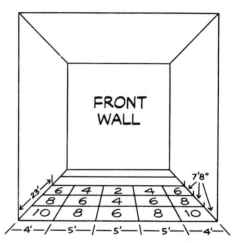

FIGURE 11-2 *Handball Service Test*

volley accuracy test

From a height of six feet downward, the front wall is marked off into squares. If a shot to a particular area is harder to return than one from another, the numerical value of that square will be greater. The player serves a ball that rebounds legally. He then hits it to the front wall in an effort to score the highest point there. His score will be the total value of five attempts (Figure 11–3).

FRONT WALL

6	4	2	4	6
8	6	4	6	8
10	8	6	8	10
4'	5'	5'	5'	4'

FIGURE 11-3 *Volley Accuracy Test*

volley speed test

The player serves, then gets behind the short line and plays the ball continually for one minute. The number of times the ball hits the front wall is his score. If a ball lands and stays beyond the short line, the player may run up and get it but must return to the short line before hitting it again.

DEFINITION OF TERMS

Ace. A service that cannot be returned or that completely eludes the receiver.

Back Court. The area between the short line and the back wall.

Crotch Ball. A ball that strikes the juncture of two playing surfaces, such as the floor and the front wall.

Cutthroat. A game involving three players, each playing against the other two.

Dead Ball. One that is not in play.

Double Fault. The commission of two consecutive errors by the server while serving.

Doubles. A game in which two teams consisting of two players each compete against each other.

Fault. A rule infraction involving a penalty.

Foot Fault. On the serve, an illegal position of the server's foot or feet.

Front Court. The area between the short line and the front wall.

Half Volley. A "pick-up" shot in which the ball is struck soon after it hits the floor.

"Hand Out". The losing of a service.

Hinder. Accidental obstruction or interference not involving a penalty.

Hop. The action of a ball in changing direction after a bounce.

Kill. A ball played so as to be unreturnable.

Lane Shot. A shot in which the ball travels straight back from the front wall very close to the side wall.

Lob. A type of shot or service in which the ball is purposely hit high and slowly into the air.

Long Ball. A serve that hits the back wall before it hits the floor.

Match. The best two games out of three.

One-wall Handball. Handball played on a court where there is only one wall, that being the front wall.

Pass Shot. A shot that goes by the opponent and cannot be played.

Point. A score. (Only the server can score points.)

Receiver. The player to whom the ball is served.

Return. A shot in which the ball hits the front wall before it strikes the floor.

Screen. Blocking an opponent in such a way as to prevent him from reaching a shot.

Service. The act of starting a play.

Service Line. A line parallel to and five feet in front of the short line.

Service Zone. A box or zone 5 feet wide. In doubles, the server's partner stands in this zone while the service is in progress.

Short. A service that does not rebound past the short line.

Short Line. A cross-court line that is halfway between the front and back walls.

Side Out. Loss of service by a player in singles or both players in doubles.
Three-wall Serve. An illegal serve which hits three walls before hitting the floor.

DISCUSSION QUESTIONS

1. In what country did handball originate?
2. Name some famous handball players of the nineteenth century.
3. What was the approximate size of the early American four-wall court?
4. Name some of the basic skills of handball and tell how each is performed.
5. Of what value is spin on the ball?
6. Why is it necessary to be in good physical condition for the game?

BIBLIOGRAPHY

Amateur Athletic Union, *A.A.U. Handball Guide,* latest edition. New York: American Sports Publishing Company.

Cummings, Parke, *The Dictionary of Sports.* New York: A. S. Barnes and Company, 1949.

Encyclopaedia Britannica, Vol. 11. Chicago: Encyclopaedia Britannica, Inc., 1950.

Mand, Charles L., *Handball Fundamentals.* Columbus, Ohio: Charles E. Merrill Publishing Company, 1968.

Mitchell, E. D., *Sports for Recreation.* New York: A. S. Barnes & Company, 1952.

Morrison, Marie, *Here's How in Sports.* Garden City, New York: Doubleday and Company, Inc., 1948.

O'Connell, Charles J., *How to Play Handball.* New York: American Sports Publishing Company, 1935.

Phillips, Bernath E., *Fundamental Handball.* New York: A. S. Barnes & Company, 1937.

Platnicki, Ben A., and Kozar, Andrew J., *Handball.* Dubuque, Iowa: Kendall Hunt Publishing Company, 1970.

Roberson, Richard, and Olson, Herbert, *Beginning Handball.* Belmont, California: Wadsworth Publishing Company, Inc., 1965.

Yessis, Michael, *Handball.* Dubuque, Iowa: William C. Brown Company, 1968.

ice hockey

12

Much of the early history of the game of ice hockey is shrouded in mystery. There is no evidence to establish the time when children, after learning to skate, began to make a game out of pushing an object over the ice. They probably kicked it at first and later employed a stick to assist in moving it. The game may have taken this form in the late eighteenth or early nineteenth century. It was probably undergoing some refinement all this time, but when records began to be kept, it was near its present form.

It is believed that a game similar to present-day ice hockey was played by the Royal Canadian Rifles stationed in Halifax and Kingston, Canada, in 1855. It is quite possible that English troops stationed in Kingston from 1783 to 1855 also played hockey.

McGill University claims that ice hockey was played in Montreal about 1875, and that many characteristics of the game, including the rubber puck, the goals, and the number of players, were developed through the leagues and games in which McGill students played.

In 1879 the first attempt was made to standardize the rules. The first hockey league was formed at Kingston in 1885 and included the Kingston Athletics, the Kingston Hockey Club, Queens University, and the Royal Military College.

The group that eventually became the governing body for ice hockey was formed in 1890 and was known as the Ontario Hockey Association. This organization controlled all amateur hockey and helped to get professional hockey off to a sound start.

In 1891, the Bandy (used synonymously with hockey) Association was formed in England, and international matches were held. C. G. Tebbett, a well-known English ice hockey player of the 1890s, is credited with spreading the game to Norway, Sweden, Denmark, and Switzerland.

The Stanley Cup, the most famous of all hockey prizes and the most cherished by professional teams, was established through the interest and effort of Lord Kilcoursie. This gentleman became interested in hockey when he saw games in Canada. He learned to play and was made a member of one of the teams. When he realized that the players battled for nothing more than the fun and enjoyment in the game, he began to look for means of establishing some sort of prize. He finally influenced Lord Stanley to donate the equivalent of fifty dollars, with which a silver cup was purchased. Through the years, it has become battered and tarnished, but the Stanley Cup is fought for by the teams of the National Hockey League as if it were a bar of gold. In amateur hockey, the Allan Cup is the emblem of the outstanding senior hockey team in Canada and the United States.

Ice hockey is most popular in Canada, but the game has successfully invaded the United States and is played in high schools, colleges, and junior hockey leagues. The teams play independently against other school teams, or they are members of a league. The first league of any importance organized in America was the American Amateur Hockey League, which was formed in the 1913–14 season. This group sponsored competition for the senior championship cup until 1917. There was no other non-professional league competition in this country until the Amateur Hockey Association of the United States was organized in 1937.

BASIC SKILLS

Ice hockey is one of the fastest games played today. The quick starts and almost instantaneous breakaway speed, coupled with quick direction changes and sudden turns make it most challenging to play and interesting to watch.

The skill fundamental to the game is the ability to skate. To become an outstanding hockey player, one must be an accomplished skater. In order to be at his best in the game, a player should develop endurance and skill by hours of skating practice when he first starts learning hockey. During this time, he should concentrate on fast starts, dodging, turns, stops, and restarts. It is important that hockey players learn to skate backward skillfully. The player should also fall on the ice and practice recovery to skating position quickly. All of these skills will be required many times during a game, and the more practice one has on them, the more successful hockey player he will become.

Today's regular sized hockey arena or playing surface is 85 feet wide and 200 feet in length (Figure 12–1). In recent years there have been four

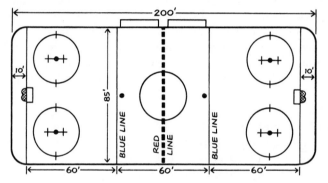

FIGURE 12-1 *Hockey Court*
Ideal Ice Area—200×85 feet
Face-off Circles—30 feet in diameter
End Zone Face-off Spot—2 feet in diameter
Center Face-off Spot—12 inches in diameter

faceoff areas added on each side of the blue line, along with a small half circle near the timekeeper's bench, where the referee goes to make all penalty reports to the announcer for relay to the spectators. Should a player come inside this half circle when a penalty has been called, he may receive an additional penalty. This rule was made to keep the players from delaying the game by continual conversation with the referees.

A good hockey player will always be moving, so he will have better position on his opponent when he receives a pass. A player going at full speed can travel about 30 miles an hour. Skating at this speed he can get more power into his shots. In present-day hockey, several players can shoot the puck about 110 miles an hour. Speed has developed out of the change from the wrist shot to the slap shot.

stick handling

Aside from the ability to skate well, the most important single skill is being able to handle the stick. The puck cannot be held with the hands in general play other than by the goalie; it must be propelled by the stick. Since most hockey players play the stick from the left side, all discussion will deal with that position. A stick is grasped by the right hand at the butt of the handle and the left hand from 18 to 24 inches above the right. In general, the hands stay in that position. An exception is made when unusual force is needed or a strong block is required, at which time the left hand may be moved almost to the blade. The grasp of the stick by the right hand should be firm but at the same time loose enough to allow for manipulation.

The puck should be carried in the center or middle part of the blade. Rarely is it necessary to hit at the puck. The player should practice moving the puck down the ice without having to look at it. This gives him a chance to watch the field ahead of him and decide where to play it next. Body faking is an excellent way to maneuver an opponent in order to go around him. The stick handler should continually use deception when working the puck down the ice and never show in advance where it is going to be played.

The player should not only be able to push the puck along with his stick, but he should also be able to lift it off the ice. Since a goal may be scored even in an upper corner of the net, the player should become skilled in shooting for every part of the goal. Most goals are made to the stick side of the goalie, along the ice, and the player should particularly practice shooting in this area.

passing

In passing to a teammate, the stick should be placed flat on the ice to the side of the puck, and pushed in the direction of the other player. This skill is extremely important in successful team play and should be practiced continually.

Each player should also be skilled in receiving a pass. As the puck nears the vicinity of the receiver, the stick is placed in its path. Just prior to the time it arrives, the stick should be pulled back slowly to allow for a gradual stop. The puck should not be allowed to rebound off the stick. The blade always must be kept flat on the ice when the player is receiving a pass.

shooting

Shooting is the method used to score, and it is necessary for the player to develop skill in this phase of the game to become a successful hockey player. He should avoid the shots that are easiest for the goalkeeper to stop, and should concentrate on those that are most likely to get through for a score. The easiest shot to stop is one through the center of the goal on the ice. The next easiest is the same shot about 3 or 4 feet off the ice. The hardest to stop are those 6 to 12 inches off the ice in the lower corners.

To make a shot, the player places the blade next to the puck and pushes forward toward the goal, at the same time elevating the edge to get the puck off the ice. The puck should be started from a point well behind the player and then swept forward. The follow-through is very important. Faking a shot is an advantage in scoring. Players should also learn to shoot backward and make slap shots.

The slap shot is like a golf shot, started with the stick above the shoulder. The force at impact is greater than the wrist shot. This shot, however, is difficult to control but has a great deal of speed behind it. This is one reason most goalkeepers wear masks for face protection.

The wrist shot is similar to a baseball swing—a smooth stroke with a wrist-snap at the point of contact with the puck, which gives the force to the shot.

The screen shot is one of the hardest for a goalie to stop. It is one in which one or more players obstruct his view when play is in his end of the ice. A goalie will sometimes move his own player out of the way by hitting him gently with his stick or pushing him with his hands. He does this all the time when an opposing player is in his way. Most screen shots are taken from the blue line. A defenseman usually shoots from this spot unless the coach places one of his better shooters at the blue line when he has a power play in progress.

In the power play, the attacking team has the advantage of one extra player because a penalty deprives the defending team of one man. Most teams have a special group of players who take the ice when they have the one man advantage. This is another situation when the coach wants his best shooters in the game. On the power play the defending team or the team with the penalty also has a group of players used to kill off the time of the penalty.

play of the positions

All ice hockey players need to know how to handle the puck, to pass, and to shoot. They need also to know how to deceive, to dodge, to check when necessary, and to exercise the other skills of the game. Certain aspects of the game, however, are more important for some positions than for others, and it is necessary to discuss these individually.

THE GOALKEEPER. The goalkeeper should be the most agile and alert man on the team. Size is an asset, but it is not to be chosen over agility and alertness. He is the one person on the team who is very much like an efficient pitcher in baseball or a good quarterback in football. In order for a team to achieve any success it needs a good goalie.

In playing the position, the goalie should stand in a slight crouch, with knees bent to some extent. He should face the puck squarely and keep his feet comfortably apart for balance. He should grip the stick with the right hand, palm in, at the point where the handle ends and the blade begins. The left hand, palm outward, is kept in a position ready to catch the puck or grasp the stick if necessary to clear the puck.

A very important requirement for playing goalie is to concentrate fully on the puck, and always to make sure no angles are open near the post for the opponent to score. An angle shot, made from the side of the net, gives most goalies trouble when they first play the position. Assuming the player closest to him is his teammate, the goalie must not hold on to the puck more than three seconds after catching it. If he does hold it longer, there is a faceoff.

Most goalies now come out of the goal crease to clear the loose puck to a teammate. More often, when the puck is shot around the back of the dasher boards behind the net, a goalie will come out to stop it for a teammate.

The goalkeeper should continually call to his teammates and let them know when an opposing player is near. This is particularly necessary when they are going after the puck in their own zone and their backs are toward the other players.

To stop a puck, the goalie may use any part of his anatomy or equipment. What he uses depends on the way the puck is moving toward the goal. Normally, a shot on the ice is stopped by the stick, backed up by the skates and pads. Usually the goalie saves with the stick and backs up with hands, body, and skates. The glove hand should be ready to stop the puck in case of a rebound. High shots must be stopped with the hand or other parts of the body, depending on what is easiest and most efficient.

If the puck has been deflected away from the goal, it must be cleared. That is, it must immediately be moved away from the goal so that an opponent may not get another shot and the offense may get under way toward the other goal.

THE DEFENSE. In addition to the goalie, two other players make up the defensive group. They are the right and the left defensemen. When the opponents recover the puck and start down the ice, the defensemen start from center-ice and skate slowly backward. The distance between them should remain about the same. As the offense closes in, the defense must first be sure that no one skates between them and then they try to intercept a pass. As the puck carrier approaches and commits himself to a pass or a shot, the two defensemen should move cautiously together to prevent him from going between or around them. The nearest defense-man should check the puck carrier with his body, and the other should drop back to recover a loose puck or to pick up the opponent if he eludes his teammate. When possible the defensemen should try to keep an attacking player as close as possible to the boards. When this is done they eliminate possible good shots on his goal.

Modern defensemen carry the puck much more than they did in the fifties and forties. A good puck-carrying defenseman can set up many goals for his team by going the full length of the ice surface. When this happens, a wingman will usually fall back into the defensive position to cover. Most defensemen are much faster skaters today than in years past.

As the goal is neared, at least one of the defensemen should keep him-self clear and out in front of the goal to assist in its defense. In case of an unsuccessful attempt for a goal, the defense gets to the puck, clears it, and begins to move up the ice. The defensemen work together as a team, one covering in front of the goal while the other tries to pass the puck up to one of the forwards or carries it out of the zone.

Some points for a defenseman to remember other than those already mentioned are that if a pass has gone to a wing, he should follow fast and cut off the opponent along the boards. Shots should be broken up with the stick, shins, or body as soon as they are attempted. He should defi-nitely not stand around and let his opponent shoot. Anytime a shot is taken, the defense should yell the word "shot" to alert the goalie. A puck should never be carried in front of the goal. High shots should be knocked down.

Center. The center roams the entire ice. He should be extremely fast, aggressive, and skilled. He should be the team leader, alert and clever. He should be an accomplished skater and puck handler because his posi-tion allows for dodging in many directions and for shooting in such a way as to deceive the goaltender. He must be quick to size up situations and determine the best play to make.

The center should be a good forechecker, which means he harasses the opponent who has possession of the puck in the defensive end of the ice. He should do this until he gains control of the puck, and then start look-ing for his wingmen or defensemen to move into scoring position.

Another important duty of the center is to gain control of the puck in faceoff situations. This is done by drawing the puck either to his left or right, depending upon the situation.

The Attack. Hockey places a great offensive load on all members of the team except the goalie, with the brunt of the attack being shared by the center and two wings. They must be alert and aggressive, always carrying the attack to the opponents and working continually together to advance the puck. The right wing should be right-handed, the left wing left-handed. The wings and the center must have enough endurance to continue at top speed throughout the game. The wings should be good defensively, since they usually must cover the opposing wings man for man.

coaching points

1. The player should always keep the head up, looking ahead, when carrying the puck.

2. When a player is unable to pass the puck to another man and cannot skate with it, he should shoot it into an open area, or at the opponent's goal if possible.

3. The best way to score is by shooting the puck along the ice, opposite the side of the goalie's stick. For a high shot, the best place is also opposite the goalie's stick.

4. A player should at all times shoot on the opposing goalie when he has the chance.

5. A player should always be in a moving position, ready to take a pass, never standing around. The stick should always be on the ice, ready to act as a target for the passer.

6. After making a shot on goal, a player should remain facing the goalie ready for a rebound. He should never turn his back to the goalie after a shot on goal.

7. A player should not pass away the puck from a blind position.

8. The player should always try to stay in position. For example, the right wing should get back to his position after giving up possession of the puck.

9. A player going down ice should always pass the puck to the teammate ahead of him, thus letting the puck do the work. This is called "headmanning the puck."

10. When the player makes a pass to his teammates, he should get back into the play ready to get the puck back.

TEACHING PROCEDURE

The first call for squad assembly should be made two to three weeks prior to the time ice will be available. During this period, conditioning exercises may be engaged in. The coach may get information about each squad member's previous hockey experience and whether he is right- or left-handed. He can also make training regulations clear to the team.

Practice sessions should be devoted almost entirely to running. No sprinting should be allowed, and at the beginning runs should be about a half mile. The distance can be increased progressively until, after two weeks, the team will be doing about four miles at an easy jog. Handball and squash are excellent conditioning games, sharpening reflexes and eyes. Chest weight drills are used to strengthen the forearm, upper arm, and back muscles for shooting.

Before the team goes on the ice to practice, a smooth gym floor may be used for shooting practice. A makeshift goal can be set up, and the players can run in gym shoes, going through all the body and stick movements required for shooting. Boards may be placed in the goals with small openings in the corners to encourage accuracy in shooting.

Initial ice practices should be devoted only to the skill of skating. Smooth skating should be developed first, with emphasis on a long coast on each stroke. After about three days of this and a warmup on the fourth day, occasional sprints involving fast, short leg strokes may be taken. Quick turns and stops should be included in such practice. Obstacles can be placed several feet apart on the ice for the players to skate between.

When skating skill and physical condition improve, each player should be supplied with a puck and a stick. Stick handling practice should include vigorous action as well as slow, lazy movements. As more skill develops, the team should be paired off in such a way that one man is on offense and the other on defense. The next step would be to group players in threes, with two on defense and one on offense. After each has had a turn on both offense and defense, two should be put on offense while one works on defense.

Considerable practice time should be devoted to shooting. At first, players should practice without the interference of a goalkeeper and develop skill in coming in at full speed and playing the corners. All the pucks available should be used for this practice. The next step is to place the goalie in the net.

As playing skill and general physical condition improve, the team should be assembled gradually and practice should be devoted to teamwork on offense. After certain plays are perfected, a defense should be set up against them. Scrimmages should be started as soon as possible. The scrimmage is a good conditioner and a good way to spot the players with the most ability. When scrimmage gets under way, the first one should be limited to one hour. Later it is possible to increase the length of scrimmage, depending on the coach's opinion of the physical condition of the players.

SKILL TESTS

When grades must be established for record purposes, it is necessary to determine adequate criteria of playing ability and provide means of testing this ability. Since shooting, stick handling, and speed are extremely valuable assets to successful icehockey play, these factors should be tested.

shooting for accuracy

A diagram should be drawn on a plywood board and placed inside the net at the end of the area. It should be the size of a goal, and the bottom should be flush with the ice. The rectangular diagram should be divided into sections, each a foot high and two feet across. (See Figure 12–2.) The

10	8	10
8	6	8
6	4	6
8	2	8

4′

|← 6′ →|

FIGURE 12-2 *Target for Accuracy Test*

player skates toward the goal and shoots from 20 feet out. He takes ten shots at the goal in this manner. His score is the total number of points he makes on the ten shots.

zigzag skating

Obstacles are placed at intervals on the ice. Skaters go around each one and return to the starting point. The score is the length of time it takes to cover the entire course (Figure 12–3).

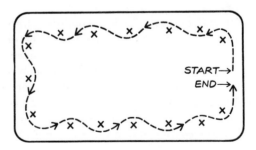

FIGURE 12-3 *Zigzag Skating Test*

DEFINITION OF TERMS

Attacking Team. The team that has possession of the puck.
Attacking Zone. This is the zone or area of the playing surface nearest the opponent's goal.

Bench Minor Penalty. This penalty requires the team against which the penalty is assessed to play a man short for a period of two minutes of actual playing time. The coach of the penalized team may designate any player on his team to serve the penalty.

Blue Line. This is the line that determines the attacking or defending zone on the playing surface, depending on which team has possession of the puck. It also acts as the line to determine offside plays.

Boxes. Areas outside ice surface where players serve penalties.

Checking. Taking the puck off an opponent's stick by using one's own stick or body. Getting in the way of an opponent when he has possession of the puck.

Defending Zone. The area of the playing surface nearest the defending team's goal.

Defensive Team. The team that does not control the puck.

Faceoff. When two opposing players face each other with stick blades on ice and the puck is dropped by a referee or linesman to start play.

Game Misconduct. A player incurring this penalty is ordered to the dressing room for the remainder of the game. A substitute for the penalized player is permitted immediately.

Goal Cage. A framework made of metal and netting that is 4 feet high, 6 feet wide, 17 inches in depth at top and 22 inches in depth at bottom. One is placed at each end of the ice.

Goal Crease. A rectangular area 8 feet wide and 4 feet deep, located in front of each goal cage. Marking this area is a red line.

Goalkeeper Penalty. No goalkeeper may be sent to the penalty box for an infraction that incurs a minor, major, or misconduct penalty. Instead, such a penalty may be served by any player of his team who was on the ice when the infraction occurred.

Major Penalty. Penalized player is ruled off the ice for five minutes actual playing time, during which time no substitute is permitted. This does not apply to a goalkeeper.

Match Penalty. Anyone incurring this penalty is ordered to the dressing room immediately for the rest of the game, and is not permitted to take part in any further games until his case has been dealt with by the league.

Minor Penalty. Penalized player, except a goalkeeper, is ruled off the ice for two minutes of actual playing time, during which time no substitute is permitted.

Misconduct Penalty. Penalized player, except a goalkeeper, is ruled off the ice for a period of ten minutes actual playing time. A substitute for the penalized player is permitted.

Offensive Team. The team that has possession of the puck.

Penalties. Penalties shall be in actual playing time, and are divided into the following classes: (1) minor penalties, (2) bench minor penalties, (3) major penalties, (4) misconduct penalties, (5) game misconduct penalties, (6) match penalties, and (7) penalty shot.

Penalty Shot. A shot that may be taken on the goalkeeper by a player designated by the referee or selected by the team. The player receives the puck in the center faceoff circle, and once the shot has been made, the play is complete. No goal can be scored on a rebound.

Red Line. This line divides the ice surface in half. It is where each period is started, and it acts as a marker on the two line offside call.

Stick Handle. To maintain control of the puck by skating around a depending player.

DISCUSSION QUESTIONS

1. Identify the relationship of the following men to the game of ice hockey: (a) Lord Kilcoursie, (b) C. G. Tebbett, (c) Lord Stanley.
2. Why is ice hockey so challenging to play and interesting to watch?
3. Diagram the floor plan of an ice hockey rink. Indicate the correct positions for each man on the team when they faceoff at center ice.
4. Describe the wrist shot and the slap shot.
5. Make an analysis of the play of (a) goalkeeper and (b) the center.
6. Describe a screen shot.
7. Suggest some coaching points for the attack.

BIBLIOGRAPHY

Athletic Handbook. Toronto: National Council of the Young Men's Christian Association of Canada, 1968.

Encyclopedia Britannica, Vol. 11. Chicago: Encyclopedia Britannica, Inc., 1950.

Fisher, Thomas K., *Ice Hockey.* New York: Charles Scribner's Sons, 1926.

Hughes, William L., and Williams, Jesse Feiring, *Sports, Their Organization and Administration.* New York: A. S. Barnes & Company, 1944.

Jeremiah, Eddie, *Ice Hockey.* New York: A. S. Barnes & Company, 1942.

Menke, Frank G., *The New Encyclopedia of Sports.* New York: A. S. Barnes & Company, 1969.

Mitchell, Elmer D., *Sports for Recreation.* New York: A. S. Barnes & Company, 1952.

Percival, Lloyd, *The Hockey Handbook.* New York: A. S. Barnes & Company, 1951.

Official N.C.A.A. Ice Hockey Guide, latest edition. New York: National Collegiate Athletic Association.

Royal Canadian Air Force, *How to Play Hockey.* Queens Printers, Ottawa, Canada, 1971.

Watt, Tom, *How to Play Hockey.* Garden City, New York: Doubleday and Company, Inc., 1971.

lacrosse

13

BACKGROUND

The first Europeans to arrive in Canada observed the Indians playing a game that was to develop into the modern game of lacrosse. The Indians called the game *baggatoway*. There is no way of knowing how long it had been in existence, but one may assume that it had been played for centuries previous to the time it was observed by the early settlers in Canada.

A game of baggatoway was an occasion for much celebration. Some games were preceded by pow-wows, wild dancing, and a feast; others had only a religious ceremony to initiate them. The gallery was composed mostly of women, who grouped along the sidelines cheering the players. The playing field could be any size. Medicine men stood at each end of it to mark the goal line, and when they moved, the goal line moved. These same men served as the referees.

The number of participants was unlimited as long as the sides were even. There might be fewer than 50 to a side or more than 200. The strategy involved getting rid of as many opponents as possible by "accidentally" hitting them over the head with sticks. As soon as the numbers had been sizably reduced, the game proceeded on a more skillful level.

A baggatoway game was the occasion for one of the worst Canadian massacres. The Chippewa and Sac Indians scheduled a game and invited the occupants of Fort Michilimackinac to attend. When they refused the invitation because they did not believe it safe to go so far away from the fort, the Indians decided to hold the game nearby. As it proceeded and interest increased, the occupants of the fort carelessly left the gates open and wandered about outside. At an opportune time, the Indians suddenly secured tomahawks from their squaws, who had been hiding them under blankets, and proceeded to kill all but two of the people from the fort.

The game was given its present name because the pioneer French-Canadians thought the stick used to play the game resembled a bishop's crozier, or cross. In describing it, they kept saying *la crosse*.

There is no way of knowing positively when the game was played for the first time as lacrosse. It is believed that it may have been staged in 1834 between the Iroquois and Algonquin Indians at the Pierre race course in Montreal, where the game was played in an enclosure and by rules understandable to the white spectators. The Olympic Club, active in the 1840s and early 1850s, sponsored lacrosse. The first organization with the sole purpose of promoting lacrosse was the Montreal Lacrosse Club, formed in 1856. Another club, called the Hocheloga, followed in 1858, but later merged with the Montreal Lacrosse Club. The Beaver Club was formed in 1859.

Dr. George W. Beers was one of the greatest lacrosse enthusiasts. Realizing that the game was handicapped by many different sets of rules, he undertook the task of standardizing them. He rewrote them and brought about revolutionary progress. Soon his rules were adopted by all the lacrosse teams. Because of his contribution to the game, Dr. Beers is now known as the "Father of Lacrosse."

Lacrosse was adopted as the Canadian national sport by an act of Parliament in 1867. Though there was a time when 5,000 to 8,000 people would come to see a professional game, this era in the history of lacrosse was short-lived. There has been no professional lacrosse since 1932. The amateur game continues to be very popular in Canada.

Late in the nineteenth century, lacrosse was being played on the Boston Common. John R. Flannery was instrumental in getting the game started there. Since then, it has spread to colleges and high schools along the Eastern Seaboard.

Lacrosse now enjoys its greatest popularity around Baltimore and in the New England States. The game is played on both high school and college levels. Its popularity is increasing, particularly on the high school level.

Early in the history of lacrosse in this country, the United States Intercollegiate Lacrosse Association was formed. It has functioned continuously and now numbers more than 100 schools in its membership. The Association makes all-American Selections and awards the Wilson Wingate Trophy to the outstanding lacrosse team in the Association.

Lacrosse is played on a field 110 yards long and 60 yards wide (Figure 13-1). The goals are 80 yards apart, and the field is divided into halves.

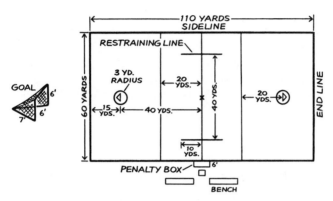

FIGURE 13-1 *Lacrosse Field*

The goal is 6 feet by 6 feet and is covered with a net. There are restraining lines and flags in each corner of the field and on the midfield lines. The penalty box is at the center of one side of the field. Around the goal is a crease or circle 18 feet in diameter.

BASIC SKILLS

Lacrosse is a very fast game requiring skill, endurance, ruggedness, and, of course, quick movement. Some of the skills required are similar to those for other sports, especially those involving body movement in offense or defense. Many, however, are peculiar to lacrosse. Skills in this category are concerned particularly with the handling of the stick. Catching, throwing, and intercepting the ball combine skills unique to the game of lacrosse.

handling the stick and cradling

The stick (crosse) used for moving the ball somewhat resembles a tennis racket and a snowshoe. The mesh used to cradle the ball is made of either ordinary or clock cord and ranges in width from 8 to 12 inches, depending on which player is to use it (Figure 13–2).

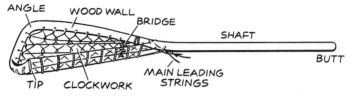

FIGURE 13-2   *The Crosse*

The stick is held in both hands. A right-handed player holds the butt end firmly with the left hand, palm down. The right hand (with the palm up) grasps the handle near the throat by holding the stick in the fingers only, thus ensuring a relaxed grip, which facilitates cradling. Cradling is the term used to describe the arc-shaped movement of the head of the stick, which is the secret of keeping the ball in the pocket.

throwing

For the beginner, the throw is very similar to the baseball pitcher's overhand delivery.

The right-handed player has his left side in the direction of the target, feet placed like a baseball pitcher's. Both hands are on the stick in the cradling position. The right-handed player should look at the target and push the butt hand slightly down and away from the target, thus extending the stick backward, aligned lengthwise in the exact direction the ball is to be thrown. He throws by stepping toward the target with the left foot and pushing the right hand (and stick). In the preparatory movement, the right arm is flexed (cocked to throw). In the actual throw, it comes through extended at the target. The player follows through by pointing the head of the stick at the target.

catching the ball

In making a catch, the player should work with relaxed arms. The eyes should be glued to the oncoming ball, and the stick should be extended into its path with the pocket open toward the ball. As the ball nears the pocket, the player "gives" to allow the stick to move in the same direction as the ball. When contact is made with the pocket, the ball is gradually slowed to a complete stop by a backward arc of the stick. At completion of the catch, the stick should be returned to cradling position. The ball is best caught at shoulder height, and the feet should be so placed during the catch that the body is in position to make a throw immediately.

scooping

When the ball is on the ground, it is necessary to pick it up with the stick. Since the ball is more frequently on the ground than in the air, scooping is one of the most important skills of the game. The head of the stick is placed nearly parallel to the ground in the path of the ball and moved toward it. As contact is made, the ball is scooped up into the net of the stick in a movement that resembles shoveling snow from a hard surface. After scooping up the ball, the player should bring the stick to a position for either cradling or throwing.

running

Running is a basic skill of lacrosse. Some positions require almost constant running combined with quick starts, turns, and stops. It is advantageous to be very fast and to be in top physical condition in order to utilize this speed continuously.

body checking

Body checking is performed on the ball carrier to prevent a possible receiver from getting the ball or to keep him off balance. It is merely a movement into an opponent to deflect him from his path or from the ball. The man doing the checking stays on his feet, makes contact hard and high, most often using the shoulder, and moves on quickly to pursue the ball or defend his position. The contact with the opponent must be made above his knees and must always be from the front. It is illegal to check an opponent who does not have possession of the ball or who is not within 5 yards of a loose ball.

stick checking

This skill is a defensive maneuver performed to prevent an opponent from using his stick to catch the ball. Upon a signal from the goalie, the defenseman hits the stick of his opponent by crossing it with his own. It is also used on the stick of the ball carrier to dislodge the ball. This maneuver is legal when the opponent has possession of the ball, when the defense is within 5 yards of a loose ball, or within 5 yards of the ball in flight.

facing off

The faceoff can be compared to the jumpball in basketball. At such times, the sticks are placed on the ground, back to back, at right angles to a line toward the nearer goal. The defensive player crouches with both hands on the stick, his back to his goal. His opponent crouches facing him, both hands on his stick. The official adjusts the sticks so that the pockets are vertical and places the ball down in the slight space between the pockets. After the whistle, each player attempts to control the ball by clever stick handling, or throws a block at his opponent to drive him away from the ball.

dodging

Dodging is a skill employed by an offensive man in order to get past the defense. It involves a fake indication of direction to get the defense to commit itself. After that, the offensive man moves away from and beyond the defensive man. The best defense against dodging is to keep the eyes on the opponent's hips, for these are the least likely to move in a faking maneuver.

switching

Switching is identical to the basketball play with the same title. It is a defensive maneuver important to the game. When an offensive block play is being made, a player may block his own teammate. He should leave the man he is attempting to guard and switch to the opponent of his teammate. His teammate then switches to the other opponent and guards him. If such a maneuver were not carried out, the two defensive men would be tangled with each other, and one offensive man would be completely free.

PLAY OF THE GAME

There are ten players on a team in men's lacrosse: the goalkeeper, three defensemen, three midfielders, and three attackers. A women's team consists of twelve players: five attacking players, six defending players, and a center who plays both attack and defense.

Each player is paired against an opponent, except the goalkeeper who always stands in front of his own goal. The goalkeeper may not be interfered with when he is standing within the goal crease, and a goal does not count if it is made within the crease or while any attacking player is within the crease.

A team must keep at least four players in the defensive half of the field and three in the attacking half.

The length of a regulation game is 60 minutes, divided into four quarters. A goal counts one point, with the team scoring the most goals the winner. If the score is tied at the end of the playing time, two five-minute periods are played after a five-minute intermission.

The purpose of each team is to score by throwing, rolling, or kicking the ball into the opponents' goal and to prevent the opponents from scoring. Each score counts one point. No player may touch the ball with his hands except the goalkeeper in the act of preventing a score. The ball is moved by carrying, throwing, batting, or kicking it in any direction within the field limits. The defensive players endeavor to keep the offensive players away from the goal by stick checking, body blocking the ball carrier, or intercepting passes of the offensive players.

Play is started and resumed after each goal by a faceoff at midfield between the two centers.

Fouls are of two kinds: (1) technical, including such acts as touching the ball, throwing the crosse (stick), being offside, and entering the goal crease; and (2) personal, including holding, tripping, slashing, and checking into the offense.

The technical foul is penalized by a free throw, which gives the ball to the opponent at the spot of the foul and permits him to throw it to whomever he pleases, or by suspension from the game for one minute. The personal foul is penalized by expulsion from the game for from one to three minutes.

attack

In most cases during the course of a game, the attack will begin at the opponent's goal and will proceed until a goal is made at the other end of the field or the ball has been intercepted. The first group involved in an attack includes the goalie, the point, the cover point, and the first defense. All these players range close to the goal and begin working the ball up the field. When on attack, they do not have possession of the ball very long at one time, for it is to the team's advantage to get it quickly to the attack group.

Also involved in attack are the midfield men, including the second defense, the center, and the second attack. They serve as intermediaries to get the ball to the next group for a chance to score. These three roam the midfield and by skillful running and passing advance the ball into scoring territory.

The major part of the attack is carried out by the attack group, but the center, the second attack, and the first attack stay reasonably closeby and assist when necessary. The close-attack group includes the first attack, the out home, and the in home.

It is their chief job to get the ball into the goal. They are assisted to some degree, but only to a small extent, by the midfield group. Members of the close-attack group stay always within 20 to 30 yards of the goal, pick up the ball coming in, and by carefully planned teamwork make efforts to score.

Members of the attack group must be extremely good shots. They must be alert, fast, and able to size up a situation quickly and to take the best advantage of it. The plays can be similar to those in basketball.

the defense

All the positions on a team are defensively important to some degree because each man has a defensive responsibility when the other team has possession of the ball. The positions vary in importance, however, depending upon how close each is to the goal in which the opponents may score. The farther away from the goal a defensive player is, the less is his importance in that capacity.

The defense must be skilled in blocking passes and body checking. They must know one another so well that they know instinctively when to switch from one offensive man to another. They must be able to analyze the attack in order to break it up most effectively. Once a play has been broken up and possession of the ball secured, the defensive group must have the ability to clear the ball by running or by passing hard, far, and accurately in order to get it downfield and away from their goal.

The most important man on the defense is the goalie. He has the specific job of preventing the ball from going in his goal. Every player is alert to the goalie and his signals. He is in a position to see the entire field of play and is always aware of the movements of both teams. He may call the type of offense or defense, and he may call plays to be made by specific individuals.

A goalie must be fast, a skillful stick handler, intelligent, alert in making decisions, and extremely cool under pressure. He is the last man on defense; if a ball gets behind him, it is usually a score.

TEACHING PROCEDURE

As a general rule, it is necessary for each player to be able to perform all the skills involved in the game. However, an exception to this rule is that the men concerned primarily with defense should be particularly skilled in defensive play and those concerned with attack should be skilled that part of the game. The training of lacrosse players, then, should center on the skills they will be most often called upon to use. Since top physical condition, speed, and ability to start, turn, and stop are essential for all players, practice designed to develop all of these should be stressed.

Other necessary skills for all players include the ability to pick up ground balls (stationary and moving, with or without opposition) and ability to pass. Drills designed to improve the attack should include dodging, cutting, and various kinds of shooting. Defense drills should include switching, and lateral and backward running.

SKILL TESTS

In order to assign grades to lacrosse players, the most essential skills should be tested. Running, turning, throwing, catching, and shooting are the ones most necessary to a successful game, and all of them are reasonably easy to test.

running

This is a zigzag run around stakes set at a distance of 100 yards (Figure 13-3). There should be nineteen stakes, one every 5 yards. They should

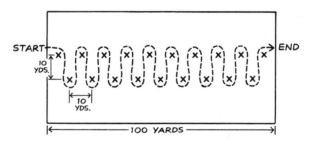

FIGURE 13-3 *Lacrosse Zig-zag Run*

be 10 yards apart laterally. The player being tested starts at the first stake and goes on the outside of every stake until he has passed all nineteen. His score is the length of time it takes him to cover the entire distance.

throwing for accuracy

A target comparable to one used in archery should be drawn on a wall, with scores specified as nine for the center circle and seven, five, three, and one for the other circles as the outer edge is approached. A player is given ten throws using a stick, and his score is the total number of points he makes on all throws. The throws are to be made 20 yards from the wall.

catching and throwing

A line is drawn 20 yards from a smooth wall. The player throws from this line to the wall, catches the ball on the rebound, and throws it again. The player's score is the number of throws he makes in one minute.

DEFINITION OF TERMS

Assist. Credit in scoring to the last offensive player to pass to the scorer.

Attack. This is a general term applied to those players charged with the offense.

Backing-up. Team play for strengthening a defense. Lending support to the teammate encountering the ball carrier.

Body Checking. A legal body block of an opponent who may be in possession of the ball, be within 5 yards of it, or be a potential receiver.

Brush-off. A maneuver used to get into the open by running an opponent into one of his teammates.

Center Draw. The faceoff taking place in the facing circle at the beginning of each quarter and after each goal.

Center Stripe. The line running through the facing circle and dividing the field into offensive and defensive halves.

Checking. Striking an opponent's stick to prevent him from playing the ball.

Clearing. The launching of an attack by the defense immediately following an interception or a stop in defensive territory.

Crease. The circle boundary around the goal, 18 feet in diameter.

Crosse. The stick used for playing the game.

Cross Checking. Illegal use of the part of the stick between the butt and the throat in stopping an opponent.

Defense. A general term applied to those players charged with the defensive phase of the game. These players include the point, cover point, first defense, second defense, center, and second attack.

Dodge. An individual offensive maneuver to get around a defenseman while in possession of the ball.

Draw. Gaining possession of the ball from a faceoff.

End Line. The out-of-bounds line at the end of the field.

End Zone. The area of the field behind the goal.

Extra on the Attack. Possession by a team on the offensive of an extra man because of a penalty on the opposition.

Extra on the Defense. Possession by a team on the defense of an extra man by virtue of a penalty.

Face Guard. Required metal or plastic protection for the face.

Faceoff. The method by which the ball is put into play at the beginning of each quarter and after each goal.

Freezing. Stalling for time in order to keep possession of the ball.

Goalie. The player protecting the goal.

Gloves. Padded gloves that are standard equipment.

Helmet. The required protective headgear.

Hugging Defense. A defenseman who guards his opponent so closely that he will go wherever the attacking man goes.

Midfield. The second line or group on the attack and the first line of defense. The midfield consists of the second attack, center, and second defense.

Penalty Box. The desk to which the player reports when he draws a penalty.

Point of the Goal. A position about 6 feet back of the goal where the goal net converges.

Pushing Off. An individual offensive maneuver to get into the open by shoving against an opponent.

Riding. Action whereby a team, after attempting a shot or losing the ball, tries to prevent the defense from clearing the ball to their attacking unit.

Save. Preventing a score.

Screen Play. An offensive maneuver to obstruct the goalie's vision.

Shooting. Various shots taken at the goal in an effort to score.

Shooting Area. An imaginary arc 20 yards from the center of the goal.

Shot. Any particular drive at the goal in an attempt to score.

Side Line. The out-of-bounds line running the length of the field on either side.

Slashing. Illegal stick checking.

Stick. The implement with which the player propels the ball, also known as the crosse.

Stop. A save made by the goalie.

Switching. A defensive maneuver to prevent attack men from getting into the open when brushing-off.

Wing Area. The lined area in midfield near each side line, within which both second attack and second defensive men are restricted until the whistle sounds, commencing the game.

DISCUSSION QUESTIONS

1. Describe an early baggataway game as played by the Indians.
2. Why was the name of the game changed to lacrosse?
3. Who was Dr. Beers and how was he related to lacrosse?
4. What method of propelling the ball is unique to the game?
5. When is body checking used?
6. What is stick checking?
7. What is switching?
8. Who is considered the most important man on the team? Why is he so considered?
9. Name the players on a team and summarize the specific duties of each.
10. Describe an attack.

BIBLIOGRAPHY

American Association for Health, Physical Education and Recreation, *Physical Education for High School Students.* Washington: 1960.

Canadian Lacrosse Association, *Rules of Box Lacrosse.* Sec. Treasurer W. W. Mickey Sims, 7964 Selkirt St., Vancouver, B. C.: 1948.

Fait, Hollis F., Shaw, John H., Ley, Katherine L., *A Manual of Physical Education Activities.* Philadelphia: W. B. Saunders Company, 1967.

Menke, Frank G., *The New Encyclopedia of Sports.* New York: A. S. Barnes & Company, 1969.

Mitchell, E. D., *Sports for Recreation.* New York: A. S. Barnes & Company, 1936.

Official N.C.A.A. Lacrosse Guide, latest edition. New York: National Collegiate Athletic Association.

Stanwick, Tad, *Lacrosse.* New York: A. S. Barnes & Company, 1940.

paddle tennis

14

BACKGROUND

The game of paddle tennis was devised by Frank Peer Beal, a minister and an ardent tennis enthusiast who was also interested in playground opportunities for the youth in New York City. He produced a paddle tennis court just one fourth the size of a regulation tennis court. By using a lower net, sponge ball, and wooden paddles, he developed a game that spread quickly throughout New York City, accelerated by the interest and assistance of James V. Mulholland, City Recreation Director.

This game first appeared in 1921 and was being played a very few years later in other parts of New York State. When the National Recreation Association approved it, nationwide interest in it proved inevitable.

In 1922, the Manhattan Recreation Department cooperated with the New York Rotary Club to stage the first paddle tennis tournament ever held. It was won by Dalio Santini.

The first paddles were made of heavy maple and were easily broken. The second type of paddle was made of three-layer plywood. It was much stronger and somewhat lighter (Figure 14–1).

FIGURE 14-1   *Paddle Tennis Paddle*

Platform paddle tennis was originated by James Cogswell and F. S. Blanchard. They built a wooden platform on which to play badminton and deck tennis as soon as possible after rain. It was a simple procedure to play the game of paddle tennis on this new facility. To reduce loss of time caused by chasing balls, a strong wire fence was put around the court. An innovation in the game was introduced when Cogswell and Blanchard began to play the ball off the wire in much the same manner as the walls are used in handball.

The enclosed length was 60 feet, which allowed a space of 8 feet from base line to the back wire. The court dimensions remained at 44 feet by 20 feet. The game has enjoyed tremendous growth and is now played in city parks and private clubs. Because the larger court proved of greater interest to adults, both paddle tennis and platform paddle tennis are now played on a court 44 feet long (Figure 14–2).

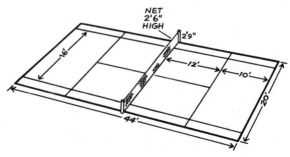

FIGURE 14-2   *Paddle Tennis Court*

Paddle tennis and platform paddle tennis are both similar to tennis with the three following exceptions:

1.   In both games only one serve is permitted.

2.   In platform paddle tennis the ball may be played off the side walls and backstop, provided it has bounced once inbounds and is struck before it bounces a second time.

3.   In playground paddle tennis singles, the full doubles court is used following the serve.

The game of paddle tennis is quite similar to lawn tennis in rules and court layout as well as in playing skills. It is a somewhat faster game than tennis because the ball goes only about half as far, though the actual flight is slower. For this reason, the game serves very well as a preliminary game to tennis. Anyone becoming skilled at paddle tennis makes the conversion to the string racket, livelier ball, and bigger court very quickly. Likewise, good tennis players prove to be good paddle tennis players after very little practice. The skill in the platform game is quite similar to that required in the other paddle tennis game except for the play off the back wall. The skill in this particular phase of the game will be discussed after the skills common to all. Since the basic strokes are so similar to those of tennis, it is suggested that the reader check the chapter on that game for illustrations of each stroke under discussion.

stance

The way a person stands both at the time of stroking the ball and when waiting for a return is important to efficient play of the game. In waiting for an opponent's service, a player should assume a position approximately one foot behind the base line, facing the opposite end of the court, with his weight evenly distributed on the toes of each foot. The knees and trunk should be slightly bent, the head erect, and the eyes carefully watching the opponent in an effort to foresee what he will do with the next shot. The paddle is held firmly so that it can be moved quickly to any position for striking the ball. The player should be ready to move in any direction in order to be at the best spot to stroke the ball most effectively.

When preparing to strike the ball, the player changes his stance. His feet should be in line with the length of the court. The player faces to the right on a forehand drive and to the left on a backhand.

the grip

The way a paddle is grasped can have much to do with how effective one's game becomes. A good grip has two objectives: (1) to hold a paddle firmly; and (2) to permit moving it easily from place to place without changing its position in the hand. The author prefers what has come to be known as the Eastern grip. With this grip, it is easy to make a powerful stroke with a minimum of extra movement. The grip is taken when the handle of the paddle is parallel to the ground and the face is perpendicular. The right hand reaches out and takes hold of the handle as if shaking hands. The fingers flex around to the right and the thumb to the left. The V made by the thumb and index finger opens directly toward the paddle. The grip should be firm but not tight. The wrist should be kept flexible so that it can snap on the stroke. For information relative to the Western grip, the reader is referred to the discussion in the chapter on tennis.

the forehand drive

This particular stroke, in terms of the frequency of its use, is the most important one in the game of paddle tennis. It can be a powerful stroke, and it is performed in such a way that the ball can be hit squarely or spin can be put on it. In order to execute this stroke, a right-handed player should take a stance so the left side of his body is toward the net and his feet are in a comfortable side-stride position with the weight on the right foot. A distinct disadvantage of the forehand drive is that the heights at which balls may be hit are limited. It is best used on balls that come by the right side of the player between his knees and shoulders. Upon making a forehand drive, the player places his feet in line with the length of the court, knees flexed, and looks closely at the oncoming ball. As it approaches, the paddle is brought back and when the arm is fully extended backward, the paddle is started forward. The paddle face is toward the oncoming ball. The grip is maintained firmly. At the moment the paddle makes contact with the ball, its face should slant slightly downward so that a topspin will be put on the ball. The arm motion continues across and in front of the body. As the arm stroke comes forward to the ball, the body weight should shift to the forward foot, which, for a right-handed person, would be the left one.

Immediately after the ball is hit, the player should go quickly to a defensive position and stance.

In teaching beginners, it is best to insist on a straight stroke at first in order for them to perfect the swing and follow-through. As skill increases, they may gradually be allowed to put some spin on the ball.

the backhand

This particular stroke is one that is used to hit balls that come to the left side of the body at knee to shoulder height. At the time the stroke is to be made, the player faces to the left, body weight equally distributed on his feet. Some players prefer the Western grip on this shot. If so, the adjustment can be made by moving the hand a quarter turn counterclockwise on the handle. The legs are slightly flexed, and the head is toward the oncoming ball. As the ball approaches, the paddle is brought to the rear, stopped, and then started forward. For the beginner, the paddle face should be perpendicular when it contacts the ball, and it should be slanted forward for topspin by the more advanced player. The follow-through should continue forward and to the right. The player should immediately resume a defensive stance and court position. In driving the ball forward, it should be aimed just over the top of the net in order that gravity and top spin can take it to the playing court and keep it low and difficult to return. On both the forehand and backhand stroke, the ball should be contacted when the paddle is just in front of the body.

When possible, the paddle should always be held so that the handle travels slightly upward on both the forehand and backhand drives.

the serve

This shot is a means of putting the ball in play at the start of each point. By constant practice, a player can develop so much skill at it that he can consistently win points on his serve alone. The object of the serve is to hit the ball from behind the base line across the net and into the service court in such a manner as to be difficult for the opponent to return.

A good serve involves points that must be taken into consideration when learning the basic movements. At least one foot must be kept in contact with the court from the start of the arm movement until the ball is hit. The front foot should be the one. The back foot comes forward on the swing but must not touch the court on or inside the base line until after the ball is hit. Keeping these legal considerations in mind, the player should begin practice on the serve.

The server stands with feet apart, weight distributed evenly, knees slightly flexed, body erect. The paddle may be held by either of the grips, but the Eastern is preferred. The arm moves downward and backward, forming an arc. As this movement gets underway, the ball is tossed high into the air. As the paddle starts upward in its backward arc, the player's back arches slightly. The paddle continues upward and then forward at such a speed as to meet the ball at the highest point that the extended arm and its own length will allow it to go. As the paddle starts forward, the body snaps forward from its arched position to give some additional power to the stroke. Just prior to the time the ball is contacted, the wrist snaps forward. At the time the paddle strikes the ball, its face is turned slightly to the left and slanted slightly forward so that a partial topspin and sidespin is put on the ball. It is emphasized here again that the height at which the ball is hit is important to greater service efficiency.

Some players prefer the Western grip for the service because they believe they get more power from it. It is questionable whether this is true. This serve does allow the paddle face to turn slightly to the right in such a way as to put a spin on the ball that causes it to break abruptly to the receiver's left. Continuous use of this stroke will eventually allow the receiver to get set for it. It is suggested that if this serve is used at all, it be mixed with the conventional serve.

the volley

To volley a ball is to hit it before it touches the court. Most volleying takes place close to the net and is generally performed in basically the same way as the forehand and backhand drives, except there is very little chance for the preliminary paddle swing and hardly any follow-through. Many times, the stroke must be made so quickly that the player cannot get into position for the shot. However, he should make every effort to pace his game so that he will be in the proper position. The paddle is kept reasonably high, and the stroke is slightly downward in order to give some bottom spin to the ball. On the backhand volley, the paddle should be controlled by the thumb. It is best if the volley is made from a position of 3 to 5 feet from the net.

the half volley

The half volley is made just after the ball rises from the court. It is a block shot, with little movement of the paddle. It is used not only as a matter of expediency, because it would be difficult to get into another position to play the ball, but also as a surprise to opponents who are expecting another type of shot.

the overhead smash

This shot is made in much the same way as the serve. It is utilized to take advantage of high, weak returns. It is a very difficult shot to time properly, for one must accurately judge the speed and height of the ball as it is dropping down to the court. It is made with the same movements as the serve in order to drive the ball back to the opponent at tremendous speed. The paddle face is vertical because spin is not necessary, and the shot is more accurate. To smash well, it is necessary to be relaxed and to keep the eye on the ball.

The smash is an effective kill stroke in paddle tennis, but in platform paddle tennis, where the ball can be played off the wire screen, it is not so effective and should not be utilized so often.

the lob

The lob is simply a ball hit upward and across the net. It is generally considered a safe shot. It is hit particularly to a player who has a weak smash and may err on the return. The average lob begins as does a forehand or backhand drive. As the paddle goes through its arc, the face turns upward so that an upward angle plus a back spin or bottomspin is put on the ball. Another time the lob is used is if the opposition is close to the net and cannot hit a ball sent high to the back of the court. It is possible to put spin on a lob by a quick backward movement of the wrist.

the chop

The chop is a shot that gives considerably more control than any of the other shots. It is not a powerful shot and, in a fast game, is considered the change-of-pace shot. It can be made either forehand or backhand. In either case, the balance and the arm and paddle motion are quite similar. The shot can be used either offensively or defensively, but it is primarily a means of defense. It is such an easy shot that if the player is not careful, he will find himself using it more and more often.

The shot is made by swinging the paddle forward and downward, with the face of the paddle slanted upward. This swing and this slant of the paddle cause bottomspin as well as forward motion. When the ball hits the court, it has a tendency to bounce upward close to where it first contacts the court. This peculiarity forces the receiver to be closer to the spot of the bounce in order to play the ball properly. Though the chop shot is an easy one to make, good players should employ it only as one of many possible strokes.

the drop shot

The drop shot is one in which the ball is dropped quickly over the net with a reversed spin in such a way as to bounce quickly and often defy return. It is used when the opponent is back near the base line and the player wants to trap him with a close shot that will not bound to him as he runs forward in an effort to return it.

The drop shot is a dangerous one to make because a slight mistake will put it into the net or so deep over the net that the opponent can return it with a smash. It is a delicate shot, requiring a sensitive touch and years of practice.

In making the drop shot, the movement is essentially the same as for the chop except that it is a shorter movement and there is a minimum of follow-through. The ball is aimed just over the top of the net so that it will drop fast, near the net.

taking a ball off the wire

In platform paddle tennis, it is legal to play the ball after it has bounced off the wall and prior to the time it hits for the second time. To take a ball off the wall does not require a stroke different from those mentioned, but it does need somewhat different timing. As the ball comes off the wall, the player should get in front of it—toward the net. If it comes to him, he can have the paddle following closely behind and finally contact it, sending it on to the opponent. If the ball does not travel quite to him, he can still send it over the net by driving the paddle from behind it. The common error in such a shot is to be too far behind a wall bounce, where it is impossible to reach it in time to send it across.

PLAYING THE GAME

hints to players

The paddle tennis player should keep his eyes on the ball. Many a shot has been missed because a player looked toward where he was planning to hit it instead of at the ball. Overhand strokes should be avoided where possible. They are difficult to time properly, and usually it is easier to hit a forehand or backhand drive. Keep the paddle generally in line with the forearm. When wrist snap is part of the stroke, however, the paddle will not be in line with the arm. Bend the knees in proportion to the height of the ball on any shot—i.e., low ball, deeper knee bend. There are few exceptions to the rule that a player should always face at right angles to the net. During a stroke, the weight should be shifted from the back foot to the front one. Play aggressive ball, always pressing the opponent. Return quickly to a defensive stance, prepared to move in any direction to play the ball.

strategy

Paddle tennis is a game in which speed and accuracy are important and should be utilized at every opportunity. The net position is of great importance in the game, and it benefits a player to acquire command of it first. Because the court is small, a player can reach nearly any shot, except a high one, that comes across.

If a person has established himself at the net, it is difficult but not impossible to beat him in the point. The ball can be hit over his head to the back court, or it may be possible to pass it by him down the outside of the court. Hitting directly to him may be effective.

In volleying, the player has a better opportunity to cover the court effectively if he stands about 6 feet in back of the net. Straight forehands and backhands are the most frequently used strokes, though other shots should be employed when the opportunities present themselves.

The opponent should be studied very carefully and his weaknesses determined. As soon as they are found, they should be exploited. Lob to an opponent often, even if the ball does not go above his head. To return such a shot requires perfect timing, and frequently it is missed. Utilize placement at every opportunity. Keep the opponent moving, and as soon as he starts in one direction, place a shot behind him where it will be impossible for him to play it. The shots should vary, in order to keep him guessing. Make every effort to guess where he will hit the ball, and be there to return it.

In the doubles game, the court should be balanced between partners, both being about midcourt. The server's partner should play slightly in on the opposite side of the court and be prepared to move up or back, depending on where the return goes. There should be some agreement between the two players as to which one will take shots coming down the middle.

TEACHING PROCEDURE

A paddle tennis class should be limited in size, depending on the number of courts and practice areas available. If there are five courts, the class should be limited to twenty members. If there is backboard space, an additional student may be included for every 15 feet of board. Each student should have a paddle and a ball. At the first meeting of the class, the background of the sport should be given and a demonstration conducted. The class should then be gathered in a semicircle, where the backhand and forehand strokes are demonstrated. A careful check should be made to see whether the class members are far enough apart to swing the paddles clear of the person next to them. Without hitting the ball, the students may practice both the forehand and backhand drives (body and arm movement). If any time remains in the class period, the students may move to the courts and begin hitting balls across the net with forehand and backhand strokes. The teacher should move from person to person, correcting faults and stimulating participation.

In each class period, the teacher demonstrates some of the various strokes and then allows time for practice, either on the court or on the backboards. After the forehand, backhand, and chop have been practiced, the students should be shown the serve and allowed to play the game, utilizing all the strokes learned up to that point plus the serve.

The students should be stimulated to play an aggressive game as they master basic movements, to vary the attack from fast to slow, and to use strategy whenever possible. It is the teacher's job to improve the techniques of each player. He should make a serious effort to analyze the play of every student so that each will show greater paddle tennis skill every day he attends class.

Each student should be urged to practice the various skills outside of class time and to play the game as much as possible. On rainy days, the class members may take turns volleying against the gymnasium walls or in the handball or squash courts.

SKILL TESTS

serve for accuracy

The player makes ten legal serves, scoring one point each time it is good and a half point if it is a let. The score for the test is the number of points the server makes in ten attempts.

For another test, a target consisting of five circles is drawn on the practice board. The center circle has a diameter of 1 foot, the next circle has a diameter of 3 feet, the next 5, the next 7, and the outside 9. The server stands back 44 feet and serves to the target. If he hits the center circle, he gets nine points; the next circle is worth seven points, the next five, the next three, and the last, one. The server's score is the total number of points he makes on five attempts. Reference is made here to the diagram showing this test in the chapter on tennis.

stroke for accuracy

The player hits a ball off the wall. When it comes back, he drives it to the same target used for the serve. His score is the number of points he makes in five attempts.

rally for speed

The player stands 10 or more feet from the wall and strokes the ball to the wall as many times as he can in one minute.

DEFINITION OF TERMS

Ace. A point scored on the service when the receiver fails to return the ball.

Advantage. The point scored by a player after the score has been deuce.

Alley. The strip lying between the singles and doubles side lines.

Back Court. The area within the court and near the base line.

Backhand. A stroke in which the back of the player's hand is toward the direction he is returning the ball.

Backspin. The spinning of a ball so that the top of it turns toward the striker, caused by a chop or downward stroke.

Backstop. The wire netting on either end of the court to contain the flight of the ball. In platform paddle tennis, the back netting off which the ball may be played.

Base Line. The line at each end of the court, back of which the server must stand while serving.

Chop Stroke. A downward motion of the paddle used to put a backspin on the ball.

Court. The territory lying within the boundaries of play.

Cut. The twist or spin of a ball caused by a chop stroke.

Dead Ball. A ball that is not in play.

Deuce. A game in which each side has won an equal number of points. Each side must have scored at least three points before a game can be considerd "deuced."

Doubles. A term used to refer to a game in which there are two players on each side.

Drive. A long, fast stroke used when a player is in his back court. The ball either has topspin or is driven flat.

Drop. The sudden downward curve of the ball, caused by a topspin.

Drop Shot. A stroke that sends the ball just over an opponent's side of the net. Usually used to catch an opponent by surprise at the base line.

Error. The loss of a point by making an inaccurate or illegal shot.

Fault. An illegally served ball, or one that does not hit in the proper court on a service.

Fifteen. The term used to denote the first point scored by a player.

Fifteen-all. The score to indicate that each player has made one point.

Fifteen-love, Thirty-love, or Forty-love. The score when the server has scored one, two, or three points, and his opponent has made none.

Foot Fault. An error indicating that a server's feet were in an illegal position, e.g., over or on a line.

Forcing Shot. A shot that puts the opponent on the defensive.

Forehand Stroke. The stroke made on the right side of the body by a right-handed player and on the left side by a left-handed player.

Game. The scoring of at least four points by a player who has at that time a lead of two points.

Half Volley. A stroke that is made at the moment immediately after the ball bounces from the ground.

Kill. To smash the ball so that the opponent cannot return it.

Let. A serve that touches the top of the net and drops into the proper service court.

Lob. A stroke that carries the ball high into the air.

Love. The term used in scoring to indicate that one player has not yet scored any points in that game.

Love Game. A term indicating that one player did not score in that game.

Love Set. A series of six games, all of which were won by a single player or team.

Net. The mesh barrier over which the ball must travel.

Place. To cause the ball to go to a particular spot on the court.

Point. A term meaning that one player or side has scored.

Position. The place on the court where a player should be in order best to return the ball.

Rally. A series of strokes made during play for one point.

Return. To hit the ball legally during play.

Serve. Putting the ball into play from back of the base line by tossing it into the air and striking it with the paddle into the service court.

Server. The player who puts the ball into play at the start of a point.

Service. The first stroke of the point to be played.

Service Court. The part of the court on the other side of the net in which the ball must be placed on the service.

Set. A series of games, of which one player must win at least six. If the players tie at five each, a player must have a two-game lead to win.

Set Point. The point that will end a set when scored.

Side Line. The boundary on either side of the playing area.

Singles. A game with only two players taking part.

Smash. To kill the ball by means of a hard drive that does not impart spin or slice.

Spin. The twist of the ball caused by making any one of several strokes.

Stroke. The act of hitting the ball with the paddle during play.

Topspin. A turn of the ball that causes it to pick up speed when it bounces.

Undercut. The stroke that puts a backspin on the ball.

Volley. To stroke the ball before it touches the ground.

DISCUSSION QUESTIONS

1. Who is responsible for the origin of paddle tennis? Platform paddle tennis?
2. For what reason was paddle tennis originated?
3. To what well-known game is paddle tennis similar? List the differences.
4. Make a list of the basic strokes and describe each.
5. What is a defensive stance?
6. When may a lob be used effectively?
7. What is the chief advantage of a change-of-pace?

BIBLIOGRAPHY

Blanchard, Fessenden S., *Paddle Tennis*. New York: A. S. Barnes & Company, 1944.

Fait, Hollis F., Shaw, John H., and Ley, Katherine L., *A Manual of Physical Education Activiites*. Philadelphia: W. B. Saunders Company, 1967.

Menke, Frank G., *The New Encyclopedia of Sports*. New York: A. S. Barnes & Company, 1969.

Mitchell, E. D., *Sports for Recreation*. New York: A. S. Barnes & Company, 1952.

shuffleboard

15

BACKGROUND

Shuffleboard resembles to some extent both curling on ice and bowling on the green. Whether it was originally intended to be a combination of the two or is like them by accident is not known. Information regarding the origin of the game is somewhat contradictory, but one source assigns its beginning to ancient Persia. Another states that it was started sometime during the thirteenth century in England.

At first, the game was variously named *shove groate* and *shovel board*. It was played on hard-packed courts. Though many people participated in it, Henry VIII banned it because he thought it interfered with the practice of archery. At no time in its history did shuffleboard enjoy the popularity of either archery or golf. But in spite of such royal disapproval, it was sufficiently popular that elaborate boards of exquisite workmanship were utilized.

The game came to America either late in the eighteenth century or early in the nineteenth. Another ban, this time because of gambling, caused a decrease in interest. Later it became more popular and came to be one of the chief parts of the recreational program aboard most ocean-liners.

At the turn of the present century, many children were playing the game. As often happens, adults began to play with their children, and before long shuffleboard had a large following.

The game was introduced at Daytona, Florida, in 1913, and it found many adherents among vacationers. Every hotel and tourist court had shuffleboard facilities, and soon tourists popularized it in other parts of the country. The first shuffleboard club was organized in St. Petersburg, Florida, in 1924; the Florida State Shuffleboard Association was founded in 1928. The lack of uniformity in the rules caused a great deal of confusion, and as a result, the National Shuffleboard Association was formed in 1931 for the purpose of standardizing rules and promoting the game. Schools, colleges, social clubs, and municipal recreation organizations began providing facilities for the game.

The first men's national championship was staged in the winter of 1930–31 in St. Petersburg, Florida. In 1932, a tournament was held that included women. These first tournaments were open to all ages. In 1934, people over fifty years of age first had a tournament of their own. Now, two tournaments are held each year: a winter meet in St. Petersburg, and a summer meet in Traverse, Michigan.

The game has grown so much in popularity in recent years that it is being taught as a part of the physical education classes in schools and organizations. It is a particularly interesting game for people who are unable to take part in strenuous sports.

The diagram below shows the uniform size of a shuffleboard court (Figure 15–1).

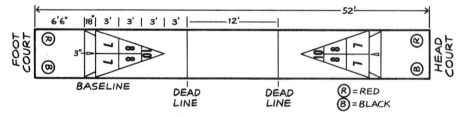

FIGURE 15-1 *Shuffleboard Court*
Lines are 3/4 to 1/2 inches wide
Separation triangle—1/4 inch line

BASIC SKILLS

The game of shuffleboard is not strenuous. It requires little energy, but a great amount of coordination is necessary. The basic skill is a good sense of "touch" so that the disc will be pushed with just the correct force to cause it to stop in the scoring spaces. The only skill involved is the push of a cue against a disc. This seems comparatively simple, but the player soon finds that it takes hours of practice to place the disc where he wants it to go. Some strategy is involved when the opponent's disc rests in high scoring areas or blocks the passageway for another disc. Different floor surfaces call for pushes of different strengths, and the efficient player needs to become so familiar with the characteristics of many types of surfaces that he needs little practice on a new surface to be able to apply the correct amount of force. Accuracy is important when one desires to push an opponent's disc out of a high scoring space and at the same time cause his own disc to remain there.

the push

The cue should be placed against the disc before the push begins. Beginners often start the push with the cue a foot behind the disc, believing that this position gives more power. It does not. It kills any sense of "touch" the player may have, and the resulting crash of the cue and disc often breaks one or both of them.

To push to the best advantage, the player should grasp the handle of the cue firmly near the end and then straighten his elbow. He should stand slightly leaning forward in such a way that the arm holding the cue is at a 45-degree angle behind the body. The feet should be about 12 inches apart, with the left foot slightly in front of the right. The weight should be equally distributed, and the knees should be flexed. As the right arm starts forward in the push from the shoulder, the left leg slides forward to shift the body and cause a more powerful stroke. As the cue forces the disc forward, the arm follows through, and the right leg may be brought up even with the left.

TEACHING PROCEDURE

Wherever there are shuffleboard courts, there is usually a level space nearby that can be used for practice. In such cases, the class should be divided in half and two lines formed. The lines should be parallel to each other at the regular shooting distance apart (about 39 feet). Each student should be equipped with a cue and a disc. The students in one line shoot to the players in the other, attempting to place the discs as close to the line as possible; then those in the second line push the discs back to the first line. As they become skilled in the basic movement of the push, the students should be put on shuffleboard courts and allowed to try to score without opposition. When this skill is mastered, the players should have opposition and should try to put the discs on the scoring areas with the possibility of getting them knocked off by the opponents.

The next and final step is the actual game of shuffleboard. At first, it should be a singles game, and later, the doubles game.

SKILL TESTS

The best indication of whether a shuffleboard player has mastered the skill of the game is the score he is able to shoot. He should shoot ten times for score. Each of the first five discs shot should be taken up after the score is registered. Each of the last five shots would remain on the court. The student's score is the total number of points he makes on the ten shots.

DEFINITION OF TERMS

Appeal. The plea a player makes to the officials because of his objection to one of their decisions.

Balk. The pushing of a disc in two motions.

Base Line. A line behind the scoring zone at each end of the court.

Correction. The replay of a half round because the wrong color disc was shot.

Court. The area upon which the game of shuffleboard is played.

Court Referee. The person who is chiefly in charge of the game.

Court Scorer. The recorder of the scores called by the court referee and umpire.

Court Umpire. The official who assumes the duties of the court referee at the opposite end of the court.

Cue. The stick used to propel the disc.

Dead Disc. A disc that, while in motion, hits a foreign object or stops in the area between the dead line. It is removed from the court.

Dead Lines. The lines 12 feet apart indicating the neutral zone.

Disc. A circular plastic or wooden object, 1 inch thick and 6 inches in diameter that weighs between $11\frac{1}{2}$ and 15 ounces.

Foot Court. The end of the court opposite the end where the game started.

Game. When a team has scored 50, 75, or 100 points, depending upon the tournament.

Ground Rules. Regulations made to suit the local playing conditions.

Half Round. A complete play at one end of the court.

Head Court. The end of the court from which the game is begun.

Match. The best two out of three games.

Mounted Disc. A disc resting on top of another. Its score is the same as the one upon which it is resting.

Red Disc. The one always shot first at the beginning of the game.

Round. A round is complete when, in singles, both players have played from both ends of the court, or, in doubles, when both members of the two teams have shot.

Scoring Disc. A disc that comes to rest completely within the scoring area.

Ten-off. The area just in front of the base line. If a disc stops in this area, the player has ten points subtracted from his score.

DISCUSSION QUESTIONS

1. Was shuffleboard ever banned in Great Britain? In the United States? If so, why?
2. Why is shuffleboard a popular sport?
3. What is the one basic skill involved in shuffleboard?
4. What were the various names given to shuffleboard in its early days?

BIBLIOGRAPHY

Butler, George D., *Recreation Areas.* New York: A. S. Barnes & Company, 1947.

Ernst, Lucia, and Horner, A. Irene, *Official Recreational Games and Sports Guide with Track and Field, 1940 and 1941.* New York: A. S. Barnes & Company, 1940.

Foote, Dareen, *Modified Activities in Physical Education.* New York: Inor Publishing Company, 1945.

Harbin, E. O., *The Fun Encyclopedia.* New York and Nashville: Abingdon-Cokesbury Press, 1940.

Lawson, Arthur, *Fun in the Background.* New York: Thomas Y. Crowell Company, 1940.

Marran, Ray J., *Games Outdoors.* New York: Thomas Y. Crowell Company, 1940.

McCoy, Mary E., *Recreational Games and Sports.* Washington, D. C.: American Association for Health, Physical Education, and Recreation, 1963.

Menke, Frank G., *The New Encyclopedia of Sports*. New York: A. S. Barnes & Company, 1969.

Schofield, Jessie, and Kellam, Mary Frances, eds. *Official Recreational Games and Volleyball Guide, 1955–57*. Washington, D. C.: American Association for Health, Physical Education, and Recreation, 1955.

Tunis, John R., *Lawn Games*. New York: A. S. Barnes & Company, 1943.

———, *Sports for the Fun of It*. New York: A. S. Barnes & Company, 1940.

skiing

16

BACKGROUND

The sport of skiing is a big business in the United States. It has grown by leaps and bounds in the number of persons participating and the number of resorts catering to these devotees. It has developed from a sport involving fewer than thirty thousand ski jumpers in the 1920s to four million today. For every skier in the 1920s, there are more than a thousand in the 1970s.

Skiing is said to be more than five thousand years old, a claim not many sports can make. The earliest ski runners were bones from large animals strapped to the shoes with leather thongs, as were snowshoes. When man sought a faster way of progressing over frozen wastes or over the icy surface of lakes, he used smaller bones, which probably were the pioneer skates. The joints of the bones were smoothed so as to produce a flat surface, which permitted a swift, gliding motion.

The Swedes learned the value of skis in warfare, using them in the War of 1521. In later conflicts in 1576, 1590 and 1610, they equipped all their troops with either skis or snowshoes. In the 1521 war, the Swedes stretched animal skins between two skis, placed injured comrades on them, and carried them off the battlefields.

The bone-runner ski had no standard size, and it was impossible for it to turn up at the ends. Several centuries after the beginning of the Christian era, wood was substituted for the bones. Wooden skis served through the early years, and no radical changes were made in their design until the sixteenth century.

It is not known who brought the first pair of skis to North America, or if they were used by Indians in Canada. It is possible that they were imported by settlers from Sweden and Norway. The snowshoe has been known for many generations in Canada, and those who used them may have constructed skis for going down steep mountainsides. It is known that during the rush to the Pacific Coast for gold in the 1850s, skis were used in the snow-covered mountains of the Sierra Nevada.

The first ski club in the United States was formed at Berlin, New Hampshire in January, 1872. The first national association was organized in 1904 with seventeen charter members, all from the middle west. It was called the National Ski Association. Later, its name was changed to the United States Ski Association.

The United States Ski Association supervises the expanding army of skiers in this country, and it has influenced the construction of ski runs and hotels. Twenty years ago no more than twenty locations in the United States provided hills for jumpers, or suitable terrain for skiers. Few inns stayed open to house the ski clan, and after a day of sport was over, skiers were faced with the prospect of traveling many miles for food and lodging. But today skiing is a business of considerable magnitude. Progress is being made in developing skiing as a school sport. The number of competitive ski programs in high school and college has risen considerably in recent years.

DESCRIPTION OF THE SPORT

Skiing is a sport with the simple objective of propelling oneself smoothly over snow on a pair of skis which are approximately 3 inches wide and from 3 to 7 feet long. It is a sport suitable for both sexes and all ages.

Four types of skiing are in general use today: cross-country, slalom, downhill, and jumping.

cross-country

In cross-country skiing, the skier slides over the snow by alternately pushing one ski ahead of the other and by pushing strongly with the poles. This type is employed when the skier hikes over winter terrain with a minimum of climbing and downhill running.

slalom

Slalom racing may be defined as controlled downhill skiing. It is usually the fearless racer who wins in a downhill race, but the individual with particularly fine skill wins in slalom racing. A number of flag-bearing poles are set in the snow from the top to the bottom of the hill. They are placed so that the skier must go around them or between them while executing complete command of all turns, and demonstrating fast reaction and coordination of body and skis. In this type of race, the skier is timed from his start at the top of the hill until he crosses the finish line at the bottom.

downhill

In downhill skiing, the skier glides down a hill with a speed in keeping with the pitch of the slope and his degree of skill. Since the ski lift has come into use, this has become the most popular form of skiing because it provides a maximum amount of skiing for a minimum of effort. The downhill is the fastest and most exciting of the races in ski competiton. But downhill skiing can be very dangerous if the necessary skills are not mastered.

jumping

Ski jumping is a thrilling part of ski competition. It is not recommended for a recreational skier because it takes considerable specialized training. The proficient jumper must have good balance and know how to judge flight. If he falls, he must be prepared to do so properly to avoid serious injury. A jumper is in the air from three to ten seconds, depending upon the steepness of the landing slope. The longer and steeper the slope, the longer the jump. The jumper is awarded points on form and distance jumped.

EQUIPMENT

The most important consideration for a beginner is determining the right fit and quality of equipment. Price is usually a good indicator of quality.

boots

The most important item of equipment is the boots, for it is through his boots that the skier controls his skis. All the force applied to controlling the ski passes through the boots. They should fit snugly with no play around the heels; the ankles should be held rigid to aid in a comfortable forward lean. The individual should try on the boots wearing normal ski socks and ski pants. When not in use, boots should be clamped in boot trees and occasionally polished with a good wax.

bindings

In addition to the boot, good bindings are needed. A conventional binding consists of a metal toeplate into which the boot tip is set. In addition, a cable circling the boot that pushes the toe firmly into the toeplate and pulls the heel down tightly on the ski is clamped forward. The binding prevents lateral movement and any lifting action of the heel on the ski. Release bindings or safety bindings are designed to release the boot and the skier from his skis should there be a sudden forward or lateral twist during a fall.

skis

There are special skis for every type of skiing mentioned, but the beginners should be concerned only with the selection of downhill skis.

Most skis are made of wooden laminations in a combination of wood and some metal. Both wooden and metal skis are graded either soft, medium, or hard according to their flexibility. In general, if a skier is light, a soft ski is preferable, and if he is heavy, a hard ski should be used. The skis should have steel edges for good control and durability. Plastic bottoms have proven to be more resistant than wood. Wood skis are cheaper but less durable. Metal skis are very durable and are easily repaired, thus providing years of service. A good skier may want a longer ski; however, the beginner should use shorter skis for better control.

ski poles

Ski poles are used for balance and movement on the level or uphill. They should be light, durable, and well balanced, with a comfortable hand grip (Figure 16–1). Poles may be made from bamboo, steel, alumi-

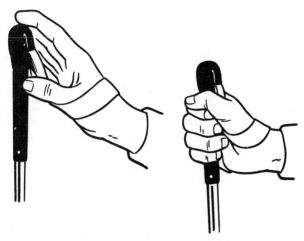

FIGURE 16-1 *Pole Grip* (From Don Cash Seaton, Irene A. Clayton, Howard C. Leibee, and Lloyd L. Messersmith, *Physical Eduction Handbook*, 5th ed. © 1969, Prentice-Hall, Inc. Reproduced by permission of the publisher.)

num, or fiberglass. A suggested length is from the ground to within a generous hand's breadth below the armpits.

clothing

The skier's clothing should be designed to keep him warm and to give protection from the wind and wet snow. It should be light enough, however, and so styled as to avoid being clumsy.

BASIC SKILLS

When an individual is learning to ski, he should plan to practice a minimum of twice a week and should learn under proper guidance, since this can be a very dangerous sport if the techniques are not properly learned. Warm-up exercises to stretch the muscles and maintain body flexibility are recommended for beginning skiers.

Elementary skiing skills are explained in the succeeding paragraphs and should be mastered in the order given. It is very important to master each skill before proceeding to the next.

walking and gliding

Walking on skis is really little more difficult than walking without skis. The difficulty the beginner encounters is that the ski is intentionally slippery. To overcome this slipperiness on the level, the skier makes use of his poles.

In walking, the skis are kept parallel and close together, and the legs are moved as in normal walking, except that the feet must glide forward. The poles are used alternately—the right going forward with the left leg and the left with the right leg. The elbows should be kept in and the pole not planted beyond the foot. The skier should push down with the arm so that the pole aids in his smooth, forward movement. The beginner should practice walking on the level until the skill is accomplished with relative ease.

A more vigorous form of walking is gliding. Each gliding step is preceeded by a slight crouch. As the skier takes a forward step, he rises out of his crouch and propels himself forward and upward, using the pole as an aid. The skis are then allowed to glide for a distance before the next step is taken.

step around

The simplest way to turn around or change direction on skis from a stationary position is to step around. This should be practiced on level ground where there is no danger of the skis slipping. The skier should start with the skis parallel, placing all the weight on one ski. He next lifts the tip of the other ski and, using the tail as a pivot, swings the tip a foot or two to the side. Then he places it back on the snow, shifting the weight to it, and brings the other ski parallel again, lifting the tip and pivoting on the tail. The poles are kept in the snow for balance and are moved only when necessary. It should be remembered that the tails of the skis always remain on the snow and that the movement of the skis resembles the motion of the hands of a clock.

Another variation of this turn is to move the tails of the skis and pivot around the ski tips. This variation is used on gentle grades, opening the tips if facing uphill and the tails if downhill.

kick turn

The most efficient way to turn the skis in the opposite direction is to execute the kick turn. The skier should learn this skill after mastering locomotion and balance. He places the skis in a traverse position, which is horizontal to the slope. In turning to the right, he sets the left pole close to the tip of the left ski and the right pole back of the left ski; then he lifts the right ski clear and swings it completely around parallel to the left ski, but pointed in the opposite direction. After transferring the weight to the right ski and balancing on the right pole, he swings the left ski and left pole around until they point in the same direction as the right ski.

falling and recovering

Everyone falls sooner or later. Only when a skier resigns himself to the idea that falling is as much a part of skiing as downhill running will he become a safe and confident skier.

The skier should be relaxed and alert, with eyes open, sizing up quickly the conditions of the snow and the slope ahead. This cannot be if he is preoccupied with fear, or even concerned about falling.

When a fall seems inevitable, the skier should assume a low crouch, controlling his fall to the uphill side by sitting to the side of his skis. To rise, the skis should be moved downhill to the body, parallel to each other and horizontal to the slope. Both ski poles are placed together. Then with the skis tucked under the body and with one hand on the top and the other on the bottom of the poles, he pushes to stand.

uphill climbing

Climbing maneuvers are designed to get the skier uphill with a minimum of fatigue. There are three different methods of climbing: the diagonal sidestep, the sidestep, and the herringbone.

In the diagonal sidestep, used on gentle slopes, the skier walks with short strides uphill at an angle.

The sidestep is used on steep slopes and is much the same as the diagonal sidestep, except that no forward motion is made. The weight is always carried upon the lower ski, while the upper is being lifted to the new position.

The herringbone is used for more speed and straight ascents, but it is more fatiguing than the sidestep. The skier must first open his skis in a

V position. He then lifts one ski upward and forward, stamps it into the snow, and places his weight over it. The operation is repeated with the other foot (Figure 16–2).

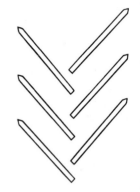

FIGURE 16-2   *The Herringbone* (Adapted from Hollis F. Fait, John H. Shaw, and Katherine Ley, *A Manual of Physical Education Activies*, 3rd ed. © 1967, W.B. Saunders Company, by permission of the publisher.)

downhill running

The skier first should practice the straight run (sliding downhill without turning) on a small slope with an adequate runoff. The most important principle in downhill skiing is balance. To maintain a balance position, a skier must ski with total motion, that is, a unity of action by the entire body. The skis should be parallel to each other and slightly apart. Their tips should always be aligned. The skier's ankles, knees, and torso are slightly flexed, with the body at right angles to the skis at all times. His elbows are flexed near the body, with the ski poles pointed down and back.

It is a good procedure in downhill running to descend by traversing, after the skier has practiced the straight run. Traversing the slope means the skis are pointed downhill at an angle no greater than 45 degrees. As the speed increases, the skier should step uphill. This is accomplished by quickly placing the weight over the lower ski and quickly lifting the upper ski ahead and into the slope. The weight is then carried by the upper ski as the lower ski is brought up to it. Once sideslipping has been mastered, a steep slope can be run with a minimum of speed, while at the same time the skier experiences the feeling of his edges biting into the slope. The greater the angle of traverse, the slower the hill is run. This is a very important skill and should be practiced in both directions.

braking

The beginner should turn his attention to braking only after he becomes proficient in straight running and the traverse. There are two techniques of braking: sideslip and snowplow.

SIDESLIPPING. This is the most important controlled braking and serves as a basis for the christies. To initiate the sideslip, the skier starts from a traverse position. This will cause the center of his weight to move downhill, flattening the ski edges. Weight distribution in sideslipping is the same as in the traverse. The body always faces the direction of the sideslip, thus insuring proper balance. By shifting weight forward and backward, a slow, controlled sideslip can be made. The sideslip can be checked, and the traverse position resumed by resetting the edges through angulation.

SNOWPLOW. This is used to slow down or stop at times when a more natural turning stop cannot be used. To snowplow from a straight running position, the skis are unweighted with an upward motion and the tails displaced at equal angles approximately a ski pole's width apart, the tips together. The skier bends the knees toward the tips of the skis, which are at right and lateral angles to the lower legs, with the weight equally distributed and slightly forward. The control of the braking force in the snowplow is essentially the skier's weight, not his strength. The poles should be kept well back. To return to a straight running position, the skis are again unweighted by an upward motion, and the tails are allowed to slide back together (Figure 16–3).

FIGURE 16-3 *Snow Plow* (From Don Cash Seaton, Irene A. Clayton, Howard C. Leibee, and Lloyd L. Messersmith, *Physical Education Handbook*, 5th ed. © 1969, Prentice-Hall, Inc. Reproduced by permission of the publisher.)

The single stem is used to achieve slight braking. The outside ski is stemmed while the inside ski bearing the weight is kept straight. The single stem is often used in a systematic drill for stem turns and stem christie. It relates to an unweighted uphill ski.

turns

Turns are simply changes in direction that require the following conditions: motion, muscular energy, and resistance.

SNOWPLOW TURN.   This is started from a straight snowplow. From this position the skier transfers more weight to one ski, which becomes the outside ski in the turn. Weight transfer is accomplished by a slight bending of the knee and angling the upper body over the weighted ski as the outside shoulder comes slightly back. The tips are kept together, and the skis remain at equal angles. To turn right, the left ski is weighted; to turn left, the right ski is weighted.

STEM TURN.   This is a slow, deliberate, controlled turn initiated from a traverse position. The uphill ski is stemmed rather than the downhill. This keeps the skier's weight on the downhill ski, making it easier to control the direction of the traverse. After the uphill ski is stemmed, his weight is gradually shifted to the stemmed ski by angling the upper body over it while the outside shoulder moves slightly back. The stem is continued across the fall line until the downhill ski points in the direction the skier wants to go. The edging of the downhill ski is increased in preparation for a new traverse. The uphill ski is then gradually allowed to run alongside the downhill ski, and a new traverse position is assumed, thus completing the turn.

UPHILL CHRISTIE.   This skill is important because it develops confidence on steep slopes and is the last half of a christie turn. The uphill christie is initiated from a traverse position by unweighting with an upward and forward motion with slight counterrotation. This is followed immediately by a sinking motion, angulation, and slight countermovement, which combine to displace the tails downhill. The turn is completed when the skier rises to resume normal traverse position.

STEM CHRISTIE.   This is perhaps the most difficult turn to master. The skier starts from a traverse position. The uphill ski is stemmed, accompanied with a sinking motion, keeping the downhill ski edged and weighted. With an upward and forward motion, he transfers the weight to the stemmed ski. The inside ski is advanced slightly and brought immediately alongside the outside ski prior to crossing the fall line. The remainder of the turn continues as an uphill christie.

PARALLEL CHRISTIE.   This has been the precursor of many variations of parallel skiing, for example, parallel christie with check, wedeln, short swing, serpent, mambo. It is considered an advanced form of skiing. The parallel christie is initiated from a traverse position with a sinking motion accompanied by a pole plant. With an upward and forward motion with counterrotation, weight is transferred to the outside ski, and the edge set is changed. Pressure is then exerted on the edges by a downward motion, angulation position with the skier's knees and hips pressing forward, and slight countermotion. Rising to a new traverse completes the turn. The tails of the skis must not swing too much past the fall line.

TEACHING PROCEDURE

The American Ski Technique, which is taught in most ski schools in the United States, was created by the Professional Ski Instructors of America in 1958 to answer an obvious need for a unified system of teaching. The idea was, and is, that a skier can move from one ski school to another without missing a step in his progress. There are six class levels from A to F, and each one has an objective "final form," or as it is now called, "demonstration form." In class A, (novice class), a student learns straight running and straight snowplowing. When that is mastered adequately, he moves on to class B (beginner) for snowplow turns and traversing. From class B the beginner goes to class C (intermediate), where the stem turn, sidestep and uphill christie are mastered. In class D (advanced intermediate), the stem christie is taught, in class E (advanced) the parallel turns, and in class F (expert) the wedeln. Each form belongs to a class and each class to a certain level of proficiency. Each is a logical step beyond the preceding one.

Before the novice ventures on the slopes for the first time, he should spend a few minutes familiarizing himself with his skis and poles. He should put them on and take them off a few times indoors or on the lawn before he attempts to go on the snow.

The skills involved in skiing can be taught effectively in classes with a maximum of twelve people. The ideal size is six. The instructor should explain and demonstrate each skill involved in the different techniques. The skills should be discussed and demonstrated before the students begin practice. When practice begins, the instructor should give individual assistance to all who are having difficulty in the movements. Skiing in class means skiing at slow speeds, and under control. The student should not be asked to attempt an exercise for which he is not ready. Since every maneuver can be divided into parts, and since exercises may be used to teach these parts, most ski instructors use the whole-part-whole method of teaching.

SKILL TESTS

When grades must be established for record purposes, it is necessary to measure ability and knowledge. The following means for evaluating are recommended:

1.   A written test of rules, techniques, and safety precautions.

2.   Observation of student's form and skill development.

3.   A test given to measure speed over a prescribed distance if students are advanced enough to perform these skills.

4.   A test course set up to evaluate the skills of *climbing*: walk, step around, kick turn, herringbone, traverse; *snowplow*: start, turn, stop and repeat; and *stem turn*: start, turn, traverse and repeat.

DEFINITION OF TERMS

Abstem. A turn in which the lower ski is stemmed.

Angulation. A body position in which the knees and hips are rolled into the hill in order to edge the skis. The upper body is angled outward and down the hill to compensate for this action. Also called comma position.

Binding. A device that keeps the boot fastened to the ski.

Boot Press. A mechanical device to hold the soles of ski boots flat.

Breakable Crust. Snow covered with a crusty surface that will not support a skier.

Camber. The built-in arc of the ski as seen from the side view; designed to distribute the skier's weight more evenly on the snow.

Check. Any maneuver to slow down the skis.

Christie. A means of turning by keeping the skis parallel as the turn is completed.

Corn Snow. A texture of snow found in the spring as a result of cold nights and warm days. Its honeycombed structure permits easy turning.

Double Stem. A running position in which the tails of both skis are pushed out into a V position. Commonly called snowplow.

Edges. The metal strip along the outside of the bottom of the ski.

Fall Line. The steepest line of descent.

Gate. Any arrangement of two flags or poles through which a skier must pass in a race.

Herringbone. A method of climbing a hill with the skis in a V position, with pressure being exerted against the inside edges.

Kick Turn. A 180-degree turn made usually on level ground moving one ski at a time.

Mogul. A bump in the terrain usually caused by many skiers turning on the same spot and pushing the snow into a mound.

Novice. A skier who has mastered the snowplow and the snowplow stop.

N.S.A. National Ski Association, the parent ski organization in this country.

N.S.P.S. The National Ski Patrol System, which is the rescue branch of the N.S.A.

Outside Ski. The ski that goes around the outside arc of a turn.

Pole Plant. A quick jab into the snow with the inside ski pole, to serve as a pivot for a turn.

Powder Snow. A dry, fluffy type of snow that is found after a fresh snowfall.

Sidestep. A simple method of ascent or descent with gradual steps with the skis parallel to each other and horizontal to the slope.

Slalom. A form of alpine compeition in which the racer must run a course designated by a series of narrow gates set in various combinations to test technique, speed, and agility.

Snowplow. Skiing in an inverted V, tips close, heels apart. A maneuver used to control speed, especially for beginners.

Stem. Preparation for a wide turn by opening the tail of the uphill ski.

Stem Christie. Turn initiated by stemming one ski, after which the skis are brought into the parallel position for the duration of the turn.

Traverse. Skiing straight or diagonally across the fall line.

Uphill Ski. The upper ski or the one that will become the upper ski in any ski turn.

Vorlage. Forward lean or shifting the weight forward prior to a turn.

Wedeln. A series of close parallel turns made in the fall line with a minimum of edge set.

Weighting. The application of weight to the skis in order to set the edges.

Wood Skis. Skis with wood as the primary strength-bearing material.

DISCUSSION QUESTIONS

1. What organization controls ski competition in the United States?
2. What safety factors should be considered before going skiing?
3. Describe the skills that should be mastered by a novice.
4. Describe the equipment necessary for skiing.
5. What is the most important piece of ski equipment? Why?
6. Where was the first ski club organized in the United States?
7. Define the following terms: (a) corn snow, (b) herringbone,, (c) kick turn, (d) snowplow, and (e) traverse.

BIBLIOGRAPHY

Bradley, D., Miller, R., and Merrill, A., *Expert Skiing*. New York: Holt, Rinehart and Winston, Inc., 1960.

Fait, Hollis F., Shaw, John H., and Ley, Katherine L., *A Manual of Physical Education Activities*. Philadelphia: W. B. Saunders Company, 1967.

Foeger, W., *Skiing for Beginners*. New York: The Ronald Press Co., 1965.

Genasci, Jean, and Genasci, James, *Skiing*. Springfield, Mass.: Springfield College, 1967.

Lund, Morten, *The Skier's Bible*. New York: Doubleday and Company, Inc., 1968.

Menke, Frank G., *The Encyclopedia of Sports*. New York: A. S. Barnes and Company, 1969.

Seaton, Don C., Clayton, Irene A., Leibee, Howard C., and Messersmith, Lloyd L., *Physical Education Handbook*. Englewood Cliffs, N.J.: Prentice-Hall, Inc., 1969.

Sports Illustrated, *Book of Skiing*. Philadelphia: L. B. Lippincott Company, 1960.

Ski Magazine Publishers, *Encyclopedia of Skiing*. New York: Harper and Row, 1970.

Ski Magazine Publishers, *The New Way to Ski*. New York: Universal Publishing and Distributing Corporation, 1964.

The Professional Ski Instructors of America, *The Official American Ski Technique*. Salt Lake City: Quality Press, 1967.

soccer

17

Soccer is essentially a game played with the feet, similar to the game of Harpastum, which is supposed to have been popular among the Greeks. The modern game has apparently resisted and survived the tendency toward variation that gave the world rugby and modern football. To avoid duplication of material already covered, this history of soccer will begin with the game as it existed in the nineteenth century.

The London Football Association met in 1863 and voted to retain, in the face of a great interest in rugby football, a purely foot game. The game this group set up by rule was first called *association football*. One version has it that the eventual name was derived from the shortening of the term *association football* to *assoc* and finally to *soccer*. Another version is that the name soccer came from the long socks that all the players

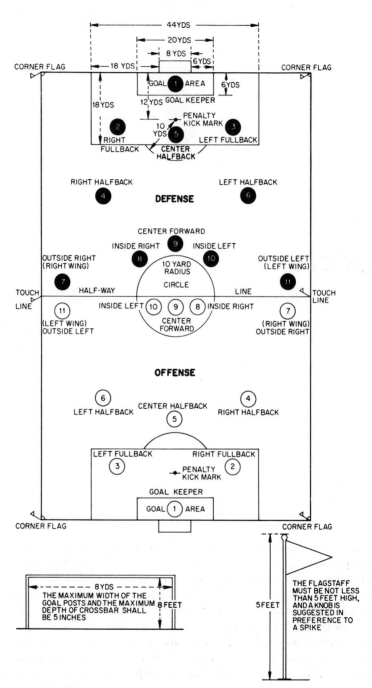

FIGURE 17-1 *Soccer Field* (From Don Cash Seaton, Irene A. Clayton, Howard C. Leibee, and Lloyd L. Messersmith, *Physical Education Handbook*, 5th ed. © 1969, Prentice-Hall, Inc. Reproduced by permission of the publisher.)

wore. With the change of a few rules and the standardizing of the playing area, the game was put into its present form (Figure 17–1).

Soccer has developed to the extent that it now holds the sort of position in England and Latin America that football and baseball enjoy in the United States. It is not unusual for crowds of over one hundred thousand people to witness soccer games.

Soccer-type football was played in America in the early nineteenth century. In fact, some of the earliest football contests between colleges were more like soccer than modern football. In the 1880s, the modern game of football was formed, but soccer continued to be played as much as usual.

The game has been played as a professional sport and by colleges and high schools on an amateur basis. It is popular in midwestern, eastern, and west coast colleges and high schools and in certain sections of the southwest. An All-American college soccer team is selected annually.

BASIC SKILLS

Soccer is an extremely fast game requiring a variety of skills and much endurance. Some of the skills, such as running and certain types of kicking, are much the same as for other sports. Some, however, are peculiar to soccer, and still others are used only in soccer and speedball. These latter skills include heading, blocking, and trapping. Correct execution of all the various skills is necessary for good soccer, and many hours of practice both in drill and in game situations must be devoted to them. Running hard, starting, stopping, and turning while manipulating the ball with the feet require stamina as well as skill, and it is necessary to include a great deal of running during practice sessions to assure good physical condition for games. The game is essentially a leg and foot game. Except for goalie play, the arms are used in no way to propel the ball, but as a balance during running steps and maneuvers. Most people have grown up employing the arms for the propelling of objects. It is usually difficult for them to learn a game in which only the legs and feet are used.

kicking

The ball is propelled and controlled principally by many kinds of kicks. These are performed in several ways, depending on the situation. Kicks may be made while the player is standing still or while running at full speed. In either case, balance is important and must be maintained to facilitate further movement after the kick. In making contact with a ball during a kick, the foot may strike it at the toe, the instep, the inside or outside of the foot, or the heel, and it may be kicked with the knee.

Each method of making contact has its peculiarities and needs to be considered separately.

TOE KICK. In all probability, the toe kick is the most inaccurate of all the kicks, because such a small part of the foot contacts the ball that it is easy to misdirect it either to the right or the left. Since it is used to some extent, it is necessary to consider it and to devote considerable time to it in practice. In this skill as in many others, it is important to keep the eye on the ball. Since the ball motion may increase the inaccuracy of the kick, the toe kick should be used only when the ball is lying motionless. (Though a good soccer player should be equally skilled with both feet, it is assumed that the kicker is right-footed in all the kicking explanations.) Just before the kick is made, the left foot is placed near to and on the left side of the ball. The right foot, being already extended to the rear, swings forward in line with the direction of the ball. The foot is pointed straight in line with the direction of the leg swing. As it passes the center line of the body, the back should arch and the arms move out and to the side for balance. The toe contacts the ball in the exact center. If a slight lift is wanted, it contacts the ball slightly below its middle but still directly in the center from right to left. The force of the kick will vary with the distance wanted and can be determined by practice.

TOP-OF-FOOT KICK. As a general rule, the top of the foot is used only to contact a ball that is moving either on a short bounce or from a longer flight. However, this kick is becoming more and more popular as a method of propelling a ball when one wants it to go in a straight line. It is especially useful on wet balls. When the ball is lying motionless on the ground, it is very seldom kicked with the top of the foot. To give any direction to the ball by use of the top of the foot, the kicker may contact it coming straight toward him, or he may turn slightly to the side and cause it to go in the direction being faced. Timing is essential and can come only through practice. The position of the ball in the air should be anticipated in order that the kicker may get set. The kick may be made from a standing position with a swing of the right leg, or it may be made in stride. If it is made in stride, the leg should swing through for the kick as a substitute for the last step. After the ball is kicked, the leg touching the ground skips while the other completes the step started by the kick.

INSIDE-OF-FOOT-KICK. This kick may be used to direct the ball to the left or to slow it down in order to gain better control. In making the kick, the leg swings through in much the same manner as it does on other kicks except that the toes are turned outward so that the inside of the foot makes contact with the ball. This kick is limited in power but is extremely useful for direction. It is essential to good dribbling. It can be made by a swing of the kicking leg while standing, or it can be, and usually is, used while the ball is in motion down the field.

OUTSIDE-OF-FOOT KICK. The movement and the use made of this kick are essentially the same as those of the inside-of-foot kick. It is a directional kick and does not utilize much force. Since it is somewhat more difficult to turn the foot in than to turn it outward as in the previous kick, it is necessary to set the body slightly to the left for a ball coming straight and very fast toward the kicker. In any case, whether the ball is approaching from the side or from straight ahead, the leg must be swung in an outward arc. In a right-footed kick, the direction given to the ball is always to the right. This kick is used alternately with the inside-of-foot kick in dribbling, in passing to another player to the right, and in blocking the ball in order to gain some control of it.

SOLE-OF-FOOT KICK. This kick is similar to the heel kick except that the sole of the foot is held perpendicular to the ground and a push is given. Though it is not so powerful as the heel kick, greater accuracy is possible.

HEEL KICK. The heel kick is used to give abrupt direction backward to the ball and to stop a ball that is rolling in the same direction as the kicker is moving. It is a dangerous kick to attempt, since the kicker may not time himself accurately, or he may step on the rolling ball, lose his balance, and fall. Much preliminary practice is necessary in order to be assured that the foot clears the top of the ball and gets ahead of it for the reverse kick. In making the kick, the kicker runs after the ball, carefully judging its speed. At a time best judged by previous practice, the left foot is planted well ahead and to the left of the ball. The right foot goes directly over the ball and in front of it. The knee is flexed so that the heel is directed backward to the ball. The kick is only slight and develops very little power. This is necessary because of the need of regaining balance quickly with the kicking foot.

KNEE KICK. This method of kicking is used to "save face" or to gain more height, though by comparison the top-of-foot kick exerts more power and gives more height. It is more difficult to achieve accuracy with the knee kick. The kick is made at a ball in flight that comes reasonably close to the kicker. In making the knee kick, the player should plant the left foot firmly, body erect, head up. As the knee goes up to contact the ball, it is flexed, while the kicker's back is arched, and his arms are extended out for balance. Balance is regained by bringing the kicking leg down and the arms in.

VOLLEYING. Volleying is kicking the ball before it hits the ground and bounces. It is used to change the direction of the ball, to advance down the field in long kicks, or to pass when moving slowly down the field. Volleying is used chiefly in a team's own end of the field. More dribbling and ground passing should be utilized at the other end of the field.

Volleying can be done either by a foot or a knee kick. The foot kick is used when power and distance are wanted. The kicker times his movements to be where the ball can best be kicked. The left leg is well planted and the kicking leg swings forward flexed at the hip and at the knee, with the greater power coming from the latter. The toe is pointed, and the contact is made with the top of the foot at a time when the ball is about two feet off the ground. The knee kick is made with both hips and knee flexed and when the ball is somewhat higher.

HALF VOLLEY. The act of kicking the ball the moment it bounces or immediately after is called a half volley. It is a valuable skill and one that will often catch opponents off guard.

PLACE KICK. A place kick is made because of some violation of the rules. It is also utilized in the goal kick. When this kick is to be made, the ball lies motionless on the ground. The kicker has free access to it and can kick it without hindrance from other players. He is allowed a short period of time in which to make the kick.

In making the place kick, the player places the left leg firmly on the ground to the left and slightly behind the ball. The kicking leg is swung backward and forward. On the forward swing, the contact is made with the ball just after the right leg has passed the left. Contact can be made with any part of the foot but generally is made either with the toe or with the top of the foot, depending on whether the kicker wants distance, height, or both on the ball. The toe kick gives distance, the top-of-foot kick both distance and height.

CORNER KICK. A corner kick is made when the defending team causes a ball to go out-of-bounds over the goal line outside of the goalposts. For such a kick, the ball is placed at a corner nearest where the ball left the playing field, and one of the opponents kicks it into the playing field. This kick will usually be a high one to a teammate, who may score on a heading play.

GOAL KICK. A goal kick is made by the goalkeeper or another defensive man near that area when the offense causes the ball to go out-of-bounds over the opponent's goal. The kick can be either long or short, depending on the type of offense the team is employing. A kick from that area will usually be a reasonably long kick in order to get the ball away from the opponent's scoring area.

PENALTY KICK. When a serious foul is committed in the penalty area by a defensive player, the offended player is given a penalty kick. The ball is placed on the penalty mark, and the player is allowed to kick directly to the goal. The area is cleared and only the goalkeeper is allowed to make any interference with the ball in the goal area to prevent it from going through the goal, but other players may contact it after it has been touched by the goalie or it has rebound off the goalposts.

INDIRECT FREE KICK. This kick is one from which a goal may not be scored until the ball has touched another player. The referee places the ball on the ground and allows the kicker free access to it. The actual kick may be made by any method of kicking best suited to the player.

DIRECT FREE KICK. This is a kick from which a score can be made directly with or without touching another player. The ball is stationary on the ground, and a toe kick is usually used. Most soccer players prefer to use the upper side of the toe and first bone connection before the ankle.

shooting

Kicking for goal during the game is an important consideration, since the type of kick often determines whether the goal is made. It is rare that a kick for goal can be made with the ball lying stationary on the ground. Most kicks for goal are attempted from within the penalty area, though goals can and have been made from far out in the field. A short, hard kick allows the goalkeeper less time to get set, thus affording a better opportunity to score. It is good playing procedure to get within the penalty area before shooting and, as soon as clear, to kick the ball hard and straight to the goal. If it is ever possible to catch the goalkeeper moving, the ball should be kicked behind him.

dribbling

Dribbling is the propulsion of a ball down the field by the use of short kicks. In most cases, it is better to dribble than to make long kicks. Dribbling helps to maintain control of the ball, whereas long kicks are frequently the cause of loss of control. Dribbling is done by kicking the ball in a variety of ways. It may be done with one leg only, by alternating inside and outside-of-foot kicks, by using only inside-of-foot kicks with one leg or only outside-of-foot kicks with one leg, or by alternating legs and types of kicks. In any case, when the field ahead is reasonably clear, the kicks should be straight for greater speed. Dribbling to the right or the left slows the attack down. Practice is important in order to perfect dribbling to such an extent that the ball can be kicked without breaking stride. Dribbling is used to get around opponents who may come up in an attempt to break it up and gain possession of the ball. To get around an opponent, it is necessary to kick to one side or the other of him while faking a movement to the opposite side. The fake should get the opponent out of step and enable the dribbler to pass him. It should be emphasized at this point that passing is the most important key to successful soccer, and dribbling should be minimized when it is possible to pass.

passing

Passing is the act of playing the ball from person to person when on offense. It is the key to successful soccer and should be emphasized and practiced over and over. The skill includes heading, the various types of kicking, running, and evading defensive players. Passing is the phase of the game that makes teamwork possible. A series of passes can be made from one player to another and back, or from one player to a second, and to a third. Most passing is done when running. In passing to a person who is running, the player should kick the ball well ahead of him so that he can meet it without having to break stride. A pass does not have to be made on the ground. When enough skill has been developed, passing can be done by air kicks. It is less accurate this way but considerably faster.

Beginners should pass by trapping the ball first to gain control of it before kicking it to a teammate. As they develop skill, kicks can be made without a preliminary trap. Very soon after the beginner is showing some mastery of the passing technique, a defensive man should be injected into the situation so that the passer will have a chance to learn evading skills.

heading

Heading is a skill that is used on occasion and, if executed properly, is very useful in giving additional propulsion to the ball in flight. Since the head is not a very maneuverable part of the human anatomy, much body play must be made in order to get into position and to play the ball. A ball that has been kicked or headed high is the type most easily headed. The player places himself where the ball will come down and flexes his knees and hips so that he is in a slightly squatting position. As the ball comes down, the legs and hips extend, causing the head to go up and contact it. The extension, plus a jump, provides important speed. The direction given to the ball depends on where the player wants it to go and how he hits it. A snap of the head in the direction one wants the ball to go is important. Skill in directing the ball is developed through hours of intensive practice.

trapping

Trapping is a method of stopping the ball and gaining control of it. It is important to the game because much greater accuracy is possible in kicking a controlled ball than in kicking an uncontrolled one. It is a very difficult skill and one that requires much attention during practice. There are many ways to trap, and practice must be devoted to all of them. The harder a ball approaches the player, the more difficult it is to trap. Trapping can be done with any part of the body other than the arms and hands, but most generally is done with the feet.

There is no chief method of trapping, but one frequently used is with the bottom of the foot. As the ball approaches the player either as a "grass cutter" or in a high bound, the foot is lifted higher, with the toe pointing upward, than it would have to be in contacting for the trap, and the wedge takes place just as the ball reaches the player. The foot should be flexed prior to the time the ball gets there, and as contact is made, extension should take place so that the ball can be held to the ground. In making any trap, it should be remembered that a minimum of weight should be placed on the ball. Sprained ankles easily result from putting too much weight on it.

If a ball approaches the player in a slow roll from straight in front, it can be stopped with the inside of the foot. If from the left side, it can be stopped by the outer, or right, side of the foot. Timing and flexibility of the foot are necessary in order to prevent a bounce from the foot.

If a ball approaches from the rear and the player does not have time to turn and stop it, the heel is brought into play. After the ball is slowed down in this manner, the player turns and brings it to a complete stop in the manner previously described.

Trapping can be accomplished also by use of the legs and the body. This type of trapping is performed when the ball is in the air. The legs are employed when the ball is relatively low, and the body when it is higher. If a ball is coming in at knee height or lower, the knees are flexed so that the shin is leaning toward the ball. As contact is made, the knees are flexed a little more so that the ball is deflected downward. At this point, the ball can be stopped in either of two ways: a foot can be lifted and placed on the ball, or the ball can be wedged between the ankles.

A method of trapping that utilizes a technique sometimes referred to as blocking but also called the stomach trap is used frequently to stop and control balls in flight. The ball is checked by the chest while the body is leaning backward. It is allowed to roll down the length of the body and is trapped by the foot in any of the previously described methods. In a chest trap, the ball is deflected by the chest directly to the ground, where it is easily controlled. Heading may also be utilized to trap the ball.

charging

Charging in soccer refers to the maneuver of taking the ball out of the control of, or away from, an opponent. It may be an attempt to use the shoulder to unbalance the opponent in order to get the ball, or it may involve only the feet. When getting ready to charge, the defensive player should set himself in the path of the oncoming dribbler. Feet should be spread apart, knees flexed, and eyes kept on the feet of the opponent and the ball. In this position, the player is prepared for a quick change of direction and knows from looking at the ball where it is at all times. When the offensive man gets close enough, the player moves in, hooks a foot around the ball, and kicks it in a direction away from where the opponent is going. Whether the defensive man moves in slowly or fast depends on the direction of the opponent. The player then follows the ball and begins a dribble down the field or passes to one of his teammates. If the shoulder is used, the player must have at least one foot on the ground, and the arms must be held close to the body. The charge must be made from the side when players are shoulder to shoulder.

POSITION PLAY

The game of soccer has eleven positions, and each requires certain maneuvers, skills, and qualities of the men who play it. There are five forwards, three halfbacks, two fullbacks, and one goalkeeper. Careful study should be made of the requirements of a position and an effort made to conform insofar as possible.

the goalkeeper

The job of the goalkeeper is to prevent the ball from going between the goalposts and to direct the defensive positioning of his fullbacks and, sometimes, his halfbacks. His area of play is limited to the penalty area for strategic purposes, although he may legally get outside that territory to play the ball. If he gets out of the area, he forfeits the privilege of using his hands. In addition to all the skills previously described, the goalkeeper needs to be able to use his hands adroitly in picking up the ball and to throw it well. The goalkeeper is governed by a rule similar to one in basketball, limiting him to four steps when he is holding the ball. He may dribble, then again hold the ball, and travel four steps. That rule varies from college to amateur or professional games:

1. College: The goalie has to bounce or lose contact with the ball in every four steps.

2. Amateur or professional soccer: After the goalie puts both hands on the ball the second time, he has to get rid of the ball.

In defending the goal, the keeper should stand about one foot in front of it and halfway between the posts. He should face the ball squarely and have his legs flexed and spread in order to move in either direction to play the oncoming ball. He should never play behind the goal. If the ball is being played toward a side, the goalkeeper should move over toward that side. He needs to be able to execute all the traps well and also to leap high into the air upon occasion.

the fullbacks

The two fullbacks have defense as their chief job but are in a position to, and often do, start offensive drives up the field. They should range within their own defensive area. A satisfactory limitation would be the center line, although some coaches teach fullbacks to move into the offensive area and go on attack. Fullbacks should play in tandem. The one on the side of the field that the ball is on should play up closer to the ball. If the ball moves to the other side, they switch positions, or the one in the rear comes forward while the other drops back.

The fullbacks should be able to perform the listed skills well. In playing as a two-man combination, one should play nearer the opponent's goal than the other, the distance depending on their skill and speed. When their team becomes the defense, the fullbacks should retreat toward their own goal. They may have to take free or goal kicks and should be skilled in performing them. When close in, the fullbacks should not play in such a way as to obstruct the goalkeeper's view of play.

the halfbacks

The center half plays a greater part in the game and requires more skill, stamina, and alertness than the wing halfbacks. He is the key of the team, defensively and offensively. Many times the wing halfbacks switch positions in a particular play. They play in tandem, starting from the side of the field where the ball is being played. If the play is on the right side, the left half plays deeper and toward the center of the field. The center half covers more ground than either of the other backs. All of them range the entire field and may be on offense one moment and defense the next. There is never a letdown in the play of the halfbacks. They are in the thick of the play at all times. Because of this, they need to be in top physical condition and must have tremendous stamina and courage. They must be skilled in all the aspects of play necessary for everyone except the goalkeeper and, in addition, because of the nature of their duties, must be able to start, stop, and change direction quickly.

The halfbacks play in front of the fullbacks and just back of the forwards. The width of the field is divided among them.

Though it should not be tried as a general rule, it is possible and highly desirable at times for a halfback to attempt to score from far out on the field. There are times when the space between the halfback and the goal is reasonably clear, and a try for goal would be more strategic than a pass to another player. The halfbacks play a large part in both offensive and defensive corner kicks. Each guards a man.

If the corner kick is to be tried near the boundary line, the halfback should be down the field in a position to assist in an offensive attack. If the kickers are of equal ability, all free kicks on the defensive half of the field should be taken by the fullbacks and the goalie (goal kicks or other kicks close to the goal). Of course, getting a ball quickly may be a point in favor of having a player very close to the ball take the kick.

the forwards

The forwards are essentially the men responsible for attack. Although their job is chiefly offense, there are times when defensive skills must be utilized. The forwards should be skilled in the various types of kicks and in evading, trapping, running, and changing direction suddenly.

The forwards need to be aggressive, able to keep going under all conditions, and able to withstand the physical punishment involved in the close play near the goal.

Besides the physical factors required for the forwards, it is necessary that they, more than the men in any other position, be alert and intelligent. A lack of alertness in any position could result in a goal for the opposition. Decisions must be made in a hurry. Teamwork must frequently be planned on the spur of the moment.

The skill of shooting is of great value to the forward, and he should spend long hours in practice in order to perfect it.

The forwards should divide the field among them in equal widths and each be responsible for his area. As the men advance, the two wings and the center forward are usually on a line in advance of the two insides. Their play should nearly always be in the opponents' territory. The forward rarely goes back in his own territory.

The two insides and the center forward play important defense roles and will often be involved with guarding the center half and the inside forwards of the other team.

It is not quite so important that the inside forwards be particularly fast, but they must be clever and good play makers. They are feeding men in many instances but also do their share of shooting. A slow forward is of little use to a team. All of them should be able to handle the ball while moving at top speed.

The center forward should be a fast and skillful player. The attack is developed around him, and he may often be the cause of a successful or an unsuccessful attack. He will be in a position to make more shots than any other player and should be skilled in that department. He should be a good team player and work well with his teammates all the time.

The wing forward needs to be fast, aggressive, and adept at getting to a ball and changing its direction to prevent it from going out-of-bounds if his own man has last touched it.

TEAM STRATEGY

Soccer is a game that lends itself well to cooperative team play. It is best to plan attacks and defense in advance, but the planning should not go so far as to deprive the players of initiative in case of a sudden situation for which no previous plans have been made.

the kickoff

Unlike other sports in which the kickoff is used to give the opposing team possession of the ball, soccer makes it possible to retain possession of the ball. The members of the defending team are 10 yards from the ball, and a kicked-off ball needs to travel forward only the distance of its circumference in order to be played by a member of the kicking team other than the kicker. Since scoring depends largely on a team's ability to retain possession of the ball, the smart kicker kicks the ball a very short distance forward to a teammate, who begins dribbling and passing to other members of his team.

Any attack should involve the use of several men working together. No one man should be allowed to monopolize the play. The attack may take four forms. First is the long-kick attack, in which the players pass to each other with kicks that cover 10 or more yards. This attack should continue all the way down the field. The second type of attack is the short-pass type, when nearly every pass is made with a kick that travels approximately 10 yards. The whole attack up the field and back holds to that pattern. The third attack is a combination of the first two, with the long pass used in a team's own end of the field and the short pass near the scoring area. The fourth type of attack is erratic and involves a variety of distance passes, many team members, and less planning. The third type of offense is recommended. The attack should be planned well ahead of time and an effort made to prepare for any emergency. However, there will be times during soccer games when there is no plan for an existing situation. As a result, the fourth method will have to be utilized until the team can get set into another offensive maneuver and establish the types of kicks and passes necessary to score eventually.

In any kind of attack, this formation has been found effective: the forwards form a semicircle, with the center closer to the opponent's end line and the outside forwards closer to the side line. The halfbacks play from 7 to 15 yards back in order to assist in the attack or to break up a fast attack if the ball is intercepted. As the scoring area is neared, the men pull closer together. When the goal is reached, they should be converged to the extend that the outside forwards are about 30 yards apart and the other three men spread equidistant between them. The halfbacks come up in their own semicircle about 4 yards behind the forwards. They are ready to assist with the offense at any time, but, more important, they are in a position to pick up the opponent who may intercept the ball. The fullbacks should come up near the mid-line, ready to intercept the opponents on a break.

In offensive strategy, it should be the policy to have an intended receiver for every pass. It is never wise, unless the element of surprise is intended, to make long, high, hard, inaccurate kicks that may be played or fought for by several players of both teams at the same time.

When the opponents suddenly gain control of the ball, a team should immediately set up defensive measures. These generally fall into a pattern. The halfbacks and fullbacks break quickly toward their own goal in an effort to get ahead of the ball, intercept a pass, and gain control. The forwards play a definite part and work into this pattern by remaining slightly back of the team. As soon as a fullback, goalkeeper, or halfback has secured possession and started the ball goalward, the forwards enter the play, and by teamwork with all team men begin another effort to score.

drills and organization for teaching

It is necessary to spend much time on the fundamentals involved in propelling the ball with body, head, and feet, and in the bodily movements. The teams should be lined up in two lines, and a soccer ball provided for every two players. If that many balls are not available, the players should be divided into as many groups as there are balls. They are stationed from 15 to 20 feet apart. The various kicks are explained, and the players then kick to their partners. The simplest kick is used first, and the other kicks are tried in their order of difficulty according to the opinion of the teacher.

This kicking practice should continue just as long as it takes the players to master the fundamental movements of the kicks. Soon they should begin kicking under game conditions. At first, they move up and down the field, kicking the ball either in a dribble or by passing without the interference of an opponent.

Later, an opponent is added to give the player the opportunity of learning to play around him.

Goalkeepers should be given specific practice in defending the goal against kicked balls. This can be done by putting the goalkeeper in his position and allowing a player to stand from 15 to 20 yards away and kick toward the goal. The kicks should be varied in direction and height to give the player practice on all types of kicks that may come his way. Remember, a goalkeeper should always put a part of his body between the ball and his nets.

The whole team should be set up and offenses should be run without opposition. Later, opponents should be added to simulate the defense of an opposing team. Other drills should be employed, involving trapping, heading, tackling, and other skills.

Since players may become bored with the game if too much attention is given to drills and since they like to scrimmage, time should be provided for it in the coaching schedule.

TEACHING PROCEDURE

Soccer is a game that requires top physical conditioning. It is rugged, for there is hardly a time when at least the halfbacks and the forwards are not moving rapidly. One cannot play soccer without having endurance and stamina. This conditioning for the game comes during the practice sessions. There should be at least three weeks of preparation for the first scheduled game. There should be much running, starting, stopping, and turning as a part of each practice session. There also should be some calisthenics each time, including stretching exercises, knee and leg exercises, and development of the abdominal muscles. The running exercise may be gained by running laps, sprinting, and doing wind sprints as well as by simulating game situations.

The ankles and feet are most likely to be injured because of their use in kicking. Shins and knees are subject to some injury from being kicked on occasion. The teacher of soccer should have a well-equipped training room in order to treat minor abrasions and sprains. Each player should be checked carefully at each session to determine the extent of his injuries, if any. A further safeguard is recommended where the budget allows and necessity dictates; ankle wraps should be employed during every practice session, and for the game the ankles should be tightly strapped with adhesive tape.

To prevent early injuries and bring a group to a peak of good physical condition, it is necessary to start slowly and have progressively longer and harder practice sessions. No sprinting or quick starts and stops should be allowed during the first week, and should be permitted later only after a good warm-up.

The first practice session should last about an hour, and each session thereafter should be increased by about ten minutes until the time has been lengthened to two hours. A typical two-hour session should consist of the following:

3:00 to 3:15   Warm-up calisthenics and running
3:15 to 3:30   Practice on fundamental kicks
3:30 to 3:45   Dribble practice
3:45 to 4:00   Passing practice
4:00 to 4:15   Practice on heading, trapping, blocking, and evading
4:15 to 4:30   Team offense and defense
4:30 to 5:00   Scrimmage

In English-style training, there is always a one mile run after scrimmage and before showers.

SKILL TESTS

Speed, accuracy in kicking, and ability to trap, head, and dribble are all included in the objectives of soccer and are the elements that go to make for effective soccer. The player should be tested for his knowledge of the background, rules, and strategy of the game, and the results should be included with the skill tests before determining the final grade.

Some subjective rating, as a part of the grading system, may be employed. The instructor can analyze good soccer playing, set up criteria for a good player, and establish points on the basis of how well each player meets these criteria. Such a method of rating will take into account such things as ability to think under pressure and cooperation with teammates, which cannot be measured otherwise.

dribble test

The dribble test is designed to test speed and kicking ability as combined to perform the dribble. The test is performed over a distance of 100 yards, and the man being tested goes from one end of the test area to the other. The subject's score is the number of seconds elapsing from the time he starts until he reaches the other end of the field. Ten obstacles are placed on the field, as shown in Figure 17–2. If there were lines running across the field as in football, there would be an object on each of the lines plus one on the goal line at the turning point. These objects alternate to the right and the left 5 yards from an imaginary line drawn straight down the middle of the field. The objects may be stakes, boxes,

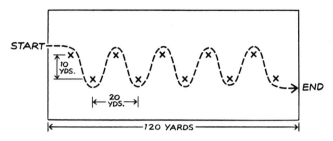

FIGURE 17-2 *Soccer Dribble Test*

chairs, people, or even line markers. At the signal "go," the man being tested runs in figure-eight fashion to the outside of every object, kicking the ball in front of him.

kick for distance

Though distance kicking is frowned upon as a general practice in soccer, the skill is necessary a few times during the game. The field should be marked in such a way as to indicate the yardage of the kicks. Figure 17–3 shows how this may be done.

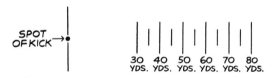

FIGURE 17-3 *Kick for Distance*

The ball is placed on the ground in front of the kicker at a designated spot. Thirty yards from this point begins a series of 5-yard zones. The first zone is No. 1, the second No. 2, and so on to No. 10. If a kick goes beyond the No. 3 mark but not to No. 4, the kicker receives a score of three.

A premium can be placed on accuracy in this test by setting limits to the right and the left inside of which the ball must hit in order for the kick to be good. If a kick is short of the first zone or too far to the right or the left, the score is zero.

heading test

The heading test is simply the act of continually heading the ball. The instructor bounces the ball high off the ground. The man being tested places himself under it and begins heading it straight into the air. His score is the number of times he heads the ball without missing it.

trapping test

The instructor passes the ball ten times to the man being tested. The player's score is the number of times he successfully traps it. The instructor should be the one to feed the ball to all the men, and each man should be given a chance to trap a variety of types of balls.

kicking for accuracy

A player stands 30 yards away from the center of five circles drawn on a bounding board and kicks five times (Figure 17–4). He attempts each time to hit in the center of the circles. He receives nine points if he hits on the line of or within the center circle, seven points for the next one, and so on down the line. If he misses all the circles, his score is zero.

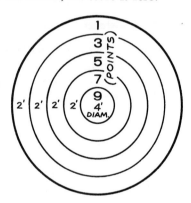

FIGURE 17-4 *Kick for Accuracy*

The heading tests and the dribble tests are scaled to a ten-point basis. The scores are then added. Each player has the opportunity of making fifty points.

DEFINITION OF TERMS

Corner Area. A quarter circle area with a radius of one yard at each of the four corners.

Corner Flag. A flag of a bright color 5 feet or more above the ground at each of the four corners.

Corner Kick. A kick taken by one of the offensive players after the ball, having last been touched by a defensive player, goes out-of-bounds over the goal line outside the goalpost.

Direct Free Kick. A kick made without interference that can score without having to be touched by another player.

Discretionary Power. An authority given the referee with which he may designate punishments for infractions not otherwise provided for in the rules.

Fair Charging, or Legal Charging. Act of attempting to unbalance the opponent and take the ball from him. Shoulders must be side by side with the opponent's and arms at side.

Free Kick. An award made to the offended team when a player commits a serious foul.

Goal Area. Area around and immediately in front of the goalposts. It comprises a rectangular area 6 yards by 20 yards.

Goal Kick. A kick made by a defensive team after the ball is kicked over the goal line by an offensive player.

Goal Line. The line across either end of the field, on which the goals are located.

Half Volley. A kick made when the ball is rising from a bounce.

Halfway Line. A line across the field which divides it in half and on which the kickoff circle is located.

Handle the Ball. The act of catching or propelling the ball with the arm or hand.

Illegal Charging. Charging an opponent using the hands, or with both feet off the ground, or when the opponent does not have the ball, or violently.

Indirect Free Kick. A kick made without interference that must be played by some other player of either team before a score may result.

Kickoff. Act of putting the ball in play at the beginning of the game.

Linesmen. Officials who have the duty of indicating when the ball has illegally left the field of play and assist referee when offside, or any foul is committed.

Offside. When a player is nearer his opponents' goal without having two opponents at the time the ball is passed to him, not when he receives it.

Penalty Area. Area in front of the goalposts from which lines run parallel to the goal lines and are 18 yards from the goalposts. A rectangular area 18 yards by 44 yards.

Penalty Kick. A kick made from the penalty mark toward the goal with no obstructions except the goalie.

Penalty-kick Mark. Spot 12 yards from the goal, from which a penalty kick is made.

Place Kick. Method of putting the ball in play in the center of the field; when his teammates are on the side, a player kicks the ball forward at least the distance of its circumference.

Punishment. Penalty for rule infractions.

Referee-drop-the-ball. The act of releasing the ball between two players when it is not known which team touched it last before it went out-of-bounds.

Throw-in. This is made because the ball went out-of-bounds on the side. The player making it stands outside the boundary line and passes the ball in by facing the field directly and throwing it in with both hands overhead with both feet touching the ground. This method of throw-in is used in all soccer games.

Touch Line. Boundary lines on the side of the field.

DISCUSSION QUESTIONS

1. How is soccer different from other types of ball games?
2. Discuss the skill of kicking a goal and the problems to be met in attempting such a kick.
3. What is charging in soccer and when is it used?

4. Explain the play of the forwards.
5. Name the four types of team attack and describe the best of these.
6. Name and describe some soccer skill tests.

BIBLIOGRAPHY

American Association for Health, Physical Education, and Recreation, *Physical Education for High School Students*. Washington, D. C., 1961.

Caswell, John E., *Soccer for Junior and Senior High Schools*. New York: A. S. Barnes & Company, 1933.

Coyer, Herbert E., *The Coaching of Soccer*. Philadelphia: W. B. Saunders Company, 1937.

Fralick, Samuel, *Soccer*. New York: A. S. Barnes & Company, 1945.

Hughes, William L., and Williams, Jesse Feiring, *Sports, Their Organization and Administration*. New York: A. S. Barnes & Company, 1944.

Menke, Frank G., *The Encyclopedia of Sports*. New York: A. S. Barnes & Company, 1969.

Mitchell, Elmer D., *Sports for Recreation*. New York: A. S. Barnes & Company, 1952.

Official N.C.A.A. Soccer Guide, Latest edition. New York: National Collegiate Athletic Association.

Seaton, Don C., Clayton, Irene, A., Leibee, Howard C., and Messersmith, Lloyd L., *Physical Education Handbook*. Englewood Cliffs, N.J.: Prentice-Hall, Inc., 1969.

Shaw, John H., *Selected Team Sports for Men*. Philadelphia: W. B. Saunders Company, 1952.

Waters, Earle C., Eiler, John R., and Florio, A. E., *Soccer*. New York: A. S. Barnes & Company, 1950.

speedball

18

BACKGROUND

The game of speedball was devised in 1921 by Dr. Elmer D. Mitchell, the director of physical education at the University of Michigan. By combining the exciting passing techniques of basketball with the kicking and dodging skills of soccer and touch football, he hoped to develop a fast-moving, vigorous outdoor sport which would have widespread appeal for people of varying abilities. It was also his intention to lengthen the fall outdoor sports season by inserting this new activity after football and prior to the start of the basketball season. Today speedball has become a regular part of the physical education program in schools all over the country, and it is fast finding a place as an exciting intramural sport for students from junior high school age through college.

THE GAME

The game of speedball is played on a large field similar to soccer or football, with goalposts placed on the end lines. The dimensions for the men's game are 100 yards long and 531 ⅓ yards wide (Figure 18–1).

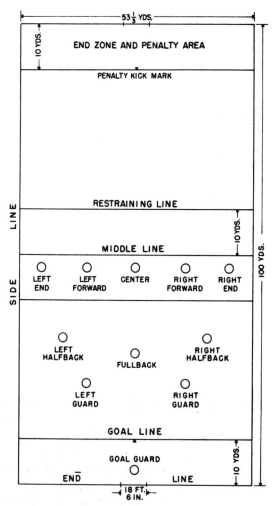

FIGURE 18-1 *Men's Speedball Field* (From Don Cash Seaton, Irene A. Clayton, Howard C. Leibee, and Lloyd L. Messersmith, *Physical Education Handbook*, 5th ed. © 1969, Prentice-Hall, Inc. Reproduced by permission of the publisher.)

Maximum suggested dimensions for the women's game are 100 yards long by 60 yards wide, or minimums of 80 yards long by 40 yards wide (Figure 18–2). A regulation speedball is slightly larger than a soccer ball, but a soccer ball frequently is used in school programs.

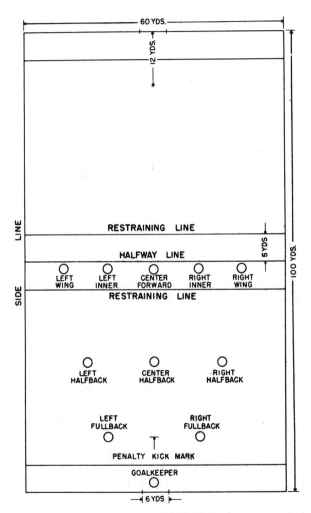

FIGURE 18-2 *Women's Speedball Field* (From Don Cash Seaton, Irene A. Clayton, Howard C. Leibee, and Lloyd L. Messersmith, *Physical Education Handbook*, 5th ed. © 1969, Prentice-Hall, Inc. Reproduced by permission of the publisher.)

A speedball team consists of eleven players who align themselves on their own half of the field as in soccer or field hockey. The object of the game is to score by passing or kicking the ball down the field over the opponent's end line or through the goalposts.

There are four methods of scoring in women's speedball, and five in the men's game.

1. *Field Goal.* A field goal is scored when a ground ball is kicked through the uprights and under the crossbar. Points awarded: 3 (men), 2 (women).

2. *Drop Kick.* A drop kick is scored when the ball is drop-kicked over the crossbar from outside the penalty area. Points awarded: 1 (men), 3 (women).

3. *Touchdown.* A touchdown is scored when an aerial ball is passed from the field of play over the penalty area to a teammate standing behind the goal line but not between the goalposts. Points awarded: 2 (men), 2 (women).

4. *Penalty Kick.* A penalty kick, awarded for certain fouls, is a place-kick taken on the penalty kick mark in front of the goal. Only the goalie may defend against this kick, and a goal is scored if the ball is kicked between the goalposts and under the crossbar. Points awarded: 1 (men), 1 (women).

5. *End Goal.* An end goal is scored whenever the ball is kicked or bodied over the end lines, not between the goalposts. Points awarded: 1 (men only).

POSITIONS

The vigorous running and passing game in speedball and the rapid shift from an aerial to a ground attack make position playing and the marking of an opponent extremely important factors in a well-played game. Players should be alert and quick to change position and direction, in order to keep pace with an opponent or keep an area properly covered.

Positions on the field are similar in the men's and women's games, with only slight differences found in the names given to the players.

Names of players, ready for a kickoff, are as shown in Figure 18–3 for men and Figure 18–4 for women.

The responsibilities of the players are similar to those in soccer, in that the forwards are the main offensive players trying to score. They are assisted by and backed up by the halfbacks, who may advance with the forwards even as far as the opponent's goal. Forwards should not play back in their own goal area, but instead should try to remain out in the clear, waiting to receive the balls kicked or passed out by their own

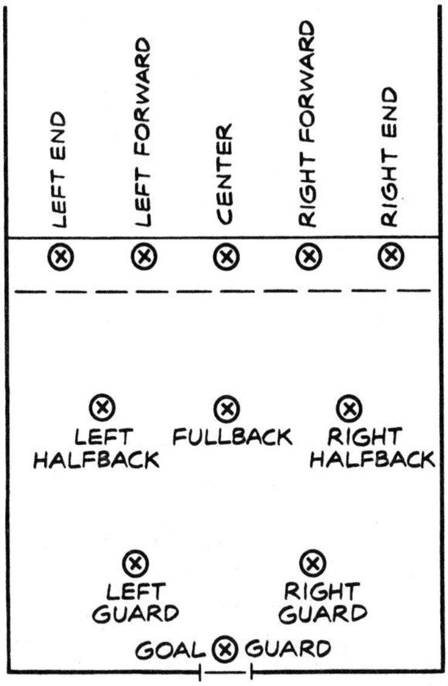

LEFT END
LEFT FORWARD
CENTER
RIGHT FORWARD
RIGHT END
LEFT HALFBACK
FULLBACK
RIGHT HALFBACK
LEFT GUARD
RIGHT GUARD
GOAL GUARD

FIGURE 18-3 *Men's Speedball*

LEFT WING
LEFT INNER
CENTER FORWARD
RIGHT INNER
RIGHT WING
LEFT HALFBACK
CENTER HALFBACK
RIGHT HALFBACK
LEFT FULLBACK
RIGHT FULLBACK
GOALIE

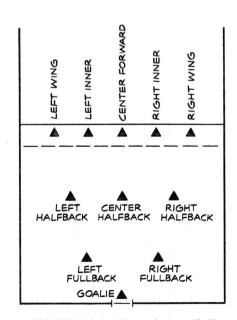

FIGURE 18-4 *Women's Speedball*

defense. Fullbacks are important defensive players, keeping the ball from entering their goal area, and assisting the goalie in preventing all types of goals. It should be noted here that the goalie has no special playing privileges in speedball as he does in soccer.

Because of the rapid exchanges of the ball, and the basketball-style game that is frequently used by the attack, a man-to-man type of defense is often utilized. For defensive purposes, therefore, all players should *mark* or be responsible for guarding a specific opponent, according to respective positions on the field. Basketball guarding techniques and rules are applicable here to the game of speedball. Specific man-to-man assignments should be designated as follows:

1. Left end (wing) versus right guard (fullback)
2. Left forward (inner) versus right halfback
3. Center forward versus fullback (center halfback)
4. Right forward (inner) versus left halfback
5. Right end (wing) versus left guard (fullback)
6. Goalie versus goalie—if necessary

   (Note: women's positions are in parentheses)

Zone defenses or a combination man and zone defense also may be used in speedball. Whichever method is used, it is important that players remain spread out, covering the entire playing area to promote better team play and passing opportunities. Too often, particularly with younger age groups, players bunch around the ball, hindering good passing and often causing fouls or injuries.

BASIC SKILLS

Many of the skills and techniques found in the game of speedball are identical to those used in other team games. For instance, good passing, catching, pivoting, and guarding are vital to the development of a rapid aerial speedball attack. These skills are discussed fully in the basketball chapter of this book, and need not be defined here. Hints for the development of good kicking, dodging, trapping, tackling, and heading may be found in the soccer chapter. These are essential fundamentals of a solid ground game in speedball, but details need not be repeated. However, there are certain skills that are unique to speedball, and this section will be devoted to them. In general, these are developed in order to change from a ground to an aerial game, and therefore they involve the conversion of a ground ball upwards so that it may be caught by the player or by a nearby teammate.

the kick-up to self

The ball may be legally converted from a ground ball to an aerial ball by a player's using one or both feet and kicking it up to waist level so that it may be caught.

1. A moving ball that is rolling on the ground toward a player may be converted easily by the player extending a foot to meet the oncoming ball. As the ball rolls onto the instep, a gentle lifting of the leg and simultaneous flexing of the foot will raise it up into the hands. A moving ball that is coming in the air toward a player may be caught, provided it has just been kicked up by a teammate or an opponent, volleyed, or headed to the player. A ball that has rebounded from the ground is a ground ball, and must remain that way, unless it is kicked up.

2. A stationary ball may be converted into the air by a player's using one or two feet:

   a. *One-foot method.* The foot that is placed directly on top of the ball gives it momentum by rolling it backward and onto the instep for the lift up to the hands.

   b. *Two-foot method.* This technique is more advanced and requires coordination and timing for successful completion. It should be attempted only when a player is in the clear and not surrounded by opponents. To perform this skill, the player places one foot on either side of the stationary ground ball, squeezing it gently with the ankles. Using the arms and upper body to help provide upward momentum, he jumps up, lifting the ball with the ankle grasp, and, at the height of the jump, releases it so that it may be caught.

the kick-up to teammate

A ground ball may also be converted to an aerial ball by kicking it up to a teammate. To accomplish this skill, the player extends his foot under a stationary or moving ball. With it momentarily balanced on the instep, he kicks it upward in the direction of his teammate. When caught, it legally becomes an aerial ball. If the teammate is unable to hold the ball, and it falls to the ground, it should then be kicked and played as a ground ball.

the drop kick

The drop kick is an additional speedball skill that is important because of its scoring value. To execute a drop kick for a score, the player with the ball must be facing his opponent's goal but no closer than the penalty area. With his eyes constantly on the ball as he drops it directly in front of him, he takes one step forward and kicks it just after it bounces. The kicking foot should send it forward and upward so that it will travel in an arc over the crossbar between the uprights.

The drop kick may be used by defensive players to put the ball in play after it has gone out-of-bounds over the end line. The punt (a drop kick without the bounce) may be used also to get the ball out of the goal area, but not to score.

TEACHING PROCEDURE

fitting it into the program

The game of speedball fits easily into the physical education program as a follow-up to a unit on soccer or field hockey. Inasmuch as hockey and soccer positions and soccer game skills are utilized in speedball, the transition is a simple one. Furthermore, the addition of basketball game skills brings real excitement and challenge into the soccer-speedball unit. This in turn provides a welcome opportunity to practice basketball skills outdoors, prior to the beginning of the indoor season.

Players are quick to recognize many other values inherent in the game of speedball. Besides basketball and soccer skills, the players realize that alertness, speed, endurance, aggressiveness and quick thinking are all essential elements of speedball. The challenge of adjusting from an aerial to a ground game, or maneuvering the ball into one of the many scoring possibilities makes offensive and defensive strategies highly complicated. Building it into the program after the other eleven-man team games helps the players to meet these challenges more effectively.

introducing the game

A brief overview of the historical development of speedball, a film, or a demonstration may help to introduce the game to a large group all at one time. Students who have participated in the previously mentioned games of soccer, field hockey, basketball, and touch football are quick to recognize the new skills needed and the variations in rules.

Practice of the basic skills for kicking the ball up to oneself and to a partner enables players to adapt quickly into the new aerial aspects of the game. Circle formations, shuttle lines or small groups may work on these skills for a part of a class period. Then an opportunity to use them in actual game play should be provided all the students as soon as possible, in order that they may understand better how they may be utilized most effectively. The drop kick and the punt should be practiced separately, as well as various team plays in which the ball is moved into scoring position.

Station teaching with squads or teams assigned for the purpose of practicing specific drills may be utilized to develop these speedball skills. Groups can be rotated through the stations in order that all students may have the opportunity of developing or improving.

developing team play

To develop teamwork and playing patterns for speedball requires formation drills as in other team sports. Players should plan together strategies to be used in the various situations that arise during a game.

KICKOFF PLAYS. Various types of kickoff plays should be developed in which the ball is kicked forward diagonally to the wings, or converted into an aerial ball for quick passes to the sidelines and down the field toward the opponent's goal.

SCORING PATTERNS. Plans for the completion of touchdown passes, or for quick changes of an aerial ball into a field goal attempt or a drop kick over the goal should be developed, making sure that both sides of the forward line have an opportunity to practice. A shifting diagonal line is often effectively used by attacking forwards, wherein the forwards without the ball run ahead in their own zones while maintaining a diagonal pattern.

THROW-IN FORMATIONS. Aerial passing patterns that result from an out-of-bounds throw-in should be rehearsed so that the halfback taking the throw-in may successfully complete his or her pass, and his team may retain control of the ball.

Other situations that may also be practiced include the *jump ball*, taken as in basketball whenever two opponents tie up the ball, a *kick-in* from the end line, which may be a drop kick, place kick, or punt taken by the guard or fullback, or a *free kick* from the middle of the field as a penalty for violations. In each of these situations all players must spread out away from the player taking the kick, and the kicker may not touch the ball again until after it has been played by someone else.

To develop effective team play, beginning players should be reminded constantly to avoid bunching up around the ball. Playing in proper lanes, and marking only the designated player should promote coverage of total playing area, as well as good defensive play. Players are less likely to be injured, also, if they remember to keep distances between themselves and their teammates. More advanced players should be able to exchange areas when necessary without difficulty.

EVALUATING SPEEDBALL SKILLS

Skill tests should be administered to all students as part of the overall evaluation of a speedball unit. Many tests may be drawn from basketball or soccer references. Others may be developed by the teacher in order to include the conversions, the drop kick, and the punting skills that are important elements of the game. One simple testing technique that may easily be utilized and administered is the rating scale, wherein the teacher indicates a score of one-to-five or one-to-ten for individual performances of skills, depending on the excellence of the outcome. Keeping an individual record of interceptions, fumbles, dodges, completions, scoring attempts, and goals made is another method of evaluation. Students may assist in maintaining these accounts, and this, in turn, becomes a learning opportunity.

DEFINITION OF TERMS

Aerial Ball. A ball that has been caught after having been kicked or volleyed, and may then be played as in basketball by passing it down the field.

Carrying the Ball. A violation of the rules in which a player makes forward progress with the ball by taking steps.

Defensive Team. The team attempting to stop the advance of the offensive team, to prevent their scoring and then to secure possession of the ball.

Double Foul. Two players on opposing teams foul at the same time.

Dribble. A ball kicked with the feet, batted, or tipped, and then advanced in a series of short kicks by one player.

Drop Kick. A kick made by dropping the ball to the ground after it has been legally caught, and then kicking it with the toe or instep just after it makes contact with the ground. May be used to score.

Field Goal. A goal made when a ground ball is kicked so that it passes through the goalposts and under the crossbar.

Fly Ball. A ball raised into the air from a kick.

Free Kick. A kick awarded the opposing team when a violation of the rules occurs. All players must stand 5 yards (women) or 10 yards (men) away from the kicker.

Ground Ball. A dead, stationary, rolling, or bouncing ball which must be advanced by means of the feet.

Guarding. Playing in such a position as to interfere with the opponent's efforts to play the ball.

Intercept. The catching of a pass or a kick-up of a ball or a dribble from the opponents.

Juggle. An aerial dribble. The ball is batted up in the air over or around an opponent. The player who juggled the ball advances down the field to catch it. Only one aerial dribble is permitted at one time.

Kickoff. A kick used to put the ball into play at the start of the game. It is also used to start the second half and following the scoring of a goal.

Marking. A system of assigning specific opponents for each player to guard.

Offensive Team. The team in possession of the ball.

Out-of-bounds. When the ball touches the ground on or over the side lines. The halfback on the opposite team receives the ball for a throw-in. When a player with the ball passes over the side lines, or a dead ball crosses over the end line it is also an out-of-bounds call.

Pass. A ball that is thrown or kicked to a teammate.

Penalty Kick. A kick awarded for a foul in the penalty area made by the defensive team. The offensive team is given a chance to try for a goal without opposition except from the goalie. The ball is placed on the penalty kick mark, and scores one point if completed.

Personal Foul. A type of rule infraction in which personal contact is made, impeding the progress of an opponent. Kicking, tripping, holding and pushing are examples. A free kick is awarded opponents when a foul is committed in the middle of the field, or a penalty kick is awarded if said foul is committed by the defense in the penalty area.

Pivot. A change of direction made by rotating the feet without walking with the ball, as in basketball.

Punt. A type of kick in which the ball is held in the hands and dropped toward the foot, which then rises to meet it, and kicks it into space before it has touched the ground.

Restraining Line. A line drawn parallel to the halfway line beyond which the defensive team may not pass until after the kickoff.

Side Lines. The lines at the sides of the field.

Tackle. A maneuver used to take the ball from an opponent by means of the feet.

Technical Foul. A type of rule infraction that does not involve personal contact, for which a free kick may be awarded.

Tie Ball. Two opponents taking possession of a ball simultaneously, and a jump ball is called.

Touchback. When the ball crosses the goal line after being last touched by the defense.

Touchdown. When the ball crosses the goal line after being passed from outside the penalty area and caught by a teammate waiting behind the end line not between the goalposts.

Trapping. A means of stopping the ball and gaining control of it by one foot, both knees, or the inside surface of the lower leg.

Violation. An infraction of a rule, such as running with the ball, for which the opponents are awarded a free kick.

Volley. Playing the ball with the head or any other part of the body except the hands, forearms, and feet before it touches the ground.

DISCUSSION QUESTIONS

1. Relate the background of speedball.
2. Indicate some of the differences and similarities between soccer and speedball.
3. Outline the various methods of scoring in speedball, and indicate the number of points awarded for each type.
4. Explain some of the skills unique to the game of speedball.
5. Originate some offensive and defensive team plays.

BIBLIOGRAPHY

Barnes, Mildred J., Fox, Margaret G., Loeffler, Pauline A., and Scott, M. Gladys, *Sports Activities for Girls and Women*. New York: Appleton-Century-Crofts, 1966.

Barton, Helen, *Speedball for Girls and Women*. Ann Arbor, Michigan: Edwards Brothers, Inc., 1937.

Dear Elaine, Kjellstrom, Louise, and Turnbull, Jenny, *Motion Pictures in Sports*. Washington, D. C.: National Section of Women's Athletics of the American Association for Health, Physical Education, and Recreation, 1939.

Division for Girls and Women's Sports, *Soccer-Speedball Guide,* current edition. Washington, D. C. American Association for Health, Physical Education and Recreation.

Hillas, Marjorie, and Knighton, Marion, *An Athletic Program for High School and College Women*. New York: A. S. Barnes & Company, 1929.

Hupprich, Florence L., *Soccer and Speedball for Girls*. New York: A. S. Barnes & Company, 1942.

Larson, Marjorie S., *Speed-a-Way Guide Book,* current edition. 1754 Middlefield Road, Stockton, California.

Mason, Bernard, and Mitchell, Elmer, *Active Games and Contests*. New York: A. S. Barnes & Company, 1935.

Meyer, Margaret, and Schwarz, Marguerite, *Team Sports for Girls and Women,* fourth edition. Philadelphia: W. B. Saunders Company, 1965.

Miller, Donna Mae, and Ley, Katherine L., *Individual and Team Sports for Women*. Englewood Cliffs, N.J.: Prentice-Hall, Inc., 1955.

Mitchell, Elmer Dayton, *Official Speedball Rules*. New York: American Sports Publishing Company, 1933.

Seaton, Don Cash, Clayton, Irene, A., Leibee, Howard C., and Messersmith, Lloyd, *Physical Education Handbook,* fourth edition. Englewood Cliffs, N.J.: Prentice-Hall, Inc., 1965.

Sevy, Ruth, *Selected Soccer and Speedball Articles* (1935–64). Washington, D. C.: Division for Girls and Women's Sports, American Association for Health, Physical Education and Recreation, 1963.

Shaw, John H., *et al.,, Selected Team Sports for Men*. Philadelphia: W. B. Saunders Company, 1952.

Vannier, Maryhelen, and Poindexter, Holly, *Individual and Team Sports for Girls and Women*. Philadelphia: W. B. Saunders Company, 1968.

swimming

19

BACKGROUND

Man's first attempts at swimming probably took place because of the challenge presented by a deep steam or lake and the fact that he saw animals propelling themselves in water. Some of his fellows may have drowned, and he might have realized that by being able to stay afloat, he could prevent himself from drowning. Since he copied animals, he almost certainly used what we now call the "dog paddle" as his first stroke.

The first existing record of swimming is depicted in mosiacs at the ruins of Pompeii. These picture men propelling themselves in water. It is believed that because of the numerous large baths, the many rivers in Greece, and the interest in all kinds of athletics, the ancient Greeks participated in swimming on a rather large scale.

The English regarded swimming as a sport early in the 1800s. The stroke, through some sort of natural evolution in an effort to improve it, had taken the form of what is now known as the breaststroke. Contests began in 1837 under the auspices of the National Swimming Society of England. English swimmers had a brief view of a type of crawl when the Society imported some American Indians in 1844 for swimming meets. Even though they swam faster than the English, their stroke was performed so grotesquely that no efforts were made to copy it.

By 1862, the Associated Swimming Clubs governed the swimming contests. The site of one meet was the German gymnasium in London. In 1869, a new ruling group, known as the Amateur Swimming Association, took control and 300 swimming clubs became affiliated with it. In 1875 Captain Mathew Webb successfully swam the English Channel, using the breaststroke to cross the long and difficult stretch of water.

Swimming speed has gradually increased through the years in all the racing distances. To illustrate this improvement, let us examine the 100-yard event. Until about 1900, the English were more successful in their attacks on that distance than the people of any other country. After 1900, the Americans began gradually to lower the record. The history of the development of speed in the 100-yard race is closely tied to the development of freestyle swimming. As the freestyle stroke shortened racing times, swimmers began to learn and use that method of swimming. The first assault on the 100-yard distance was with the breaststroke in 1878, and the time recorded was 76.75 seconds. A second time of 68.5 seconds is recorded for the same year.

Trudgen, an Englishman, took a trip to South America sometime in the 1860s and learned a new swimming stroke that involved bringing the arms out of the water alternately in windmill fashion. Since it appeared to result in faster movement through the water, he introduced it to English swimmers upon his return. It became known as the trudgen crawl. In addition to the arm movement, the legs used a scissor-like motion on each complete arm stroke. There may have been a flutter kick between each scissor. The success of the stroke in reducing the swimming time for the 100-yard distance is seen in the gradual lowering of the record over a period of fourteen years to one minute flat. Trudgen was the leading proponent of swimming in his day. He became extremely famous in the swimming world. Though his stroke is not employed in competition, it is still used by many swimmers today, and his name is used to identify it.

The crawl type of stroke came upon the swimming scene in 1902, when Richard Cavill set a new record of 58.6 seconds for 100 yards, using this method. The history of this stroke goes back to 1878, when Cavill's father, who had made an unsuccessful attempt to swim the English Channel the year before, took a trip with his family to the South Seas. On this trip they noticed the same stroke that Trudgen had observed, but they went further than Trudgen and analyzed the leg movement carefully. It was found to be an up and down movement resulting in a splash. The family eventually settled in Australia and introduced the new style of swimming. The Australians quickly dubbed it the splash stroke, but since it was later described by one of Cavill's sons as a type of crawling through the water, it eventually became known as the Australian crawl.

The other sons of Cavill began to spread the fame of the new stroke in other parts of the world. Sydney Cavill was chosen to direct the swimming activities of the San Francisco Olympic Club, where he stayed for twenty-five years. One of his pupils was J. Scott Leary, who became the first American to swim 100 yards in one minute. After accomplishing this and winning seventeen straight races, he became known as the outstanding American swimmer.

Up to Leary's time, Charles Daniels of the New York Athletic Club was the most renowned swimmer in the country. At the first opportunity, Daniels observed Leary's stroke and immediately saw the difference between his own trudgen scissors kick and Leary's flutter kick. Assuming this to be the reason for the extra speed, Daniels developed his own kick and in so doing created what is now known as the American crawl.

Using the American crawl, Daniels swam 100 yards in 57.6 seconds in New York in 1906, tying the record Healy set in Australia in 1904. However, later in the same year, Daniels set a new world's record of 56 seconds in a meet in St. Louis. Before his swimming career came to an end, he swam the distance in 54.8 seconds in 1910.

Duke Kahanamoku, a Hawaiian, arrived on the swimming scene with a stroke that was quite similar to the two crawls. He managed to break the world's record in 1913 by swimming 100 yards in 54.6 seconds, and he lowered this over a period of four years to 53 seconds flat. His swimming time remained the lowest until 1933, when Johnny Weissmuller reduced it to 52.6. Notable among men swimmers have been Peter Fick and Alan Ford. The latter, in 1945, established a record of less than 50 seconds for the 100-yard race. While these men were working hard to reduce the 100-yard time, other competitors were attacking other distances successfully, using other strokes. In the 1960s Don Scholander did more than any other individual to bring the U. S. to the forefront in Olympic swimming.

Women were also in the picture. Two most successful in the freestyle were Helene Madison, who did her best swimming in 1932, and Ann Curtis, who in 1946 and 1947 improved nearly all of Madison's work. Eleanor Holm Jarret Rose was the outstanding backstroke swimmer. Katherine Rawls was one of the greatest women breaststroke swimmers. Recently Debbie Meyer set several Olympic records.

BASIC SKILLS—STROKES

In this chapter no space is given to the teaching of beginning swimming, It is assumed that everyone who reads this material will be able to propel himself in the water, turn in any direction, tread water, bob, surface dive, swim under water, do a standing dive from the pool deck, and, when in fair physical condition, swim a quarter mile using one of the three accepted speed strokes. The techniques here are concerned directly with the skills involved in swimming competition and how to perfect those skills in order to perform with reasonable efficiency as a member of a senior high school or a college swimming team.

The student who desires proficiency in competitive swimming must have a love of water and water activity. He must realize that in order to develop the skill and endurance required, a great deal of hard work in the form of kicking and arm stroke drills and many laps using special strokes must be endured. Swimming competition is one of the most tiring of all sports, and adequate conditioning must take place in order to meet its rigors.

Each of the three strokes used in competition consists of four distinct phases, each of which must be mastered in order to excel. These are the arm stroke, the kick, breathing, and the coordination of these phases. Each one of the first three is extremely important, and the last is so important that, if the first three are performed to perfection but not coordinated, nothing is gained. Two other very important fundamentals of good swimming that make for more effective stroking are body position and glide. A position in the water that creates the least resistance and enables the legs and arms to work most effectively is the one to be sought by the swimmer. There are times, however brief, during a complete stroke when neither the legs nor the arms are driving. At such times, the body must glide through the water. It is important that such a body position be maintained that minimum resistance is caused.

Any type of swimming is performed more effectively when the swimmer is not tense. He should feel so much at home in the water that he is able to relax and concentrate on the skill at hand. Some individuals with possibilities as competitive swimmers never really become efficient because they cannot work relaxed. The good teacher will work first on body position and then on relaxation, endurance, and skill.

the crawl stroke

Teachers of swimming who skip the elements of beginning swimming and progress to the strokes, generally teach the crawl stroke first. It is a speed stroke, as indicated by the fact that the fastest swimming times are made using the crawl. When performed correctly, it is not very tiring and, once it has been mastered, other strokes are learned comparatively easily. Most people have a desire to learn the crawl stroke but have trouble mastering it if they have learned some other stroke first. A student who profited from good swimming instruction early and has mastered the elements of the crawl has a good chance of making the swimming team in the freestyle events.

The crawl stroke is performed in a horizontal position in the water. The instructor can demonstrate this position to pupils by pushing off at one side of the pool and doing a face float. The face is underwater, the hands and arms are extended beyond the head, the back is arched, the legs are straight and together, and the toes are pointed. The body should be relaxed and allowed to float on top of the water. If the person lacks the buoyancy to float, momentum will hold him up a while. The potential crawl strokers will then see that all that is necessary for the crawl stroke is to move correctly the arms, legs, and head.

The four phases of the crawl stroke are the flutter kick, the overarm stroke, breathing, and the coordination of these three. Some coaches insist on teaching all four as a unit, stressing coordination. The writer believes coordination should be stressed, but he believes also that peak performance can be achieved only by teaching the first three phases separately and gradually putting them together.

THE FLUTTER KICK. The kick is executed by moving the legs alternately in an up and down thrash. At the feet, the thrash at its widest will be from 12 to 15 inches. The legs move from the hips down with enough bending at the knees to cause a circular motion of the feet. Resistance, which is the basis for motion in water, comes from the entire leg and not from just the shin down. Some novice instructors even today insist that the legs remain rigidly straight during all movements of the flutter. If this advice were adhered to, the result would be no motion at all, since there would be as much backward as forward resistance, and the forward thrust would be zero. On the other hand, if a beginner is allowed to bend his knees during the flutter-kick drill, he may bend them too much, thrash air, and get nowhere. A suggestion would be to allow some knee bend but with the caution that it should be kept at a minimum. Some power is obtained on the downthrust of the leg, but it is pointed out here that emphasis for propulsion is on the upthrust. The downthrust is more of a recovery than a power movement.

The swimmer should make no effort to point the toes and turn them inward. This usually results in a tense leg kick. Actually, with a powerful kick, the proper position will come without any conscious effort. The legs are below water, but the feet at the end of the upward thrash should barely break the surface so they will cause a splash about 6 inches high.

If the splash is higher than 6 inches, the feet come out of the water too high, flail air, and lose much of their power.

The teacher should demonstrate the flutter kick on land and analyze each movement carefully. He should then get into the water and, pushing off from the bank, flutter kick across the pool so that the swimmers may see how it is done. The pupils should then get into the water, grasp the pool gutter with one hand, and place the other about 20 inches below, fingers pointing down, supporting the body in a prone position so that the kick can be practiced.

Starting with relaxed legs extended, close together, they practice the crawl kick, which consists of a series of alternate up and down leg thrashes of even lengths. The leg movements are started slowly, and then the speed is gradually increased until an easy rhythm is established. Such a practice in some form or other should be a part of every class period, because it is highly important to have a correct flutter kick for an efficient, strong crawl.

Another form of kicking practice is to push off from the side of the pool in a prone position and flutter kick across. As the kicking skill improves, swimmers should be put on kick boards and assigned several laps each practice period.

some coaching points for the flutter kick

1. Check height of feet out of water and knee bend. If too much knee bend, insist on student's kicking from the thighs.

2. Check leg and foot extension, and insist that legs be kept in longitudinal line of the body, with back arched.

3. Check width of leg drive or thrash.

4. Insist on smooth, even, rhythmic movement.

5. Check how far feet are apart; if too far apart, bring them together.

6. The crawl stroke flutter kick is usually made from a prone position. Many coaches, however, utilize the back flutter to train the legs for the crawl stroke flutter.

THE ARM STROKE. Teaching the arm movement also should start with a demonstration by the instructor, both on land and in the water. The pupils should then stand in shallow water, submerge the chest, and lean forward slightly. The relaxed left arm is extended backward near the hips in its position at the end of the drive. The right arm is extended forward, palm down, touching the water. The fingers are together, and the hands are slightly cupped. The right hand and then arm dip into the water. When 10 to 12 inches under, it begins what is known as the catch and

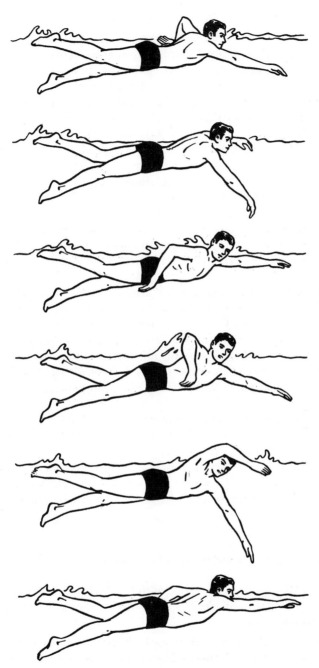

FIGURE 19-1 *Crawl* (From Don Cash Seaton, Irene A. Clayton, Howard C. Leibee, and Lloyd L. Messersmith, *Physical Education Handbook*, 5th ed. © 1969, Prentice-Hall, Inc. Reproduced by permission of the publisher.)

drive, and the left arm begins what is known as the recovery. At the catch, the right hand starts down and back, following the imaginary center line of the body. The first fourth of the pull is taken with the arm extended; the drive is continued and finally completed with the arm bent.

When the right-hand drive is being made, the left hand is in the process of recovering. The left elbow is lifted out of the water, and the forearm is allowed to relax and follow. As the elbow comes out of the water, it moves forward. When it is even with the head, the forearm begins moving forward ahead of the elbow until the arm is almost completely extended. The left arm is now ready for the drive. The movements are continued with the arms always alternating—while one is driving, the other is recovering. When the left arm is driving, the body should be rolled slightly to the left. The right shoulder should be slightly higher than the left to allow complete water clearance and less resistance on the recovery (Figure 19–1).

The students should practice the arm stroke while standing in the water. They should then have a land check, particularly for the drive. They should then go back into the water and be told to push off from the side and swim across, using the arm stroke only. They should be urged to pull hard when the drive is started, but not so hard as to break up the rhythm of the stroke. The movement should be made with as little splash as possible, chiefly to cut down resistance but also to make for a smoother stroke.

The coach should stress again that the fingers should be held together in order that they may more efficiently form a paddle with which to pull the body forward through the water.

During the time the beginner is practicing the crawl arm stroke, he should keep his head under water. This tends to aid relaxation and keeps him in a prone position so that the movement can be done with more ease.

some coaching points for the crawl arm stroke

1. Insist that recovery be started with hand relaxed and in a normal position. Palm up and arm rigid results in shoulder tension and increased resistance.

2. High, straight arm recovery, which many beginners try, is a needless expenditure of energy. It increases the body roll and makes breathing more difficult.

3. The arm that is recovering should be completely out of the water to cut down resistance. Slight increase in the roll and a more relaxed arm will often prevent arm drag.

4. Avoid forcible extension of the arm forward, since this consumes energy and prevents necessary relaxation.

5. Crossing hands in front of face or around the head on the recovery and at the catch limits the drive and adds unnecessary motion. Correct by having the swimmer slowly straighten the arm forward and catch slightly to the outside of the body's center line.

6. Have students avoid overreaching on the recovery, for it will cause a body twist and greater body resistance.

When the student has mastered the crawl arm movement to a certain degree, he is instructed to push off from the side and coordinate the arm movement with the flutter kick, which should have a six-beat kick for each complete arm stroke. Drill on this particular coordination should continue for long periods of time in order that movements may become habit.

BREATHING. Proper breathing—that is, the ability to get air to the lungs in many swimming situations without strangling and without interfering with the stroke—is a skill that is very difficult to acquire, and much time, effort, and basic instruction are necessary. It should be emphasized that the key to proper breathing is never to inhale when the mouth is underwater. Inhalation and exhalation both should be done, at least by the beginner, through the mouth.

The next step should be to inhale and exhale rhythmically. All good swimmers start their exhalation immediately after the inhalation and continue the exhalation until time for the next breath. In this way, there is little if any breath holding and a more relaxed stroke. Following this, the swimmer should stand in the water so that the mouth will be at surface level. This fills the mouth half full of water. If the head is tilted slightly forward, the water level does not affect breathing through either the nose or the mouth. After much breathing practice in this manner, it is comparatively simple to jump into and out of the water or to breathe as part of each swimming stroke without becoming strangled.

It is necessary at this point to begin the head movement and the type of breathing used in the crawl stroke. Some swimmers breathe from the left side and others from the right. When the swimmer has decided on which side he prefers to breathe—we will assume it is the left—he stands in waist-deep water, bends his knees slightly, leans forward, and puts the right side of his face into the water. The head movement consists of nothing more than a quarter turn to allow the face to move from the side to a downward position.

Several practice sessions should be conducted in which the student practices the skill of timed breathing. After it has become a set habit, the arm movement should be added. When timed correctly, breathing is comparatively simple with the arm stroke. When the left arm is completing the drive, the head turns to that side, and a breath of air is taken. When the arm starts the recovery, the mouth goes underwater, and the movement is completed, ready to be made again.

The students should be put in water about waist-deep again and should practice the coordination of the arm stroke with the breathing while they walk along.

A land drill to a six-beat rhythm may be of help in getting better coordination. The six counts can represent the six beats of the kick, the first three the right-arm drive, and beats four, five, and six the left-arm drive. After water and land drills on breathing coordination, the students should get into the water and attempt to swim across the pool, using the flutter kick and the alternate arm stroke while breathing at the same time. Much practice time should be devoted to this coordination, because for many it proves to be the hardest part of the learning process.

coaching points

1. Students may have a tendency to roll too much to be sure the mouth is far enough out of the water. Show them again how breathing can be done while the mouth is close to water.

2. Insist on students' starting leg action first, then going gradually into arm movement and breathing.

3. Have the head make only a quarter turn, a slight roll but no lift of the head.

the alternate overarm back stroke, or back crawl

The alternate overarm is the backstroke that is used in the speed events. To the casual observer, it is quite similar to the crawl stroke and is therefore popularly called the back crawl. It is true that the kick movements are virtually the same. The arm stroke movements, however, are the reverse of those used in the crawl stroke.

The back crawl is performed, as the name indicates, while the swimmer is lying in the water on his back. The head is turned toward the feet, looking down the length of the ventral portion of the body. The swimmer should be in a very slight "sitting up" position, which serves to keep the head just above the water, to keep the face from being splashed, and to give plenty of open area for easy breathing. Two distinct functions performed by the body in this stroke cause the person to move: the flutter kick and the overarm stroke. The coordination of these two makes it possible to swim smoothly and swiftly (Figure 19–2).

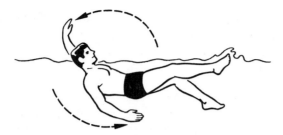

FIGURE 19-2 *Back Crawl*

THE FLUTTER KICK. If one has acquired a good crawl kick, it will be easy to apply the action in a reversed position. The movements of the legs, knees, ankles, and feet are much the same for both strokes. The thrash should be rapid, at least six beats to an arm stroke, and it should cover, at the feet, a distance of from 10 to 15 inches. The knee bend should be greater than in the crawl kick, and the thrash should break the surface a little higher. If the kick is done correctly, it should be possible to see the shin and part of the foot come above the water on each beat.

The propelling power is derived from the scissoring leg action and from the resistance of the entire length of the leg during each beat. The kick should originate at the hip and by coordinated action of the knee and ankle continue down the leg. The toes and the ankles should be relaxed and flexible. The feet should perform paddlewheel circles through the flexible action of the knees and hips.

The kick should be demonstrated on land and analyzed. The teacher should then swim across the pool on his back, using legs only. The students should be lined up on the side of the pool, told to sit on the deck, and put their feet in the water. If the swimming place is a lake, the pupils can lie in shallow water upon their backs and practice the kick in that position. After many drills on the kick in this position, they should be ready to go into the water, lie upon their backs, and perform the kick across and back without much effort.

It is emphasized here again that the student should use nothing but his legs in the first efforts in order to develop confidence in the power of the kick. When a person can feel the power he is getting from the kick alone, it will be very easy for him to begin using the back crawl arm movement in combination with the kick.

coaching points

1. Urge leg relaxation to facilitate knee and ankle flexibility.

2. Emphasize even leg thrash in an effort to get driving power for both the upward and downward movement of the leg.

3. Check body position in water to be sure slight sitting position is maintained.

The Alternate Overarm Stroke. Beginning with the start of the recovery, the hand should be near the thigh and the arm nearly straight. The hand is lifted out of the water and started up toward the head following a path near the center line of the body. It is lifted high enough to cause the elbow and the remainder of the arm to clear the water in order to lessen resistance. The shoulder of the arm recovering should be slightly higher than the other. The elbow bend should be just enough to allow the hand to follow its designated course. When the hand gets as high as the face, it begins to go laterally out from the body. The arm begins to straighten until both hand and arm are out over the water. The arm is in such a position as to form a V if the other arm were in the same relative position. Just prior to and during the catch, the wrist is flexed completely, the fingers are together, and the hand is slightly cupped. The hand and forearm form an L, and the palm of the hand is in such a position as to effect the most backward resistance when it goes into the water. After the arm "catches" the water and reaches shoulder level, flexion begins in the elbow, and the hand pushes and then rotates until the palm finally pushes downward to full extension. When the hand reaches the thigh, the recovery is started again. The right arm is driving while the left is recovering.

A land and a water demonstration of the arm stroke should be conducted, and the pupils should be drilled on its movements first on land. After it appears that the correct movements are mastered, the swimmers should be put in the water and allowed to practice the arm stroke there. The use of the feet should be avoided insofar as possible at first. When the arm stroke has been developed to the point of habit, the kick may be added.

The coordination of the feet and arms is much the same as in the crawl stroke. There should be a six-beat flutter with each complete arm stroke. There needs to be little emphasis on proper breathing, since the head is not underwater.

coaching points

1. Make sure the arm does not drag water on recovery.

2. The hand should not cross over the center line of the body on recovery. This is wasted effort.

3. Insist on a shallow arm pull. Deep pull causes body roll and is not so effective.

the breaststroke

The breaststroke was one of the earliest strokes used by man and was universally employed in competition until late in the nineteenth century, when the crawl and sidestroke began to take its place. At the present time, very few people use the breaststroke exclusively. Not very long ago, the breaststroke was the one taught first. It is a very difficult stroke to teach because the head must be supported above the water a great portion of the time.

The breaststroke is emphasized as one of the three strokes in swimming competition. Because the swimmer's head is up and looking straight ahead, it is used as an approach in lifesaving. The kick is powerful and can be utilized as the propelling power in some of the lifesaving carries. The breaststroke is the slowest of the three speed strokes.

Like the crawl stroke, the breaststroke has four basic phases: the arm stroke, the kick, breathing, and the coordination of the three. The body position for the breaststroke is prone. The back is arched, and the head is up, looking straight forward (Figure 19–3).

THE ARM STROKE. The arm stroke serves as a powerful propelling force, though not quite so powerful as the kick. Again it is important that the fingers be kept close together and the hand slightly cupped to add to the power of the stroke.

From the starting position, the arms are extended overhead just below the surface. The brief power phase is initiated as the arms rotate slightly inward and move laterally. The wrists and elbows flex slightly to expose a greater surface area of the palms and forearms away from the intended line of movement. The forceful pull of the hands and forearms is slightly downward and backward to the shoulder line. The elbows continue to flex outward to bring the hands closer to the mid-line of the body at the end of the drive. The hands follow a semicircular path during the power phase.

When the arms have almost completed their movement, the recovery should start. The first part of the recovery overlaps momentarily with the final push of the hands. The arms recover against the chest, and the hands slide together, palms downward, in front of the chest. The recovery action is completed as the fingertips lead the arms into the extended overhead position.

After the students have been shown these movements, they should have some land drill on them. They may practice them in a prone position, but while standing and bending forward at the hips is preferable. Swimmers should be encouraged to continue such practice at home. After the students have mastered these movements on land satisfactorily, they are put into the water and told to push off from the side of the pool and perform the proper arm movements while keeping the head underwater.

Start

Finish and Glide

FIGURE 19-3 *Breaststroke* (From Don Cash Seaton, Irene A. Clayton, Howard C. Leibee, and Lloyd L. Messersmith, *Physical Education Handbook*, 5th ed. © 1969, Prentice-Hall, Inc. Reproduced by permission of the publisher.)

coaching points

1. Palms should be kept in such a position as to afford most resistance to the water.

2. Care should be exercised to see that hands resist water as little as possible on the recovery.

THE BREASTSTROKE KICK. At the end of a kick, the legs should be straight, the feet together, and the toes pointed. The recovery begins by flexion at the knees and at the hips. The knees are kept together until flexion has gone halfway. The knees and feet begin to come apart and start out laterally. At the same time, the feet are flexed in such a way as to cause the toes to be nearer the knees. It is to be emphasized here that the recovery must be as slightly resistant as possible in order for the drive to be more effective. The legs are now in a position to start the drive. The knees come farther apart, as do the feet, and a whiplike motion begins, with the feet and knees going outward from the longitudinal axis of the body and performing a circle, which is completed when the legs come together. The feet should be guided in such a way that the toes are the farthest point out in the circle, and the heels lead the movement. When the feet are about 12 inches apart toward the end of the drive, they should be rotated inward and flexed away from the direction of the knees. The final position is that described in the first sentence of this paragraph.

coaching points

1. The whiplike motion is important to propulsion and should be developed carefully.

2. It is important that the heels lead the leg movement on the whip.

THE COORDINATION OF THE ARM AND THE LEG MOVEMENTS. Probably the most likely place to start an explanation of the coordination of the arms and legs is the beginning of the arm drive. It should be explained at this point that the arms and legs alternate in their driving action, and there is a glide during the arm recovery. When the arms are driving, the legs are being flexed and made ready for the drive. At the end of the arm drive, the legs are ready to whip. Very quickly and as the arms begin their recovery, the legs drive hard. The movement is fast and is completed before the arms have entirely recovered. The arms move forward, getting ready for another drive, while at the same time the legs are extended to the rear. This last is known as the glide. The legs are ready to recover and the arms to drive. The head is out of the water, and a breath may be taken during the arm drive. During the leg drive and the arm recovery, the head is underwater, and an exhalation is made.

the butterfly

This stroke has come into prominence rather recently. Since its introduction, it has been responsible for the lowering of previous breaststroke marks. Its advantage lies in the fact that the arms are brought out of the water for the recovery, thus cutting down some of the resistance. A few swimmers coordinate it exactly as the original breaststroke is coordinated, but most butterfly swimmers drive the legs and arms simultaneously and recover them likewise. Because the body must be lifted slightly higher out of the water in the butterfly, it is necessary that the arm stroke drive be deeper. Not all swimmers can adapt themselves to the butterfly because it takes much strength and flexibility of the shoulders.

BASIC SKILLS—STARTS

The ability to start fast and to begin stroking easily often makes the difference between winning and losing a race. It begins when the gun sounds. Between the time the starter says "take your marks" and the instant the gun sounds, the swimmer is getting in position to begin the race. His balanced movement, his stance, and his ability to anticipate the firing of the gun make for a good start.

freestyle and breaststroke starts

With the exception of the leg position upon entry and a slight difference in depth, the starts for the breaststroke and the freestyle are exactly the same. When the starter says "take your marks," the swimmer moves to the edge of the pool, places his feet 12 to 18 inches apart, and crimps his toes over the edge of the deck. He flexes the knees, bends at the hips, and extends the arms back and slightly higher than the hips. The head is up and looking straight ahead. At the sound of the gun, the arms immediately move in an arc forward. They do not move back and then forward, for this would tend to delay a start. As they are moving forward to an extension, the body is doing the same at the hips and knees until, by the time the feet are leaving the deck, the body is in complete extension out over the water. The swimmer makes every effort to get as far over the water as he can before hitting it. His chest and head hit first, and the back is arched. The feet and legs are spread the width of the leg thrash on a freestyle start so that as soon as the feet contact the water, they can begin work. The legs are kept together on the breaststroke start, and the body is allowed to go beneath the surface for a slight glide. On the freestyle start, the body is kept as near the surface as possible. One arm is allowed to drop down and back so that the two will be in opposition to each other, and the stroke begins there. Stroking begins more quickly in the freestyle start than in the breaststroke start, although there is some glide in each. Emphasis is placed on a powerful drive with the legs from the pool deck and a coordinated swing of the arms forward.

the backstroke start

The backstroke is started from the water. The swimmer is in the water grasping the gutter at the command "take your marks." He then places his hands firmly on the gutter about 18 to 24 inches apart. The legs are flexed, and the feet are placed against the wall of the pool about 6 inches apart and slightly below the hands. He then alerts himself to the sound of the gun. When it sounds, he instantly uncoils backward. The chief propulsion of the backstroke start comes from the powerful extension of the legs. The motion of the complete start is toward the long end of the pool and slightly up, so that the body will skim the surface of the water. As the body goes back, the arms extend back of the head, forming a V and ready for a drive. At the instant the swimmer settles in the water, one arm begins a drive. As soon as it has completed a drive, the other begins, so that alternation can go on effectively. The legs begin the flutter kick as soon as they are extended at the start.

BASIC SKILLS—TURNS

A good turn, well executed, is faster than straightaway swimming. A turn poorly executed has been the cause of many lost races. All swimmers should work hours on turning technique in order to master it completely and to be able to turn efficiently under any conditions. Each style of swimming requires an essentially different type of turn, and each needs to be practiced much in order to approach perfection.

the freestyle turn

There are several types of freestyle turns, many of which require much skill and top swimming ability. The turn described here is very effective, is used extensively, and is relatively easy to learn. The freestyle turn begins when the hand touches the end of the pool. Under no circumstances should a swimmer alter his stroke or change the rhythm in order to cause a certain hand to touch first. If the right hand contacts the end first, the turn is to the left, or to the right, if the left hand touches first. In view of this, the freestyle swimmer should perfect two distinct turns—one for the right hand and one for the left.

For explanation purposes, the turn to the left will be used. The contact of the right hand at the end is accepted by the body as a signal to begin the turn. Hours of practice should have developed the reflexes so that the body starts coiling for the return. After the hand contacts the side, momentum causes the legs and other parts of the body to "gather" without much effort at the end of the pool. The palm is placed flat against the side of the pool and the fingers point downward. As the hand turns to point downward, the body is flexing and turning to the left. By the time it is completely flexed, it has turned and is in a position to go back. The feet are placed squarely on the side of the pool from 8 to 12 inches apart and about 18 inches below water level. The right hand is taken from the side, placed with the other, and extended forward. This is done to cut down drag. The head is submerged, and a powerful leg thrust drives the body away from the end. The body is extended in order to cut down resistance. Because of the additional resistance caused by surface tension, the swimmer should remain underwater until he is about 10 feet from the side. The kick begins the instant the head breaks water, and the arm stroke as soon as the shoulders break water.

the breaststroke turn

The turn used with the breaststroke is somewhat more simple than the freestyle turn because both hands must contact the end simultaneously. This allows the swimmer to turn in either direction. He should decide which is easier and work hard in order to perfect a turn to that side. The turn is essentially the same as the freestyle turn after the hands have made contact. One hand becomes the pivot. The coil, turn, and leg drive are performed in that order, and the swimmer glides out underwater for about 12 feet. Just at the moment the head breaks water, the arms begin the drive. The legs start when it comes their time, depending on the coordination of the stroke.

the backstroke turn

The backstroke turn contains a factor not present in the other turns, which complicates it and makes it more difficult. The swimmer is on his back and cannot see the edge of the pool where he is to make the turn. Previous practice should have acquainted him with certain landmarks on the sides and ceiling that indicate proximity to the end. When he sees these, he is alerted to his nearness and can be ready for the turn. The backstroker must, by rule, stay on his back until his hand contacts the end of the pool. At that instant, the other arm comes across the body. If the right hand touches first, the left hand comes violently across the chest, and at the same time the body turns to the right to get in a prone position. Both hands grasp the gutter. Momentum has carried the feet to the end of the pool, and the swimmer takes the same position there that he assumed for the start. From this position, the movements are exactly the same as they were for the start.

turn drill

In order to develop skill on the starts and turns, the swimmers should devote fifteen minutes during each swim practice to work on these two very important phases of the activity. In order to get a great deal of turning practice, the swimmers should start and turn from the side of the pool. Each sprint should include a start and at least three turns. This would be a minimum of four laps of the pool and would permit the coach to see at close range the start and the turn made on the starting side. The swimmer should continue doing these laps for the full fifteen minutes, always under the watchful eye of the coach. Additional starting and turning can be a part of the conditioning laps and most certainly should be a part of the special race practice.

RELAYS

Relays are races between groups of either three or four participants. Only one from each team swims at any one time. The relay race may be freestyle, backstroke, or breaststroke, or it may be a combination of the three. If the race is of one stroke, four contestants make up a team; if it is medley, three compete. In any case, all members of a team swim equal distances except in a distance medley, in which case how far each swims is specified.

the freestyle relay

There are four swimmers on a team in the freestyle relay, and if the distance is 400 yards, each swims 100 yards. The fastest member should be the last to swim. He is known as the anchor swimmer. The next fastest should swim the first leg, and the other two in the second and third spots.

Each leg of a relay is quite similar to any other swimming event except in one respect. There is the start, and there may or may not be a turn. The one difference lies in the changeover from one contestant to another during the course of the race. After the start, no one in the relay may begin his leg until the swimmer ahead of him has touched the end of the pool. Judges are stationed at each end to see that the changes are performed according to the rules.

The relay start and change may be practiced on the width of the pool. The first and third swimmers are on the side from which it begins, and second and fourth are on the opposite side. The first swimmer, who is started in the conventional way, crosses the pool and touches the other side. The second is in a starting position and leaves the instant after the touch. It is extremely easy to foul on the relay change by leaving too early; thus, much practice must be conducted to assure the contestants do this phase of the race legally.

TEACHING PROCEDURE

Since swimming is very strenuous, proper diet and sufficient rest are highly important. Each player should be impressed with the importance of keeping himself in top physical condition and should be educated as to the proper foods and amounts that he should eat and the rest he should get.

During the first two weeks of training, the swimmer should develop endurance slowly by swimming freestyle for long periods of time and by doing several laps on the kick board. This is also a good time for instruction in starts and turns. At no time during the first two weeks should a swimmer be allowed to swim "all out" on any event. During the third week, conditioning is still stressed, with laps added, and starts and turns continually practiced. Added at this time, but only after a warm-up, are wind sprints involving a start, a length of the pool, and one speed turn.

From the fourth week on, a typical practice session should include the following:

40 laps in the swimmer's specialty

15 minutes of starts and turns

Relay-team practice

Sprint for time in the swimmer's special event

10 laps on the kickboard, using the swimmer's special kick

20 laps in the swimmer's specialty to end practice

Such a schedule may appear rather rigid to the average swimmer. Competitive swimming requires top physical condition, and there is only one way to get in that condition—by very hard work in practice.

DIVING

basic rules

A dive consists of five essential phases upon which a judgment is made and a score given:

1. *The Start.* The diver stands on the back of the board at a spot where he can conveniently take three or more steps and a hurdle to the end. He stands at attention, head up, feet together, and arms extended straight forward level with shoulders. Hands should be as far apart as the shoulders are wide. Fingers should be together.

2. *Steps and Hurdle.* The diver should take not fewer than three steps followed by a hurdle. The hurdle is a jump that takes the diver to the end of the board. At the end of the hurdle, both feet must contact the board simultaneously.

3. *The Takeoff.* The takeoff should be from both feet, high, and denote confidence on the part of the diver.

4. *The Dive.* During the dive proper, the body should be in a straight, pike, or tuck position.

5. *The Entry.* The body must be straight and vertical, toes pointed, arms extended on head-first entries and close to body on feet-first entries.

scoring of dives

Dives should be graded by judges standing at advantageous positions around the board. Each dive is scored within a range of ten points, depending on how well it is performed from the starting position to the entry. As a dive is performed, the judges flash cards to the recorder.

Each dive has a difficulty rating ranging from 0 to 2.6. If a diver receives a score of 5 on a dive rated 1.3, his total score for that dive is 6.5. This figure is determined by multiplying the score of the dive (5) by the degree of difficulty (1.3).

The remainder of this section will concern swimming in college competition, swimming in dual meets, and utilizing only the one-meter board.

In a dual meet, there must be eight dives, three compulsory and five optional. The three compulsory dives must be performed first and may be any three of the five compulsory dives listed. The five optional dives must include four of the several groups specified by rule. Reference is made here to the various groups of dives and the list of compulsory and optional dives in the *Official N.C.A.A. Swimming Gide.*

diving fundamentals

The ability to dive depends on many qualities, among them poise, strength, coordination, grace, and timing. A diver is naturally endowed with some of these. The others he must acquire by constant practice. Diving depends to a large extent on the diver's being able to use the board. Before he begins diving, he should practice the steps, the hurdle, and the spring. Several efforts will establish the approximate spot to start. He should confine his movements to three steps and a hurdle. He should soon determine on which foot he prefers to begin the hurdle. If he hurdles from the left foot, he should step from the left at the start. His movements then are: left, right, left, hurdle. During the steps, the body is held erect, and the arms are swung in such a way as to keep it in balance and on the upswing at the beginning of the hurdle. The left foot (assuming the left foot is the hurdle foot) presses the board downward. As it comes up, the right knee is flexed reasonably high to help give lift. The higher the hurdle, the more the board is bent at the end of it, and the higher the diver is thrown. He comes down on the board flat-footed, with legs straight and knees locked. Since he is testing the board reaction, he should not go into a dive but should bounce up and down to learn the coordination involved in getting maximum height for a dive. This bouncing should consume several minutes of each practice session and meet warm-up. Many beginning divers leave the board too soon; they do not wait for its lift. This bouncing practice aids in developing the correct timing for the lift.

When the board reaction is determined and approach skill is well advanced, diving can begin. The student should study the diving illustrations contained in two publications: *The Official Swimming, Water Polo and Diving Rules of the Amateur Athletic Union* and the Red Cross Manual, *Swimming and Water Safety.*

A few general suggestions for diving that may prove helpful to the beginner are given here. Almost all forward dives begin exactly alike. The takeoff from the board is with a very slight, almost imperceptible lean forward. It is not necessary to lean out over the board in order to get more turn or to be sure of clearing it. Turn is regulated by the movements of the body after leaving the board, and clearance is achieved by the momentum gained in the three steps and hurdle. It is well for the beginner to remember that the tighter the tuck, the faster the turn. He should also be told that he is quite likely to hit flat many times and should wear protection, such as a sweatshirt, to prevent pain. Whenever any swimmer hits flat on a dive, he should return to the board immediately and attempt the same dive again and again until he can enter the water correctly. A day's lapse before correcting a flat dive builds up a terrific mental hazard.

In any sport, and particularly in diving, perfection is neared only through practice, practice, practice, plus sincere, authoritative, constructive criticism.

SKILL TESTS

Swimming lends itself to testing as well as any other activity. The chief criteria for excellence in the strokes described in this chapter are speed and form, with emphasis on the former. When taught as a part of class procedure, scores can be established on the basis of the time required to swim a specified distance.

Form is a factor in speed and does not necessarily have to be judged separately. If it is decided to grade form, a point basis can be established on the various phases of a stroke, and a student may be graded on his ability to perform each of these.

Diving is graded in competition on a point basis, and there is no reason why the system could not be used to test and to establish grades. To eliminate the factor of difference in the way two or more people may judge, only one person should score all divers when testing for grades.

DEFINITION OF TERMS

Anchor. The last leg of a relay.

Catch. The movement of the hand in beginning resistance to the water at the start of a drive.

Championship Meet. An event in which several teams have entered to determine the best organization or individuals within a group.

Course. The path of the swimmer.

Drive. The drawing of the hand or leg through the water to give propulsive force.

Dual Meet. A meet in which only two teams compete.

False Start. The act of a swimmer in leaving his mark before the signal.

Foul. An infraction of the rules during a race.

Freestyle. A designation meaning that a swimmer may use any stroke he believes will carry him through the water the fastest.

Heat. A preliminary race run to pick the fastest competitors for the final race.

High Board. A diving board the upper surface of which is three meters from the water.

Hurdle. The slight leap at the end of the third step preliminary to a dive.

Long Course. Pool 50 or more yards in length.

Low Board. A diving board the upper surface of which is one meter from the water.

Mark. A swimmer's position at the edge of the pool at the start of the race.

Medley. A term indicating that more than one stroke or different distances are employed in a race.

Record. Best performance in an event over a specified period of time in a specific group.

Recovery. The movement of the arm or leg in getting back into position to start a drive.

Relay. A race in which several swimmers—usually four—participate as a team, each swimming in one leg of the event.

Short Course. Pool between 25 and 50 yards in length.

Start. The beginning of a race.

Take-off. Act of leaving the board on a dive.

Turn. The act of turning at one end of the pool.

Twenty-yard Course. A pool 20 yards long.

DISCUSSION QUESTIONS

1. Identify the relationship of the following men to the development of swimming: (a) Trudgen; (b) Richard Cavill; (c) Charles Daniel; (d) J. Scott Leary; (e) Johnny Weissmuller.

2. Name some women prominent in swimming history.
3. What are the attributes necessary for a student to become a good competitor?
4. Analyze the crawl stroke.
5. Name five important coaching points on the crawl.
6. Go through the steps employed to teach breathing.
7. Describe the coordination of arms and legs in the performance of the breaststroke.
8. Analyze a freestyle start, considering carefully why each movement is made.
9. Why develop a good turn?
10. Evaluate a dive on the basis of the five essential phases.
11. How is diving scored?

BIBLIOGRAPHY

Amateur Athletic Union, *Official Swimming, Water Polo and Diving Rules,* latest edition. New York: Amateur Athletic Union.

American National Red Cross, *Swimming and Water Safety.* Washington, D. C.: 1968.

Barr, Alfred S., Grady, Ben F., and Higgens, Lt. Comdr. John H., *Swimming and Diving.* New York: A. S. Barnes & Company, 1950.

Brown, Richard L., *Teaching Progressions for the Swimming Instructor.* New York: A. S. Barnes & Company, 1948.

Cureton, Thomas K., *How to Teach Swimming and Diving.* New York: Association Press, 1934.

Harris, Marjorie M., *Basic Swimming Analyzed.* Boston: Allyn and Bacon, Inc., 1969.

Kiphuth, Robert J. H., *Swimming.* New York: A. S. Barnes & Company, 1942.

Lawson, Victor E., and Mader, Priscilla, *Swimming.* Philadelphia: J. B. Lippincott Company, 1937.

Luehring, Frederick W., *Swimming Pool Standards.* New York: A. S. Barnes & Company, 1939.

Mann, Matt, and Fries, Charles C., *Swimming: Fundamentals.* New York: Prentice-Hall, Inc., 1940.

Menke, Frank G., *The Encyclopedia of Sports.* New York: A. S. Barnes and Company, 1969.

Mitchell, Elmer D., *Sports for Recreation.* New York: A. S. Barnes & Company, 1952.

Official N.C.A.A. Swimming Guide, latest edition. New York: National Collegiate Athletic Association.

Olen, Harold S., and Larcom, Guy, *The Complete Swimmer.* New York: The Macmillan Company, 1939.

Shaw, John H., Troester, Carl A., Gabrielsen, Alexander M., *Individual Sports for Men.* Dubuque, Iowa: William C. Brown Company, 1964.

table tennis

20

BACKGROUND

The game now officially known as table tennis has in the past been called many other names, including ping-pong, miniature tennis, and gossima. There is no doubt that it is an outgrowth of lawn tennis, but the process by which it came into existence is somewhat unclear. One source has it beginning in the United States, another places its birth in England, and the third credits a British army officer on foreign duty with devising it. Since the game is so closely linked to tennis, there is reason to believe that several people, not even remotely connected, could have devised it in the process of modifying tennis to fit the top of a table.

The oldest claim dates its beginning as 1880 in England. Equipment for playing the game is supposed to have been manufactured and sold by a British sporting goods firm, which called the game *gossima*. The equipment supplied included both a rubber and a cork ball, wooden paddles, and a cloth net. Prior to the year 1901, but after table tennis had been played for some time both in the United States and in England, James Gibbs saw the celluloid balls in use in the United States and carried the idea to England, where the new piece of equipment was adopted.

A group in America that developed a type of table tennis employed the Parker Brothers of Salem, Massachusetts, to manufacture equipment for it. This firm started by producing the orthodox wooden paddles and both rubber and cork balls and later began the manufacture of the celluloid ball.

In England, E. C. Goode introduced the rubber-faced racquet to take the place of the sandpaper or rough-surface wooden paddle. This type of surface was used almost exclusively until the early or middle 1950s, when sponge-covered racquets were introduced in Japan. Though pebbled rubber is still used, most tournament or top-ranked players now prefer what is called sandwich sponge racquets, consisting of a layer of cellular rubber or sponge, covered with pebbled rubber with the pips turned either inward or outward. When they are turned inward, the bat is known as an inverted sandwich sponge bat.

Americans first called the game indoor tennis; the British called it gossima, indoor tennis, and later ping-pong. This latter name was applied because of the sound of the paddle and the table when the ball struck. Ping-Pong was a name copyrighted by Parker Brothers to identify their product. The name of the sport is properly table tennis.

The game came to be played extensively by the English nobility and by the people in the higher socio-economic levels in several European countries. It increased in popularity, and before long enthusiasts of these countries were holding tournaments to decide the world championship. Czechoslovakia soon excelled the other countries and won the championship several years in succession.

In the United States, the game was mildly popular in the early part of this century. Its popularity did not last very long, however, and it faded almost completely from the sports scene until about 1927, when interest began to revive.

This renewed interest resulted in the formation of the American Ping-Pong Association in 1930. The next year, a tournament was conducted, using Parker Brothers equipment. Interest ran so high that the firm could not supply enough for all those who wanted to play. It was not long, however, before other companies began marketing equipment for the game. The United States Table Tennis Association was formed to regulate all play in the game, known either as Ping-Pong or table tennis. This organization is still taking leadership in the sport and is closely affiliated with the groups that govern the game in Europe.

Sectional, national, and international championships are conducted yearly. These championships and the challenging aspects of the game have stimulated its growth tremendously. Millions of people play, and table tennis facilities are found almost anywhere. Schools, colleges, agency groups, municipal recreation associations, private clubs, and homes frequently have table tennis equipment. The relatively inexpensive equipment can be used in a very small area. The game challenges the skill and coordination of all who try it.

the table

The table is rectangular, 9 feet in length by 5 feet in width. It is supported in such a way that its upper surface will be 2 feet 6 inches above the floor and will lie in a horizontal plane. It may be made of any material that will yield a uniform bounce of not less than 8¾ inches nor more than 9¾ inches when a standard ball, preferably of medium bounce, is dropped from a height of 12 inches above its surface. The upper surface of the table is called the playing surface; it is dark green, with a ¾-inch white line along each edge. The lines at the ends of the playing surface are termed end lines and those at the sides are side lines (Figure 20–1).

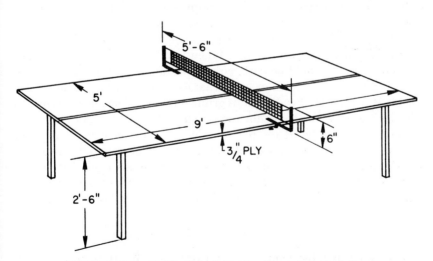

FIGURE 20-1 *Table Tennis Table* (From Don Cash Seaton, Irene A. Clayton, Howard C. Leibee, and Lloyd L. Messersmith, *Physical Education Handbook*, 5th ed. © 1969, Prentice-Hall, Inc. Reproduced by permission of the publisher.)

the net and its supports

The playing surface is divided into two courts of equal size by a net running parallel to the end lines and 4 feet 6 inches from each. The net, with its suspension, is 6 feet in length; its upper part along its whole length is 6 inches above the playing surface; its lower part along the whole length is close to the playing surface. The net is suspended by a cord attached at each end to an upright post 6 inches high, the outside limits of which are 6 inches outside the side line.

the ball

The ball may be made of celluloid or a similar plastic, white and matte, not less than 1.46 inches nor more than 1.50 inches in diameter, and weighing not less than 37 grains nor more than 39 grains.

the racket

The racket may be of any size, shape, or weight. Its surface is dark colored and matte. The blade of wood is continuous, or even, in thickness, and is flat and rigid. If the blade is covered on either side, this covering may be either plain pimpled rubber, with pimples outward, and a total thickness of not more than 2 mm., or "sandwich," consisting of a layer of cellular rubber surfaced by plain pimpled rubber turned outward or inward, in which case the total thickness of the covering of either side will be not more than 4 mm. When rubber is used on both sides of a racket, the color should be similar. When wood is used for either side, or for both sides, it should be dark, either natural, or stained (not painted) in such a way as not to change the character of its surface. The part of the blade nearest the handle that is gripped by the fingers may be covered with cork or other materials for convenience of grip; it is to be regarded as part of the handle. If the reverse side of the racket is never used for striking the ball, it may all be of cork or any other material convenient for gripping. The limitation of racket cover materials refers only to the striking surface. A stroke with a side covered with cork or any other gripping surface would, however, be illegal and result in a lost point.

BASIC SKILLS

The game of table tennis can be extremely fast. It requires a high degree of coordination and skill and has all the elements of a regular tennis game, though on a smaller scale. It requires endurance, a good eye, and extremely close mental concentration. The game demands that strategy, timing, accurate stroking, precision play, and quick thinking be used. To perfect these skills and other factors leading to creditable performance, the table tennis player must make a careful study of the phases involved and practice long and determinedly toward improvement.

form

Good form is necessary in table tennis, probably more than in most other games. Because of the speed of the ball and the limited time to get in position to make a stroke, unnecessary movement must be minimized. Good form is concerned with the position of the arms, the trunk, the head, the legs, and the feet. Good form is the first step toward good stroking.

the grip

There are two basic ways to grasp a paddle: the tennis grip used by nearly all American and European players; and the penholder grip, used by the majority of Oriental players. The tennis grip is shown in Figure 20–2 and the penholder grip in Figure 20–3. A good grip is one that holds a paddle firmly but that permits moving it to any position necessary to play the ball efficiently without making any change in the placing of the fingers.

FIGURE 20-2 *Tennis Grip or "Shake Hands"*

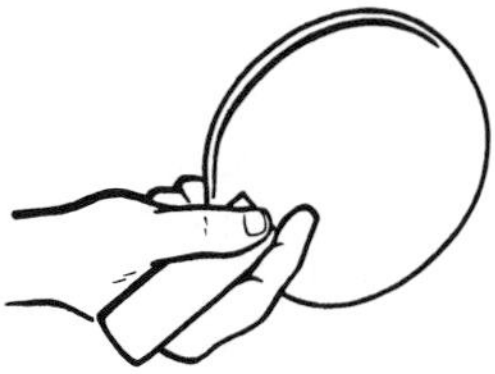

FIGURE 20-3 *Penholder Grip*

To grasp the paddle correctly using the tennis grip, its face should be turned perpendicular to the table surface. The player should then take hold of the handle as if he were shaking hands with it. The index finger rests on the portion of the face near the handle. The other three fingers encircle the handle to the right, and the thumb encircles it to the left. The grasp of the paddle should be firm but not tight.

Such a grasp enables the player to stroke a ball in any position, forehand, backhand, underhand, overhand, up near the net or back, without making any change in finger placement. The ball may be hit from either side of the paddle, depending on the position from which the stroke is made. Because the index finger rests on a portion of the paddle face, care should be taken that the ball does not hit it. However, it is not illegal for the ball to be played by that finger while it rests on the paddle.

the stance

The position in which one stands is important to successful play. It is a part of form in that correct stance makes for more efficient play. The player must be able to turn quickly to the left or the right, to back up fast, or to lean forward and play a shot above the table.

The body should stand within a foot of the end of the table or further back, depending upon the type of play the opponent forces on a player. The feet should be about 12 inches apart and placed so that a line extending from one to the other will be parallel to the end of the table. Weight should rest evenly on both feet. The knees should be relaxed and flexed slightly, ready for quick movement in any direction. The trunk should lean slightly forward. The head should be in a position that it can move freely to follow closely the flight of the ball. The paddle is grasped firmly and held higher than the table. The arm should be kept relaxed but able to move the paddle quickly to any spot necessary to play the ball. If a forehand drive is necessary, the body turns slightly to the right, and the right foot drops back slightly. If a backhand shot is needed, the left side turns to the left, and the left foot drops back. After every shot, however, the player should return as near as possible to his original stance.

the swing

This skill is discussed not from the standpoint of pattern, but to stress its importance. The way a swing is made depends on what stroke is being attempted, and there will be a different swing for every stroke. A smooth swing made in the right direction is necessary to contact the ball correctly and at the right time. As the player learns each stroke, he should concentrate on the movement of the arm before and after the ball is contacted and practice making the proper motion.

the wrist movement

The action of the wrist is another important factor in effective stroking. Correct wrist movement can give speed and accuracy that cannot be applied to a stroke in any other way.

The wrist should be kept flexible and moved whenever necessary to execute a stroke properly. Snapping the wrist toward the direction the ball is to go, just prior to the instant it is hit, gives it speed. The paddle can be adjusted by wrist movement to a better position for hitting the ball. Attention to wrist movement during practice can do much to hasten improvement in the game. Because some shots are made with a locked wrist, one should determine in practice when it should be locked and when it should not be.

spin

Very seldom is a shot made that results in a dead ball. In nearly every stroke, the ball spins to a certain degree. The spin on the celluloid ball affects the flight and rebound more than the spin on a ball used in any other sport. The direction and amount of spin determine to a great degree the direction of the ball in the air and upon the rebound. For this reason, it is necessary for the table tennis player to take into consideration on every shot the amount and direction of spin he is imparting to the ball. Because of the spin factor, he must also observe the stroke movement of his opponent so that he will know what sort of spin is put on the ball and, as a result, the probable direction of it in the air and on the bounce.

the serve

This shot is included at this point in the discussion for two reasons. First, it is the first stroke made in a game, and second, it is a convenient way to put the ball in play for practice stroking. The player may use a practice serve every time he starts a practice rally with another player.

The ball is placed on the palm of the free hand, which must be stationary, and above the level of the playing surface. Service will commence by the server projecting the ball by hand only, without imparting spin, nearly vertically upwards so that it is visible at all times to the umpire. As the ball is descending from the height of its trajectory, it will be struck so that it touches first the server's court and then, passing directly over or around the net, the receiver's court. In any serve, the flight of the ball should be kept low so that it barely clears the net. A high bounce is slower and much easier hit.

A variation of the conventional serve is one in which spin put on the ball causes it to go from one side to another during flight and on the rebound. In order to make a ball move toward the left, the player puts left-to-right spin on it. This particular spin is possible from the forehand, but it is more powerfully and efficiently done from the backhand. The player stands with the left foot slightly back, extends the paddle out to the left, and by stroking both forward and to the right starts the ball spinning from left to right. The right-to-left spin is accomplished from a forehand position. As the ball is dropped, the paddle, from a position out to the right and back, starts forward and to the left in such a way as to start the ball forward and spinning. As it moves, it tends to the right and on each bounce turns abruptly in that direction.

The table tennis player should make his preliminary movements for all kinds of services as nearly alike as possible in order not to give away his intentions to his opponent.

the block

This shot is frequently referred to as the half volley. It may also be called the push shot. It is a basic defensive shot and one that the beginner will also use for offense. In order to perform it correctly, the player stands about a foot away from the back edge of the table, with feet comfortably spaced, in line with the end of the table. The knees are flexed slightly. The body faces the length of the table with the right forearm approximately parallel to the top of it. The shot is made most frequently with the backhand face of the paddle, which is nearly vertical, with the top edge slightly back to elevate the ball when striking it. It is important in all shots, and particularly in this one, to keep the eye on the ball at all times.

The block is, basically, just that. The ball is stopped by the paddle with very little force and is allowed to bounce off and back over the net. The paddle is pushed forward at the correct moment, determined by much practice, so that the ball is contacted just after it rebounds from the table. The basic shot imparts a little spin to the ball. However, by an additional movement of the paddle either upward or to either side, the ball can be made to turn in any one of several directions.

Though rarely used by the more advanced player, this shot is one that he must know in order to play the game successfully. He will use it only on rare occasions when he is on the defensive.

forehand drive

The basic characteristic of all drives is that the ball is hit hard, has speed, and is given an overspin. Since most drives are made against balls that have been hit hard by the opponent, the player must stand back about 2 feet from the end of the table. The right foot should be dropped back slightly and should bear the major portion of body weight. The eyes should be on the ball. The right hand drops back to about shoulder height and circles downward at the back of the swing to a spot about table height or lower. The paddle is then brought upward and forward extremely fast. The body weight shifts at this moment to the left foot. The paddle face is closed—that is, the top is farther forward than the bottom. The ball is contacted and sent on its way, and the paddle follows through forward, upward, and finally back to a defensive position (Figure 20–4).

FIGURE 20-4   *The Forehand Drive*

backhand drive

This shot is more difficult than the forehand drive, but because he must use it for top performance, the table tennis player should spend considerable time improving it. The reasons for its difficulty are that the shot is made from a more unnatural position than other shots and that the ball is partially hidden from sight at the moment of contact. The backhand drive is used for two purposes: for defense and for setting up a shot for a kill (Figure 20–5).

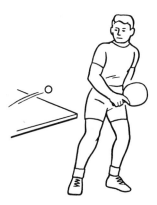

FIGURE 20-5   *The Backhand Drive*

To make the shot, the player's trunk faces somewhat to the left. The left foot is back, and most of the body weight is on it. The right elbow is near the side. The paddle is brought back high, down, around, and forward to make the stroke. The movement should be timed so that the ball is contacted near the top of its bounce. As the swing takes place, the player's weight changes to the right foot. As the ball is contacted, the paddle is moved upward as well as forward in order to put topspin on the ball. In order to get more power on this shot, the wrist should be snapped slightly forward. As soon as the stroke is completed, the player should resume a defensive stance, ready to make the next play.

forehand chop

The basic chop movement puts backspin on the ball, but the power common to most drives is not present. The effect of the chop is to cause the ball to hold a more nearly level path when crossing the net and to come to a partial stop after the bounce on the other side. The chop can be used defensively, but generally it is used to mix up shots, depending on the strategy in progress. In the forehand chop, the right foot is about a foot from the left, back and to the right. The weight is on the left leg, and the knees are flexed. The trunk is leaning forward slightly. The eyes are on the ball. The right arm extends in front of the body with elbow flexed somewhat, and the paddle is kept at about shoulder height or slightly above. During the stroke, the weight stays predominantly on the left foot. To make the shot, the paddle moves down and forward in such a way as to put forward motion and back spin on the ball at the moment of contact.

the backhand chop

This stroke has the same effect on the movement of the ball as the stroke just described. It is used to play a ball that comes to the left of a player and for cross-table shots from left to right. The feet are about 12 inches apart, with the left leg back. The weight is on the back foot. The stroke is started from about shoulder height, and the movement is forward and downward across the back of the ball. The arm continues to extend on the follow-through until it is straight.

When either of the two basic chop strokes is being learned, there should be no wrist action at all. After they are mastered, wrist action may be applied to a mild degree.

the flick

This stroke is appropriately named; the movement is little more than a mere flick of the wrist and forearm. It is generally performed backhand, though it can be a forehand shot. It is an extremely difficult stroke to carry through successfully, and only a few of the most skillful table tennis players have ever mastered it. It is included in this discussion to offer a challenge to the player who is progressing rather rapidly in developing the basic skills. It requires as nearly perfect timing as any other stroke.

The player stands with trunk facing to the left, feet apart and in line with the length of the table. The weight is fairly well distributed on both feet. The arm and paddle have very little preliminary movement. As the ball comes up from the table, the paddle starts from a backhand position at a time when the forearm is parallel with the end of the table. The stroke from that point on is nothing more than a quick forward movement of the forearm and the wrist. There is an absolute minimum of follow-through. The defensive stance is then quickly resumed.

The shot is used frequently to throw the opponent off balance. He generally expects, because of preliminary arm movement, some indication of what the shot is going to be like, and he is completely surprised by the suddenness of the flick.

the loop drive

This relatively new stroke is believed to have been originated in England about 1961 or 1962, and introduced in this and other countries shortly thereafter. It has had a profound effect on the offensive game. The only type bat that can be used is the inverted sandwich sponge. This stroke imparts very great topspin to the ball (opposite of a heavy chop) and can be performed most effectively when the opponent is pushing or chopping. It is similar to the forehand drive, except the bat is brought nearly straight up in the vertical motion with much speed, so that it gently contacts the ball for a longer time than other strokes, resulting in terrific topspin. Even championship class players when first encountering this shot could not return it safely, because the topspin forces the ball to bounce from the bat much higher normal, either going over the table or presenting the looper with a set-up. Much practice is required to return a good loop, which has a much greater amount of topspin than any other stroke. Some players have developed a backhand loop, but this is rather uncommon.

the smash

This shot is used to "put away" a point. It becomes possible either as the culmination of a series of shots leading to a kill or because the opponent accidentally hits the ball slow and high, allowing it to bounce above the net.

When such a return is made, a player often spoils his opportunity to stroke successfully because of his eagerness. The smash is a power stroke. It is a shot that employs brute strength, body weight, timing, and a minimum of skill. Little or no spin is put on the ball. It is made straight to the table across the net, with no curve on the ball. To carry out a smash successfully, a player must be alert to the opportunity to make such a shot. As the chance presents itself, he should move close to the table into position for either a forehand or a backhand smash, depending on which side of him the ball may be approaching.

FOREHAND SMASH.   This shot is made when the ball bounces near the middle or on the right of the receiver's half of the table. The player drops the right foot back slightly but keeps the weight on the front foot. The player leans forward, and the right arm is brought up so that the paddle is about shoulder height. From this position, the stroke is a terrifically hard smash forward in the direction the player desires the ball to go. There is no slice. The paddle is completely open toward the ball. The stroke from the start to the time the ball is contacted is straight forward and downward. The follow-through brings the paddle down, around, and to the left. Because there never ceases to be a possibility that the ball may be returned and the player is more off balance after this shot than after any of the others, he should make a strenuous effort to get back quickly into the defensive position.

BACKHAND SMASH.   The basic movement of this shot is quite similar to that of the forehand smash. The ball rebounds from the center or the left side of the player's half of the table. The player stands with the trunk toward the left side of the table, the left foot slightly back and about a foot from the right. The paddle is brought up across the body so that it is at shoulder height or slightly higher, with the backhand face turned toward the ball. When it has bounced high and is nearing the spot where it should be hit, the paddle starts directly forward and slightly downward. It does not travel in an arc but in a straight line toward the point where it is intended for the ball to go. The shot is a power drive. There is no effort to place spin on the ball. The player may expect considerable power, but it is difficult to get as much with the backhand as with the forehand smash.

It is possible to chop a smash, and players sometimes employ such a shot, but because it is not particularly effective and it requires considerable additional skill, it is not done very often.

the drop shot

This particular shot is more than a simple movement of the arm and wrist. It is a strategic shot used only when the opponent expects something altogether different. The player should, generally, follow a hard-hit drive with the drop shot, particularly if the opponent returns with a more or less defensive chop. The player should move into this chop shot as if he were going to drive it. He places his paddle at the spot just back of where the ball will bounce and then holds it. The bounce should be fairly close to the net for the drop to be effective. The ball hits the paddle, bounces back just over the net, and drops quickly down on the other side. The opponent has expected a hard-hit drive and is back where he can play such a shot effectively. The ball drops so suddenly that he does not have an opportunity to get to it in time to play it.

The shot should be made with the paddle face open so that the ball goes upward and over the net as it rebounds from the paddle. There should be no follow-through whatsoever. Such a shot is very effective if used sparingly. Too much use causes the opponent to expect it and to be prepared for it. The shot is an easy one for a player who expects it.

the shovel shot

This stroke is made just as it is named. The paddle action is similar to a shovel movement. It is a method of creating backspin and at the same time hitting the ball high in such a way that it bounces just over the net. If the shot is performed correctly, the backspin will cause it to return directly over the net without being hit. It is strictly a trick shot and should not be used often. There is a danger of the ball bouncing too high and giving the opponent time to get to it and actually hit it back.

STRATEGY

Table tennis is a terrifically fast game that requires not only refined technique and considerable skill but thought as well. Because of the speed of the celluloid balls, decisions must be made very quickly. Basic strategy may be worked out ahead of time, but many decisions must come within a split second.

A player needs to study his own game and specific skills very carefully and then map out his strategy accordingly. He should know his weaknesses and avoid making shots that will allow opponents to play to them.

No player should play a slow, defensive game continuously, and neither should he, on the other extreme, play a fast, hard, driving game all the time. Rather, he should mix easy shots with hard ones. He should take advantage of opportunities to smash, to shovel, to flick, and to use any of the other shots that may catch the opponent napping. Straight shots should be varied with cross-court shots. Even though a player should vary his game, his variations should never fall into a pattern so that the opponent will come to know what type of shot is coming next.

The player should make a serious study of his opponent so that he can play to his weaknesses and avoid his strong points. In making such an estimate, he is taking the first step toward the ability to anticipate shots. A part of strategy is to calculate correctly where a shot is going. The player should first know approximately what to expect his opponent to do—series of shots, driving game, and chopping game. He then should watch the arm, wrist, eyes, and stance of the man at the other end of the table, with the idea of determining what he is planning to do. If the next shot can be anticipated from these signs—and it often can—the first move toward a successful return shot has been made.

No player should take chances with shots not yet perfected but should continue to play the type of game known to be effective. The element of surprise should be used at every opportunity. The table tennis player should play every point seriously in an effort to win.

The player should keep his eyes on the ball. He should always play as if he expected to win. He should never lose his temper, but should stay cool and even-tempered. The first step to defeat is to become angry during a game.

TEACHING PROCEDURE

A class should be limited to four times as many students as there are tables on which to play. Of course, it is possible to have a class with fewer facilities, but it is never satisfactory. Each of the class members should have a paddle, and there should be a ball for every two people.

During the first class period, the students should be given a general background of the game. A demonstration of correct table tennis playing should be staged to give them an idea of what they are supposed to be working toward. A method the writer sometimes uses is suggested here. The students are allowed to go to the table and begin a table tennis game so they may become aware of their inadequacies at the very outset and may be more willing to practice the skills.

The next step should be to teach the stance and the grip. Since a convenient way to put the ball in play each time is a serve, it should be next, followed by the forehand and backhand drives. It is impossible to get beyond a serve at the first class meeting; the other strokes should be taken up during subsequent meetings of the group.

Each time the class meets, it should practice the skills taught previously, and at least one new skill should be taken up. After about a week, the students should be allowed to play short games of seven or eleven points. As the class advances, more of the period can be devoted to playing. Toward the end of the quarter, the class may be divided into doubles teams and a round robin tournament may be conducted to determine the best team in the class.

During the time the students are practicing the skills, the teacher should be walking from table to table analyzing player difficulties and making corrections. As playing skill advances, the teacher should give instruction on strategy.

SKILL TESTS

speed rally

A player teams with another, and they oppose each other across the net. The ball is served by one of them, and a rally begins. The score of each is the number of times the ball crosses the net in one minute. In order to balance the effect of a strong player being paired with a weak one and, as a result, getting a low score, each one of the students should have at least five chances at the speed rally with as many different partners. It is assumed that the law of averages will place each with others of varying ability, so that the final score will actually be an approximate indication of his ability.

serve for accuracy

The table should be marked off on one side of the net into rectangles of varying scores depending on the particular area's importance in preventing a good return. A player serves five times, and his score is the total made on all five serves.

stroke for accuracy

A partner across the table serves a relatively easy ball to the player being tested. Using the same marked area on the table, the player attempts to return the ball so that it will hit in one of the squares of higher value. His score is the total made on five attempts.

demonstration of strokes

All the strokes taught should be demonstrated. A player receives a score ranging from zero to five points for each shot, depending on his ability to execute it correctly.

DEFINITION OF TERMS

Attack. The process involved in being aggressive.

Backhand. A stroke that involves reaching across the body to make a shot.

Backspin. A way of rotating a ball by hitting down on it so that when it bounces it will slow considerably.

Ball Flight. The path of the ball through the air.

Blade. The striking surface of the paddle.

Block. A paddle stroke that consists of placing the paddle in front of the ball to cause it to return across the net.

Chop. The act of hitting down a ball to give it both direction and backspin.

Defense. The art of preventing an opponent from making points.

Down-the-line. A shot made straight down the table.

Drive. A type of shot that gives speed and topspin to the ball.

Drop Shot. A shot that places the ball barely over the net while the opponent is far back awaiting the drive or smash.

Edge Ball. A legally played ball that strikes the edge of the table and bounds abruptly off.

End. The edge of the table near where the player stands.

Finger Spin. A way of beginning a service, now illegal, by which a spin is given to the ball before the paddle hits it.

Flat. A way of hitting the ball so as to impart no spin.

Flat Swing. A stroke made in such a way that the paddle follows a line parallel to the floor.

Flick. A quick stroke involving wrist and forearm action, designed to catch the opponent off guard.

Follow-through. The continued path of the arm and paddle after the ball has been hit.

Forehand. The act of hitting a ball with the right hand from the right side of the body.

Free Hand. The hand other than the one doing the stroking.

Gymnasium Player. An individual who does not play well under game pressure.

Half Volley. A shot in which a ball is hit almost immediately after it bounces.

Handle. The part of the paddle that is gripped by the hand.

Let. If the ball served in passing over the net touches it or its supports, provided the service be otherwise good or volleyed by the receiver, or if a rally is stopped for some reason described in the rules, before the point is completed, which will then be replayed.

Loop Drive. A stroke that imparts very great topspin to the ball, usually a forehand shot.

Net. The mesh cloth dividing the court in half.

Net Ball. A serve or other shot that hits the net.

Overspin. The twist of a ball that causes it to gain speed when it bounces.

Paddle. The instrument employed to propel the ball.

Paddle Hand. The hand in which the paddle is held when playing.

Placement. The act of putting the ball where the opponent cannot successfully return it.

Playing Surface. The top of the table on which the game is played.

Push. The act of meeting the ball gently and getting it back over the net.

Receiver. The person to whom the ball is served.

Receiving Position. A way of standing in order to play a serve.

Score. Point made by opponent when player fails to make a successful shot. A game consists of twenty-one points, with the winner scoring at least two more points than the loser.

Serve. The method of putting the ball into play. The serve changes from one player to the other at the end of every five points, and alternates every point after the score of twenty each is reached.

Service Line. A line dividing the table in half longitudinally; used in the doubles game.

Set-up. A ball that is easy to play, usually a high ball near the net.

Side Lines. The longitudinal edges of the table.

Sidespin. A turn of the ball that causes it to twist to the right or left when it bounces.

Smash. A stroke designed to put blinding speed and little spin on the ball.

Spin. The rotation of the ball in flight.

Stroke. The act of hitting the ball.

Throat. The point where the blade and handle join.

Topspin. Some as overspin.

Underspin. Same as backspin.

Volley. To hit a ball before it touches the table.

Wood. The blade or wide part of the paddle.

DISCUSSION QUESTIONS

1. Relate the history of table tennis.
2. List and describe some of the skills of table tennis.
3. Relate the differences between table tennis and tennis.
4. How is wrist movement important to the game?
5. Describe a successful block.
6. How would one go about teaching a class in table tennis?

BIBLIOGRAPHY

Clark, Coleman, *Table Tennis*. Englewood Cliffs, N.J.: Prentice-Hall, Inc., 1939.

Fuller, Emily M., *Top Notch Table Tennis*. Englewood Cliffs, N.J.: Prentice-Hall, Inc., 1942.

Miles, Richard, *The Game of Table Tennis.* Philadelphia: J. B. Lippincott Company, 1969.

Purves, Jay, *Table Tennis.* New York: A. S. Barnes & Company, 1942.

United States Table Tennis Association, *Laws of Table Tennis,* 1970.

tennis

21

BACKGROUND

The game of tennis may have received its name from a command heard frequently in France in a game called *la paume* (the palm). In French the command is *tenez*, which means "Take it! Play!" When English-speaking people heard the French word, they supposed that it was the name of the game. As time passed, *tenez* finally became *tennis*. Another source states that tennis is a corruption of the word *tamis*, meaning "sieve," because in the French game the ball was bounced on a sieve.

La paume was a crude type of tennis played by hitting a ball across a net with a paddle. Originally the ball was hit with the hand, and it may have been adapted from Irish wall handball. The paddles were adopted either to relieve the stinging hands or to propel the ball faster. La paume was played only outdoors at first. It was taken indoors by the clergy early in the thirteenth century, but Louis IX later banned the clergy from play-ing it because he thought it was not dignified enough to be played by priests. The outdoor game continued to increase in popularity, and the English soon imported it to Britain.

Sometime during the fourteenth century, Edward III became interested in tennis and had a room in his palace fixed for play. Because of the King's interest and the game's natural appeal, tennis continued to increase in popularity. The game became so popular in France that addi-tional edicts had to be issued to continue to enforce the ban against the clergy participating.

Considering its popularity, there surely were some rules to the game; but if any were ever written, they were eventually destroyed or forgotten. It is known that a net was used during the game's entire history, and it is believed that at some time a wall was involved in part of the play. There seems to have been no regulation size for the court, standards for the ball, or rules for the size and construction of the paddle or racket. It is believed that there were more than 2,000 courts of varying sizes in France during the seventeenth century.

The French eventually began to apply the term "tennis" to their game. Gradually the English and French games became more and more similar, until representatives of the two countries found it possible to hold tourna-ments. A great deal of international rivalry developed, and world cham-pionship tournaments were held.

As has been true of several other sports, gambling on tennis games became widespread. The joy of winning became secondary, and the players were after money and didn't mind who knew it. As a result, the best players sold out to gamblers for a share of the profits. Tennis courts came to be the scene of gambling on a tremendous scale—so much so, in fact, that France eventually banned the game completely. England took the same steps soon after. If it had not been for the European nobility who continued to play the game, tennis might easily have disappeared completely from the sports scene.

American tourists heard about tennis early in the nineteenth century. They liked what they could learn of it, and, as a result, many Americans began playing the game in the United States. The name used at that time was "court tennis." It was played generally at private homes and in a few clubs.

As we know it today, the game of lawn tennis was originated by Major Walter Wingfield at a lawn party in 1873 in England. He patented it under the name of *Sphairistike* in 1874. The game was tremendously popular at the very beginning and almost overnight spread to Bermuda and then to the United States. One of the men of Major Wingfield's party took it to Bermuda, where it became immediately popular. Miss Mary

Outerbridge, an American, saw the game there and carried it back to the United States. She was influential in having a court constructed at the Staten Island Cricket and Baseball Club late in 1874.

There were no standardized rules until 1881, when one of the Outerbridge boys called together a group of the tennis leaders in the East for a meeting in New York. They standardized rules and equipment and formed themselves into the United States Lawn Tennis Association, which is the governing body of the game today. (See Figure 21–1 for court dimensions.)

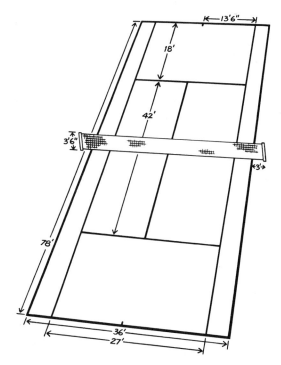

FIGURE 21-1 *Tennis Court*

National championships were held in 1881 at Newport, Rhode Island, and Richard D. Sears was crowned the first winner. Women's championship matches were started in 1887. In 1900, Dwight F. Davis donated a cup for which teams from all nations might compete. This stimulated interest in the game, and to this day the Davis Cup matches are an important part of lawn tennis.

By early in the twentieth century, tennis had thousands of followers. It was played not only on private estates but also in clubs and public recreation areas. It is no longer a game played solely by the elite, but by people on nearly all socio-economic levels.

Within the past 30 years, a great interest has developed in the professional game, and thousands today pay high prices to see the best professionals play.

BASIC SKILLS

Tennis is an interesting game and one to which millions of people are attracted. It is adaptable. It can be slow or it can be extremely fast. depending on the skill of the players or the type of game that is desired at the moment. Many people like it because it does not take very long to develop enough skill to enjoy it. It is played outdoors and thus attracts those who want both to play an enjoyable game and at the same time benefit from healthful outdoor activity.

When all or many of the game's very definite skills are mastered, it provides an extremely fast form of physical activity. To develop these skills and to learn strategic use of them requires that the player devote much time to practice on the court and on the backboard.

stance

The way a person stands both when waiting for a return and at the time of stroking the ball is important to efficient play of the game. In waiting for an opponent's service, the player should stand with feet in line with the base line (cross-court), weight balanced evenly on the toes and balls of the feet. The knees and trunk should be bent slightly. The head is erect, eyes looking straight ahead in order to see what the opponent will do on his next shot and to observe the ball as it approaches. The racket is held firmly in the Eastern grip so that it can be moved quickly to any position for stroking the ball. The player should be ready to move in any direction in order to be at the best spot to stroke the ball most effectively. The position described, if carefully maintained while waiting for shots, will enable the player to start quicker for the spot from which he can return the ball most efficiently.

When the ball is being struck, the stance changes. The feet should be in line with the length of the court. The player faces to the right on the forehand drive and to the left on the backhand.

the grip

The way a racket is held can have a lot to do with how effective one's game becomes. A good grip has two objectives: to hold a racket firmly, and to have it in such a position that it can be moved easily from place to place without changing its position within the hand. The writer prefers what has come to be popularly known as the Eastern grip.

EASTERN GRIP. It is possible to make a powerful stroke with this grip and to hit from many different positions with a minimum of extra movement. It is taken when the handle of the racket is parallel to the ground and the face is perpendicular. The right hand reaches out and takes hold of the handle as if it were shaking hands. The fingers flex around to the right and the thumb to the left. The V made by the thumb and index finger opens directly toward the racket head. The grip should be firm but not tight. The wrist should be kept flexible prior to contact with the ball The wrist should lock upon impact. The Eastern grip is best used on forehand shots (Figure 21–2). When making a backhand shot, the hand must

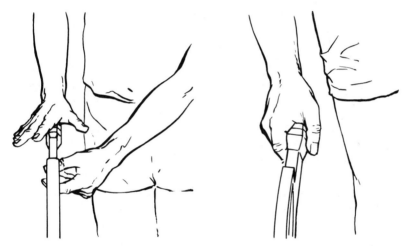

FIGURE 21-2 *The Grip* (From Wayne Pearce and Janice Pearce, *Tennis.* © 1971, Prentice-Hall, Inc. Reproduced by permission of the publisher.)

be shifted slightly to provide greater strength. In order to have more than the thumb supporting the racket against the ball in a backhand, the hand should be shifted on the handle about a quarter turn in the direction of the thumb. In this position the base of the thumb is giving support to the racket.

WESTERN GRIP. Although the Western grip is virtually obsolete among better players, there are some few individuals who prefer it. Because the tennis student should know what it is like, it is described here. With the racket face parallel to the ground, the racket is grasped near the end of the handle as if the player were shaking hands with it. The V formed by the thumb and index finger opens toward the face of

FIGURE 21-3 *Forehand Drive* (From Wayne Pearce and Janice Pearce, *Tennis.* © 1971, Prentice-Hall, Inc. Reproduced by permission of the publisher.)

the racket. Such a grip is considered good for the forehand drive, but it is poor for the backhand and overhand smash.

the forehand drive

In preparing the forehand shot, the player should assume a "ready for action" position. He faces the net with the throat of the racket resting on the palm of the left hand, his body in a slightly crouched position, standing on his toes and ready to move. After moving close enough for the stroke, the player should turn his body almost sideways to the net, with the front foot pointing more toward the net and the back foot pointing toward the side. By pointing the front foot toward the net, he can transfer his weight forward more easily at the time of racket impact with the ball. The knees should be slightly bent as the backswing begins. For beginners a level backswing is recommended. The backswing should be carried back at about waist level with the arm extended and wrists locked to a point about opposite the right hip. The racket head should be kept higher than the wrist throughout the entire swing. The body weight must be transferred to the back foot on the backswing. As the forward swing begins

with the racket, arm, shoulders, and hips moving together as a unit, the weight is transferred to the front foot. The ball should be contacted just in front of the forward foot, with the arm extended and the wrist still locked. After impact with the ball, the racket should follow through the line of flight of the ball. From the time the racket starts back and the forward movement begins, there should be a continuous flowing action with the same speed throughout. A player should not attempt to hit the ball with great speed or a jerky or punchy movement. Speed may be acquired after control has been mastered (Figure 21–3).

the backhand drive

This particular stroke is one that is used to hit shots that come to the left side of a right-handed player. There should be a slight adjustment in the backhand grip. The best way to grip the racket for a backhand stroke is to grasp the handle in the Eastern grip with the throat of the racket resting on the left hand. The left hand then moves the handle about an eighth to a quarterturn to the right. The thumb can either extend along the edge of the handle or curl around the handle. The fingers should be comfortably spread for the forehand and backhand grips.

As the backswing for the backhand begins, the body should be turned toward the left side with the right shoulder pointing toward the net. The player should swing the racket straight back toward the left hip or slightly lower. Many players support the racket during the backswing by lightly grasping its throat. As the forward swing begins, the racket slides off the left hand. As the swing moves forward, the arm should be comfortably extended. The front knee should be bent so that the body weight will be transferred forward. One of the most common causes of poor backhand shots is allowing the ball to come in too close to the body. The swing should be timed so that at the time of impact, the ball will be about even or slightly in advance of the front foot. The swing should be completed with a smooth, natural follow-through.

the serve

This shot is the means of putting the ball in play at the start of each point. By constant practice a player can develop so much skill that he can consistently win points on the serve alone. It is the object of the serve to hit the ball from behind the base line across the net and into the service court in such a manner as to be difficult for the opponent to return.

Preparatory to serving, the player stands with feet parallel toward the direction the ball is to be served. The feet should be approximately 12 inches apart, with the knees slightly flexed, so that the weight can be easily shifted from the rear to the front foot. The side should be pointing toward the net. The beginning player should use either the forehand grip or one between the forehand and backhand grip. The serving arm is bent

FIGURE 21-4 *The Flat Serve* (From Wayne Pearce and Janice Pearce, *Tennis.* © 1971, Prentice-Hall, Inc. Reproduced by permission of the publisher.)

FIGURE 21-5 *Total Service Swing* (From Wayne Pearce and Janice Pearce, *Tennis.* © 1971, Prentice-Hall, Inc. Reproduced by permission of the publisher.)

so that the forearm and the upper arm are approximately at right angles. The racket head is dropped down in back of the shoulder. From the position just described, the server brings the racket head above the height of his head. The ball should be contacted at a point well above the head. (See Figure 21–4) Just prior to the time the ball is contacted, the wrist snaps forward to give further power. At the time the racket strikes the ball, the face of the racket is turned slightly forward to the left and slanted, so that a partial topspin and sidespin are put on the ball. It is emphasized here again that the height at which the ball is hit is important to greater service efficiency. The server continues the follow-through by finishing down and across the body. As players advance, the total service swing should be used as shown in Figure 21–5.

the volley

To volley a ball is to hit it before it touches the court. Most volleying takes place close to the net and is generally performed in basically the same way as the forehand and backhand drives, except there is very little chance for a preliminary swing and there need not be much follow-through. Often the stroke must be made so quickly that the player cannot get into position for the shot. However, he should make every effort to pace his game so that he will be in the proper position. The volley should be hit in front of the body with a punch stroke. There is no time for a backswing on the volley. The ball should be hit with a locked wrist instead of a flick of the wrist. The body should face the net when volleying. The left foot should be advanced forward for a forehand volley, and the right foot should be advanced toward the net for a backhand volley. This type of foot action moves the weight into the ball better and gives a crisper shot. The half volley is a shot that is made just after the ball rises from the court. It is a block shot with little movement of the racket. It is difficult to make and requires much practice.

the overhead smash

This shot is made in much the same way as the serve. It is utilized to take advantage of high, weak returns on the part of the opponent. It is a very difficult shot to time accurately because one must judge properly the speed and height of the ball as it is dropping down to the court. It is made in the same movements as the serve in order to drive the ball back to the opponent at tremendous speed. The racket face is flat simply because spin is not necessary and also because such a shot is more accurate. To smash well, it is necessary to be relaxed and to keep the eyes on the ball. This is a kill shot and, executed properly, can clinch many a point. The overhead smash is made, as a general rule, before the ball bounces, but it can be executed on a high-bouncing ball also.

the lob

The lob is simply a ball hit upward and across the net. It is generally considered a safe shot. It is played particularly to opponents who have a weak smash and may err on the return. The average lob begins similarly to a forehand or backhand drive. As the racket goes through its path, the face turns upward so that the ball is sent high in the air and bottomspin is put on it. Another time the lob may be used to advantage is if the opposition is up close to the net and cannot get to a ball sent high to the back court. It is possible to put backspin on a lob by a quick backward movement of the wrist.

the chop

The chop is a shot that allows considerably more control than any of the other shots. It is not a powerful shot and, in a fast game, is considered the change-of-pace shot. It can be made either forehand or backhand. In either case the balance and the arm and racket motion are quite similar.

Because it can be made from a position closer to the body than the regular drives, it is sometimes used in their stead when the player cannot get to the ball quickly enough. The shot can be used either offensively or defensively, but it is primarily a means of defense. It is such an easy shot that the player will be using it more and more often if he does not exercise care.

It is made by swinging the racket forward and downward, with the face of the racket slanted upward. This swing and slant of the face causes the racket to impart bottomspin as well as forward motion to the ball. When it hits, the ball has a tendency to bounce upward close to the place where it first contacts the court. This peculiarity forces the receiver to be closer to the spot of the bounce in order to play the shot properly.

Though the chop shot is an easy one to make, the good player should employ it only as one of many possible strokes. He should not rely on it exclusively, however.

the drop shot

The drop shot is one in which the ball drops quickly over the net with backspin in such a way as to bounce quickly and often defy return. It is used when the opponent is back near the base line and the player wants to trap him by a close shot that will not bound to him as he runs forward in an effort to return it.

The drop shot is a dangerous one to make, because a slight mistake will put it into the net or so deep over the net that the opponent can return it in such a way as almost certainly to clinch the point. It is a delicate shot that requires a sensitive touch and years of practice.

In making the drop shot, the movement is virtually the same as for the chop except that it is shorter and there is a minimum of follow-through. The ball is aimed just over the top of the net so that it will drop fast and near the net.

scoring

Tennis is scored somewhat differently from other sports both in number of points necessary to win a game and the name applied to each point. Four points scored by a player before his opponent scores three are enough to win the game. After the opponent scores three, it is necessary for a player to be two points ahead in order to win.

The names of the various points are as follows: one point is called either 5 or 15; two points are called 30; three points, 40; and four points, game. In calling a score, the server's score is given first. Some of the scoring combinations that may exist in the course of a game are as follows:

POINTS		SCORE
Server	*Receiver*	
1	0	15–love
2	0	30–love
2	1	30–15
2	2	30–30
2	3	30–40
3	3	Deuce
4	3	Advantage server
5	3	Game won by server

hints to players

The tennis player should keep his eyes on the ball. Many a shot has been missed because the player looked toward where he was planning to hit the ball instead of at the ball. Overhead strokes may sometimes be used, especially from the forecourt. They are offensive, fairly easy shots. They are difficult to time properly, however, and often it is easier to hit a forehand or backhand drive. The knees should be bent in proportion to the height of the ball on any shot—that is, the lower the ball, the deeper the knee bends. Except in unusual situations, the player should face at right angles to the net. During a stroke, the weight should be shifted from the back foot to the front one. The player must not allow a ball to get too close to his body during the stroke. Play should be aggressive, with the opponent continually pressed. A player should return quickly to a defensive stance and be prepared to move quickly in any direction to play the ball.

strategy

The opponent should be studied very carefully and an attempt be made to determine his weaknesses. As soon as they are found, they should be exploited. Lob to an opponent frequently even if the ball does not go over his head and behind him. To be returned, such a shot requires perfect timing, and frequently it is missed. Placement should be utilized at every opportunity. The opponent should be kept moving. As soon as he can be caught going definitely in one direction, a shot should be placed behind him so that it will be impossible for him to play it. The shots should vary with the situation. Players usually stand behind the base line at the center of the court until the opponent's next stroke is anticipated.

The player should develop his service ability so that he can frequently ace his opponent. If the first shot is not effective, the second shot should be just about as hard as the first. Never should the second shot be lofted over easily just to get it inbounds. This often results in a driving kill on the service return.

The successful tennis player should play an aggressive game at all times. As in other sports, a good offense is a good defense. Any player who goes on the defensive is admitting that his opponent is getting the better of him. The game should be planned carefully and on an aggressive basis. However, the player should not hesitate to change the attack whenever he sees fit and to go so far as to take a chance occasionally. In singles, the player should vary from a backcourt game to a net game, making every effort to keep his opponent back as much as possible.

In playing doubles, each player should have a clear understanding of just what the other is most likely to do in any given situation. Most movements on the court are generally based on fundamental position. A concept by which a player may guide his play is that of maintaining court balance. When one player is back to the right, the other should be up and to the left. The factor that guides a player in the choice of his position is the position of the player who is hitting the ball. If player A is stroking the ball at the net on the right, player B should get quickly to the left side toward the back.

In general, a player's game can be improved if he follows certain suggestions:

1. Never change the tactics in a winning game, but feel free to revise a losing game.
2. Keep the eyes on the ball.
3. Play aggressive tennis.
4. Do not play too close to the net.
5. Play to the opponent's weaknesses.
6. Keep the opponent guessing about your next move.

TEACHING PROCEDURE

A tennis class should be limited in size, depending on the number of courts and practice areas available. If there are four courts, the class should be limited to sixteen players. If there is backboard space, an additional student may be included for every 15 feet of board. Each student should have a racket, and at the first meeting of the class the background of the sport should be given and a demonstration conducted. The class should then be gathered in a semicircle where the backhand and forehand strokes are demonstrated. A careful check should be made to see whether the class members are far enough apart to swing their rackets clear of their neighbors. Without hitting the ball, the students practice the body and arm movement associated with both the forehand and backhand drives. If any time remains in the class period, they may move to the courts and begin hitting the ball across the net in the forehand and backhand strokes. The teacher should go from person to person, correcting faults and stimulating participation.

At each class period, the teacher demonstrates some of the various strokes and then allows time for practice on them either on the court or on the backboards. After the forehand and backhand have been practiced considerably, the students should be shown the serve and allowed to practice it. Not more than three or four class periods should go by before they begin to play the game, utilizing all the strokes learned up to that point plus the serve.

The students should be encouraged to play an aggressive game as they master the basic movements of the strokes, to vary the attack from fast to slow to fast, and to use strategy whenever possible. It is the teacher's job to improve the skill of each of these players, and he should make a serious effort to analyze the play of everyone so that each will show greater tennis skill every day he comes to class.

Each class should be urged to practice the various skills outside of class time and to play the game as much as possible. On rainy days, the class members may take turns hitting the ball against the gymnasium walls or in the handball or squash courts.

SKILL TESTS

serve for accuracy

The player makes ten legal serves and scores a point each time one is good and a half point if the serve is a let. The score for the test is the number of points the server makes in ten attempts.

serve for accuracy, using the practice board

A target consisting of five circles is drawn on the practice board. The center circle, the middle of which is 5 feet from the ground, has a diameter of 1 foot, the next circle a diameter of 3 feet, the next 5, the next 7 and the outside one 9. The server stands back 39 feet and serves to the target. If he hits in or on the edge of the center circle, he gets nine points;

the next circle is worth seven points, the next five, the next three, and the last one. The server's score is the total number of points he makes in five attempts.

forehand and backhand tests

This type of test can be used most effectively with the aid of the automatic tennis ball throwing machine. Ten or fifteen balls may be thrown to the forehand side and the same number to the backhand side. A point is awarded for each shot returned back over the net and inside the boundary lines. A string should be hung across the court about 6 or 8 feet above the net so that the players will not lob the shots back. There can be several variations of this test, such as marking certain areas of the court to test accuracy. Additional points may be given for balls hit into more difficult areas. If a tennis-ball machine is not available, this type of test may be administered by designating someone to toss the ball underhanded from the net to the students being tested. It is important that the thrower have good control of the balls tossed.

stroke for accuracy

The player hits a ball to the wall and, when it gets back to him, drives it to the same target used for the serve. His score is the number of points he makes in five attempts.

rally for speed

The player stands 10 or more feet from the wall and strokes the ball to the wall as many times as he can in one minute.

the dyer backboard test of tennis ability[*]

This test is similar to the ones just described except that the time is limited to 30 seconds. Norms have been worked out for it since the test was first published.

DEFINITION OF TERMS

Ace. A term to explain a scoring point when the opponent failed to touch the serve.
Backcourt. The section of the court lying between the base and service lines.

[*] Dyer, Joanna T., "The Backboard Test of Tennis Ability." *Supplement to Research Quarterly, American Association for Health, Physical Education, and Recreation,* March, 1935, Vol. IX, No. 1, pp. 62–74.

Backhand. A stroke on the left side of a right-handed player, taken with the arm and racket across the body.

Backspin. Rotation of the ball that causes it to spin toward the striker.

Backswing. The swinging of the racket behind the body when preparing to hit the ball.

Base Line. The line at either end of the court, which is parallel to the net and behind which the server stands.

Center Mark. A line 4 inches long and 2 inches wide that bisects each base line and insures the server's standing behind the correct half of the base line.

Center Serving Line. A line that is equidistant from the side lines and divides the right and left service courts.

Center Strap. A white canvas strap 2 inches wide, which is necessary to hold the net down at the center.

Chop. A stroke in which the racket is drawn down sharply with a chopping motion, giving the ball a back spin.

Cross-Court. A shot that goes diagoally across the net at a sharp angle.

Deep. A shot that hits in the backcourt near the base line.

Default. The victory given to a player because for some reason the opponent refuses to play or is absent.

Depth. Something gained by hitting the ball deep in the backcourt, near the base line.

Deuce. The score when each side has three or more points and the score is even.

Double Fault. A situation when the server fails to make his two serves good, and the point is lost to his opponent.

Doubles. A game in which there are two players on each side.

Doubles Court. A singles court with a 4½-foot alley added on either side.

Drive. To hit the ball forehand or backhand on the first bounce and with enough force so that it will land near or on the line.

Drop Shot. A very easy shot that barely clears the net and bounces only slightly.

Eastern Grip. A grip formed by placing the hand on the racket handle as if shaking hands with it. The face of the racket is perpendicular to the ground.

Error. The failure to make a legal return even though the ball is hit.

Fault. A served ball that is not in the proper court or is otherwise illegal.

Fifteen. A term used when a player scores his first point in a game.

Five. Another term that is often used instead of "fifteen" for the first point that a player makes.

Flat. A way of hitting a ball so squarely that it does not spin.

Flat Serve. A very hard and high serve that has little or no spin.

Foot Fault. The failure to keep the feet in the right position when serving.

Forcing Shot. A shot intended to put an opponent out of position.

Forecourt. The territory between the service line and the net.

Forehand. A stroke made with the arm and racket on the natural side of the body, leading with the palm.

Forty. A term used when a player has won three points in a game.

Ground Stroke. A stroke that is made immediately after the ball bounds from the ground.

Kill. To place a ball or to hit a fast ball in such a way that the opponent cannot return it.

Lawn Tennis. The official name for the game of tennis.

Let. A served ball that touches the net, but goes over into the correct court. It is also any stroke that is played over.

Line. The boundary and division lines of a court.

Lob. A soft stroke that has a high arc, used to place the ball behind the man at the net.

Love. A term used when a player has not scored.

Match. A series of sets to determine the best in three or the best in five.

Match Point. A single point that stands between the player and victory in a match.

Mixed Doubles. A game in which a man and a woman play as partners on each side.

Net Man. The player of a doubles team who plays near the net.

No Man's Land. Usually denotes midcourt territory where a player cannot volley properly, nor can he play very well those balls that are on the bounce.

Official. One who supervises in some capacity during a contest.

Pass. A stroke causing the ball to pass out of the reach of a net man.

Place. To direct the ball so that it hits a special part of the court.

Placement. The placing of the ball accurately when hitting it into the opponent's court.

Rally. A series of legal returns during play.

Receiver. One to whom the ball is being served.

Recover. To return a difficult shot that seems impossible.

Retriever. One who covers a great deal of territory and regularly returns hard shots.

Right Service Court. The half of the court on a player's right when he faces the net.

Seeding. The deliberate placing of strong players so they will not meet early in a tournament.

Serve. To put the ball in play at the start of a game.

Server. One who puts the ball in play at the start of each point.

Service Court. The court in which the served ball must hit if it is good.

Service Line. A line 21 feet from the net, running parallel with it.

Serving Order. The order in which players serve.

Set. A series of games won by the first player to win six games unless both sides have five games each; in that case, the winner must be ahead by two.

Set Point. A point that, if won will give a player the set.

Singles. A game in which two people participate, one on each side of the net.

Smash. A shot made with a hard overhead sweeping stroke.

Stop Volley. A very easy shot that places the ball just over the net away from the opponent.

Take the Net. Rushing to the net to volley.

Tape. The band of canvas found at the top of the net.

Thirty. A term used when a player has won two points.

Topspin. The rotation of a ball in such a way that the top of the ball spins forward.

Volley. A stroke in which the player hits the ball before it hits the ground.

Volleyer. A person who plays near the net and prefers to volley.

Western Grip. A grip made by "shaking hands" with the racket when its faces is parallel to the ground.

DISCUSSION QUESTIONS

1. From what French game did tennis originate?
2. Relate some of the difficulties tennis had in getting started.
3. How was the game brought to this country?
4. What are the advantages of the Eastern grip?
5. What is a volley? When is it used?
6. Describe tennis strategy.
7. How may a class be organized for teaching?

BIBLIOGRAPHY

Barnaby, John M., *Racket Work, The Key to Tennis*. Boston: Allyn and Bacon, 1969.

Bowers, Chester, *Advanced Tennis*. New York: The Macmillan Company, 1940.

Budge, John Donald, *Budge on Tennis*. Englewood Cliffs, N.J.: Prentice-Hall, Inc., 1939.

Budge, Lloyd, *Tennis Made Easy*. New York: A. S. Barnes & Company, 1945.

Cummings, Henry I., *Tennis as a Hobby*. New York: Harper and Brothers, 1940.

Driver, Helen Irene, *Tennis for Teachers*. Philadelphia: W. B. Saunders Company, 1941.

Dyer, Joanna T., "The Backboard Test of Tennis Ability." *Supplement to Research Quarterly, American Association for Health, Physical Education, and Recreation*, March, 1935, Vol. IX, No. 1, pp. 62–74.

Fogleman, Harry, *Tennis for the Beginner and the Average Player*. Portsmouth, Ohio: Johnson Publishing Company, 1937.

Gonzales, Pancho, *Tennis*. New York: Cornerstone Library, 1965.

Harman, Bob, *Use Your Head in Tennis*. Port Washington, New York: Kennikat Press, Inc., 1966.

Jacobs, Helen Hull, *Tennis*. New York: A. S. Barnes & Company, 1941.

Jaeger, Eloise M., and Leighton, Harry "Cap", *Teaching of Tennis*. Minneapolis, Minnesota: Burgess Publishing Company, 1959.

Kramer, Jack, *How to Win at Tennis*. Englewood Cliffs, N.J.: Prentice-Hall, Inc., 1949.

Moss, Major T., *Lawn Tennis*. London: George Allen and Unwin, Ltd., 1949.

Perry, Frederick J., *Perry on Tennis*. Philadelphia and Chicago: The John C. Winston Company, 1937.

Tilden, William Tatem, *Aces, Places and Faults*. London: R. Hale, 1938.

Vines, Ellsworth, *Ellsworth Vines' Quick Way to Better Tennis*. New York: Sun Dial Press, 1939.

touch football

22

BACKGROUND

Touch football developed naturally from its mother game, tackle football. To determine exactly when it first began would be impossible. It is safe to say that it has been used for years by football teams during practice sessions. Boys on sandlots have been playing it in place of tackle football since the beginning of the century. Intramural programs in junior and senior high schools and colleges, as well as physical education classes, have included touch football in one form or another for an indefinite period of time.

Some attempts have been made to standardize the rules, but because the game has never assumed the proportions of tackle football, with schools from scattered parts of the country coming together for games, there has not been a concerted or successful effort to frame a basic, uniformly accepted set of regulations.

Touch football is an excellent game to use in the intramural program and to develop certain football skills. It is extremely enjoyable for the participants, and much enthusiasm and spirit can be developed in league play. The game is comparatively inexpensive, requiring essentially only a football and a well-marked playing field.

In order to develop touch football in a school program, it may be well to include instruction in the basic skills in the service program. Then the intramural program should be organized and supervised so that the students will have a place to perform the skills learned in class.

Most of the fundamentals used in tackle football apply to touch football with the following modifications:

1. In blocking, the player must remain on both feet before, during, and after contact.

2. Instead of tackling, the player makes a one-hand touch between the opponent's shoulders and knees.

3. All players are eligible to receive a pass.

4. If the ball is loose or is fumbled, it is automatically dead, with a loss of down.

An official touch football team is composed of seven players, but a six, or even a nine-man team may be used with slight rule adaptation. The adoption of the seven-man team is recommended so that the rules and game will become relatively uniform in all parts of the country. This number appears to allow the greatest flexibility and maximum versatility for players, while at the same time reducing the number of injuries. It is now generally recognized that when more than seven men play on college intramural teams, there is an increased percentage of injuries. The nine-man team produces the highest rate of casualties.

The scoring is patterned after college football with the attempted play after a touchdown counting either two points if made while running or passing or one point if made by kicking. To obtain a first down, a team must advance the ball beyond the next zone within four attempts, regardless of the initial starting position. (See Figure 22–1 for drawing of touch football field and marking of zones.)

The length of time required to play a touch football game is four ten-minute periods. There should be a three-minute rest between quarters and a five-minute rest between halves. If the game ends in a tie, there are three methods of determining a winner: (1) award the game to the team with the greatest number of first downs; (2) give each team four downs from the 20-yard line and award the game to the team advancing the ball the farthest; (3) award the game to the team with the greatest number of penetrations inside the opponent's 20-yard line.

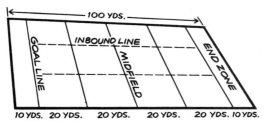

FIGURE 22-1 *Playing Field* (Adapted from Hollis F. Fait, John H. Shaw, and Katherine Ley, *A Manual of Physical Education Activities*, 3rd ed. © 1967, W.B. Saunders Company, by permission of the publisher.)

flag football

Flag football is steadily increasing in popularity in this country as a physical education activity. It is a variation of touch football in which cloth flags are worn by all players. Instead of a touch, the flag is detached from its place on the ball carrier by the defensive player. Flags should be strips of cloth 12 to 15 inches wide.

Flag football eliminates subjective judgment as to whether a player is tagged. When one of the flags is removed, the play is dead, and a tackle has been made. The basic rules governing flag football are similar to those used in touch football, and they must be strictly enforced in relation to blocking and tackling to minimize hazardous play. Strong measures are recommended to eliminate blocking, tackling, or the holding of the ball carrier by a defensive player attempting to secure the flag. Blocking with the shoulder with no intent to grasp the flag is illegal and results in a 15-yard penalty. It should be pointed out also that a defensive player must maintain contact with the ground when attempting to secure the flag.

PUTTING THE BALL INTO PLAY

The ball is put into play halfway between the kicking team's 20-yard line and midfield at the start of the game, beginning of the second period, and after a touchdown. The ball may be put into play by a drop kick or a place-kick and must be kicked forward at least 10 yards.

All players of the kicking team must remain behind their restraining line throughout the kick. This is an imaginary line drawn across the field even with the forward point of the ball. The receiving team must stay behind its restraining line, which is 10 yards in front of the kicking team's restraining line, until the ball is kicked.

At all other times the ball must be put into play from the line of scrimmage by a snap pass to a backfield man. The snap pass refers to handing or passing the ball with a quick motion of the hand or hands.

BASIC SKILLS

blocking

The block is an attempt to keep the opponent away from the ball carrier by placing the body between the ball carrier and the defensive man. The blocker should attempt to force the defensive man away from the ball carrier or away from the path he is to take. Since the player is not permitted to leave his feet in executing the block, he must become adept at maintaining body balance. The forearm and the shoulder provide the blocking surface, which makes contact at the opponent's midsection. While in a semicrouched position, the blocker places his head between the opponent and the ball carrier and attempts to drive the opponent back or to either side. It is usually advisable for the blocker to keep contact with the defensive man after the initial charge to prevent his slipping away.

The blocker should not "telegraph" the direction of his charge by leaning or looking in the direction he intends to go, but always should assume the same position on the line of scrimmage and make no move until the ball is snapped.

touching

For a legal touch, the defensive player makes contact with either hand between the shoulder and the knee of the ball carrier while keeping both feet in contact with the ground. Rule variations that increase the difficulty of touching include the two-hand touch between the shoulders and the knees or a one-hand touch below the waist. Rather than remaining stationary in a waiting position, a potential tackler must move toward the ball carrier, with a slight decrease in speed, just before the touch is made. The defensive player's eyes should be fixed on the belt area of the ball carrier as he approaches. Body balance is very important for the ball carrier, since he may sidestep or pivot away from the defensive man. It is easier to make a touch when approaching from the side than head on.

passing

In executing the forward pass, the passer grips the ball at the end that will be pointing over his shoulder. The index finger is placed about two inches from the point of the ball, with the thumb opposite. The remaining fingers are comfortably spread on the laces of the ball.

He brings his arm back slightly above and behind his ear, with the weight of his body shifted to the rear foot. The nose of the ball is kept slightly upward as the front foot steps toward the receiver, while the free hand leaves the ball and moves to the side of the body for balance. The ball is thrown with an overhand motion similar to the throwing movement made by a baseball catcher, as his weight shifts to the leading foot. The ball is released with a considerable amount of wrist snap, which causes it to spin in a clockwise movement. This type of spin overcomes air resistance with a minimum loss of speed and accuracy. Short passes require little or no lead for the receiver and must be thrown with great velocity to avoid interception. Long passes, which cover more than twenty yards, must be thrown with a much higher trajectory path that necessitates a lead to reach the receiver.

receiving passes

When receiving passes, a player should catch the ball with the fingers while using both hands. The ball should not be caught with the body when it is possible to use the fingers. They should be spread and relaxed, and the hands should give as the ball comes in contact with the fingers. The eyes must watch the ball until the pass is caught. Many passes are fumbled because of a player's failure to keep his eyes on the ball and to catch it on his fingers. After the ball is caught, it is drawn to the body. Sometimes this happens so rapidly that it appears the pass receiver catches the pass with his body.

If the receiver can get open, there is a great possibility of pass completion. An outstanding receiver must know how to alter his pace and direction.

A change of pace is a good technique for getting open. The receiver runs at a moderate rate, and as he nears the defensive man, he puts on a burst of speed. When the defensive man sees the pass receiver advancing at a certain speed, he will assume that is his fastest and will set his own pace accordingly. When the pass receiver accelerates, the defensive man is not ready to cope with this change and will often lose a few steps. These steps are the difference in the receiver being open or covered.

Change of direction is another method used for deceiving the pass defender. This consists of a sudden change from one direction to another. It may be made to either side at any angle or by cutting directly back toward the passer. The change of direction must be accompanied by fakes just before the cut is made. The receiver may run in one direction for a few steps before cutting in another. Crossovers, side steps, and pivoting are excellent techniques to be used with the change of direction. It should be remembered that all players are eligible to receive a forward pass.

punting

Punting is an important fundamental of football requiring concentration, balance, and leg power. The punt is most frequently used on the fourth down when the offensive team is on its half of the field, and the possibility of making a first down is doubtful.

The kicker usually stands about 10 yards behind the line of scrimmage, placing the kicking foot slightly ahead of the other foot. While in the waiting position, the punter should place the arms waist-high, with the palms up, and the elbows and trunk flexed slightly. He must move the elbows and hands backward slightly upon receiving the ball in order to cushion the impact. It should come to him about waist-high. The right-handed kicker usually holds the ball with the right hand under and in the middle of it and the left hand on the side to steady it. Some kickers prefer to have their hands in positions other than the one mentioned above, which is all right if this does not affect their kicking.

The kicker should take as few steps as possible to make contact with the ball. Generally, he will take one step forward with the left foot preceding the kick with the right. The two-step approach is recommended over the three-step, since it is quicker and does not place the kicker as close to the line of scrimmage.

The downward drop of the ball is so slight that it may be said it is laid upon the kicking foot. The ball should be dropped to land partially on the instep and partially on the toe with its center directly over the point where the instep begins, lying across the instep at an angle. Punting consistency is greatly dependent upon dropping the ball at the desired angle because this largely determines the distance which the ball will travel.

The kicking foot should meet the ball about knee-high and continue to follow through to finish above the head. The ball is kicked with the instep, with the toe pointed downward and the ankle locked. If the toe is turned too high, the ball will go straight up instead of going forward. The kicking leg is flexed at the start of the kick, becoming extended at impact.

place-kick

The place-kick is used to start the game, to start the play after each touchdown, or to try for an extra point. During the place-kick, the ball is held for the kicker by a teammate. The holder places the point of the ball on the ground with the fingers of his right hand on top of it (Figure 22–2). It is held slightly tilted toward the kicker.

During the kickoff, the kicker stands four or five strides back of the ball and runs forward so that his left foot stops at a distance of four to

FIGURE 22-2 *Place Kick* (Adapted from Hollis F. Fait, John H. Shaw, and Katherine Ley, *A Manual of Physical Education Activities*, 3rd ed. © 1967, W.B. Saunders Company, by permission of the publisher.)

eight inches behind and slightly to the left of it. After planting his left foot, he brings his right foot forward so his toe meets the ball just below its center. The kicker should keep his eyes upon the ball until it is kicked.

In the kick for the extra point, the ball is centered from the line of scrimmage. The player who is to receive the pass and hold the ball should be on his knees from 10 to 12 yards behind the center. Usually a place is marked where the ball will be held so that the kicker may keep his eyes on that spot until the ball is kicked. The holder places the ball on the ground in the same manner as in the kickoff. The kicker usually takes the same steps as described in punting.

The kicker's head is held down with his eyes on the ball at all times, and his toes are pointed straight ahead. The kicker should never raise his head until after he has kicked the ball.

lateral passes

The term lateral is used to describe any pass that is not thrown forward. Such a pass is a very effective way of advancing the ball in touch football, since blocking is difficult. Also, the pass is not so hazardous in touch football as in tackle football, for in touch football a fumbled lateral pass becomes dead at the point of contact with the ground, while in tackle football it is a free ball.

The lateral is used when the defensive man has committed himself and is about to touch the ball carrier. A one-handed underhand pass or a two-handed chest pass may be used to execute the play. A lateral should never be used until the ball has been advanced forward as far as possible.

centering

The center on a football team should be a versatile player, since he is responsible for all the duties of an interior lineman. In addition he must safely center the ball to a quarterback, make the long center to the punter, call the huddle, and maintain team spirit.

The stance of the center varies somewhat, depending on the type of offense, single-wing or T formation, and on the individual. Basically, the feet are spread a shoulder's width apart and slightly staggered, with the right foot, or the foot on the side of the centering hand, forward. From this position, he bends at the trunk, places his left hand on his thigh, and grasps the ball in a grip similar to the passer's grip. The centering hand is extended downward from the shoulder, the weight is on the balls of the feet, the head and eyes are up, the back is erect, and the shoulders are squared.

In centering to a tailback in a single-wing formation or in a direct snap for a punt, the passer alters his basic stance slightly by lowering the shoulders below the buttocks, distributing the weight of the body on the heel and toes of the right foot and the toes of the left foot, and placing a minimum amount of weight on the football. The ball is grasped in a fashion similar to the grip for a forward pass. The arm sweep and a wrist snap provide the force for the spiral pass to the backfield area. When two hands are used, the left hand provides support and aids in direction. Centering to a punter is a difficult skill even though it is similar to the one described for the single-wing snap. Speed and accuracy are important to perfect this skill, and to develop it will require concentrated practice.

ball carrying

One end of the ball is placed in the outside armpit, which should be the arm farthest from the defensive player. The other end of the ball is held by the palm and fingers, which should be comfortably spread to provide a firm grip. The ball should be changed from one arm to the other, depending upon the position of the defensive player, to permit the free arm to ward off the tackler. The ball carrier should master the various head, shoulder, eye, and leg points as well as various spins to dodge potential tacklers effectively. The ball carrier has the responsibility of following his interference and of assisting in making downfield blocking easier by setting up blocks through various feints prior to breaking in the desired direction.

TEACHING PROCEDURE

Each skill presented in class should be demonstrated, analyzed, and then practiced. With large groups, it is necessary to work formally, and movements should be made on commands. The men should be lined up for practice so that the teacher can observe the entire group and make corrections.

Scrimmage is important in touch football, especially since it is almost the perfect game situation. However, it is believed that the average teacher spends too much time in playing groups against each other. He must be sure to devote adequate time to developing fundamental skills. Touch football is a game that requires fast thinking, a great degree of skill, speed, and strength, and a teacher should plan thoughtfully in developing the talents of the class.

Frequently, only one person will be teaching a particular skill such as blocking, and some thought should be given to the organization of the group so that he may see the largest possible number of players. This is particularly important for a large number performing a skill such as blocking. The blockers should stand side by side in a straight line facing the men being blocked, who face them in a straight line. Each blocker is a No. 1, and each man being blocked is a No. 2. At a signal, the blockers charge and practice blocking. The teacher, standing at the end of these lines, can see most of the mistakes and correct them immediately. At a word, the assignments reverse.

One of the activities a player must begin very soon after practice gets under way is ball handling. The players should be supplied with footballs —one ball for each pair. They should be shown the skills of passing and catching and then should line up to practice each of these. After several minutes of practice, they should line up as if beginning a scrimmage, and the ball should be snapped to a passer, who passes to the receiver going out.

SKILL TESTS

Touch football is a game where ability can best be measured in game situations. However, in order to determine the ability a person possesses in the various skills, tests may be set up that will reveal passing accuracy, pass catching ability, kicking skills, centering accuracy, and running speed. Testing should be kept to a minimum, since it tends to cause loss of interest on the part of the participants. The teacher should determine in advance what he wants the players to learn and perform, and then test them on the basis of these objectives.

passing tests

Form. Points can be assigned for stance, grip, body balance, and spiral. If the player does all of these well, he receives five points; if any one is not done well, one point is deducted from the total.

Distance. One factor in good passing is the ability to throw a long pass. Each student should be allowed to throw for distance, and each throw should be measured. Students throwing the pass the farthest will get the highest number of points.

Accuracy. Circles should be drawn on a wall with points assigned to each. The passer stands back 20 yards and throws five times. He is given credit for the circles he hits.

punting tests

These tests may be conducted in much the same way as the passing tests and should measure the same factors: form, distance, and accuracy. The accuracy test can be made by kicking toward circles laid out on the ground, the most credit being given for hitting the center.

running tests

The only two factors that lend themselves to testing are form and speed, and they can be tested simply. In such testing one should list all the factors involved in good running form: position of head and body, the stride, and the swing of arms. Assign a point for each, and give the student credit for all he performs creditably.

STRAIGHTAWAY RUNNING. This can be checked by timing a student on a set distance. It is suggested that 220 yards be used because of the greater variation of times that will be indicated, and also because the factor of fatigue will enter in many cases over this distance.

ZIGZAG RUNNING. Hurdles or some other objects should be set up around which the student is to run. They are arranged so that the student must change directions several times.

DEFINITION OF TERMS

Back. A player who starts each scrimmage more than a yard behind the scrimmage line and who is trained in the skills of that position.

Blocking. The act of impeding the progress of a defensive player by an offensive player through causing contact with his shoulder, forearm, or other parts of the body.

Buttonhook. The action an offensive player takes in suddenly turning a step or two back toward the line of scrimmage in order to evade the defense.

Defense. Opponent of the offensive team.

Double-wing. An offensive formation in which both halfbacks line up behind and usually slightly outside the ends.

Down. Action beginning with a snap or free kick and ending when the ball becomes dead.

Fair Catch. A receiver's gaining control of a kick in flight without opposition, thereby forfeiting any right to advance the ball.

Field Goal. A score made by kicking the ball legally over the opponent's goal. Cannot be scored from a kickoff.

Flag. A strip of cloth suspended from a player's belt. When a defensive player pulls the flag, the act constitutes a tackle.

Flat. That part of the field on both sides of the defensive team extending from 2 to 15 yards beyond the line of scrimmage.

Forward Pass. A ball thrown toward the opponent's goal line.

Fumble. The act of losing possession of the ball.

Huddle. The act of a team in coming together for the purpose of learning the next scrimmage play.

Interception. Catch of a pass or fumble by an opponent.

Kickoff. The method of putting the ball in play at the beginning of each half and after each touchdown, usually at the kicking team's 40-yard line.

Loss of Down. Loss of right to play over the down.

Lineman. A player who begins each down within a yard of the scrimmage line and who has been trained in that position.

Neutral Zone. A space the width of the football's length between the two scrimmage lines.

Offense. Team in possession of the ball.

Offside. The position of a player who is beyond his restricting line when the ball is put in play.

Out-of-bounds. A ball or a player in possession of the ball going beyond the boundary lines.

Pass. The act of propelling the ball with the hands.

Place-kick. A kick made when the ball is in a fixed position on the ground or on a tee.

Punt. A kick made by dropping the ball and making foot contact before it touches the ground.

Quarterback. Player who designates the various offensive plays.

Runner. A player in possession of a live ball.

Safety. The offensive team's causing the ball to go above or behind its own goal line, and its becoming dead there while in their possession. Two points are scored for the defensive team. After a safety, the team scored upon kicks from its own 20-yard line.

Screening. An offensive player staying momentarily between a member of his team and defensive players.

Scrimmage Line. A line extending across the field at the point of the ball nearer the players' own goal.

Secondary. That part of the playing field immediately back of the defensive lineman protected by the backs and any lineman that may have been pulled back to assist them.

Shift. Two or more players changing positions just prior to the snap.

Snap. The motion of the center in putting the ball in play from the scrimmage line.

Stance. Body position taken by a player on offense or defense.

Tee. Device used to elevate the ball and hold it in a fixd position.

T Formation. An offensive formation characterized by the quarterback's being over the center and near enough to receive the ball as it is handed to him directly from the center's hands.

Touchdown. A score of six points made by getting the ball across the opponents' goal line legally.

DISCUSSION QUESTIONS

1. How many players constitute an official team?
2. How is a first down achieved?
3. Are fumbles alive or dead when they touch the ground?
4. How is the ball put in play following a touchdown?
5. What basic fundamentals are different in touch and tackle football?
6. What amount of time constitutes a regulation game?
7. Who is eligible to receive a forward pass?
8. What methods may be used to determine a winner if the game ends in a tie?
9. Is blocking a legal action?
10. Describe the "change-of-pace" technique for a receiver getting open.

BIBLIOGRAPHY

Birmingham, Frederic A., *How to Succeed at Touch Football.* New York: The Macmillan Company, 1962.

Dintman, George B., and Barrow, Loyd M., *A Comprehensive Manual of Physical Education Activities for Men.* New York: Appleton-Century-Crofts, 1970.

Fait, Hollis F., Shaw, John H., and Ley, Katherine L., *A Manual of Physical Education Activities.* Philadelphia: W. B. Saunders Company, 1967.

Grombach, J. V., *Touch Football.* New York: The Ronald Press Company, 1958.

Menke, Frank G., *The Encyclopedia of Sports.* New York: A. S. Barnes and Company, 1969.

National College Physical Education Association, *Official National Touch Football Rules.* Chicago: The Athletic Institute, 1963.

National Federation, *Football Rules,* latest edition. Chicago: National Federation of State High School Athletic Associations.

Seaton, Don C., Clayton, Irene A., Leibee, Howard C., and Messersmith, Lloyd L., *Physical Education Handbook.* Englewood Cliffs, N.J.: Prentice-Hall, Inc., 1969.

Shaw, John, *Selected Team Sports for Men.* Philadelphia: W. B. Saunders Company, 1952.

Stanbury, Dean, and Desantis, Frank, *Touch Football.* New York: Sterling Publishing Company, Inc., 1961.

track
and field

23

BACKGROUND

Many of the track and field events we know and practice today originally were skills necessary for man's survival. He used them to attack his enemies aggressively or to defend himself. There is little evidence to show just when all this started, but it can be assumed that when man came into existence hundreds of thousands of years ago, he developed for purposes of survival ways and means of escape and attack that have continued to the present. He had to run to escape his attackers, to catch animals for food and clothing, and to pursue his enemies. His running took the form both of sprints and of distances. A good guess would be that often rocks, tree branches, and other obstructing objects in his path were the origin of present-day hurdle races. Primitive man used rocks and shafts for throwing, which could very well be the basis for our shot, discus, and javelin events. It may be assumed also that the necessity of jumping over ditches or wall-like rocks gave rise to the long jump, pole vault, and high jump.

As ages passed and primitive man began to learn ways of doing things more efficiently through the discovery of fire, pottery, and archery, he found that he had some leisure time on his hands. This time was employed in many ways, one of which was to play at running and throwing, with the dual purpose of recreation and improvement of efficiency. Men made a game out of these skills by racing one another, jumping to see who could jump the farthest, and throwing to see who could throw with greatest accuracy.

As far as is known, such was the history of track and field events until the rise of civilization in Greece. Track and field were developed to a high point in that country for two reasons. The Greeks, especially the Athenians, idolized the human body and worked toward its development through athletic contests. The Spartans fought neighboring states frequently, and many of the battle skills were developed in contests of running, jumping, and throwing the discus and javelin.

The Greeks became so interested in the contests that they began to offer prizes for excellence in each of them. This led to the celebration of the deities in games, songs, and dances. The festivals included the Dionysia, Eleusinia, Panathenaea, and Pan-Hellenic. The latter included the Isthmian, Nemean, Olympian, and Pythian.

The first of the Pan-Hellenic festivals was held in 776 B.C. at Olympia. It became the most famous of all and took place every fourth year until 394 A.D., when the Emperor Theodosius abolished it. The Olympian festival included races of various distances, jumping, and throwing the javelin and discus. The javelin was a spear similar to that used in warfare but with a dull point. The spear had thongs wrapped near the middle to give a firmer grip and, as a result, greater distance. At first, the discus was a round stone but it later took its present form.

The Olympian festivals included events other than track and field, such as boxing and wrestling. Track and field, however, were always considered more important than all the other sports combined. The Olympian games were revived in 1896 in Greece through the efforts of a Frenchman, Baron Pierre de Coubertin; and except for the years 1916, 1940, and 1944, they have been held every four years since. After nearly three thousand years, track and field events are still the most important part of these games.

Whether types of track and field competition existed anywhere from the time the Olympic festival was abolished by Theodosius until about 1100 A.D. is purely a matter of conjecture, since no known records exist. The English revived practices of jumping, running, and throwing during the twelfth century, and the sport has continued in different forms and with varied interest since that time.

As participation increased and interest became greater among the English, an effort was made to organize the sport. This extended only to a standard of performance that would allow a man to participate in major contests.

In 1864, Oxford and Cambridge held the first track and field meet. Several years later, a meet was held in London to determine the national champions in the various track and field events.

The sport began to assume organized form in the United States with the formation of the New York Athletic Club about 1867. In 1868, this organization sponsored the first amateur track and field meet, which was held indoors.

Since colleges first came into existence in the United States, there has been some form of track and field in their athletic programs. There have been rules and regulations to govern the sport since the early 1870s. At that time, the eastern colleges were holding intramural track meets. The first intercollegiate meet was held in 1874 in Saratoga, where teams representing Columbia, Cornell, Harvard, Princeton, Yale, and other colleges met. This event became an annual affair and was the beginning of the first intercollegiate athletic association. Except for greater participation, improvement of facilities and equipment, and the hiring of coaches, the sport has not changed much through the years.

BASIC SKILLS

the sprints

The sprints are composed of three races: the 100-yard dash, 220-yard dash, and the 440-yard dash. These races require good innate speed, proper conditioning and correct training in the techniques of speed running. Quick clearance of the starting blocks, "all out" effort throughout the race, and a strong finish are the basic essentials of these three races.

Most authorities recommend relaxation as the key to fast starting and fast running. It is felt that by running with a relaxed confidence, the runner can run just as fast as a straining runner because he is stronger at the finish and does not decelerate as much. In the 220 and 440, there is a short distance in the middle of the race usually termed a "float." This is a period of about 25 or 75 yards in which the runner will "coast" to allow himself to gather strength for the final burst to the finish line.

THE STRIDE. The basic movements of the running stride are natural developments that start at an early age and progress as the individual progresses physically. However, work can be done to improve these movements. Coordinated, springy leg movements are required for good sprint performance. In making a stride, the track ahead is first contacted with the toes of the forward foot. The ball of the foot then contacts the track. Very little weight is placed on the heel. When the foot contacts the ground, momentum is carrying the body to and beyond this point. While the body is moving forward, powerful extension is taking place at the hips, which gives added forward push. The knee is slightly flexed, and as the leg goes back beyond the perpendicular line of the body, it begins extension along with the ankle. This extension both lifts the body upward and drives it forward. The opposite leg is performing the opposite movement (Figure 23–1).

FIGURE 23-1   *The Running Stride*

A normal stride for a sprinter will measure approximately 7 to 9 feet. It will be longer or shorter depending upon the length of the legs of the individual runner. The stride will be shorter during the first fifteen yards of a race than in the latter part, since it is necessary to dig hard and quickly to develop momentum.

Looking at a stride from the side, one sees what appears to be floating motion caused by the spring and drive forward. As the foot leaves the ground flexion occurs at the knee, and the thigh is then brought through, folding the leg up and causing the sprinter's rear heel to "kick" up as high as the buttocks. This is a natural reaction to the previous powerful leg extension. During all phases of the stride, the legs should move directly forward and back, and should never have even the slightest lateral movement. The feet should point straight ahead, in direct line with the direction the legs are moving.

The sprint stride is different from the other strides only in that the movement is faster.

ARM MOVEMENT.   The arms are moved in an orderly manner and in relation to the legs to maintain balance. Well-coordinated arm movement will often make the difference in the winning margin over a man who has poor arm movement. This possibility should be made clear to runners, and much emphasis should be placed on the proper arm movement. It is the opinion of the writer that little if any forward thrust is given by the arms themselves. The arm swing merely facilitates balance in order that the legs may operate at nearly maximum efficiency.

When the leg goes forward, it is counterbalanced by the movement of the opposite arm going forward. To sum up the total arm movement, the right arm moves in the same direction as the left leg, and the left arm moves in the same direction as the right leg. In addition to the forward arm movement, there is a slight cross arm action also. The more nearly the arm stays in rhythm with the opposite leg, the less lost motion there will be, the smoother will be the action, and the more efficient will be the running.

The arm should be locked at approximately a 90-degree angle and held in this position. The arm movement originates in the shoulder, but the shoulders must not turn from side to side. The fingers should be flexed loosely, with only slight flexing of the wrists. The "grab" caused by the alternate flexion of fingers and arms, should be avoided, for it is lost motion and a hindrance to efficient running. The arm movement should be forward and back and very slightly across the chest.

POSITION OF THE BODY. During all runs there is some leaning forward or slight overbalancing. This position keeps the legs from having to "pull" the body along. Since in sprints the movement is faster, the body is leaning more forward than in the slower events. During the first 10 to 15 yards of a run, the body is leaning further forward, to assist in picking up momentum, than during the remainder of the race. The head is held naturally erect.

THE START. At the start of an event, the runner takes the position that will get him off fast. There are many positions a runner may assume when ready to begin a race, and many variations of these positions. The two factors involved in the type of start used are, first, the philosophy of the coach, and second, the feeling of the runner. There are at least two types of positions from which runners and coaches may choose. It will be assumed that the runner will place the left foot forward, for explanation purposes, though this is not to be construed as a recommendation, since the choice is left solely with the runner.

The two types are the bunch start and the elongated start. The chief difference is the distance between the feet. In the first, the feet are close together (about 4 to 12 inches) but may be at varying distances from the starting line. In the elongated start, the feet are 18 inches or more apart and again at varying distances from the starting line. A secondary factor is that the farther apart the feet are, the nearer the forward foot is to the starting line. In the bunch start, the left foot is placed from 18 to 20 inches from the starting line, depending on the size of the runner and the length of his legs.

In the second start, the knee of the right leg is placed beside the toes of the left foot, which are approximately 14 inches from the starting line, again depending on the length of the runner's legs and, in addition, his comfort.

The starting position discussed thus far is the position assumed when the starter commands, "take your marks." On the "get set" command, the runner comes up out of his complete crouch to a partial leg extension so that the arms are perpendicular or forward. When the gun sounds, the legs immediately begin a dynamic extension, particularly the left leg. After a slight extension by the right leg, it flexes and moves forward for its initial complete thrust. The body is kept low during the first few yards. The head is down at "take your marks," but comes to a natural position on "get set," and faces straight ahead at all times thereafter. The arms work in wider arcs at the start than during the normal run. The drive at the gun is first, hard forward with a hard thrust of the lead arm, and then a gradual upward thrust until a normal running position is attained (Figure 23–2).

FIGURE 23-2 *The Sprint Start* (From John M. Cooper, James Lavery, and William Perrin, *Track and Field for Coach and Athlete*, 2d ed. © 1970, Prentice-Hall, Inc. Reproduced by permission of the publisher.)

THE FINISH. Since the sprint requires an "all out" effort all the way, there is not much possibility of putting on an extra burst of speed at the finish. It might be better urged that, at the finish, the runner determine to continue putting complete effort into what he is doing, although he can aid in cutting down deceleration by lengthening his stride, pumping the arms faster, or taking a deep breath and gathering mentally for the finish. He should not jump or raise the arms at the tape. This sometimes gives the feeling of extra effort, though in reality it is not. The rules require that the runner "breast" the tape. Touching with the hands or arms is not allowed.

After the distance has been completed, the runner should not stop immediately but should come to a gradual stop by slowing down and jogging several yards. This method of ending a run may prevent pulled or strained muscles, which are frequently caused by stopping too suddenly. Physiologically, muscle use is slowed down gradually, and in turn the heart action follows the same course.

100-YARD DASH. This race is the fastest of all outdoor races. It is over an extremely short distance, and every phase of the race is vitally important to the end result. There is no time or distance to rectify a mistake by extra bursts of speed. The start must be practiced and run so that it is made "with the gun." For the first few yards, the runner stays low and slightly forward. Steps are short at first, with a gradual lengthening of stride. By the time the runner has traveled 10 to 15 yards, he should be up to a normal running position, and his stride should be as it is going to be over the total distance. From there on, it is a matter of coordination, relaxation, and a will to win.

220-YARD DASH. As a general rule, the same man who runs the 100 will also run the 220. The form is the same for the 220 as for the 100, and it requires of the runner the same bursting dynamic speed. The same advantages must be taken of the start and all the other phases of the race, but in this distance the runner must learn to coast for about 25 to 50 yards during the last three quarters of the race. It should be strided carefully and swiftly from the start, saving some extra energy for the finish. The same rule in regard to the finish applies in all races, so there is no need for further discussion of that phase here. Again the runner should coast to a stop after the finish. He should never lie down after any race. He should, instead, continue walking around until he feels reasonably recovered from it.

440-YARD DASH. Some coaches and runners believe that this distance is the hardest of all races, and that it requires more stamina, speed, and endurance than any of the other events. Others argue that, if an all out effort is made in every type of race, one is just as hard as the other and, there is no real difference except in the length of time taken to complete a race. The 440 is, except for a slight coast of about 75 yards at approximately the middle third of the distance, a sprint race from the gun to the tape.

Unfortunately, there are many runners who do not obtain sufficient conditioning for the event. They underestimate the effort needed for the race and fail to get into the necessary condition. The runner should pace himself over the distance so that he will have enough strength left to put on a burst of speed toward the end of the race. Basically, the race is still run wide open and hard all the way. All the cautions and advice on other races apply to this one, also.

THE HURDLES.   These are races that involve not only running but also jumping over obstacles. Speed is an important factor, but the man who may not be so fast but can get over the obstacles smoothly and in stride often has a chance. General conditioning, as far as running is concerned, is much the same for the hurdles as for the 100 and 220-yard dashes. The hurdle factor in these events is the one needing attention. Hours and hours of practice must be devoted to this event in order to master, first, the technique involved in getting over the hurdle, and second, the spacing of strides between hurdles.

There are a number of different hurdle races. This discussion will be concerned with the 180-yard low hurdles and the 120-yard high hurdles. They are chosen because these distances are the ones most often used, particularly on the high school level. If an athlete learns the fundamentals involved, such skill can be transferred easily to other distances. The low hurdles are 2 feet, 6 inches high and 20 yards apart. The high hurdles are either 3 feet, 3 inches (high school) or 3 feet, 6 inches (college) in height. Reference to races other than the high hurdles will be made only briefly.

Since the technique of getting over a hurdle is an important factor in the winning of a race, it is necessary to spend much time and meticulous practice perfecting this skill. The first thing a hurdler should remember is that the hurdle movement is just another stride, though slightly higher and more elongated. He should bear in mind also that the legs should go over the hurdles one at a time. Many beginning hurdlers find this statement hard to believe.

Since the high hurdles are more difficult to master than the low ones, the discussion will be devoted principally to the former. Almost the same movements are involved in the other hurdle actions, except for some slight changes in spacing and height.

A hurdler may take seven or eight strides before he crosses the first hurdle and he must take three between hurdles. The number of initial strides depends in a large measure on his anatomical structure and to a lesser degree on his ability and his personal feeling. If he has relatively long legs and average ability, or average length legs and exceptional leg drive, he possibly may cover the distance to the first hurdle in seven strides. If he is shorter and has average or less ability, he will take eight strides to the first hurdle. It is recommended that he always use the same leg crossing the hurdle (the left leg is preferred), and, if he has the anatomy and skill, to take the minimum number of strides. Particular attention is given the starting leg position, since after seven strides he should be in a position to cross the barrier in the manner he prefers.

An analysis of the hurdle skill will show that the takeoff foot leaves the ground at a point approximately 7 feet in front of the hurdle. At the actual takeoff, the left foot (assuming the runner leads with the left foot on all hurdles) lifts upward and extends forward. The right arm extends forward with the left leg to facilitate balance. The legs, as the left leg gets over the hurdle, assume an almost level plane not unlike a dancer's "split." The left leg extends straight toward the hurdle and holds to that line through the entire movement. As the left foot barely crosses the hurdle, the trailing leg begins flexing at the hip and at the knee. The knee and foot are kept up, and the entire movement is parallel to the ground so that the entire leg clears the top of the barrier at about the same height. After the trunk has gone beyond the barrier, the left leg cuts down to the track. The trailing, or right leg begins extension forward and starts into as normal a stride as possible under the circumstances. The left leg stride ends when the foot touches the track approximately 4½ feet from the hurdle. The right leg moves into the first of the three strides that must be executed between hurdles (Figure 23–3).

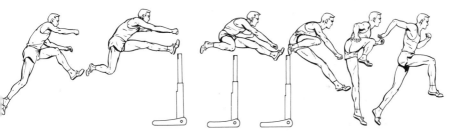

FIGURE 23-3 *The Hurdles* (From John M. Cooper, James Lavery, and William Perrin, *Track and Field for Coach and Athlete*, 2d ed. © 1970, Prentice-Hall, Inc. Reproduced by permission of the publisher.)

The takeoff and finishing distances will vary to some degree, depending on the runner and on the number of the hurdle. If it is the first hurdle, the takeoff distance is less and the finishing distance greater than for the other hurdles. There is some variation on these distances for hurdles of other heights, but not enough to be significant for the average track man.

The average beginning hurdler will want to take eight strides to the first hurdle, because of the additional "dig" enabling a quicker reaching of top speed, though more experienced men find it more efficient to use only seven. If seven strides be the case, the starting position should be such that the takeoff leg, or trailing leg, is in front, and the leading leg is behind. The strides are short at the beginning of the race but lengthen as the first hurdle is reached. A good hurdler takes a hurdle in as close to a normal stride as possible.

There are a few specific ways in which the act of hurdling may be broken down so that a single phase of it may be worked on. Since the trailing leg is the most difficult to maneuver over the hurdle, it is necessary to spend the greatest amount of time perfecting that skill. Stretching exercises, particularly at the crotch, are of great benefit and should be taken as a part of every practice. Another practice that will develop the precise movement of the skill is to stand at one end of the hurdle and rotate the trailing leg in such a manner that it goes across the hurdle exactly as it should. After crossing the hurdle, the leg recovers at the side, and the movement is repeated. It is assumed that the runner will use the same foot for the step-off in crossing all ten hurdles. This is preferable in order that the skill may best be learned in one way rather than in two. If the right leg is the one that trails, this practice is done while standing on the left foot.

Another aid to hurdling useful in everyday workouts is a padded top for the hurdle. Cut a piece of foam rubber or other material into a slice one inch thick and four inches high. Tape it to the top of the hurdle slat so that the highest measured point is 40 inches (for high school). Then let the runner work on the hurdles in normal manner. He should hurdle so that his left upper leg just scrapes the foam rubber, and then he will know that he is hurdling at the proper height. He can tell also if he hits too hard, showing he is hurdling too low, but he does not run the risk of injury and being afraid of the hurdles.

When moving between hurdles, the runner should take three strides, much like those of a man running the sprints. Because of a loss in momentum due to the hurdle, the first stride is of necessity shorter than the next two. After a runner has cleared the last hurdle, he has 15 yards in which to consider himself a sprinter and should run accordingly. This is the time he puts everything he has into the race from the sprinter's standpoint—burst of speed, stride, and a good finish at the tape.

180-Yard Low Hurdles. In this event, there are eight hurdles 30 inches in height set 20 yards apart. Since the height is less, it is possible to get over them faster, though the basic mechanical movements are the same. It is 20 yards from the start to the first hurdle and 30 yards from the last hurdle to the finish line. The stride plan is ten for the start and seven between hurdles. This race demands more endurance than the shorter distances and, as a result, requires better conditioning. It is easier from the standpoint of skill because there is more leeway in proportioning strides and greater ease in clearing hurdles.

Intermediate Hurdles. In this event there are ten hurdles 36 inches in height. They are 35 meters apart with 45 meters to the first hurdle. The stride plan here is twenty-two or twenty-three strides to the first hurdle and fifteen or fourteen between hurdles. The hurdle action is much like clearing a high school high hurdle, but general conditioning is very important, and workouts in the 440- and 880-yard runners are not uncommon.

the distances

The writer, contrary to some track authorities, places the 440-yard dash in the sprint category because most of the coaching points for it are the same as for the sprints. Since that would leave only the 880-yard run in the middle distance group, this event will be discussed as a part of the distance group.

The distance runs require stamina, endurance, and a smooth, easy, springy stride. They require also what may be an innate sense of knowing how fast each lap is being run and how much effort is being put into it physiologically so there will be something left for the final stretch run. The distance man may be of any anatomical structure, but there seems to be some advantage in a height of approximately 6 feet and a slender build. He must love to run and must spend hours at it each day, weeks and weeks before the season opens.

The stride is usually shorter than that employed in the sprints, and it has more "float" in it. On each stride after maximum speed has been reached, the foot takes off the track from a toe spring, and the body glides as the recovering leg reaches far ahead for contact with the ground. In the distance events as compared to the sprints, there is slightly more lag by the leg at the end of the drive before the recovery begins.

The arm movement helps to maintain balance and works in coordination with the legs. The elbows are locked at about a 50- or 55-degree angle. The movement is slightly across the body.

The body position is low and slightly overbalanced during starting acceleration but straightens as maximum speed is attained. During the regular run, the body is leaning slightly forward, head up, and legs moving directly forward and backward. The longer the distance, the more upright the body.

All distance races at an adequate track are run over a course in which there are turns. As a general rule, the oval will be an exact quarter mile, and the number of turns will depend on the length of the race. In some instances, the events will be run in lanes, and the runners will be staggered at the start. In most cases, however, there will be no lanes, and it will be necessary for the runners to race for the inside at the curve. In this situation, the start should be on a straightaway that will vary in distance from 50 to 100 yards to the curve. Since there is a definite advantage in getting the inside lane, it is necessary for the runner to make a dash for the curve. The closer the curve, the faster the dash. Upon reaching the turn, the runner should assume and maintain a normal stride.

There is an advantage in maintaining a steady rhythmical stride that is below the runner's full potential ability. The runner should not be upset over the dash of a competitor, since somewhere in the race he will have to slacken speed, and the distance lost will be made up.

A contestant should keep enough energy in reserve to pick up speed for passing and to finish strong. He should maintain good balance and be prepared at all times for jostling and bumping by opponents. He should avoid passing on a curve, because such a maneuver increases his running distance. Passing is also somewhat more difficult on the curve than on the straightaway. When passing, the runner must get wide enough not to interfere with his opponent and must be far enough ahead not to cause him to break stride when cutting into his path.

THE 880-YARD RUN. The 880 is run reasonably fast. The pace should be such that the runner will be almost sprinting at the end. In the pacing, the first quarter is run the fastest, but it must be possible to meet a challenge at the finish. There will be some slackening on the second quarter that will make it the slowest. The pace is quickened during the last half to better than average for the total elapsed time.

Even though the runner should keep an even pace and not challenge every man who passes him, he should not let an opponent get much more than ten yards ahead, because it will be very difficult to close the gap later.

THE MILE RUN. Much of what has been stated for the 880 is true for the mile. It is a hard race from the standpoint of both pacing and endurance. When gauged on the effort basis, the first 220 yards should be run at a reasonably good rate of speed. This is necessary to establish a pace well up in front of the group and to get to the inside of the curve. For about the next 600 yards, the race should be run at a normal mile pace. For about 100 yards in the middle of the race, the runner may coast by easing up on the amount of effort put forth. The stride during this coasting should be maintained. For the remainder of the mile the pace should be picked up until, toward the end, the runner has opened up to nearly maximum capacity.

On the basis of time, the runner should gauge each quarter in such a way that it may be run at about the same speed. For illustrative purposes, let us assume that a man can run the mile in 4 minutes 20 seconds. The average speed toward which he should strive is 65 seconds per quarter. The first quarter is usually run in slightly less than 65 seconds, the second quarter in slightly more, the third in about the same, and the fourth in slightly less, or the same.

THE TWO- AND THREE-MILE RUN.   These races are much the same as the mile as far as distribution of effort and the speed of each quarter that will be adjusted to the distance. But the spacing of effort and the timing should be applied to these races the same as to the mile. The overall expenditure of energy is not much greater than in the mile, but the speed is slower, and the stride is slightly longer and slower.

the relays

A relay is one of the most interesting events in a track meet. It is one contest that requires some teamwork. It generally is placed toward the last in dual meets and often decides the winner. The actual running phase of each leg of a relay is conducted the same as that distance event would be in a race; so it is not necessary to dwell on it. There are two factors in relay racing that are different, and the discussion will be centered about them. These are the placing of the runners in the different positions according to their abilities, and the baton exchange.

The four runners making up the relay team should be the fastest men on the squad for the required distance. They should be ranked one, two, three, and four. The fastest man or the one with the soundest judgment should run the last, or anchor leg, in the race. The second fastest man or the best starter should run the first, or lead-off, leg. Usually the slowest man will run the second leg, and the number three man will run the third leg.

The baton exchange can be so poorly done by the men of the fastest team as to cause them to lose the race. Coaching should aim to teach the passing of the baton in such a way as to interfere as little as possible with the running ability of the men. For all relay races, a 20-meter passing zone is provided wherein the exchange must take place. The man to run the next leg of a relay places himself just inside this exchange area and gets set to start his part of the race. When the runner coming in reaches a spot about 6 yards from the exchange area, the next runner starts. By the time he has picked up some momentum, the incoming runner will have come up close enough to pass the baton to him. In the sprint relays (legs of 220 yards or less), the outgoing runner will have a pickup zone of 10 meters that is provided for him to accelerate in preparation for the baton exchange in the normal zone. A pass may not be executed in the zone, called the "international zone", but it is merely used for coordination of the incoming and outgoing runners.

There are a number of ways in which runners may exchange batons, but it is not the purpose here to explain all these methods. One method is most common for distances of 440 yards or longer. The coach may add modifications as he sees fit. As the runner is coming in at the end of his leg of the race, he should be holding the baton in his left hand. The major portion of it should be extending forward. The man to receive the baton should be to the left of the man finishing, not directly in front of him. This position is to prevent the feet of the two men from touching and causing an upset. The man to take the baton holds his right hand back as he is picking up momentum. The palm is up, and the thumb is toward the inside. The man ending the race lays the baton firmly in the hand of the next man in line, and when he feels that it has been grasped firmly, releases his grip. The next runner grasps the baton firmly when it is placed in his hand and begins the race in real earnest. When the runner is getting under way, he must change the baton from his right to his left hand in order to execute the next exchange in the same manner. A weakness of this method of passing is that in order to bring the two hands together to change the baton from the right to the left hand, there is some loss of balance. There is also the possibility of dropping it, though this is remote. It is believed that the exchange from the runner's right to his left hand should be made soon after securing the baton, preferably while stride and momentum are developing and there is less loss of balance or proficiency in running. Some coaches eliminate this by having each man retain the baton in the hand in which he receives it and pass it from the same hand. For distances of 220 yards or less a blind pass is usually employed. This requires each runner to use only one hand in the exchange. The lead-off runner carries the baton in his right hand. He passes to the second man's left hand and so on until the anchor man finishes with the baton in his left hand. The exchange is made during the running action. The outgoing runner turns and starts as the incoming runner hits a spot about 5 yards away from him. When it is time for the exchange, the receiving runner extends the correct hand back, palm upward, thumb pointing in toward the body. It is the responsibility of the incoming runner to lay the baton in the outgoing runner's hand, as close to the end of the baton as is reasonable. Then the receiver can resume his natural sprinting arm action, and the baton is ready for the next pass. This method of exchange requires much practice, but it is a good method to use if practice time is available.

the weight event

The weight events are engaged in by the heavier, stronger athletes. Not much total body stamina is involved. However, the weights require strength, explosive force, and meticulous attention to the various details involved in each particular skill. Each event has its own set of skills and rules that will be explained as the event is discussed.

THE JAVELIN THROW. The javelin is a modification of the spear and is propelled in much the same way now as it was when used as a weapon. Our present day spear or javelin is made of good hardwood or metal and has a metal point. It must be at least 8.53 feet in length and cannot weigh less than 1.765 pounds. In order to facilitate grasping, it is equipped with a whipcord wrapping 6.3 inches long near the center. The distance around the outside of the whipcord shall not be more than 0.984 inch greater than the distance around the shaft at that point.

The javelin is thrown from behind a scratch line. This line is the back edge of a board 2.75 inches wide and 157.5 inches long. This board must be flush with the ground. During the throw the javelin must be held by the whipcord wrapping. It must hit the ground point first, but it does not have to stick up. The throw is measured from the scratch line to the spot it hits first.

Although javelin throwers come in all sizes, generally the larger men do the best job of throwing. Power and coordination are the chief factors in successful competition. If there is an ideal size, it would probably be a well-muscled person of from 180 to 195 pounds.

Two methods generally are accepted as being best for throwing the javelin: the Finnish style, and the American style. The first requires a cross-step, and the latter the hop. The Finnish method is generally believed to be the superior, but it requires much practice.

The Finns originated the javelin throw as a form of contest, and their method of throwing continues to bear their name. A run of from 80 to 90 feet is employed to build up momentum and to carry the thrower to a point immediately back of the scratch board. To help him check steps and know when to begin the cross step, a check mark is made about 35 feet from the scratch board. Just where this is placed depends in large measure on the thrower himself and the size of his steps.

The thrower starts at the original mark and heads toward the scratch line. When he reaches the check mark, he should hit it with his left foot and be traveling at three-quarter speed. On the next step, the right foot hits the ground toward the area of the throw (passing in front of the left leg), toe pointing to the right. Then the left foot hits with the toe pointing to the right and so on for five steps, always with the toes pointing to the right. At the last step the man should be ready to throw the javelin. The javelin, which has been drawn back to the rear, comes forward over the shoulder hard and fast and is released at a forward point. The thrower follows through on the right foot. To obtain full power, he moves through these steps as rapidly as possible. If he slows down or hesitates, his momentum for the throw is greatly decreased.

The American style is similar in many respects to the Finnish style.

The difference is that the thrower hops on the right foot just after he passes the check mark and gets into the throwing position. The actual throw is the same as for the Finnish style (Figure 23–4).

FIGURE 23-4 *The Javelin Throw* (From John M. Cooper, James Lavery, and William Perrin, *Track and Field for Coach and Athlete*, 2d ed. © 1970, Prentice-Hall, Inc. Reproduced by permission of the publisher.)

It is possible to attain more speed with the Finnish style, and this results in greater momentum, and, in turn, greater distance. Some men have a tendency to hesitate slightly on the hop and lose momentum. Regardless of the method chosen, the throw can be made from a carry high over the head or by a carry from way back and low.

At the throw it is important that the javelin be held in a firm grip. The little finger, the one next to it, and the thumb, are gripped securely around the cord. The lateral edge of the second finger is placed over the edge of the whipcord away from the point. This is done in order to give additional grip so that the hand will have little or no chance to slip. As the throw is made, the arm performs a wide high arc forward while the body weight is being put into it, and forward momentum is utilized. When the hand is high and forward, the release is made.

THE DISCUS THROW. An official discus should be made of a combination of wood and metal. The core and rim are the metal parts, and the remainder is wood. An official college discus should weigh not less than 4 pounds 6.4 ounces, and it cannot be less than 8⅝ inches in diameter. For competition on the high school level, it weighs not less than 3 pounds 9 ounces and is not less than 8¼ inches in diameter. The discus is hurled from a circle 8 feet 2½ inches in diameter into a sector marked by the radial lines, 2 inches wide, which form a 60-degree angle, extended from the center of the circle. In order to be given credit for a legal throw, the athlete must stay in the circle during the attempt and until it is marked. The discus must land within the sector provided. The distance of an attempt is measured from the edge of the circle to the spot where the discus first hits.

Weight is an advantage for a discus thrower. Long arms enable him to swing the discus in a much wider arc, which develops a great deal more whip than does a shorter arc. In the final analysis, however, turning speed, good hip action, and an explosive thrust on the release are actually most important.

When a man is ready to throw, he steps into the circle and stands as far back in it as he can legally. His right foot is in line with the circle and almost touching it. The left foot is placed 12 to 18 inches from the right foot. The distance apart depends in large measure on the height of the participant and his comfort and balance. The toes of the left foot should be toward the direction in which the throw is to be initiated. Both the knees and the hips should be reasonably relaxed and flexed to a certain extent. Weight distribution should be equal on both feet. The discus is held in the right hand (assuming a right-handed person), under the palm, with the fingers spread wide and the last joint of each flexed over the edge.

Several factors are involved in the force that propels the discus. The best throws are made as a result of a double body turn or spin that develops centrifugal force. In addition, the large muscles of the leg and back furnish the basic power and should be utilized to the greatest degree. Another important point is that the right hip should be kept well ahead of the discus during the spin. The actual swing that takes place should increase in speed and be not unlike a spring uncoiling. After the spin begins, the athlete changes from the left foot to the right and back as necessary for force and balance in such a way as to bring him toward the front of the circle at the end of two complete revolutions. During the spin it is necessary that the body be flexed or crouched, and the hand holding the discus should be behind the body and back of the hips.

At the moment before the release, the right foot is planted firmly and straightened. The right hip moves forward and around as does the body, and the discus follows. The coordination is such that the line of force moves to the discus through the arm, hand, and fingers. A wrist flip is developed by skilled throwers, but the beginner should concentrate on basic movements. Effort should be made to have the discus twirl parallel to the ground or with the forward edge slightly elevated in order to utilize aerodynamics as far as possible (Figure 23–5).

A   G   I   K   L

FIGURE 23-5 *The Discus Throw* (From John M. Cooper, James Lavery, and William Perrin, *Track and Field for Coach and Athlete*, 2d ed. © 1970, Prentice-Hall, Inc. Reproduced by permission of the publisher.)

THE SHOT PUT. To make a legal put, the participant must stay within a circle 7 feet in diameter from the time he steps in the circle until the throw is marked. He may not step on the line during this time, but he may touch the inside of the toeboard. The shot is put from the shoulder and not from behind it. It is not thrown but is put or pushed. The shot weighs 8 pounds, 12 pounds, or 16 pounds, depending upon the level of competition.

Good shot putting requires strength, above all else. However, the big man with great strength can heave with all his power and get only fair results if he does not direct his muscular efforts with the correct form. A smaller more skilled athlete who coordinates efficiently the movements involved in a put can win consistently from a larger, poorly coordinated individual. Since size and strength are important factors, combining them with well coordinated effort will make for successful putting.

The shot is held on the fingers with the four fingers spread behind it and with the thumb used as a support and guide. The putter steps into the circle and assumes a position at the back of it, resting most of his weight on the right foot. He faces directly away from the area of the sector. The shot is cradled at his neck and shoulder. The eyes focus about 10 feet behind the circle, and the left arm may be bent or straight for balance. The putting action is initiated by a bend of the trunk, flexion of the right leg, and a slight push directly back by the left leg. Then the right knee bends, and the back becomes almost parallel with the ground. The glide now begins without hesitation. In a quick movement the right foot and leg extend, and the left leg kicks directly toward the toeboard.

When the right leg is straight, the foot leaves the original position at the back of the circle and glides across to midcircle, keeping the right foot pointed about 50 degrees to the back of the circle. The body remains as close to the original position as possible during this time. The left foot should now be flush against the toeboard, and the hips should turn through leftward as do the shoulders.

The right shoulder begins to lift, and the left arm extends for balance and driving help. The shot is pushed out from the cradle at a 37- to 42-degree angle. This whole motion is quick and explosive with the shot traveling in a straight line upward and outward. At extension of the arm, a finger flip completes the follow-through and helps the putter recover. The reverse (recovery) is carried on so that the feet shift position in a reverse motion, and the right foot comes against the toeboard with the left foot back. The left arm swings around to maintain balance (Figure 23–6).

FIGURE 23-6 *The Shot Put* (From John M. Cooper, James Lavery, and William Perrin, *Track and Field for Coach and Athlete*, 2d ed. © 1970, Prentice-Hall, Inc. Reproduced by permission of the publisher.)

the jumping events

THE HIGH JUMP. The jumping pit may be not less than 16 feet wide by 12 feet long, filled to a height of at least 2 feet with foam rubber or other soft material. The upright standards are at least 12 feet apart. The top of the upright which supports the crossbar must be $1\frac{1}{2}$ by $2\frac{3}{8}$ inches in size, with the long part parallel to the crossbar.

The judges of the high jump determine the height of the bar at the start and the successive elevations. Each competitor is allowed three trials at each height. Names are drawn and jumps made in that order. If a man fails a jump, he may try again in his order. Any man may pass up jumping at a height, but if he fails at the next height, he will not be allowed to try again at the height he passed. A jumper is eliminated when he has three consecutive misses, no matter what height is attempted.

A trial is counted if the competitor displaces the bar, passes under it, crosses the line of the bar extended, or leaves the ground in an attempt. The jumper may go over the bar in any manner he wishes as long as he leaves the ground from one foot only.

In a high jump, the force in the takeoff comes not so much from speed as from the leg drive upward. The run builds up momentum to allow the body to stay off the ground longer, but the leg lift and spring are what gets the body high enough to clear the bar. For this reason, much emphasis should be placed on the actual jump and not so much on the run.

There are two styles of jumping the straddle jump, and the Fosbury flop. The latter style involves jumping over on the back and will not be discussed here.

THE STRADDLE JUMP. The angle of approach is approximately 30 degrees with about a twelve-stride approach. The rate of approach varies but is usually about three-quarter effort at the point of takeoff. The last stride is shortened, and the jumper uses a heel-ball landing with the take-off foot. Assuming an approach from the left side, the right knee is bent slightly. When the takeoff foot hits the ground, the right leg is swung up high and toward the top of the crossbar. Both arms swing up to aid the drive. The left knee is straight. The eyes must focus on the crossbar so the jumper knows where the target is located. The right foot will strive to go higher than the head, and the left hand will be pulled in close to the body to aid clearance. As the body turns or rolls around the crossbar, the left toes should be turned outward to complete clearance.

THE POLE VAULT. Pole vault rules are much the same as high jump rules in regard to the number of trials and what constitutes a trial. The uprights include pins and holes for the pins. The pins must be round and uniform in thickness, not to exceed ½ inch in diameter, and not longer than 3 inches. They are placed parallel with the ground and protrude from the uprights toward the pit.

Although pole vaulters may be of any build, it is necessary that they have strong arms and shoulder girdles. They should be well coordinated, be fairly fast runners, and be adept at gymnastics work.

The vaulter needs to practice the approach many times to determine his exact step pattern in order to know where to start the run and the exact point from which he will take off. By experience he should also know where the hands will be placed on the pole. Placing them too high requires greater momentum to take him up high while placing them too low limits his height capabilities. After determining the proper handhold, the vaulter begins his approach.

FIBERGLASS VAULTING. The pole is planted in the box when the box is reached. As the pole makes contact with the box, the leading foot (right) is thrust forward and upward. The hands remain spread 14 to 18 inches apart. In the swing position the legs hang parallel, and the hips are pushed forward. The right arm is straight, and the left bent to compensate for the hand spread. During the rock back, the pole bends, the head rocks back, and the legs rotate around the hips to start upward. The vaulter continues to pull through to attain the upsidedown position. As the pole straightens out, the vaulter's body comes to the upsidedown position. Then the vaulter turns his body around, and the legs shoot up past the cross bar. The hips bend around the crossbar as the hands complete the pushoff from the pole. The hands are released from the pole, and the arms and head thrust back to assure clearance of the bar (Figure 23–7).

FIGURE 23-7 *The Pole Vault* (From John M. Cooper, James Lavery, and William Perrin, *Track and Field for Coach and Athlete*, 2d ed. © 1970, Prentice-Hall, Inc. Reproduced by permission of the publisher.)

FIGURE 23-8   *The Long Jump*   (From John M. Cooper,
James Lavery, and William Perrin, *Track and Field for
Coach and Athlete*, 2d ed. © 1970, Prentice-Hall, Inc. Re-
produced by permission of the publisher.)

THE LONG JUMP.   The long jump pit must be not less than 5 feet wide
and 15 feet long, filled with a relatively soft substance. A takeoff board,
placed level with the surface of the pit, is eight inches wide and four feet
long. The scratch line is the edge of this board nearest the pit. The
jumper must take off from behind the scratch line. If he steps over the
line or runs past it, the error is counted as a jump.

By practice the jumper should determine just how far he needs to run
to get his longest jump. He should then determine a check mark that
shows him where to begin his run so that he will hit the toeboard correctly and at full speed.

Speed and leg spring are the two most important factors involved in
the jump. When the foot hits the toeboard, a terrific leg extension takes
place. This is designed to lift the body as high as possible. The hips are
flexed immediately after the takeoff, and the legs are tucked high. The
arms are extended forward. As soon as the pit is contacted, the body
extends forward to avoid dropping back, and the knees bend to aid the
forward movement of the body (Figure 23–8).

THE TRIPLE JUMP.   This event formerly was called the hop, step, and
jump, because this name best describes its three phases. The present system of the triple jump places equal importance on each phase, and so the

change in name. The first phase is a hop, as the same foot is used to take off and to land. Care must be taken to avoid hopping too high because extreme height causes the leg to buckle on landing and reduces effectiveness in the other phases. The step is performed as a continuation of the hop. The opposite leg is now extended to achieve the step. This is the important phase of the event because a poor step definitely limits the total distance. The last phase is a jump performed exactly like the long jump.

Under no circumstances should the track or the field man make total effort in his special event at too early a time in his workout sessions. He should also avoid any fast starts during this period. Many coaches become overanxious to learn what each man can do this year in his special events and put the watch on him too soon. As a result, there are pulled muscles and tendons to plague the athletes for the remainder of the season. Injuries received in such a way have been known to hamper an athlete throughout his track career. Running time and physical condition will be better if time is taken to bring an athlete along slowly to top physical condition.

Diet and rest are important in physical conditioning. The track man should avoid tobacco and alcohol. He should make a serious effort to go to bed at a normal hour and get sufficient rest. A minimum of eight hours is recommended.

If a runner is preparing himself for some event such as the hurdles, in which an additional skill is involved, some time should be devoted to it during the first month. The specific practice need not involve more than work on one or two hurdles with an emphasis on leg movement in getting over the hurdle.

During the month preceding the first meet, each practice should include easy running for at least a mile as a warm-up. The stretching exercises should be continued. Fast starts should be practiced with emphasis on getting in front in a hurry at the gun. The starts should be stressed for at least a week prior to the time the complete race is run at full speed. During this fifth week the specific events should be run at three-quarter speed to accustom the runner to the event. Time trials also could be held at three quarters of the race distance.

To end each practice throughout the season, the athletes should warm down slowly after the workouts and then take a good shower.

Weight lifting should be included in the workout program regardless of the event. The field event men should take part in it in a very serious manner probably three days per week. The runners should have a general body conditioning program for at least two days per week.

SKILL TESTS

Testing in track is simplified by using the times in the running events and the distances and heights in the field events as scores. No other testing devices are necessary, though the coach may desire to score on form and give points on each of the factors necessary to good form for each of the events.

DEFINITION OF TERMS

Anchor. The last leg of a relay.

Baton. A hollow cylinder made of wood, cardboard, metal, or plastic used in a relay to pass from one runner to the next.

Crossbar. A square or triangular piece of wood or metal about 16 feet long over which pole vaulters and high jumpers must vault or jump.

Course. The path of the runner.

Dead Heat. A tie finish between two or more runners.

Exchange Zone. An area one lane wide and 22 yards long in which the baton must be changed from one runner to the next.

Flight. A round of trials for all participants in the field events.

Foul Throw. An official throw that is not measured because of some violation of the rules.

Heat. A preliminary race to pick the fastest competitors for the final race.

Hurdle. A wooden obstruction over which runners must leap in the hurdle races.

Lane. The path marked on the track in which a runner must stay during his race.

L-type Hurdle. A hurdle with the base and upright construction resembling the letter L.

Marking Board. A board used to indicate the scratch line in the javelin throw.

Mark. A runner's position directly behind the scratch line, assumed at the start of a race.

Overturning Force. The pull in pounds necessary to turn a hurdle over.

Planting Box. Wooden, plastic, or metal box located at the pole vault pit in which the vaulter places the end of the pole.

Pace. A speed maintained throughout most of a race.

Pole. The instrument used by vaulters to clear the crossbar. The inside lane on a running track.

Preliminary. A group of attempts to determine who qualified for the finals in an event.

Qualify. To win the right to participate in the next round of competition.

Relay Leg. The distance traveled by one runner in a relay.

Scratch Line. A marking line used in the long jump, the javelin throw, and the races. Jumpers and throwers must not step over this line in a trial, and runners may not step on this line until the race has started.

Sprint. A sudden burst of speed in a distance event. One of the short distance races.

Stop Board. A rectangular board used to stop the pole in a pole vault competition.

Stride. The act of taking a step in running a race.

Takeoff Board. A board on which a jumper plants his foot to start the jump.

Throwing Sector. A 65-degree area marked off by lines within which the weight implements must land for a legal throw.

Toeboard. A board on or over which the shot putter may not step during his put.

Trial. An attempt in the field events.

DISCUSSION QUESTIONS

1. Trace the early history of track and field events.
2. Show how track and field competition developed in this country.
3. Name the necessary physiological attributes an athlete must have in order to be a good sprinter.
4. Describe a good sprint stride.
5. Of what importance is arm movement in running?
6. How should the 440-yard dash be run?
7. Describe the movement required to get over a high hurdle.
8. Describe how the mile should be paced.
9. How should a baton be exchanged?
10. Differentiate the two methods of throwing the javelin.
11. Describe the straddle style of jumping.
12. Outline a suggested procedure for training a sprinter.

BIBLIOGRAPHY

Bresnahan, George T., and Tuttle, W. W., *Track and Field Athletics*. St. Louis: The C. V. Mosby Company, 1969.

Conger, Ray M., *Track and Field*. New York: A. S. Barnes & Company, 1939.

Doherty, J. Kenneth, *Modern Track and Field*. Englewood Cliffs, N.J.: Prentice-Hall, Inc., 1963.

Lowe, D. G. A., *Track and Field Athletics*. New York: Putnam, 1935.

Menke, Frank G., *The New Encyclopedia of Sports*. New York: A. S. Barnes & Company, 1969.

Mitchell, E. D., *Sports for Recreation*. New York: A. S. Barnes & Company, 1952.

Official N.C.A.A. Track and Field Guide, latest edition. National Collegiate Athletic Association, Kansas City, Missouri.

Official Track and Field Rules, latest edition. Chicago: National Federation of State High School Athletic Associations.

Seaton, Don Cash, *Safety in Sports*. Chapter XII. Englewood Cliffs, N.J.: Prentice-Hall, Inc., 1948.

Track and Field Rules and Athletic Almanac, latest edition. New York: Amateur Athletic Union.

Werner, Charles D., Ryan, Frank J., and Snyder, Lawrence N., *Track and Field*. New York: A. S. Barnes & Company, 1950.

volleyball

24

The game now known as volleyball was originated under the name of *minonette*. William G. Morgan, Y.M.C.A. director in Holyoke, Massachusetts, invented it in 1895.

Morgan was impressed with the type of play necessary for the new game of basketball. He probably wanted to contribute something to sports just as one Dr. Naismith had done when he developed basketball. Morgan devised what is now known as volleyball. The first game was played indoors with a tennis net and the bladder from a basketball.

At first the game developed slowly. For some time it was played only at the Y.M.C.A. in Holyoke. The players liked it and later moved to surrounding towns to teach the game to others. Thus the game appeared in a number of Massachusetts cities, particularly Springfield.

It was in Springfield that Dr. A. T. Holstead suggested that the game's name be changed from minonette to *volleyball*, since that would more clearly describe the basic play utilized.

More and more people became interested and began to play the game. Indoor space was limited, so they began to stretch nets between trees. As a result, the game began to gather tremendous popular momentum. Children and teenagers were the first to play it, but as these children grew into adults and other adults joined them in their enthusiasm for the game, they began to see possibilities for complex skills, team play, and strategy.

High schools, colleges, and municipalities began making volleyball facilities available and promoting active participation in the game. In 1916, men who were playing it regularly wrote a new set of rules that were universally adopted. Its popularity became so great that in 1922 the Y.M.C.A. sponsored a tournament designed to determine the national champion. The United States Volleyball Association was formed in 1929 for the purpose of governing the game. Dr. George J. Fisher was named the first president of this group.

During the past decade in the United States drastic changes have occurred in volleyball. A close study of the rules as they appeared in 1960 compared to the 1970 edition of the *Official Volleyball Guide* would reveal many differences. The big change has been the adoption by the United States Volleyball Association of the principal features of the rules of the International Volleyball Federation. There are still some minor differences, but the long dispute over which rules are preferable seems to be ended.

Volleyball in the 1970s is a faster, more exciting game than it has been in the past. Coaches are more knowledgeable, and players are better trained. Players are more highly skilled and have improved the status of the United States in world competition.

BASIC SKILLS

Volleyball is a game with much more involved in it than meets the eye of the casual observer. For this reason the novice takes to the game rather slowly but in time develops much love for and interest in it. It requires skill in several areas in order to be played at its best. It is fast, allows for aggressiveness, and requires a high caliber of teamwork. Because it is a game of considerable activity demanding fast starting, stopping, and jumping, the player must be in reasonably good physical condition. Even though a satisfactory game can be played after a short period of instruction and drill, it is much better to spend considerable time in practice on the several skills needed for it.

the serve

Because the serve is the initial skill to be employed in the game, it is discussed first. In the class plan, it also should be the first skill to be taught. It is best procedure to teach the beginner an easy underhand type of serve that has a single objective—the ball falling within the court. This easy, safe kind of serve is preferable for beginners who do not have the strength and coordination to execute the overhand serve. Many successful volleyball teachers still hold to this objective. As game strategy has developed through the years, players have learned that the volleyball serve, like the tennis serve, is a strong offensive weapon and can be used effectively to gain points. It has often been said, "Control the serve and you control the game." The easy serve can be returned easily, whereas the hard, fast serve with spin is very difficult to return and will often result in points for the serving team.

Reference is made here to the rules governing the serve so that the limitations and scope of this particular skill will be clear. A legal serve is one that is hit by the hand of a person who is standing within the service area, back of the end line, the ball going over the net without touching it or any other object and falling into the court on the opposite side. There are no restrictions about hitting overhand or underhand, with open or closed fist. (See Figure 24-1 for volleyball court.)

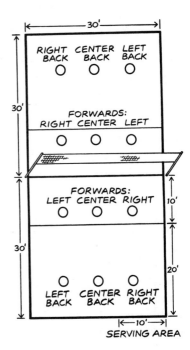

FIGURE 24-1 *Volleyball Court and Positions of Players*

THE UNDERHAND SERVE.   Since the underhand serve is the simplest, easiest, and safest to play, the beginner should learn it first. Then, too, even if the beginner develops into a first-rate player and learns other types of serves, times will come when he must fall back on the underhand serve.

In order to execute the underhand serve, the player stands with his left foot advanced and pointed toward the net. He should face the net squarely, with knees bent slightly. The left arm is flexed slightly across the body, and the ball is held in the palm and tossed lightly, for the rules do not allow the server to hit the ball as a golf ball is hit off a tee. The right arm is kept extended during the serve, with the right hand held like a claw, and the ball is hit with the heel of the hand. Some players use a closed fist and hit the ball with the heel and flat surface of the fist. But it is difficult to have the control with the fist that one has with the open hand.

The serve is not arm motion alone; the total body enters into it. As the right arm goes backward, much of the weight of the body is transferred to the right foot. As the right arm goes forward to strike the ball, the body weight is shifted to the left foot. Special care should be taken to keep the foot from touching the end line, which would constitute a foot fault and result in the loss of serve. The underhand serve, made with the palm and heel of the hand, causes the ball to go over the net reasonably dead. This makes it jump and slide, resulting in a very effective serve. Some authorities agree that a dead ball is more difficult to return than a ball with some spin on it. Even so, the underhand serve is not nearly so effective as an overhand serve.

THE OVERHAND SERVE.   The overhand serve is preferable for advanced volleyball because it can be hit hard and fast, and because of the high point of contact, it can get into the other court with less of an angle than the underhand serve. This serve is essentially easier for the volleyball player who has a tennis background, since the movements are almost the same as those of a tennis serve.

The stance for the overhand serve is with the feet in close proximity to and laterally in line with the length of the court. Some servers prefer to stand several feet behind the end line with one foot forward. This is a matter of individual preference. The ball is held in the left hand (assuming that the player is right-handed). It is thrown into the air—practice will indicate how far—and. when it starts down, the right hand begins a downward and backward arc. It continues back, up, and over so that it makes contact with the ball, hand open. The ball should be thrown straight up and in front of the right arm and shoulder. Just before the hand contacts the ball, the head is up, the eyes are on the ball, and the back is arched. The ball should be head-high or slightly higher when contact is made.

Such a serve requires considerable practice in order to develop the correct timing. After the movements have been mastered, practice can begin on the skills of putting spin on the ball. The act of hitting the ball for an "in" or an "out" is virtually the same as in the underhand swing. To curve the ball "out" or to the right, the hand moves to the left on contact, and for an "in," it moves to the right. One of the most effective shots made with the overhand serve is the drop shot. As the touch is made, the wrist is bent inward, the ball is contacted near the top, and the hand moves forward on top of the ball to add top spin to it. This causes it to go over the net fast and suddenly take a quick drop, making a good return reasonably difficult.

THE FLOATER OVERHAND. A floating or drifting serve has been developed by many efficient players. It is easy and very effective. Once the essentials are mastered, it is not difficult to control. The chief difference between this and the orthodox serve is that the ball is held with the air valve toward the net. On the actual serve, the ball is not tossed very high and is struck with the heel of the hand, with little follow-through.

When correctly executed, the flight resembles that of the knuckle ball in baseball, with no spin. Any action is likely to take place, including sudden drift down, up, or to either side. It often results in a poor pass being made by the receiver, thus lessening the efficiency of the attack.

In making this serve, some players plant both feet at right angles to the net and take no step. The danger of foot-faulting is thus eliminated.

THE ROUNDHOUSE OR DROP SERVE. A very effective overhand serve that has much force and gives considerable forward spin to the ball may be developed. The stance is with the left side to the net and with feet parallel to the end line. The ball is tossed directly overhead, with both hands so that it will be directly over the right shoulder. The right arm swings back away from the court and is then swept upward and forward, making contact directly over the head at the highest point the server can reach. The ball is contacted with the heel of the open hand above the mid-line and slightly on its right side, causing a clockwise spin. The ball is very difficult to return because of the dropping movement and forward spin.

Where the ball is directed on the serve will have much to do with whether it can be returned. A high ball dropped anywhere in the receiver's area is easy to return. Any other type of ball can be returned more easily if hit to either of the forwards. The best placement is to the back corners, and next best is down the sidelines toward the net. A hard serve with top spin is hard to recover and pass wherever placed.

The serves should be varied to the extent that easy, lofted ones are mixed with hard, straight ones, long ones with short ones, and curves to the left with curves to the right. Serves should be directed also to the different opponents in order to determine individual weaknesses on particular serves. Every effort should be made to make as many points on serves as possible—to treat the serve as an offensive weapon and not merely as a means of starting the game.

When the server gets the ball away, he should always consider the possibility of a return, no matter how effective he thinks a particular serve may be. He should come immediately into the court and begin a defense of his particular area.

passing

Passing is the means by which a ball is moved from one person to another on the same team. However, much of the technique and skill involved carry over into the attack. Passing is a more refined term for the act that gives the game its name, the volley, and refers particularly to propulsion of the ball from one player to his teammate.

As a general rule, overhand passes should be utilized whenever possible, and they are possible almost always except on hard-driven spikes. Many of the better players will even get down on their knees in order to use the overhand pass in preference to the underhand, since it is the more accurate and the easier pass to control.

A volleyball may be handled by what is known as the ten-point touch —that is, eight fingers and the two thumbs contact the ball. In the ten-point touch, the fingers are slightly flexed, forming something of a bowl. They are spread well apart, and the inside of the hand is toward the ball. This bowl or pocket should be such that a volleyball can fit on it but not completely in it. The contact is momentary, since the ball cannot be grasped, held, or carried. Every effort should be made to effect such a touch and avoid the uncontrollable palm contact. When the ball comes over the net, the player nearest where it is dropping should make every effort to get under it.

A good guide would be to place the body in such a way as to have the ball coming directly toward the nose while the head is held up and slightly back. The fingers and thumbs, held face high, form a sort of bowl with thumbs nearly touching, move toward the ball. Since the contact with it is for such a brief span of time, it is necessary that the bowl be set in the intended direction. Along with the movement of hands and arms, the whole body moves in a pass. The knees and back, which have been flexed, straighten, as do the arms.

It is impossible to get the body in the same position each time to pass the ball, which may be far to the right or far to the left, high or low. It may be so far out of reach that the contact must be made with one hand instead of two.

If the ball comes high to a player, he gets under it, with knees flexed, head up, and eyes on it, holding his hands slightly above his head, with elbows flexed. The thumbs are in, the fingers up, and the palms away from the face. Leaning back slightly will aid a player in getting the pass up into the air so that it can be handled easily by the set-up man. At the time of contact, the arms are moving up and in the direction of the pass, while at the same time the body and knees straighten up to add strength to the touch.

If the ball comes in low but directly in front of the player, the knees are flexed perceptibly with feet apart, hands are below the waist, palms are up, fingers are pointed away from the body, and thumbs are out. A moment before contact, the arms start up, and the knees and the body straighten. At contact, the hands and the whole body should give direction to wherever the player wants the ball to go.

There will be times during a volleyball game when it is impossible to get directly under a ball to hit it, and it will be impractical or even impossible to play it with both hands. In such a situation, one hand can be used, and the ball is struck clearly with the fleshy parts of the fingers and the thumb. The single forearm pass, played in an underhand manner, may be used in this situation. The forearm held away from the body acts as a surface from which the pass can be made. Among championship teams, the double forearm pass is the most common technique in receiving the serve. In the drills to develop passing, it is necessary to practice all types of passes and methods of passing. In the one-hand pass, the player is not always in balance and should become skilled in using the forearm motion combined with a flip of the wrist.

Many of the most skillful players have been quite successful in playing low balls with one hand, often with the fist closed. By doing this, they avoid the danger of being penalized by a strick interpretation of the holding or "lifting" rule.

the set-up and attack

A phase of game strategy involves the set-up and attack. Beginners usually will try to get the ball back across the net the first time it is hit. This frequently works but does not allow the control or the placement that can be achieved by the set-up and attack or spike. One type of offense that has proved effective in the past is to divide the members of the team into three attacks and three set-ups, each alternating with the other in the rotation scheme. At one point in the rotation, the front line will consist of one attack in the middle with a set-up on each side, and the back line of a set-up in the middle with an attack on each side. After the first rotation, the arrangement will be exactly the reverse of this, and after the next, it will be the same again.

The players are selected for their order in line according to their ability. A good spiker should be an attack man. The taller and best jumpers also should be attack men. The set-up men do not necessarily have to be tall but should be the best at gaining control of the ball and high placement. They should be the best passers of the six.

When a ball comes over the net to an attack, the player passes it always to a set-up man, who is generally but not necessarily on the net line. The set-up then sets the ball up to an attack man on the front row, with an overhand pass reasonably high and fairly close to the net. The takeoff from both feet adds to the height of the spiker's jump to meet the set-up and prevents him from landing over the center line of the court. The attack or spiker goes high into the air and hits the ball hard and downward in such a way as to make it most difficult for the opponents to return. If the ball comes over the net to a set-up, he either sets it up to an attack man on the net line or to a set-up man on the back or the net-line row. This set-up then sets the ball up for an attack to spike.

Spiking the ball requires height, jumping ability, excellent timing, and coordination. The spiker goes up at such a time as to reach his fullest height when the ball is above the net. He contacts the ball with the palm and heel of the hand and drives it downward over the net. The higher he contacts the ball, the better the chance to drive it downward and prevent the opponents from returning it. In today's rules, a spiker's follow-through may pass over the net, which has given the spiker a better opportunity to spike successfully those sets which are close to the net. It is good general policy never to return a ball directly over the net but to set it up and spike it.

the block

The block is the most difficult playing skill to master in the game of volleyball and one that only a few volleyball players have learned to perform well. It requires most careful timing, based on the lightning movements of the opponent across the net, and frequently it is a game gamble, a difficult chance to take. A block simply is meeting the ball at the net with the arms and hands and causing it to bound back to the opponents' side. If the block is successful, the ball gets back across the net and down before the attack has even reached the floor and certainly long before he has had a chance to recover for a return. The player who makes a block sets himself up across the net directly opposite the one who is doing the spiking. An instant after the spiker leaves the floor, the blocker goes up.

This timing allows the blocker to be at exactly the right height when the ball comes across. The arms are held high, straight, and about 6 inches apart. The hands are open, palms to net, with fingers spread. It is rarely possible to do more than form a wall with the arms and hands against which the ball will bounce back into the opponent's court. However, in unusual cases a player with quick reflexes may be able to control the ball and place it. Blockers may have their hands over the net at any time, provided they do not touch the ball before the spiker makes contact. This rule change has led to aggressive blocking, which has become a major way to win points or cause a side-out. In today's rules only the frontcourt players may block. This restriction has eliminated the backcourt players from assisting in the block. Hence, four-man blocks are no longer a part of the game, and three-man blocks are a rarity. The two-man blocks are the standard technique used against spikes.

playing the ball off the net

Frequently a ball that goes into the net bounds back into the same court from which it was hit. If this occurs on a pass play other than a serve and before it has been hit the third time, it can and should be played. It is important that the net be very tight, and it should be checked frequently for tautness. If the ball rebounds from the net, it should be played by the player nearest to it. It will rebound low and will have to be handled the same as any low ball. If this is the second time it is passed, it can be either set up or played across the net in any way possible.

TEAM DEFENSE

The team offense, which has been discussed above, is far more important than the defense. It is necessary, however, for a successful volleyball team to concentrate on some form of defense.

There are two crosses on a regulation court that serve to indicate the territory each player should cover. By taking equally divided spaces on the court, the players are in better position to field any ball that comes over the net. By having designated areas, they know exactly the part of the court for which they are responsible and can play a more coordinated game. This procedure also helps a coach to place blame for poorly played balls in certain areas.

When a ball is inaccurately placed in such a way as to go out-of-bounds, any player near that area may go over, out-of-bounds, and play the ball back into the court or over the net. It is essential to team defense that he do this.

There will be many times during a volleyball game when a player will move quickly, play the ball, lose his balance, and fail to recover in time to play the ball again immediately. In such a case, someone near that area should assume responsibility for him until he can get back into position.

The frontcourt net players sometimes have a tendency to play too close to the net. In such a case, when a ball drops down just behind them, there often is some question about who should play it. The result is that it often is not played at all but allowed to drop into the court.

general game hints

1. Treat the serve as an offensive weapon and attempt to make points with it.

2. Never play haphazard volleyball. Make every play a team play.

3. Play the ball up and easy when passing. Play it down over the net and hard when spiking.

4. Analyze the opponents and play for their weaknesses and away from their strong points.

5. Serve to the weak player or to the sidelines.

6. Whenever at all possible, play the ball three times on each side of the net.

TEACHING PROCEDURE

Many people look upon volleyball as a comparatively easy game to play and one that does not require top physical condition. This is true if the participants play it slowly and without great skill and coordinated teamwork. However, if the game takes place in a league where competition is comparatively stiff, the individuals making up the team must spend long hours improving physical condition, game skills, and team play.

Regular practice sessions should be divided into four parts:

1. Discussion of rules and game strategy.

2. Calisthenics and running.

3. Game skill drills

4. Team offense and defense

A thorough knowledge of the rules is considered essential for a successful volleyball player. No matter how well a skill is developed, if it is performed contrary to the rules, it is useless. Too little time is spent in studying them. It is hoped that in the future volleyball players will take the rules seriously and make every skill the very best according to them. Game strategy should be discussed during this period in order to lay plans concerning the direction offense and defense practice will take.

The calisthenics practice can serve two purposes: to warm-up and to develop strength and endurance for the game. Much time should be given to running and jumping. Jumping ability is essential to the game, and there can hardly be too much practice in it.

Even toward the end of the season, all practices should include some work on individual game skills, such as passing, setting up, spiking, and blocking.

Well-coordinated offense and defense can never be overemphasized. It is necessary that these be a part of every practice session.

organization for teaching the serve

After the serves have been demonstrated, the players should be organized into groups in order that they may go about learning the different serves most efficiently. There should be at least one volleyball for every two students or, if possible, a ball for each. If there is a volleyball for every two, two lines are formed, one on each end line. There will then be two lines facing each other with the entire court between them. Each line is asked to number off, and the numbers are paired. Like numbers serve to each other, each pair oblivious for all practical purposes to all the others (Figure 24–2).

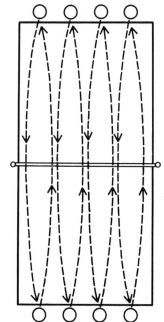

FIGURE 24-2 *Volleyball Service Drill*

If each person has a ball and there is enough smooth wall surface, targets can be chalked up so that each player can serve to the wall. This speeds up service efforts because of the rebounds, and each participant gets much more practice than he might otherwise have.

While this practice is progressing, the teacher should move among the students and make corrections continually through analysis and demonstration.

passing drills

In organizing a group for passing drills, there should be one volleyball for each two players. If that many balls are not available, the number in the group should be divided by the number of volleyballs. For example, if there are fifteen students and five volleyballs, there should be five groups of three. The groups are placed around the gym floor, and the players in each are asked to pass the ball among themselves in a specified manner. It is suggested here that they hit high passes to each other at first. After five minutes of this, they should hit low ones. The ball should then be hit so that the players will have to reach for it and possibly have to handle it with one hand.

This practice may be varied in a number of ways:

1. The group can be timed to see how long they keep the ball in the air without a miss.

2. The passes may be counted to see which group can pass the greatest number of times without a miss.

3. Each group in turn may be placed at the net in such a way as to have the ball crossing it high on each pass.

4. Drill number 3 may be repeated except that the ball should just barely miss the top of the net.

One of the chief places for developing interest in volleyball is the physical education class. By modifying the rules to lower the net to about 5 feet and to decrease the playing area greatly, the game can be played in the elementary school. On the junior high school level, the net should be 6½ feet high and the court 40 feet by 30 feet. At this age the students are ready for team games on a coeducational basis. As played by them, volleyball will not be too strenuous and will serve as a fine medium for physical and social development.

In any physical education class, whether it be on junior high, senior high, or college level, the period will consume between 30 and 40 minutes. If the students are beginners, they should be given as a part of the first week's class periods pointers on rules, conditioning exercises, and practice on game skills. As time goes on, the rules and exercise sessions should decreae, the skill practice continue, and the actual game be added. In about three weeks, each period should consist of 2 or 3 minutes of calisthenics, 10 minutes of practice on game skills, and 25 to 30 minutes of the game.

SKILL TESTS

When it is necessary to assign grades to the students in a class of volleyball, it is necessary to test them objectively. The skills of the game plus knowledge of rules and strategy should be tested. The skills should be selected, the objectives fixed, and tests devised that will determine how well these have been achieved.

service tests

It is possible to test accuracy in placement of the serve, but rather difficult to determine the effect curves and fast serves may have on an opponent and his ability to return them.

There are two ways of testing service accuracy: to serve over the net to marked areas in the opponents' court, and to serve to a wall target. In the first test, the marked areas will be assigned different point values depending upon the difficulty of returning a ball from each. A player stands behind the base line and serves over the net to the marked area. If he hits the net or if the ball goes out of bounds, the try is no good. If the ball goes into the marked area, he is credited with the number of points assigned to the square in which he hit. If he hits on a line, he gets credit for the highest square the line bounds. He takes ten serves and can make a possible score of seventy (Figure 24–3).

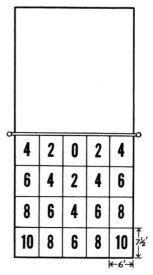

FIGURE 24-3 *Volleyball Service Test*

In the target serve for accuracy, the student stands 30 feet from a wall and serves to a circular target, the bottom of which is 8 feet high. The target, chalked on the wall, is 10 feet in diameter and contains five circles. The center circle is 2 feet in diameter and the other four are 4, 6, 8 and 10 feet, respectively. The server wins points depending upon the circle he hits. He makes ten attempts at the target and can score a possible ninety points.

volley and passing tests

Value should be placed on ability to volley fast and accurately. To approximate a game situation, another player and the net should be involved. It is necessary that each player rotate from one player to another in a series of volley tests in order to eliminate the factor of the difference in ability. Lack of rotation would tend to be a help to the weaker player and a hindrance to the more skilled one. Players are paired across the net, and a volleyball is furnished each set. At a signal, the students volley back and forth across the net for one minute. Their score is the number of volleys made in that time. Each member of a pair makes the same score. At the end of one minute, scores are recorded and a rotation is made. Each player except No. 1 moves one place to the right, and the end student on the right moves over to the other side of the net. In Figure 24–4, No. 1 is paired with No. 10 on the first test, with No. 9 the second time, and with No. 8 the third time. When they have had nine one-minute tests, the scores are totaled. The one with the highest total is assumed to have mastered best the skills of volleying and passing, and the player who scores lowest is the weakest of the ten in these skills.

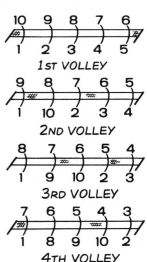

FIGURE 24-4 *Rotation for Volley Test*

Another volley and passing test does not involve the game element, but at the same time it eliminates the factor of the other player. This is a volley test against the wall. A horizontal line is drawn 8 feet from the floor. A player stands 5 feet from the wall and volleys against it. The number of volleys he makes in one minute is his score. Several participants can take this test at the same time, provided there is adequate smooth wall space, and it is necessary to test each only once. If the factor of time is important, it is well to consider this test.

jump and reach test

The ability to jump high is an important factor in successful volleyball. The height of a player's jump can be used as a factor in volleyball ability and tested accordingly. While standing flat-footed, the student being tested should reach as high as possible and with a piece of chalk make a mark on the wall. He then jumps as high as possible and makes another mark. The difference in inches between the two is his score.

DEFINITION OF TERMS

Alternation. This is when the serve is alternate as "side out" is called.

Block. Defensive play by certain players in the forward positions in which any part of the body, including the knees, is used in an attempt legally to intercept the ball.

Catching or Holding the Ball. When the ball momentarily comes to rest in the hands or arms of a player. The ball must be clearly batted. Scooping, lifting, shoving, or following it shall be considered as holding.

Dead Ball. The ball is dead after "point," "side out," or any other decision temporarily suspending play.

Double Foul. An infraction of the rules by both teams at approximately the same time.

Dribbling. A player touching the ball more than once with any part of his body when the ball meanwhile has not been touched by another player. In receiving a hard-driven spike, a defensive player is allowed to make multiple contacts even if they are not simultaneous, provided they constitute one continuous play and all contacts are above the knee.

Game Point. That stage of the game at which the winning of a serve will result in victory.

Own Court; Opponents' Court. The court occupied by a team shall be called its own court; that occupied by the opponents, the opponents' court.

Out-of-bounds. The ball is out-of-bounds when it touches any surface or object or the ground outside of the court. A ball touching a boundary line is good.

Over the Net. The act of reaching over the net to play the ball.

Playing the Ball. A player who touches the ball, or is touched by the ball, when it is in play shall be considered as playing the ball.

Point. "Point" shall be called when the team receiving fails to return the ball legally to the opponents' court.

Rotation. The shifting of the men in position.

Service. The putting of the ball into play by the player in the right-back position, by batting it over the net with one hand into the opponents' court in any direction. Both feet must be entirely behind the end line of the court until the ball is struck.

Serving Order. The order in which the teams are to serve.

Side Out. "Side out" shall be called when the team serving fails to win its point or plays the ball illegally.

Touch the Net. Contact of any part of the body with the net at any time. Contact of the ball with the net on the serve.

DISCUSSION QUESTIONS

1. Relate the background of volleyball.
2. Describe a good serve and tell why it is important to have that skill.
3. How may teamwork be employed in volleyball?
4. Describe the set-up and attack.
5. Where and how may interest in volleyball be developed in the school?
6. List the skills of volleyball and explain the tests for them.
7. What was the first name given to volleyball?
8. What kind of ball was used in the first volleyball game?
9. Describe the "roundhouse" serve.
10. Describe the "double forearm" pass.

BIBLIOGRAPHY

Anthony, Don, *Volleyball: Do It This Way.* London: John Murray Company, 1964.

Clarke, H. Harrison, *The Application of Measurement to Health and Physical Education.* Englewood Cliffs, N.J.: Prentice-Hall, Inc., 1945.

Cohen, Harlan, *Power Volleyball Drills.* Hollywood, California: Creative Sports Books, 1966.

Egstrom, Glen H., and Shaafsma, Frances, *Volleyball.* Dubuque, Iowa: William C. Brown Company, 1966.

Menke, Frank G., *The Encyclopedia of Sports.* New York: A. S. Barnes & Company, 1969.

Mitchell, Elmer D., *Intramural Sports.* New York: A. S. Barnes & Company, 1945.

Official Volleyball Guide, latest edition. Boston: The United States Volleyball Association.

Trotter, Betty Jane, *Volleyball for Girls and Women.* New York: The Ronald Press Company, 1965.

Wardale, Peter, *Volleyball: Skills and Tactics.* London: Faber and Faber Limited, 1964.

Welch, J. Edmund, *How to Play and Teach Volleyball.* New York: Association Press, 1969.

wrestling

25

BACKGROUND

Man has been grappling with other men in play or in mortal combat, and with animals, generally in mortal combat, since he has been on the face of the earth. The first recorded instance of wrestling is a group of pictures chipped in stone. These drawings of Sumerians are believed to be five thousand years old.

There is record of the Jews participating in wrestling sometime between 3,000 and 2,000 B.C. They produced excellent wrestlers and at that time looked upon wrestling as the greatest sport.

The Greeks developed wrestling to a high degree. It was a part of all celebrations and was taught as an essential in the education of the Grecian youth. Greek wrestling observed few rules and was extremely brutal. Eventually it combined boxing and wrestling in what was termed

Pankration. No holds were barred and anything was permissible, no matter how brutal.

Milo of Croton, who won the wrestling championship in the Olympian and Isthmian games, is supposed to have been the greatest wrestler in the history of Greece. Homer wrote of wrestling in both the *Iliad* and the *Odyssey*. The rules of Greek wrestling were standardized by Theseus about 900 B.C.

The Romans modified the methods of the Greeks so that the holds were limited to grappling above the waist. Some of the brutal phases of wrestling were also eliminated.

Wrestling became popular in the Middle Ages as a sport on programs attended by royalty. Kings took pride in the development of good wrestlers and matched their men against those of other countries.

The Japanese have looked upon wrestling as their national sport for hundreds of years. They even planned and carried out marriages of wrestlers' sons to wrestlers' daughters in order to improve the stature of the people. By such a process, modern-day Japanese wrestlers are giants among their people and weigh more than 300 pounds. Their wrestling at first was similar to that practiced in Rome, but in recent history it has undergone an evolution into jujitsu.

England and Ireland sanctioned wrestling, but there was never any attempt to organize it and unify the rules.

During the colonial days in this country, wrestling was one of the sports engaged in for recreation on Sunday afternoons. As first practiced here, it followed the Roman tradition of above-the-waist grappling. Two famous wrestlers of this type were Ernest Roeber and W. S. Muldoon.

In groups where the participants did not pay heed to wrestling rules, the idea of catch-as-catch-can began to take hold. Tom Jenkins, a rolling-mill employee, was an advocate of this latest method and gained much popularity because of his triumphs. He was successful for many years until he met Frank Gotch, a smaller, faster, and younger man, in 1905, and was defeated. Gotch fought 160 bouts, winning 154 of them, during which time wrestling enjoyed great popularity.

Upon Gotch's retirement in 1913, wrestling began a decline that has continued to the present. Popular professional wrestling today is not a sport but a stage show, planned ahead, rehearsed, and executed with the idea of entertaining the spectators.

Amateur wrestling is less popular but participated in to a great extent. The Amateur Athletic Union has kept the sport alive by standardizing rules and sponsoring contests.

Colleges sponsor intramural and intercollegiate contests under a set of regulations formulated by the National Collegiate Athletic Association. High schools conduct wrestling under a set of interscholastic rules. The college and high school rules are somewhat similar, but both are quite different from those of the A.A.U.

BASIC HIGH SCHOOL WRESTLING RULES

Competition is divided into twelve weight classes on the high school level. Wrestlers are evenly matched by weight, within a few pounds, and no one may wrestle in a category in which he is even a fraction of a pound overweight (but a wrestler may participate in one class above his actual weight if he so chooses). Weight classes are as follows:

98 lbs.	126 lbs.	155 lbs.
105 lbs.	132 lbs.	167 lbs.
112 lbs.	138 lbs.	187 lbs.
119 lbs.	145 lbs.	Unlimited (Heavyweight)

Matches on the high school level consist of three two-minute periods. In the first period the wrestlers begin from a standing position opposite each other (known as *neutral position*). When the match begins, one wrestler attempts to bring the other down to a prone position on the mat (known as *gaining a position of control*, or *riding*). This act of bringing the opponent to the mat and gaining control is called a *takedown*. From the riding position, the controlling wrestler will attempt to *pin* his opponent. If the two minute period ends with no pin being recorded, the second period is initiated. One of the wrestlers is given a choice of decision by the referee (arranged before the match), and may elect to begin the period on his hands and knees (the *down* position) or in a kneeling position with his arm draped across the back of his opponent (called the *top position*, with his opponent in the down position). When the referee blows his whistle, the down wrestler tries to escape to a neutral position, or reverse into a position of control on top of his opponent. The top wrestler tries to break his opponent down (controlling him) and ride him, or work toward a pin.

If the second period ends with no pin being scored, the third two-minute period commences with the earlier down wrestler in the top position, and his opponent now in the down position. (Unless a pin is scored, both wrestlers have the opportunity to wrestle from both positions.)

If the match ends without a pin being recorded, the winner is chosen according to the number of points he accumulates during the total six minutes. If a pin is scored, all match points are neglected as the pin nullifies the opponent's score. A pin is recorded when one wrestler holds both of the opponent's shoulders, or shoulder blades, to the mat for a period of two full seconds. The match is ended with a pin, no matter what period is in progress, and the man who pins his opponent is declared the victor. A near pin is recorded when the controlling wrestler holds his opponent's shoulders to the mat for a period of only one second, or one shoulder is touching the mat and the other is within one inch of the mat over a two second period. (The near pin adds points to the individual wrestler's score, but the match continues without a break.)

A *predicament* is recorded when the controlling wrestler holds his opponent's shoulders momentarily stopped within four inches of the mat, or when one shoulder is touching the mat and the other is held within a 45-degree angle of the mat but not close enough to be considered a pin or near pin. Penalty points also are given to the opponent if a wrestler uses a variety of illegal holds, is unsportsmanlike, or disobeys any of the rules of the match. Match points are used to decide the winner in event of no pin or an apparent tie, but they are not used to add up the team scores during the ensuing meet. The scoring systems for both the individual matches and for the meet follow:

Individual match points (to be awarded to the opponents of the match in progress):

Takedown .... 2 points

Escape .... 1 point

Reversal .... 2 points

Predicament .... 2 points

Near pin .... 3 points (also known as near fall)

Penalty .... usually 1 point (varies with number of times committed and severity of penalty. In certain cases a warning is first issued, then points)

The above points are added by the scorer and referee to determine the individual match winner. In addition, the referee may award a wrestler as many as two additional points if he has controlled or ridden his opponent during most of the match. If the total points of the two wrestlers in a match are exactly equal, the referee awards a draw.

Team points (to be awarded each team and used to determine the winning team at the end of the match):

Decision .... 3 team points to the team of the winner only

Draw .... 2 team points to both teams

Pin .... 5 team points to the winner's team only

Forfeit, default, or disqualification because of overweight of wrestler, injury forcing halt of match, or expulsion of wrestler for bad conduct adds 5 points to the opponent's team score.

Example #1: Wrestler from team "A", in the 98 lbs. class, scores 15 points in a match, versus wrestler from team "B" who scores 7 points. A decision would be ruled in favor of the wrestler from team "A", and the team score would be Team "A"—3, Team "B"—0.

Example #2: In the 105 lbs. class, the wrestler from team "A" is leading the wrestler from team "B" in match points by a score of 1 to 0. "B", however, reverses "A" at the beginning of the third period (scoring 2 match points) and then quickly pins wrestler "A". By virtue of his pin (and not his match points) wrestler "B" wins the match, and his team is awarded 5 points to be added to their total. Thus, at the end of two matches, the team score would be Team "A"—3, Team "B"—5.

PRELIMINARY CONSIDERATIONS

Wrestling is the oldest sport known to man and one of the finest. There is no coach or quarterback to call the plays, no one to substitute, and no one to tell the participant what to do. Every wrestler is on his own. It is a sport that gives all a chance to participate, no matter how small the individual may be. It builds self-confidence and pride along with developing a person physically, mentally and socially. It is a demanding sport requiring flexibility, agility, strength, endurance, quickness, and toughness. True, not all will be gifted with these natural abilities, but they may be developed to the maximum within each individual if he works hard and applies himself. Wrestling is complicated and there are many possibilities for the development of a series of maneuvers leading to a fall or to the amassing of points. The strong, fast, intelligent wrestler who practices long and vigorously is usually the superior one.

BASIC SKILLS

The following skills are very basic, and the individual should master them before he is taught the more advanced techniques.

the stance

A general rule that fits most situations in wrestling is to keep the feet well apart and the body weight evenly balanced. This position makes for greater stability. There are several variations of standing positions but, basically, there are only two types.

the open stance

The feet should be at least shoulder width apart with the weight evenly distributed. (One foot may be staggered if so preferred.) The wrestler should have his knees slightly bent, his back straight, and his head up. His arms should be in close to his side and slightly bent at the elbows. The palms of the hands should be turned down (Figure 25–1).

FIGURE 25-1   *Open Stance*

In this stance the wrestler is in the best possible position to take his opponent down and gain control and at the same time to counter his opponent's move from the neutral position. While in this posture the wrestler should be very alert, watching every move of his opponent for an opening or an aggressive move on his part. The eyes should not be centered on one specific spot, but by peripheral vision should be observing the opponent as a whole.

the engaged stance or closed tie-up

In this stance, the body position is basically the same as in the open stance. The only difference is that the men are actually contacting each other. The wrestler should grasp his opponent's bicep firmly from inside

FIGURE 25-2   *Engaged Stance*

out with the left hand while keeping the left elbow slightly raised. His right forearm should be placed firmly against his opponent's neck, with the palm of the right hand clasped behind it (Figure 25–2). It is very important that he gain the inside position with his arms while approaching this tie-up. Each wrestler now makes an effort to take the other to the mat and gain control.

takedowns

A wrestling match begins with the wrestlers in an upright position. From there to eventual victory, the next step for each is to take his opponent to the mat. For such a maneuver the wrestler gets two points. Many factors are involved in a successful takedown. The wrestler must be alert to possibilities and move immediately when the opening presents itself. At the same time, he must realize that his opponent has the same objective as he and must stay in a defensive position, ready to counter a move by the other man.

The wrestler should never make any move that will inform his opponent of his intentions. Instead, he should try by feinting and faking to cause the opponent to expect something different from the real intent.

the double-leg takedown

This is sometimes called the leg dive and is included here because the average boy already has gained some skill through performing virtually the same maneuver in football.

The double-leg takedown may begin from either of the starting stances. The boy should rise up quickly to make the opponent believe he is going to grasp him about the shoulders; then he should drop fast, putting a shoulder into the waist or hip of the opponent and, at the same time, reaching the arms around the legs slightly above the knees. After the

FIGURE 25-3 *Double Leg Drive*

grasp is made, the legs are pulled in together, and the shoulder goes forward to start the opponent backward. The feet are kept on the mat so that they can exert force forward to take the man down. Because this takedown may be a form of slam if the opponent is lifted off the mat, it may be necessary for the aggressor to put one knee on the mat immediately prior to the takedown in order for it to be legal (Figure 25-3).

The basic counter to the double-leg dive is the *sprawl* and *crossface*. When the opponent attempts the takedown, the wrestler should flatten out and drop his hip on the opponent's shoulder. His knees should be off the mat in this position with his weight balanced on his opponent's shoulder. He should be alert, ready to move in any direction. He should then drive his forearm across the aggressor's face and attempt to control his head.

the single-leg pick-up

This is sometimes called the "leg steal" and can be used from either the open or engaged stance. The aggressor's left foot should be planted and his right knee should land just outside and to the rear of the opponent's left heel. At the same time, his right arm should grasp the left thigh, with his right ear inside and against it. His left hand should grasp the opponent's left heel. From this point he may clear the opponent's leg from the mat by standing up, or he may drive him back by forcing his head against the thigh (Figure 25-4).

FIGURE 25-4   *Single Leg Pick-up*

The basic counter is the sprawl, which has been explained, and the hiplock. The hiplock is accomplished by overhooking the aggressor's near arm. The arm is forced up so that the leg may be freed from the aggressor's grip.

the fireman's carry

This takedown is more effective when used from the engaged stance. The aggressor should grasp the opponent's right bicep firmly with his left hand. He then raises the opponent's right arm with the bicep grip and ducks his head under the armpit. He should keep a firm grip on the bicep and pull the arm down firmly around his neck. He then steps in deep with his knee, which should be placed between the opponent's legs and on the mat. He should then grasp the right leg of the opponent with his right arm while dropping his left knee to the mat. The aggressor now can take his opponent to the mat by dropping his left shoulder and thrusting his right arm upward (Figure 25–5).

FIGURE 25-5   *Fireman's Carry*

The best defense to this takedown is never let the opponent duck under either arm nor control the biceps.

the heel pickup

This takedown is executed only from the engaged stance and is used when either of the opponent's legs is forward. The aggressor controls the opponent's head and drops in deep on both knees. The neck is pulled down as he drops in, and he picks up the near ankle with his free hand. The ankle is pulled forward, and the neck is driven backward, causing the opponent to fall to the mat and the aggressor to gain control (Figure 25–6).

The defense for this move is to keep the legs back and not allow the head to be controlled.

FIGURE 25-6   *Heel Pick-up*

the arm-drag takedown

This particular move is performed best from the open stance. The aggressor reaches out with his left hand and grasps the back of the left wrist of his opponent. His chest moves to the left so that the right arm can circle the opponent's upper arm, beginning on the inside. Pull is started forward and to the left. If necessary to cause the opponent to fall forward, the wrestler may put a foot against or on his near foot. When the takedown is completed, the wrestler executes a pinning hold (Figure 25–7).

FIGURE 25-7 *Arm Drag*

To prevent this takedown, the wrestler should not allow his wrist to be grasped. If it is grasped, he should keep his feet wide and away from the opponent's feet, and should move with the aggressor until the arm is eventually released.

the lateral drop or pancake

In this move, the contact must be close. The right arm goes under the opponent's left arm and on his back. The aggressor's left arm goes outside and around the opponent's right arm and wings it by bearing down hard, pressing in toward the center. The takedown is a lever movement, with the right arm acting as the lever and turning the wrestler to the left and down (Figure 25–8).

In defending against such a takedown, the wrestler should not allow his opponent to get close.

FIGURE 25-8 *Lateral Drop*

the referee's position

When the two wrestlers get off the mat during the course of a match, at the beginning of the first or second period, or if for some reason the match has come to a stalemate, they are put by the referee in what is called the referee's position in the center of the mat. One man is placed on his hands and knees beside the referee and is called the offensive wrestler (Figure 25–9). These are frequently called the position of disadvantage and the position of advantage, respectively.

FIGURE 25-9   *The Referee's Position*   **A**   **B**

Wrestler "A" in Figure 25–9 is in the position of disadvantage, or the down position. The knees are on the mat the width of the shoulders apart, and the lower legs are parallel to each other. The buttocks should be back on the heels. The feet should be flexed so that the toes will be contacting the mat preparatory to moving forward. The heels of the hands are placed on the mat not closer than a foot to, and directly in line with the knees. The arms are flexed and the fingers are straight. In this position, a wrestler is rather difficult to move.

Wrestler "B" in Figure 25–9 is in the position of advantage. He may be on either the right or the left side, though the majority prefer the left. He must be on the side and slightly over the other wrestler. He is on his knees, which are apart to make for good balance. His right knee may be very close to but not over the leg of his opponent. He may sit back on his heels, but, for best offensive functioning, he should not. The left hand is placed loosely on the opponent's arm just above his elbow. The right arm should rest loosely around the opponent's waist. The major portion of the weight of both wrestlers should be on the knees.

The object for wrestler "A" is to escape, for which he scores one point, or to go even further and gain control of his opponent, for which he scores an additional point. It is the object for "B" to maintain control and attempt to put his opponent on his back.

maneuvers from the position of advantage

A wrestler can make many moves from this position that will help him maintain control and lead to a pin. These maneuvers are referred to as *breakdowns* and *rides*. The following moves will be explained with the offensive wrestler starting on the left side in the referee's position.

WAIST AND FAR ANKLE. At the referee's whistle, the offensive wrestler's left hand is quickly changed from the opponent's elbow to his waist and his right hand from the waist to the far ankle. He then moves to the opponent's rear. He attempts to break him down on the mat by picking the ankle up and at the same time driving his left shoulder into the defensive wrestler's back (Figure 25–10).

FIGURE 25-10 *Waist and Far Ankle*

THE FAR-ARM DRIVE. On the signal to wrestle, the offensive wrestler in the up position moves his hand from the opponent's elbow under the chest and grasps the far arm above the elbow. At the same time he moves his right arm from around the waist and grasps the far leg on the thigh region. He then begins to drive his left shoulder into the defensive man's side and while doing so draws the far arm and far leg to him. By this maneuver he attempts to turn his opponent over for the pin (Figure 25–11).

FIGURE 25-11 *Far Arm Drive*

HEAD LEVER AND CROTCH PRY. At the whistle, the offensive wrestler drops his left hand from his opponent's elbow down to his wrist, and his right hand from the defensive man's waist down to his thigh, with the palm of his hand against the inside of the thigh. He then should drive his forehead forward into the back of his opponent's armpit, at the same time pulling back and up on his left wrist. With his right hand he should push back and out against the opponent's thigh in order to control the far leg (Figure 25–12).

FIGURE 25-12 *Head Lever-Crotch Pry*

THE FIGURE-FOUR BODY SCISSORS. On the signal from the referee, the offensive wrestler jumps astride the defensive man's back. He forms a figure-four with his legs around the opponent's body by hooking his right leg around the waist and attaching his right toes behind his own left knee. His left leg should be straight, with his left foot hooked behind the defensive wrestler's left leg. He may break his opponent down by simply leaning forward and applying pressure on the opponent's upper torso (Figure 25–13).

FIGURE 25-13 *Figure Four Scissors*

maneuvers from the position of disadvantage

Many different maneuvers that can result in either a reversal or an escape may be executed by the defensive wrestler. He has not lost a match by any means when he is put in the position of disadvantage on the mat. Most wrestlers prefer it at the start of the third period because to score by reversal or an escape is easier than to maneuver a man of equal strength into a pinning situation.

THE STAND UP. On the signal to wrestle, the defensive wrestler will drive up on his inside leg and at the same time thrust his head up. He should tuck his inside arm tightly against his side. With his right hand he grasps his opponent's hand that is around his waist. He should now step up with his outside leg, making sure his hips are out and away from his opponent's body. When the offensive man brings his left arm around his opponent's body for control, the opponent should use his left arm to pry it out and away from his body. With his right hand he should rip the opponent's right hand from his waist and turn sharply to the inside for an escape (Figure 25–14).

FIGURE 25-14   *Stand Up*

FORWARD ROLL.   This maneuver also is used primarily as a means of escaping for one point. It is very simple. At the referee's whistle, the defensive wrestler drops his inside shoulder, ducks his head, and pushes off with his feet into a forward roll. It is an easy move to counter, and it is not recommended for use against an experienced wrestler, because the defensive wrestler exposes his back to the mat.

WINGLOCK AND STEP-OVER.   This particular reversal is performed when the top wrestler attempts to get a half-nelson. When he reaches his left arm under the bottom man's left arm and up to his neck, the bottom man winglocks—that is, bears down with his left arm on the opponent's left arm. He then begins stepping to the left with both legs and hands directly sideward. The opponent will be forced over on his back. The man now assuming the advantage gets at a right angle to his opponent, secures a half-nelson with his right arm, and begins to bear down for a pin (Figure 25–15).

FIGURE 25-15   *Wing Lock and Step Over*

This same basic movement can be performed without an original half-nelson movement if the bottom man will grasp the left wrist of the top man with his right hand. By holding firmly with this grip, the same movement can be made, and a pin may result.

THE HIP ROLL. The wrestler on the bottom begins moving his right knee over to his left to be a little nearer the man on top. At the same instant, he reaches up with his right hand and grasps the right wrist of the top man. He then begins rolling quickly to the right, bringing the top man over him, across, and to the mat on the other side. The maneuver should end with the original top man in a pin position on the mat.

There are several blocks for this particular move. If the top man will flatten out on the bottom man, it may be possible to stop the move at the outset. If the roll is started, the top man may move quickly to the opposite side of the opponent and avoid being rolled.

SIT-OUT AND SWITCH. On the referee's whistle, the bottom man sits out—that is, he quickly brings his knees off the mat and to the right in a sitting position. At the same time, his right arm swings to the right and back in an effort to pin the opponent's right arm against his side. This same arm holds down the opponent's arm, and the hand reaches back inside his right leg and grasps it. After this move is made, the aggressive wrestler—the one who was on the bottom—bears the other's right shoulder to the mat. When this is done, he rolls quickly to the right across the top of his opponent and into a pin position (Figure 25–16).

FIGURE 25-16   *Sit-out and Switch*

If the top wrestler will move quickly enough when he realizes that the sit-out is coming, he can counter by shifting his leg out quickly and around the opponent's left leg to begin a scissors. All he has to do then is merely roll with the aggressor to avoid being pinned.

pinning holds

There are many ways in which an opponent's shoulders may be put to the mat and kept there at least two seconds. A wrestler needs to learn them in addition to ways of leading up to their final execution. He should also learn defenses for each in order to avoid being grasped as well as how to escape from them after they have been secured. In most holds, a wrestler utilizes strength, agility, leverage, and his own body weight to hold a person to the mat for a pin. Some of the pin holds most frequently used are described here.

HALF-NELSON. A wrestler frequently uses a half-nelson to lever a person on his back so that a pin may be secured. Since the half-nelson is a good way to hold a person as well as to turn him, it can be continued after the turn is made. More pins result from the half-nelson than from any other hold.

HALF-NELSON WITH CROTCH HOLD. The top man should put all his chest weight on his opponent. Defenses for this hold include the bridge and quick turn as well as the elbow roll (Figure 25–17).

FIGURE 25-17 *Half-nelson with Crotch Hold*

HALF-NELSON AND CRADLE. This is almost the same hold as the preceding one, but it is somewhat more effective because the legs of the bottom man are completely taken out of the combat. The head is held down by the half-nelson with one arm while the other bundles up both the opponent's legs and holds them firmly at the knees.

HALF-NELSON AND NEAR-LEG COMBINATION. In this hold, the wrestler controls the head and shoulders of the bottom man with one hand while he reaches across on the outside of the near leg and pulls to himself at the knee (Figure 25–18).

FIGURE 25-18 *Half-nelson and Near Leg Combination*

DOUBLE ARMLOCK. This is a means of completely immobilizing the arms and holding the opponent so that both his shoulders are on the mat.

BAR ARM AND HALF-NELSON. The offensive man must have his opponent broken down in order to execute this pinning combination. The maneuver begins on the left side of the defensive wrestler. The offensive man should trap his opponent's left wrist by reaching around his waist with the right arm and grasping his left wrist with the right hand. He then should place his left arm between the opponent's left arm and his lower back region. He now should drive forward with his left shoulder to further trap the arm. He next should remove his right hand from the opponent's left wrist and apply a half-nelson on the right side with his right arm. He now can turn the defensive man over by stepping to the right side and applying perpendicular pressure with the half-nelson (Figure 25–19).

FIGURE 25-19   *Bar Arm and Half-nelson*

HINTS TO WRESTLERS

1.   The attack should be planned carefully on the basis of the opponent's strong and weak points.

2.   Aggressive wrestling is preferable to defensive wrestling.

3.   Fast, specific action is necessary for success at the sport.

4.   While preparing for the next move, the wrestler should not unconsciously allow himself to get in a position vulnerable to the opposition.

5.   A wide base both in the upright stance and in the down positions makes one difficult to be moved about by the opponent.

6.   To break a grip, try working against the thumbs.

7.   The legs should be kept away from an opponent. On the other hand, effort should be made to immobilize the legs of the opponent.

8.   When wrestlers are down, it is preferable for the top man to get at right angles to his opponent.

9.   A wrestler should never support his own weight when it can be supported by the opponent. When a boy must support the other's weight as well as compete with him, fatigue sets in more rapidly.

10.   Stay close to an opponent when on offense and away from him when on defense.

11. Do a great deal of faking and feinting.

12. Never establish a pattern of attack. Keep the opponent guessing about the next move.

13. Utilize leverage and conserve brute strength until absolutely necessary.

14. Spend hours each day getting into condition for wrestling, for it is one of the most fatiguing sports.

TEACHING PROCEDURE

In wrestling as in other sports, there should be no more students in a class than facilities and leadership can accommodate. Sixteen students should be the absolute maximum for a wrestling class. These can do much of their workout on one regulation mat all at the same time. When activity requiring greater space is engaged in, part of the class can retire to another mat. Certain drills should be engaged in each day for the purpose of conditioning the wrestlers. Not more than 10 minutes should be devoted to them and, if possible, the time should be cut to 5 minutes. These include:

1. Push-ups

2. Sit-ups

3. The bridge

4. Neck exercises

5. Roll-outs

After these are completed, the class should be taught the fundamentals of wrestling. During the early class meetings, they should be given the basic rules of the sport and have clearly demonstrated to them those phases that are barred. In logical sequence the instructor should then teach one or two new skills each day and provide time for practice first in slow motion and then with resistance. The takedown should be taught first, followed by several pinning holds, and then maneuvers from both the position of advantage and the position of disadvantage. After these are reasonably well mastered, more of the basic wrestling holds should be taught with their counters and defenses. When enough of the skills of the sport have been taught that a student can wrestle with some intelligence, he should be allowed to engage in brief matches with another student of his approximate weight. During the last week of the class, a tournament should be conducted in which the students may compete with others of their own weight.

In organizing for conditioning and practice, the students should be placed on the mat where they will not interfere with others and be put through the conditioning exercises all at the same time. When practicing the holds in slow motion, they may all work at the same time. When the holds are tried against resistance, only one pair should work on any one mat. The pairs may be spaced around the mat. The instructor goes to a pair who are ready and commands, "wrestle." They try the holds or takedown, the instructor corrects them, and then he goes to the next pair. In this way little or no time is wasted, and the students may go on about learning the sport without interference.

Under no circumstances should the counters, defenses, or blocks be taught at the same time as a hold or maneuver. The wrestler should be allowed to experience each one successfully in order to develop confidence before the method of resistance is indicated.

SKILL TESTS

demonstration of takedowns, holds, and pins

The instructor may ask a wrestler to demonstrate a series of holds, and points can be awarded depending on whether they are performed correctly.

explanation and demonstration of defenses, blocks, and counters

These can be graded the same as the takedowns.

wrestling procedure

A point system can be set up by which a wrestler is judged subjectively on his aggressiveness, speed, strength, and wrestling intelligence as demonstrated with another student of equal weight.

standing in a tournament

Grades can be based on the advancement a wrestler makes in a tournament.

DEFINITION OF TERMS

Arm Drag. A method of grasping the arm and pulling the opponent for a takedown.

Arm Lever. A way of using the arm to cause the opponent to move to another position.

Armlock. The pinning of an opponent's arm between the wrestler's own arm and his body.

Block. A movement or position designed to stop an offensive maneuver.

Body Slam. The violent throwing of the opponent to the mat. Illegal unless the slammer has one knee on mat.

Bridge. The arching of the back so that the shoulders do not touch the mat.

Counter. An offensive movement, following one by the opponent, that is designed to counteract or overcome it.

Crotch Hold. A hold by which the arm goes between the legs and grasps the opponent at the buttocks.

Defense. To ward off attack or offense.

Elbow Roll. The turning of an opponent by locking his arm at the elbow.

Engaged Stance. Two wrestlers grasping each other by the neck and arm preparatory to starting a match.

Escape. To get away from an opponent who had control. One point is scored.

Fall. To pin an opponent's shoulders to the mat, ending either the time period or the match.

Fall Back. To drop backward either by accident or design.

Figure-four Scissors. A leg hold in which a wrestler runs one leg almost completely around his opponent and catches his other leg with his foot.

Full-nelson. From the rear of an opponent, running the arms under his arms and clasping the hands over them or back of his neck. It is illegal.

Half-nelson. The placing of one arm under the opponent's arm and over his neck to lever him onto his back or hold him in a pin position.

Hammerlock. The holding of an opponent's arm behind his back. Illegal if taken beyond a right angle.

Headlock. The placing of an arm around the opponent's head. It is illegal unless the opponent's arm is involved in the lock also.

Head Scissors. The locking of the legs around the opponent's head.

High Bridge. Arching the back extremely high to keep shoulders off the mat.

Hook Scissors. The locking of the legs around a leg of the opponent.

Locked-heel Pull. The placing of the feet at the heels of the opponent and pulling him backward.

Pin. To put an opponent's shoulder to the mat for a period of two seconds.

Near Fall. To put one of the opponent's shoulders to the mat and holding the other within two inches of the mat for a period of two seconds.

Quarter-nelson. A way of levering a wrestler's head by forcing down with a hand that is blocked or held in a position by the other hand under the opponent's arm.

Referee's Position. A position assumed on the mat because of a command by the official.

Scissors. A way of locking the legs around the opponent.

Sitting Out. A way of escaping from an opponent by throwing the legs out and away from him in a scissoring movement.

Slugging. The striking of an opponent. Illegal conduct resulting in disqualification.

Square Stance. To stand facing the opponent with the feet equidistant from him.

Stance. The position a wrestler assumes when meeting an opponent at the start of a match.

Straight Falls. Two pins in succession.

Stranglehold. To grasp the opponent around the neck. Illegal.

Switch. To shift from a position of disadvantage to one of advantage.

Twisting Hammerlock. A hammerlock in which the arm is also turned.

Waistlock. To put the arms around the opponent's waist and grasp the hands. It is illegal to overlap or interlock the hands around a defensive man's waist or both legs while he is on the mat. It is legal if he is in a standing position.

Wrestling. A contest between two individuals in which each tries to bring the other to the mat and hold him there.

Wristlock. The act of a wrestler in grasping the wrist of one arm with the hand of the other.

Winglock. The gripping of an opponent's arm between the wrestler's arm and body.

DISCUSSION QUESTIONS

1. Trace the early history of wrestling.
2. Who were some of the early well-known wrestlers?
3. What are some of the factors involved in successful wrestling?
4. Describe the engaged stance.
5. Name some important points to remember when attempting a takedown.
6. List several points for a wrestler to remember when successfully participating in the sport.
7. Name several pinning holds and describe the one you think best to execute.
8. How does one go about teaching a wrestling class?
9. What are good conditioning exercises for wrestling?

BIBLIOGRAPHY

Athletic Institute. *How to Improve Your Wrestling.* Chicago: latest edition.

Dratz, John P., Johnson, Manley, and McCann, Terry. *Winning Wrestling.* Englewood Cliffs, N.J.: Prentice-Hall, Inc., 1966.

Gianakaris, George, *Action Drilling in Wrestling.* Springfield, Virginia: George Gianakaris, 1966.

Keen, Clifford P., Bartelma, David C., and Speidel, Charles M., *Wrestling.* New York: A. S. Barnes & Company, 1950.

Menke, Frank, *The New Encyclopedia of Sports.* New York: A. S. Barnes & Company, 1969.

National Collegiate Athletic Association, *Official N.C.A.A. Wrestling Guide*. New York: National Collegiate Athletic Association, latest edition.

Sparks, Raymond E., *Wrestling Illustrated—An Instructional Guide*. New York: The Ronald Press Company, 1960.

Stone, Henry A., *Wrestling, Intercollegiate and Olympic*. Englewood Cliffs, N.J.: Prentice-Hall, Inc., 1950.

Umbach, Arnold, and Johnson, Warren R., *Wrestling*. Dubuque, Iowa: William C. Brown Company, 1966.

index